Practical Chess Endings

PAUL KERES

Translated by John Littlewood

B.T.Batsford Ltd, *London*

First published in West Germany, 1973

First published 1974
Reprinted 1977 – first paperback edition
First algebraic edition 1984
Reprinted 1985, 1986, 1988
ISBN 0 7134 4210 7(limp)

Photoset by Andek Printing, London
and printed and bound in Great Britain by
Biddles Ltd, Guildford and Kings Lynn
for the publishers
B.T.Batsford Ltd, 4 Fitzhardinge Street,
London W1H 0AH

A BATSFORD CHESS BOOK
Adviser: R.D.Keene GM, OBE
Technical Editor: Ian Kingston

Contents

Preface

In chess literature throughout the world countless books have been written on opening theory, the middlegame, chess tournaments and game selections. Within this vast production, however, books on the endgame are comparatively few in number, despite the fact that this is one of the most important parts of the game of chess.

It is indeed difficult to over-estimate the value of good endgame play and time spent on this department is amply repaid. The purpose of this book is to give the reader practical help in endgame technique.

Many chessplayers are averse to studying the endgame, in the belief that it is boring. To a certain extent they are right, for most theoretical endings are relatively dry in content, requiring precise calculation and offering few opportunities for individual flights of imagination. Nevertheless, there is much of interest in this phase of the game, and all chessplayers should strive to improve their play by mastering the necessary technique.

In order to pinpoint basic principles, I have decided to cut down on the number of examples but to examine them in greater detail than is customary. In this way I hope to make endgame theory a little more palatable. This has necessarily led me to reject many purely theoretical analyses and restrict myself to material which will be of most benefit to the practical player.

In offering this volume to the reader I hope not only to stimulate interest in the subject matter but principally to raise the average level of endgame technique among chessplayers everywhere.

Paul Keres
Tallinn, July 1972

Introduction

A normal game of chess usually consists of three phases; opening, middlegame and ending. In the opening a player attempts to develop his forces in the most effective manner and create favourable middlegame chances. The middlegame is the richest and apparently the most difficult part of the game, in which the player aims for a decisive superiority or at least an advantageous endgame. And, finally, the ending is that part of the game in which we must convert into a win any advantages won during the opening or middlegame.

As a result, it is clear that the ending is one of the most critical stages of the game. A player can sometimes afford the luxury of an inaccurate move, or even a definite error, in the opening or middlegame without necessarily obtaining a lost position. This is explained by the fact that in both these complicated phases of the game there are great practical difficulties in detecting and exploiting our opponent's mistakes. In the endgame, on the other hand, an error can be decisive, and we are rarely presented with a second chance.

There could be no clearer proof of the vital need to perfect one's endgame technique. The world's leading chessplayers pay special attention to this aspect of their game, and we can find numerous modern examples of finely conducted endgames.

It must be admitted that, from a purely technical point of view, endings are much less interesting to study than, for example, opening theory or the strategy of the middlegame. However, this study is essential, and there is at least the advantage that most endings lend themselves to exact analysis of winning or drawing possibilities.

In the following pages, we shall attempt to provide the reader with the most important principles for the correct handling of various practical endings. We all know that present endgame theory in its entirety would fill many hefty tomes, the mere sight of which is a deterrent. The aim of this book, therefore, is to lighten the burden somewhat by selecting from the vast material available those endings which are of most practical value. For example, we shall be examining all basic endgame positions, presenting an indispensable ABC of chess usage. Do not underrate such an approach. Even great players have been known to have weaknesses in this phase of the game.

1 Elementary Endings

In this section we shall examine positions which in fact belong to the ABC of every player and scarcely need any further elucidation. However, we mention them briefly here for the sake of completeness, first of all looking at the force required to mate a lone king.

King and Queen against King

This is always a win, the only danger being a possible stalemate.

One possible winning method from diagram 1 is the following: **1 ♕c3 ♔e4 2 ♔b7 ♔d5** the black king obviously wishes to remain in the centre as long as possible **3 ♔c7 ♔e4 4 ♔d6 ♔f4 5 ♕d3 ♔g5 6 ♔e5 ♔g4 7 ♕e3 ♔h5 8 ♔f5 ♔h4 9 ♕d3 ♔h5 10 ♕h3 mate**.

This is perhaps not the shortest way, 1 ♔b7 being possibly quicker, but the given method shows how easily the enemy king can be mated in such positions.

King and Rook against King

This too is always a win. As in the above example, the enemy king must be driven to the edge of the board before he can be mated, although the task is slightly more difficult. Whilst the queen can drive the king to the edge without the help of its own king, it is essential for the rook and king to co-ordinate their action to achieve this aim.

In diagram 2, White's task is not especially difficult. In order to force the black king to the side of the board, it is simplest to cut off the king by using the rook along the rank or the file, beginning with 1 ♖a4 or 1 ♖e1. However, as no further progress can be made without the help of the white king, the clearest method is **1 ♔b7 ♔e4 2 ♔c6 ♔d4 3 ♖e1** to force the enemy king towards the a-file **3 ... ♔c4 4 ♖e4+ ♔d3 5 ♔d5** now the black king is denied access to both the e-file and the fourth rank **5 ... ♔c3 6 ♖d4 ♔c2 7 ♔c4 ♔b2 8 ♖d2+ ♔c1** the king already has to go to the back rank **9 ♔c3 ♔b1 10 ♔b3 ♔c1 11 ♖d3 ♔b1 12 ♖d1 mate**. Note especially the use of waiting moves by the rook.

King and two Bishops against King

It is clear that king and one bishop cannot possibly mate a lone king, but two bishops easily force the win, as can be seen in the play from diagram 3.

3

The winning procedure is the same as in the previous examples. The black king is gradually driven to the edge of the board by co-ordinating the bishops to control its escape squares. The following line of play is readily understandable: **1 ♔b2 ♔e4 2 ♔c3 ♔d5 3 ♗f3+ ♔e5 4 ♗g3+ ♔e6 5 ♔d4** the black king is now completely cut off by the bishops and can easily be forced into the corner **5 ... ♔f5 6 ♔d5 ♔f6 7 ♗g4 ♔g5 8 ♗d7 ♔f6 9 ♗h4+ ♔g6** the black king's movements are even further restricted but he must be driven into the corner **10 ♔e5 ♔f7 11 ♔f5 ♔g7 12 ♗e8 ♔f8 13 ♗g6 ♔g7 14 ♗e7 ♔f8 15 ♔f6 ♔h8 16 ♗f5 ♔g8 17 ♔g6 ♔h8 18 ♗d6 ♔g8 19 ♗e6+ ♔h8 20 ♗e5 mate.** There may of course be quicker ways but the winning method remains in all cases the same.

King and two Knights against King

Whilst it is clear that a single knight and king cannot mate the enemy king, it is not so obvious that there is no way to force a win with two knights. In this case there is a theoretical mating position, but White cannot bring it about against correct defence. Diagram 4 makes this clear, for White cannot strengthen his position even though the black king is in the corner.

4

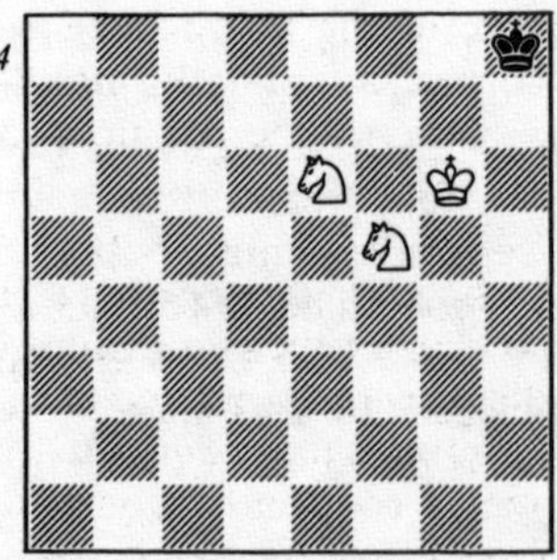

The attempt to restrict the king's movements by 1 ♘e7 or 1 ♘h6 leads to stalemate. White can try **1 ♘f8 ♔g8 2 ♘d7 ♔h8 3 ♘d6 ♔g8 4 ♘f6+** and if 4 ... ♔h8? 5 ♘f7 mate, but Black simply plays **4 ... ♔f8** and White must start all over again. However hard White tries, there is no forced way of mating the black king with two knights only.

King, Bishop and Knight against King

White can indeed force mate in this ending, and it is worthwhile to acquire the necessary technique. Once again the black king must naturally be driven into the corner of the board, and mating positions are possible in all four corners. However, mate can be forced only in the two corners which are of the same colour as the bishop controls. In the two other corners, mate is only possible if the defender makes a mistake, as was the case with the two knights.

This means that the task of the attacker is fairly tricky. Firstly, the enemy king has to be driven to the edge of the board, then into the corner, and finally into the other corner if the colour is the wrong one for his bishop. And whereas with the queen, rook or two bishops it was easy to cut the king off along the ranks, files or diagonals, with knight and bishop such control is more difficult. The two pieces constantly require the support of their own king, so that the knight and king can guard those squares which the bishop cannot control. Let us see how it all works by examining the play from diagram 5.

5

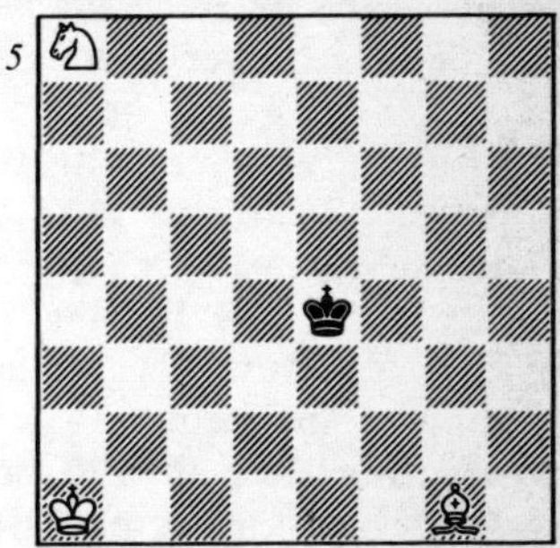

White must of course first bring up his king, whilst the black king tries to remain in the centre for as long as possible. As soon as he is driven away, he heads for the 'wrong' corner, a8 or h1, where he cannot be mated with correct defence. Play might continue as follows: **1 ♔b2 ♔d3 2 ♘c7 ♔c4** to hold back the enemy king **3 ♘e6 ♔d5 4 ♘d4 ♔c4 5 ♔c2 ♔b4** no better would be 5 ... ♔d5 6 ♔d3 **6 ♔d3 ♔c5 7 ♗h2** as we can see, the white pieces supported by the king have taken many squares away from the black king **7 ... ♔d5 8 ♘b3 ♔c6** the king must retreat, so he heads for a8, whereas 8 ... ♔e6 9 ♔e4 would drive him towards h8 **9 ♔c4 ♔b6** better than 9 ... ♔d7 10 ♔d5 **10 ♘c5 ♔c6 11 ♘a4** reaching a similar situation to the one after White's 8th move and showing a typical method of driving back the enemy king with bishop and knight **11 ... ♔b7 12 ♔b5 ♔c8** after 12 ... ♔a7 13 ♔c6 we reach a position which occurs later in the main variation **13 ♔c6 ♔d8 14 ♔d6 ♔c8** if Black tried to escape by 14 ... ♔e8, he would be driven over to h8 after 15 ♔e6 ♔f8 16 ♗e5 or here 15 ... ♔d8 16 ♘b6, without being able to slip away towards a8 **15 ♘b6+ ♔b7 16 ♔c5 ♔a6 17 ♔c6 ♔a5 18 ♗d6 ♔a6 19 ♗b8** barring the king's retreat towards a8 and beginning the manoeuvre to drive him towards a1 **19 ... ♔a5 20 ♘d5! ♔a4** White's task is simpler after 20 ... ♔a6 21 ♘b4+ ♔a5 22 ♔c5 ♔a4 23 ♔c4 ♔a5 24 ♗c7+ etc **21 ♔c5 ♔b3 22 ♘b4!** a very important knight move and a typical way of driving the king from one corner to the other **22 ... ♔c3 23 ♗f4** and we can see that the splendid position of the knight stops the black king escaping **23 ... ♔b3 24 ♗e5 ♔a4 25 ♔c4 ♔a5 26 ♗c7+ ♔a4 27 ♘d3 ♔a3 28 ♗b6** a waiting move; the black king is now compelled to go to a1 **28 ... ♔a4 29 ♘b2+ ♔a3 30 ♔c3 ♔a2 31 ♔c2 ♔a3 32 ♗c5+ ♔a2 33 ♘d3 ♔a1** at last! The black king is now mated in three moves **34 ♗b4 ♔a2 35 ♘c1+ ♔a1 36 ♗c3 mate**.

The reader will now realize that this ending is by no means easy. It is worth noting standard positions such as those after White's 8th, 19th and 22nd moves, and the beginner would do well to try to drive the black king into the corner from various positions on the board, in order to get used to the way in which the three white pieces co-operate. It must not be forgotten that the king must be mated within 50 moves, or else a draw can be claimed. This makes it all the more imperative for us to be thoroughly conversant with the winning method, so as not to lose valuable time driving the enemy king back.

King and Pawn against King

We could have examined this ending in the section on pawn endings, but as we are dealing with simpler examples here, it seems best to include it in this section on elementary endings. In this type of ending it is difficult to give general principles, as everything depends on the placing of the pieces. It goes without saying that a win is only possible if the pawn can be promoted, so our task is to establish when this can or cannot be done.

Of course, White wins easily when the enemy king is too far away to prevent the pawn queening. It is equally clear that the game is drawn when the white king cannot prevent the capture of his pawn. We are primarily concerned with those positions where the black king is placed somewhere in front of the pawn. Let us begin by examining the basic situation given in diagram 6, with the pawn on the 6th rank and the black king on the back rank in front of the pawn.

On the left is a typical position in this ending, always attainable even with the pawn originally further back, as its advance to the 6th rank cannot be prevented. The win here depends on who has the move. With White to move the game is drawn, as **1 c7+ ♔c8 2 ♔c6** gives **stalemate**, and White cannot bring about the same position with Black to move. For instance, after **1 ♔d5 ♔c7 2 ♔c5**, Black plays the correct move **2 ... ♔c8!** and now both 3 ♔d6 ♔d8 and 3 ♔b6 ♔b8 amount to the same situation. Black's defence is easy: he keeps his king for as long as possible on c7 and c8 until the white king reaches the 6th rank when Black must immediately place his king directly in front of the white king.

In connection with this ending, I would like to stress one extremely important point concerning the position of the two kings. In all pawn endings, when the kings face each other as above (i.e. standing on the same rank or file with one square in between), they are said to be in 'opposition' or more specifically in 'close opposition', as compared with 'distant opposition' when the kings are 3 or 5 squares apart. Diagonal opposition occurs when there are 1, 3 or 5 squares between both kings.

We say that a player 'has the opposition' when he has brought about one of the above-described positions with his opponent to move. In such cases the latter has lost the opposition. We could now define the left half of diagram 6 as follows: the win in this position depends on who has the opposition. If White has it, he wins; if Black has it,the game is drawn.

This rule applies to all similar positions, except those where a rook's pawn is involved. For example, in the right half of diagram 6, White cannot win even with the opposition, as **1 ... ♔h8 2 h7** gives **stalemate**.

If the pawn is not on the 6th rank but further back, Black's drawing chances increase significantly. Consider the bottom half of diagram 7.

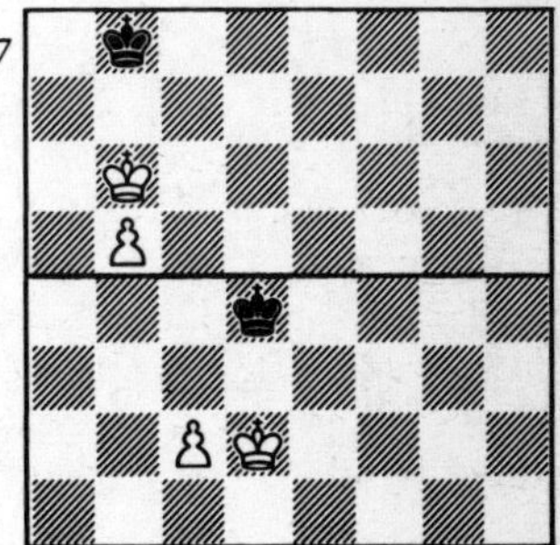

This and similar positions are drawn, whoever has the move. Black defends according to the principles we have given above, with the play going as follows: **1 c3+ ♔c4 2 ♔c2 ♔c5 3 ♔d3 ♔d5 4 c4+ ♔c5 5 ♔c3 ♔c6 6 ♔d4 ♔d6 7 c5+ ♔c6 8 ♔c4 ♔c7 9 ♔d5 ♔d7 10 c6+ ♔c7 11 ♔c5 ♔c8! 12 ♔d6 ♔d8!** and we have reached the known drawing position in which Black has the opposition.

One might think that we have now finished with the king and pawn ending, but this is far from being the case. What happens, for instance, when the white king occupies a square in front of his pawn? In this case equally there are no general rules for winning, but White's winning chances are much greater, especially if the pawn is advanced, as in the upper half of diagram 7.

The white king has managed to reach the important square in front of his pawn and this fact ensures the win in all cases, whoever has the move and however far back the pawn may be. With Black to move, there is a simple win after **1 ... ♔a8 2 ♔c7** or **1 ... ♔c8 2 ♔a7**, followed by the advance of the pawn. Even with White to move, there are few problems, for after **1 ♔a6 ♔a8 2 b6** White has the opposition, so wins as we have seen above. All similar positions are won, except for those which again involve the rook's pawn.

It is, however, worth pointing out one small fact about positions with a knight's pawn. Returning to the upper half of diagram 7, with White to move, it may seem at first sight that White can also win with 1 ♔c6, as 1 ... ♔c8 2 b6 is lost for Black. However, 1 ♔a6! is the correct move although White can reach this position again even after **1 ♔c6** which Black answers with **1 ... ♔a7!** If White now carelessly plays 2 b6+? Black replies 2 ... ♔a8! with a draw, for both 3 ♔c7 and 3 b7+ ♔b8 4 ♔b6 give stalemate. So White must swallow his pride and play **2 ♔c7 ♔a8 3 ♔b6! ♔b8 4 ♔a6!** returning to the winning plan.

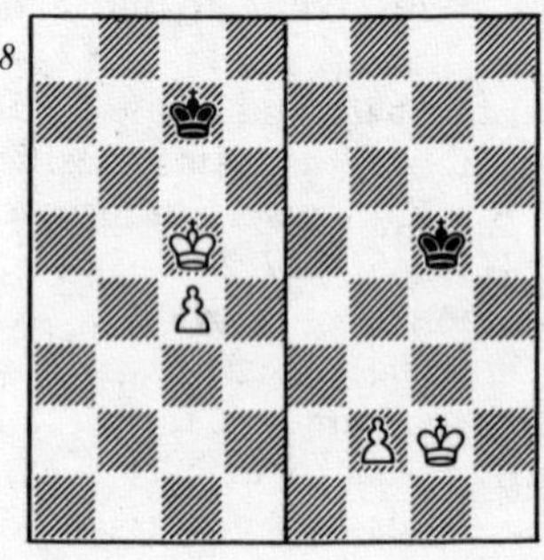

If the white king is in front of the pawn but not so advanced, we arrive at the left half of diagram 8. In this typical position the win depends on who has the move. If White has the opposition, then Black loses after **1 ... ♔b7 2 ♔d6 ♔c8** or 2 ... ♔b8 3 ♔d7 **3 c5 ♔d8 4 c6 ♔c8 5 c7** etc. However, with White to move, Black draws after **1 ♔d5 ♔d7 2 c5 ♔c7 3 c6 ♔c8! 4 ♔d6 ♔d8** with the well-known drawing position.

From this example, it is clear that White wins easily if his pawn is further back, for in this case he can always gain the opposition by moving the pawn. Hence a useful rule for conducting this type of ending is as follows: the white king is advanced as far as possible in front of his pawn (of course, without losing the latter), and only then is the pawn moved.

The right half of diagram 8 illustrates the application of this rule. If Black has the move, he draws easily with 1 ... ♔g4 or 1 ... ♔f4, but White to move wins in the following instructive way: **1 ♔g3!** gaining the opposition, as compared with 1 ♔f3? ♔f5! when Black has the opposition and draws **1 ... ♔f5 2 ♔f3!** maintaining the opposition; note that 2 f4? ♔f6 would again draw **2 ... ♔e5 3 ♔g4 ♔f6 4 ♔f4!** once more White takes over the opposition and applies our rule of advancing his king without moving the pawn; a mistake would be 4 f3? ♔g6 5 ♔f4 ♔f6! drawing **4 ... ♔e6 5 ♔g5! ♔f7 6 ♔f5** 6 f3 is possible, but not 6 f4? ♔g7! drawing **6 ... ♔e7 7 ♔g6 ♔e8 8 f4** only now, with the white king on the 6th rank, is the pawn advanced; 8 ♔g7 would be pointless, as 8 ... ♔e7 9 f4 ♔e6 would force 10 ♔g6 **8 ... ♔e7 9 f5 ♔f8 10 ♔f6!** it is vital to gain the opposition once more, as 10 f6? ♔g8 only draws **10 ... ♔e8 11 ♔g7 ♔e7 12 f6+** and the pawn queens.

In conclusion we would like to mention two exceptional cases involving the rook's pawn. The defence has better chances in this type of ending, drawing from positions that would be hopeless with any other pawn. For example, in the left half of diagram 9, even with the move White cannot win.

9

After **1 ♔a7 ♔c7 2 a6 ♔c8 3 ♔a8** or 3 ♔b6 ♔b8 **3 ... ♔c7 4 a7 ♔c8** White himself is stalemated for a change. As a rule we can state that Black draws if he can reach the critical square c8 (or f8 on the other wing). An obvious exception to this rule is when the white king already occupies c6 or b6 and 1 a7 can be played.

The right half of diagram 9 gives us another draw for Black in a situation that would be a loss against any other pawn. Again White cannot win even with the move, as **1 h5 ♔f6 2 ♔h7 ♔f7 3 h6 ♔f8** gives us the drawing position we have just seen. So in general Black draws against a rook's pawn.

With this example we complete our treatment of elementary endings and move over to more complicated cases, dealing in turn with pawn, queen, rook, bishop, and knight endings. We shall however examine only those positions illustrating general principles which can be applied to various endings. As already stated, we are not compiling an endgame reference book but presenting important basic positions which every chessplayer must know how to handle.

2 Pawn Endings

It may perhaps seem rather strange that we should begin with pawn endings, but there are good reasons for this. Firstly, pawn endings are relatively simple in form (though not necessarily in content!), consisting as they do of few men, and thus provide us with the best overall view of endings and their treatment. Secondly, pawn endings usually arise from other endings and represent so to speak the cornerstone of the whole of endgame theory.

We have already examined those elementary pawn endings which are the basis of all pawn endings. If these examples have given the reader the impression that pawn endings are the easiest of the endgames, he is sadly mistaken. As we shall see later, some pawn endings are very complex and difficult to play for the uninitiated.

King and Pawn against King

We return again to this ending which we have already examined in our section on elementary endings. As a test-piece we shall consider diagram 10 which cannot be solved immediately by applying our given principles. We shall also explain more fully the term 'distant opposition'.

10

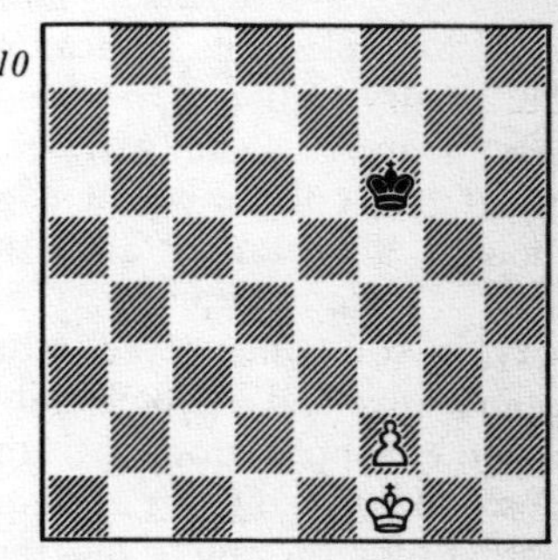

If Black has the move he cannot be prevented from reaching f4 with a draw, as we have already seen. The matter becomes more complicated, however, if White has the move. What will the result be then? To answer this question, we must examine the position in a little more detail. As we have seen in previous examples, White wins if his king can reach f6 with Black to move. His first move is naturally **1 ♔e2** (or 1 ♔g2 giving similar variations) and it is Black who must select the best defence. Obviously after 1 ... ♔f5? 2 ♔f3! White has attained his objective, and the same applies after 1 ... ♔e5 2 ♔e3 ♔f5 3 ♔f3. The only correct defence lies in **1 ... ♔e6!** in order to answer **2 ♔e3** with **2 ... ♔e5** and **2 ♔f3** with **2 ... ♔f5** gaining the opposition and drawing. The move 1 ... ♔e6! gave Black the distant opposition and this is converted into the close opposition as the kings approach each other. This example shows us the basic form of the distant opposition; we shall later examine much more complex examples of its application.

The theory of the opposition is important and reasonably straightforward, but a player can manage without it if he understands the theory of 'related squares'. This theory is sometimes even more comprehensive and comprehensible than the application of the opposition rule, so let us examine it further by returning to diagram 10.

What are 'related squares'? Let us assume that the white king is on f3 and his black counterpart on f5, when it is now known that White wins if it is Black to move. We can call these 'related squares' i.e. when the black king is on f5, White's king needs to be on f3 to win; or if Black wishes to draw, he must play his king to the related square after White's king goes to f3.

Now let us try to find other pairs of related squares, from the defender's point of view. We know that the white king cannot be allowed to reach f4, when he wins in all variations. This means that if the white king is on e3, threatening to go to f4, the black king must be ready to play to e5, f5 or g5; but g5 is no good, for with ♔e4 White wins at least the f4 square; nor is f5 suitable for the black king, as he must be ready to occupy this square, in case the white king goes to f3. There remains only e5, making this the related square of White's e3. To continue this logic, which black square corresponds to White's e2? As White can go to e3 or f3 from this square, Black must have a related square from which he can reach e5 and f5, i.e. e6 or f6.

By this process we have rediscovered the correct defence for Black. After **1 ♔e2**, only **1 ... ♔e6!** is sufficient to draw. As we have seen above, all other moves lose.

This is, of course, a simple illustration of related squares, but we shall later give instructive examples of the usefulness of this method of calculation.

King and Pawn against King and Pawn

Once again, for this type of ending there are no general rules for winning or drawing, as everything depends on the placing of the pieces. Normally these endings result in a draw, so we are primarily interested in those cases where White can force a win. First of all, let us divide our material into two groups:

A: THE PAWNS ARE ON THE SAME FILE

In this case, we can take

diagram 11 as our basic position.

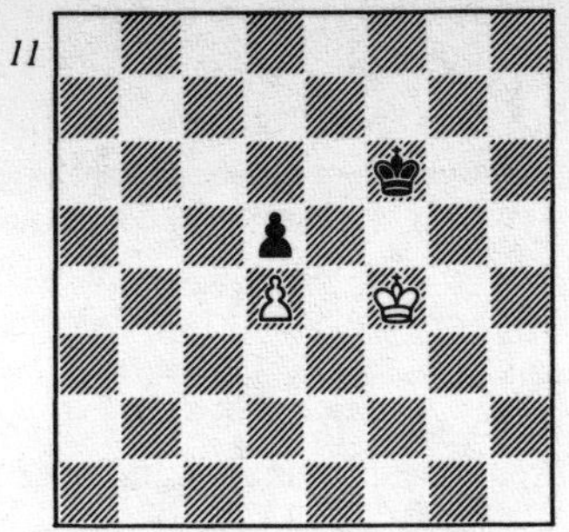

Such positions are drawn whoever has the move and however many ranks back we move the pawns. If White has the move, Black has the opposition and clearly draws after 1 ♔g4 ♔g6 2 ♔f4 ♔f6 etc. If Black has the move, then he must lose the pawn as follows:

1	**...**	**♔e6**
2	**♔g5**	**♔e7**
3	**♔f5**	**♔d6**
4	**♔f6**	**♔d7**
5	**♔e5**	

and the pawn falls, as 5 ... ♔c6 6 ♔e6 would still win it. However, Black can still draw by applying the principles we gave in our elementary endings.

5	**...**	**♔e7!**
6	**♔xd5**	**♔d7!**

gaining the opposition and drawing as already seen.

The situation changes drastically, however, if the pieces in diagram 11 are moved up one or two ranks. Admittedly, White to move cannot win, but if Black has the move, he is lost. He loses his pawn as we have just seen, but the white king meanwhile reaches the 6th rank, with pawns other than the rook's pawn, produce the same result. An exceptional case is when the black pawn is on g7 or b7. The black king can then head for the corner where he is stalemated if the white king approaches. Rook's pawn positions are drawn, as always.

Let us next examine a few positions in which both kings have more room to manoeuvre, beginning with diagram 12.

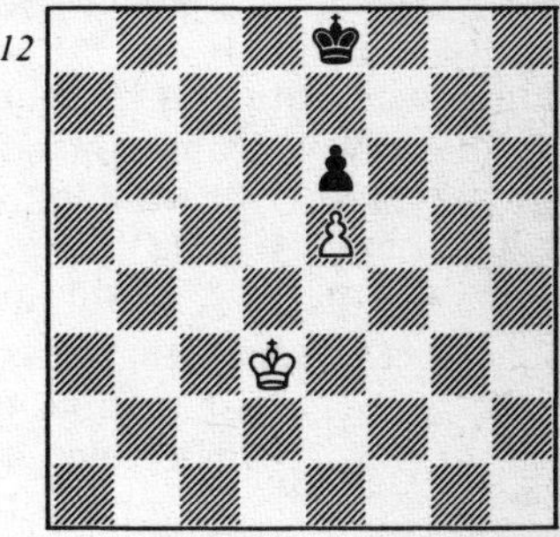

Such positions often occur in practice and their correct evaluation is therefore important. We know that White wins if he can capture the pawn, and if he has the move he can win comfortably, as Black cannot gain the opposition. Play might continue as follows:

1 ♔c4!

The only way to win. If 1 ♔d4 ♔d8! Black has the opposition and draws.

1	**...**	**♔d7**
2	**♔b5!**	

Again taking the diagonal

opposition. Not 2 ♔c5? ♔c7! drawing.

2 ... **♔c7**
3 **♔c5** **♔d7**
4 **♔b6** **♔d8**
5 **♔c6** **♔e7**
6 **♔c7** **♔e8**
7 **♔d6** **♔f7**
8 **♔d7** and wins.

This is one possibility, but Black can also attempt to set up a counterattack on the white pawn by 1 ... ♔f7. We then have:

1 **♔c4!** **♔f7**
2 **♔c5** **♔g6**

Once again, this is a common situation, with both kings coming in at the pawns from opposite wings. A typical error would now be 3 ♔d6? when 3 ... ♔f5! would even win for Black! A useful rule to remember in such situations is that the winner must be able to attack the pawn from one square below (here d7), in order to maintain the attack whilst guarding his own pawn next move (♔d6). So White continues:

3 **♔c6!**

As before the white king heads for d7, whereas Black heads for f4. It is clear that in this case White arrives first.

3 ... **♔g5**

If 3 ... ♔f5 4 ♔d6 wins at once.

4 **♔d7!** **♔f5**
5 **♔d6** wins.

Of course, with rook's pawns the winning chances are reduced, but diagram 13 shows us a subtle and unexpected winning manoeuvre.

13
W

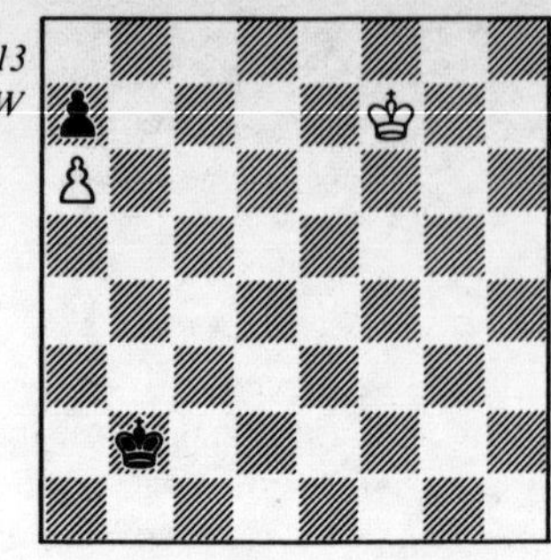

Schlage-Ahues, Berlin 1921

This position occurred in a tournament game Schlage-Ahues, Berlin 1921. With White to move, Black must obviously lose his pawn, but this seems unimportant for, in the five moves it takes White to win the pawn, the black king can reach the drawing square c7. Is the position drawn then? The game continuation was in fact 1 ♔e6 ♔c3 2 ♔d6? ♔d4 3 ♔c6 ♔e5 4 ♔b7 ♔d6 5 ♔xa7 ♔c7 etc, with a draw.

But White could have won by choosing the correct route for his king. In pawn endings it is sometimes possible for the king to choose a diagonal route which is no further in move count but which restricts the route of the enemy king. White should have played:

1 **♔e6** **♔c3**
2 **♔d5!**

As can be seen, White still captures the pawn in 5 moves but prevents the black king's approach via d4, e5 and d6. As a result he cannot reach c7 in time and is lost.

2 ... ♔b4

If 2 ... ♔d3 3 ♔c6 ♔e4 4 ♔b7 ♔d5 5 ♔xa7 ♔c6 6 ♔b8 wins.

3 ♔c6 ♔a5
4 ♔b7 ♔b5
5 ♔xa7 ♔c6
6 ♔b8

and the pawn queens.

A simple but instructive example. It is interesting to note that if Black's king had originally stood on the seemingly worse square h2, instead of b2, the game would have been drawn, as White cannot prevent the approach of the black king without wasting time himself.

B: THE PAWNS ARE ON DIFFERENT FILES

In such positions, if the pawn can be stopped by the opposing king, the result is usually a draw, unless White can capture the enemy pawn under favourable circumstances. As an example of this, consider diagram 14.

14

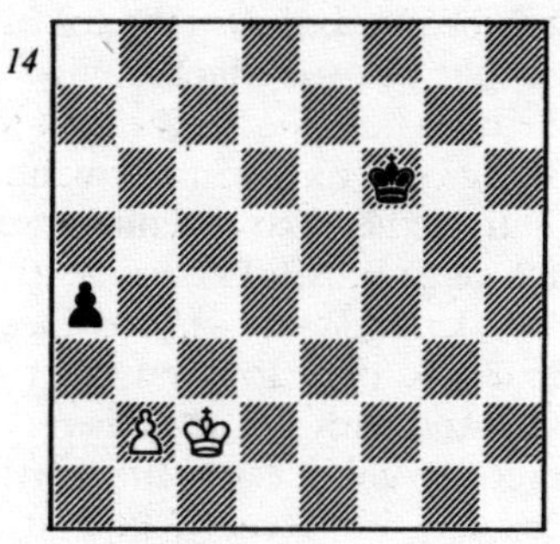

F.Dedrle 1921

White easily wins the black pawn and it appears as if 1 ♔c3 ♔e5 2 ♔b4 ♔d5 3 ♔xa4 etc would clinch matters. However, Black has the resource 1 ... a3! which draws after both 2 ba ♔e6 3 ♔c4 ♔d6 and 2 b4 ♔e6 3 ♔b3 ♔d6 4 ♔xa3 ♔c6 5 ♔a4 ♔b6 etc. In order to win, White must plan for this black defence and be ready to capture the pawn with his king whilst keeping his own pawn as far back as possible, as follows:

1 ♔b1 a3

The best defence, as White wins easily after 1 ... ♔e5 2 ♔a2 ♔d4 3 ♔a3 ♔c5 4 ♔xa4 ♔b6 5 ♔b4! etc.

2 b3!

As will soon be seen, 2 b4 would only draw.

2 ... ♔e5
3 ♔a2 ♔d5
4 ♔xa3 ♔c5
5 ♔a4 ♔b6
6 ♔b4! and wins.

It is clear that, with the pawn on b4, this last move would be impossible, whereas now we have reached a well-known winning position.

There are very interesting possibilities when both passed pawns cannot be stopped. Often the game can be won by instructive king manoeuvres, using the above-mentioned idea that in chess the shortest distance between two points is not necessarily a straight line. Let us examine an ending by grandmaster Duras (diagram 15).

A cursory glance might lead us to believe that the position is equal, for both pawns still stand

15

on their original squares and the placing of the white king is only slightly better. In the event, however, this minimal advantage, combined with the fact that White has the move, surprisingly gives him a forced win. Nevertheless, he must play most accurately to achieve this result, in particular when choosing the correct positioning of his king.

1 ♔c5!

Clearly the white king must in some way support the advance of his pawn, as otherwise the black king can stop it. But why this move which apparently places the king on an unfavourable square, in the firing line of a future black queen? The remaining moves provide an explanation.

A

1 ... ♔g6

Black attempts to stop the white pawn. 1 ... g5 will be discussed in B.

2 b4 ♔f7
3 b5 ♔e7
4 ♔c6!

Now we see why 1 ♔c5 was essential. The game would be drawn after both 4 b6 ♔d7 and 4 ♔b6 g5 5 ♔c7 g4.

4 ... ♔d8

The point is that the black king is now unfavourably placed on the back rank where he can subsequently be checked by the white queen.

5 ♔b7! g5
6 b6 g4
7 ♔a7 g3
8 b7 g2
9 b8♕+ and wins.

B

1 ... g5

Instead of trying to stop the advance of the enemy pawn, Black attempts to push his own through, a line which is all the more tempting because he would queen with check. However, the white king now reveals his flexibility with the following subtle win:

2 b4 g4
3 ♔d4!

The black pawn will now require support from his king, but this means that White can drive the king onto a square from which he can be checked. Note that 3 b5? g3 would win for Black.

3 ... ♔g5

3 ... g3 4 ♔e3 ♔g5 5 b5! would lead into the text variation, but not here 5 ♔f3? ♔f5 drawing.

4 b5 g3

If Black tries to hold off the white king with 4 ... ♔f4 then the white pawn queens first with check.

5 ♔e3 ♔g4
6 b6 ♔h3
7 b7 g2

8	**♔f2**	**♔h2**
9	**b8♕+** and wins.	

A magnificent study, revealing with limited material the complexities that some pawn endings can contain. Among countless compositions we could quote many other examples illustrating surprisingly deep ideas arising from relatively simple positions. For the moment, let us consider one more study which is probably the most famous example in chess literature of king and pawn on either side.

16

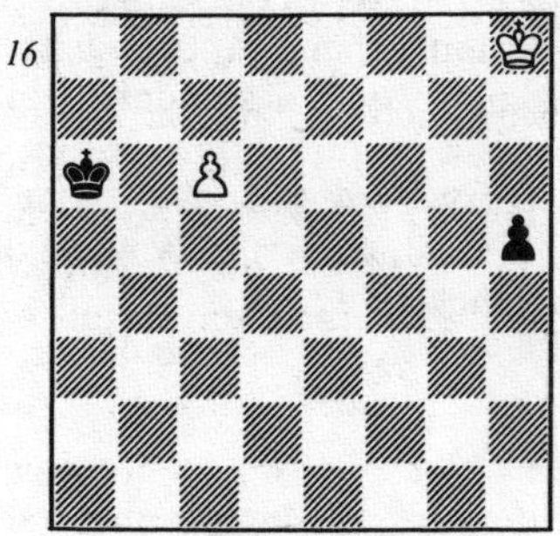

R.Réti 1922

Although White is to move, he appears hopelessly lost, for the black pawn is going to queen and White needs at least two tempi to stop it. His own pawn seemingly offers little hope as it can easily be stopped by the black king. However, the geometrical motif once more comes into play, as the white king performs wonders:

1	**♔g7**	**h4**
2	**♔f6**	**♔b6**

So White has already won one tempo by forcing Black to make a time-wasting move. If instead 2 ... h3, then 3 ♔e7 h2 4 c7 draws, as both pawns queen at the same time. Black's first two moves could have been inverted, for after 1 ... ♔b6 2 ♔f6 the threat of 3 ♔g5 would force 2 ... h4.

3 ♔e5!

The point of the whole play. As White now threatens to catch the pawn with 4 ♔f4 Black has no choice.

3	**...**	**h3**
4	**♔d6**	**h2**
5	**c7**	**h1♕**
6	**c8♕**	

with a clear draw.

Who would have assumed this possible in the initial position? These examples are by no means comprehensive, but they indicate some of the various possibilities contained within the simplest pawn endings. Later we shall meet further examples, when more complicated positions simplify during the solution.

King and two Pawns against King and Pawn

Positions with king and two pawns against king and pawn represent a very complicated section of pawn endings. There are many and varied possibilities so we must be systematic if we are to obtain an overall picture of collected material. As a rule, the side with the greater material wins especially if his passed pawn is at a distance from the other pawns and can thus drag the defending king away.

There are also, however, many positions which admit of no easy win, and it is these positions which interest us most and to which the following section is mainly devoted.

A: ISOLATED PAWNS WITH A PASSED PAWN

We intend to classify endings of two pawns against one by separating them into various groups depending on the position of the white pawns. Firstly we shall examine those in which the white pawns are isolated and one of them is passed. As already mentioned, White wins fairly easily here if the pawns are some distance apart, so we shall only examine those positions where there is one file between the pawns, which means that the passed pawn cannot take the black king too far away from the scene of action. A typical position is diagram 17.

17

As could be expected, this position is a win for White, whoever has the move. Let us assume that White is to move.

1 d5 ♔d7

White wins easily after 1 ... ♔c5 2 ♔e5 ♔xb5 3 d6 ♔c6 4 ♔e6 etc.

2 ♔e5 ♔e7

3 d6+ ♔d8!

The most cunning defence, setting White a few problems. After 3 ... ♔d7 4 ♔d5 wins, whereas now 4 ♔d5 ♔d7 or 4 ♔e6 ♔e8 5 d7+ ♔d8 would not help White. However, White can now transpose to one of the elementary endings.

4 d7!

The simplest winning method, giving up the pawn but gaining the opposition, then capturing the black pawn with a standard win. There is a more complicated way to victory by 4 ♔d4 ♔e8 5 ♔e4 ♔d8 6 ♔e5!, a possibility we shall come back to again.

4 ... ♔xd7

Or 4 ... ♔e7 5 d8♕+ ♔xd8 6 ♔d6 wins.

5 ♔d5 ♔c7

6 ♔e6 and wins.

Now let us see what happens if we bring the pieces one rank further back, giving us diagram 18.

18

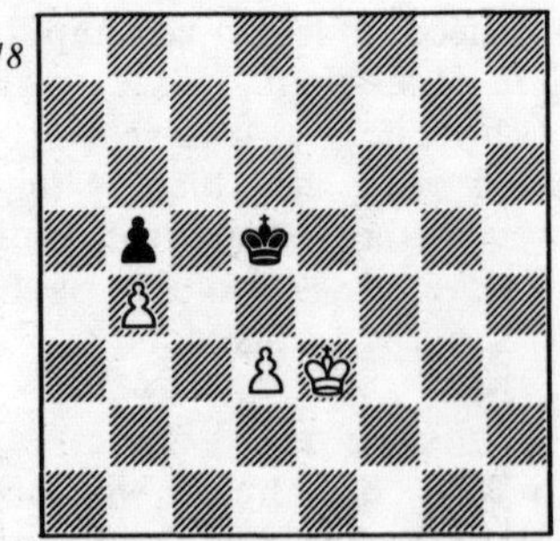

This position is equally won for White, but he must here be more careful about a counterattack on his own pawn. Play could continue:

1 d4 ♔c4

Hopeless would be 1 ... ♔d6 2 ♔e4 ♔e6 3 d5+ ♔d7 4 ♔e5 ♔e7 5 d6+ ♔d7 6 ♔d5 followed by 7 ♔c5 winning.

2 ♔e4 ♔xb4
3 d5 ♔c5

Black has to place his king on this unfavourable square to stop the white pawn queening first.

4 ♔e5 b4
5 d6 b3

5 ... ♔c6 6 ♔e6 would not alter the situation.

6 d7 b2
7 d8♕ b1♕

Both sides have a queen but Black's queen is lost after:

8 ♕c8+ ♔b4
9 ♕b7+ and wins.

One might think that all positions like diagram 18 are won for White but there is a surprising exception. This is when the black and white pawns are on the bishop's file, as in diagram 19.

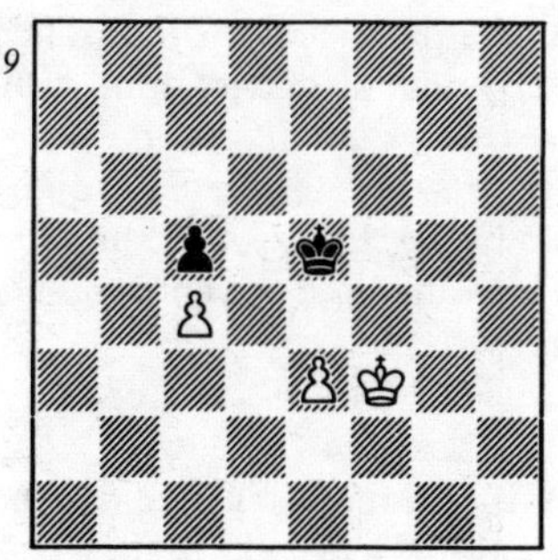

At first glance there seems no difference, as after 1 e4 ♔e6 2 ♔f4 ♔f6 3 e5+ ♔e7 4 ♔f5 ♔f7 5 e6+, or 1 ... ♔d4 2 ♔f4 ♔xc4 3 e5 ♔d5 4 ♔f5 c4 5 e6 c3 6 e7 c2 7 e8♕ c1♕ 8 ♕d8+ followed by 9 ♕c7+, White wins in the same way we have seen above. However, there is one subtle difference, as follows:

1 e4 ♔d4!
2 ♔f4 ♔xc4
3 e5 ♔b3!!

With this move Black exploits the peculiar fact that a queen cannot win against a bishop's pawn on the 7th rank when the king is too far away. Insufficient would be 3 ... ♔d3 4 e6 c4 5 e7 c3 6 e8♕ c2 7 ♕e3+ winning.

4 e6 c4
5 e7 c3
6 e8♕ c2

and the ending is drawn because White cannot stop Black's king reaching b2. We shall look at this in more detail in our section on queen endings but feel that it is worth a mention here.

It is clear that if positions similar to diagram 18 are moved one rank down, they are drawn, as Black can always attack the white pawn. Yet, surprisingly, if we push the position two ranks up, so that the black pawn is on its original square, this also limits White's winning chances. The black king remains in front of the pawns and usually escapes with stalemate, but it would lead us too far astray to examine this aspect now.

In conclusion we should mention

that positions similar to diagrams 17 to 19 are easily won for White, if Black has the move. In this case, the white pawn cannot be attacked, so White has only to advance his passed pawn, the sole exception again being positions with the black pawn on its original square.

Usually, rook's pawns significantly reduce White's winning chances, but in the positions examined this is surprisingly not the case. Consider diagram 20.

20

Fahrni-Alapin

This position could have arisen from our analysis of diagram 17 moved one file to the left with White having advanced his passed pawn. With Black to move the win is easy, but how does White win if he is to move? The same play as in diagram 17 does not work here, as 1 ♔d5 ♔c8 2 c7? ♔xc7 3 ♔c5 ♔b7, or here 2 ♔d6 ♔d8 3 c7+ ♔c8 both give Black a draw. So the win is not to be achieved by simple means and we must look a little deeper. As White would win if Black had the move, could we perhaps lose a tempo and bring about this situation?

Let us for a moment return to our theory of related squares. We have seen that Black must answer ♔c5 with ... ♔c7 and ♔d6 by ... ♔d8, so here are two pairs of related squares. Which Black square corresponds to White's d5? The white king can go to c5 or d6 from this square, so the black king must be able to go to the related squares c7 and d8. The only square is then c8, giving us another pair of related squares.

Continuing this process, we find that White's c4 (controlling d5 and c5) corresponds to Black's b8 and d8 (controlling c8 and c7); it can indeed happen that two squares relate to one only. And what about White's d4? As this square controls d5 and c5, Black's related squares are b8 and d8.

By doing all this preliminary work, we have already solved our problem. Let us assume that White has played ♔c4 and Black has selected the related square b8. White then plays his king to d4, compelling Black to go to the related squares b8 or d8. But he is already on b8 and cannot move two squares to d8. So he has to move to an unrelated square, when he loses. Let us see how this works out in a given sequence of moves:

1	**♔d5**	**♔c8**
2	**♔c4**	

It does not matter here whether c4 or d4 is selected, as they both lead to the same result.

2 ... ♔d8

Or 2 ... ♔b8.

3 ♔d4! ♔c8

If 3 ... ♔c7 4 ♔c5 wins quickly.

4 ♔d5! ♔c7

5 ♔c5

and White has reached the diagrammed position with Black to move. After 5 ... ♔d8 6 ♔d6 ♔c8 7 c7 ♔b7 8 ♔d7 ♔a7 9 ♔c6 (not 9 c8♕ stalemate) White mates in two moves.

Let us close this section with one example of this type of ending.

21

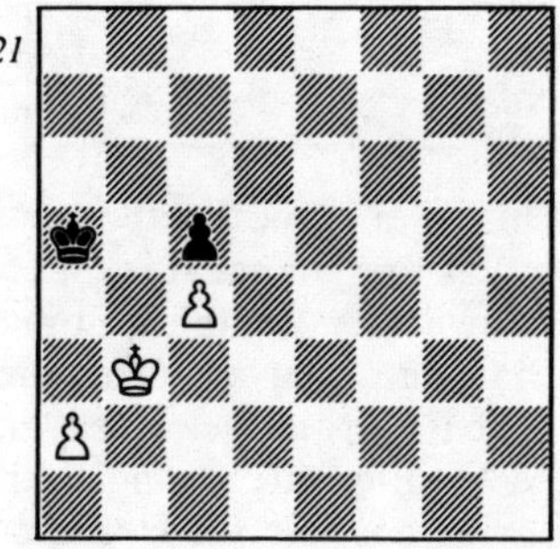

White's task is made extremely difficult by the fact that his passed pawn is on the rook's file and that he has no manoeuvring space for his king to the left of this pawn. His only chance is to attack from the right, when he must continually reckon with a counterattack by the black king. For example, after the direct attempt 1 ♔c3 ♔a4 2 ♔d3 Black plays 2 ... ♔b4! (not 2 ... ♔a3 3 ♔e4 ♔xa2 4 ♔d5 winning easily), winning one of White's pawns, with a clear draw. Again we must look a little deeper.

In order to win, the white king must reach d5 without allowing Black in the meantime to capture the a-pawn and be in a position to guard his pawn by ... ♔b4. When Black plays ... ♔b4 White must be in a position to play ♔d3 after which Black is in zugzwang and cannot prevent ♔e4-d5. So our first pair of related squares are White's d3 and Black's b4.

Let us proceed further. When the black king is on a3, threatening to take the a-pawn, White must be ready to answer this threat with ♔d5, so White's e4 and Black's a3 are related squares. Consequently Black's a4 (controlling a3 and b4) corresponds to White's e3 (controlling e4 and d3), and Black's a5 (controlling a4 and b4) corresponds to White's d2 (controlling d3 and e3).

Once again we have now carried out the most difficult part of our task. There only remains for White to reach d2 by careful manoeuvring and Black cannot prevent the white king's advance to d5. For completeness we might mention that if the black king is on a6 or b6, the white king can occupy c1, c2 or c3, when he can always answer ... ♔a5 with ♔d2.

From our last comment it is clear that Black to move loses quickly, for after 1 ... ♔b6 (or a6) White plays 2 ♔c3 (or c2) 2 ... ♔a5 3 ♔d2! immediately. With White to move, matters are more complex, but the win can be forced as follows:

1 ♔a3!

The only move, otherwise Black plays 1 ... ♔a4 and White's king is too far from the related square e3. The text move wins an important tempo.

1 ... ♔b6
2 ♔b2 ♔a5

The best, as other moves allow 3 ♔c3 with an easy win. It goes without saying that Black would get nowhere by playing his king to the centre.

3 ♔b3!

Again winning a tempo.

3 ... ♔b6
4 ♔c3 (or c2) **♔a5**

If 4 ... ♔a6 White wins by ♔c2(c3)-d3-e4 d5 etc.

5 ♔d2!

The winning move, not found until later by Kling. The theory of related squares, however, makes it all so easy!

5 ... ♔a4
6 ♔e3! ♔b4
7 ♔d3

and White reaches his goal, winning easily after 7 ... ♔a3 8 ♔e4 ♔xa2 9 ♔d5 or here 8 ... ♔a4 9 ♔d5 ♔b4 10 a3+ etc.

There are many such examples in which the apparently complicated solutions can be readily understood in the light of related squares, whose importance will be seen in other positions to which we shall now proceed.

B: ISOLATED PAWNS WITHOUT A PASSED PAWN

This kind of position gives the defending side much greater chances of obtaining a draw, especially if the attacker has no tempo moves available with his pawns. The deciding factors here are the placing of the kings and the gaining of the opposition. Consider diagram 22.

22

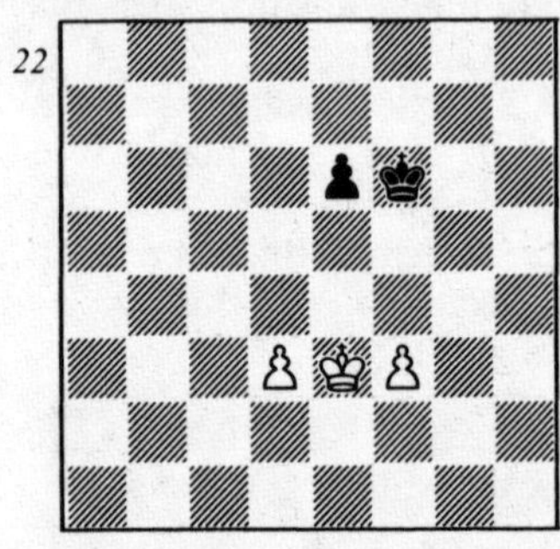

This is a typical situation in which at first glance it is difficult to say whether White wins or not. A thorough analysis is required. As a general rule, we can say that the defending side should restrict as far as possible the freedom of the white pawns, so that they have no tempo moves at their disposal. On the other hand, the attacking side must try to maintain this freedom and attempt to bring his king as far forward as possible. If the reader keeps these points in mind, he will easily understand the following variations. We shall begin with the simplest case, with Black to move.

1 ... e5!
2 f4

King moves do not help, e.g. 2 ♔e4 ♔e6 or 2 ♔d2 ♔e6 3 ♔c3

♔d5 etc. The text move is the sole winning attempt.

2 ... ♔f5

Black's only move to draw, as 2 ... ef+ 3 ♔xf4 ♔e6 4 ♔e4 ♔d6 5 ♔d4! would win for White, whereas now 3 fe ♔xf5 is completely drawn.

Apart from this simple line, Black also has another drawing method, requiring accurate play, as follows:

1 ... ♔e5

But not 1 ... ♔f5 2 d4 ♔g6 3 ♔f4 ♔f6 4 ♔e4 followed by 5 ♔e5 winning, as will be seen later.

2 ♔e2

After 2 d4+ ♔d5 or 2 f4+ ♔f5, Black threatens 3 ... e5 and if 3 f4 (or d4), we would arrive at a symmetrical position to the one arising after Black's 1 ... e5.

2 ... ♔f4

Other king moves also draw, but the text move is the most instructive.

3 d4 ♔g5!

This time the only move, for 3 ... ♔f5? 4 ♔e3 wins for White as we have seen. Black must make sure that he can answer ♔e3 with ... ♔f5, and the draw is forced, as White cannot strengthen his position.

Going back to diagram 22, with White to move, he wins as follows:

1 ♔e4!

Obeying our rule about advancing the king as far as possible! This is the only way to win, as 1 ♔f4? e5+ 2 ♔g4 ♔g6, or 1 f4 ♔f5 2 ♔f3 e5 only draw, as does 1 d4 ♔f5 2 ♔d3 ♔f4 3 ♔e2 ♔g5! etc.

1 ... ♔f7

The best chance. After 1 ... e5 2 f4! or 1 ... ♔e7 2 ♔e5 ♔d7 3 d4 ♔e7 4 f4 ♔d7 5 d5 (or 4 ... ♔f7 5 f5) White wins comfortably.

2 ♔e5 ♔e7
3 f4 ♔d7

3 ... ♔f7 loses at once to 4 f5.

4 ♔f6!

If 4 d4? ♔e7! Black would draw, as the reader can check for himself.

4 ... ♔d6
5 d4

Winning the opposition and the game. Also possible is 5 ♔f7, as 5 ... e5 6 f5 wins.

5 ... ♔d7
6 ♔f7 ♔d6
7 ♔e8! ♔c6
8 ♔e7 ♔d5
9 ♔d7 ♔xd4
10 ♔xe6 and wins.

It is worth noting that White won this ending only because he had the tempo move 5 d4 at his disposal. For instance, if we look at the position after White's 6th move and give him the move instead of Black, with best defence it is only a draw. Let us examine this in more detail.

In order to win, White must gain the opposition with his king on f7 when Black's king is on d7, as we have seen. Other related squares are White's f6 and f8 corresponding to Black's d6 and d8, and if White's king is on the knight's file, then g8 and g7 correspond to Black's e8 and e7.

But what about g6? Black's e6 is occupied by his pawn so he has here only the distant opposition on c6, a square to which Black must be ready to play as soon as White plays ♔g6.

This means that the game might continue **1 ♔f6 ♔d6 2 ♔g7 ♔c7!** not 2 ... ♔e7? 3 ♔g6! ♔d6 4 ♔f6 ♔d7 5 ♔f7 winning **3 ♔g6 ♔c6! 4 ♔f7 ♔d7 5 ♔g8 ♔c8!** again the only move, as both 5 ... ♔e8 6 ♔g7 ♔e7 7 ♔g6! and 5 ... ♔c6 6 ♔f8 ♔d6 7 ♔e8 lead to a loss **6 d5** there is nothing else **6 ... ♔d7!** not 6 ... ed? 7 f5 and White queens with check **7 ♔g7** or 7 de+ ♔xe6 and 8 ... ♔f5 **7 ... ed** and both pawns queen together.

If White's two pawns are doubled, he can only hope to win if his rear pawn has important tempo moves available. Consider the interesting position in diagram 23.

23
W

As the black king is much more actively placed than the white king, it seems at first unlikely that White can win. However, his pawn on f3 gives him a vital tempo at the critical moment, and he wins nicely as follows:

1 ♔f5!

If his pawn were on f2 he would have no problems and could win at once with 1 ♔g5 ♔e5 2 f3, but in this position 1 ♔g5 would only draw after 1 ... ♔e5 2 f4+ ♔e6 3 f5+ ♔e5, and 1 ♔g4 fails to 1 ... ♔e6 2 ♔g5 ♔e5 when he is in zugzwang. He must first bring his pawn to f4 to guard e5 from the black king.

1 ... ♔d6

White was threatening 2 f4 followed by the penetration of his king to h6 via h5. For example, if 1 ... ♔d4 2 f4 ♔d5 3 ♔g4! (not 3 ♔g5 ♔e6! and White is in zugzwang) 3 ... ♔d6 4 ♔h5 ♔e6 5 ♔g5 and 6 ♔h6 wins. So Black goes back with his king to prevent entry.

2 f4 ♔d7

3 ♔g4!

Again 3 ♔g5? ♔e6! draws for Black.

3 ... ♔e8

4 ♔h5

As will be seen later, 4 ♔g5 ♔f8 again puts White into zugzwang.

4 ... ♔f8

5 ♔g5

Now it is Black who is in zugzwang and he must allow White in on one side or the other. It is interesting to note that if the whole position were one rank further back, Black would draw by 5 ... ♔f8! waiting to see which way White goes, but he lacks the necessary space here.

5 ... ♔g8

Or 5 ... ♔e8 6 ♔h6 ♔f8 7 ♔h7 winning easily.

6 ♔f5 ♔h7

It is now too late for 6 ... ♔f8 7 ♔e5 ♔e8 8 ♔d6 ♔d8 9 f5! (the winning tempo!) 9 ... ♔e8 10 ♔c7 winning.

7 ♔e4!

White must still proceed carefully. 7 ♔e5 ♔g6! gives Black a draw, as White wants this position with Black to move.

7 ... ♔h6
8 ♔d5 ♔g6
9 ♔e5 ♔h5
10 ♔d6 ♔h6
11 ♔e7 ♔g6
12 f5+ and wins.

A beautiful study with a subtle solution.

C: CONNECTED PAWNS WITH A PASSED PAWN

When White's pawns are connected and one of them is passed, he usually has excellent winning chances. Black's defensive possibilities are limited and he can only hope for a draw when White's pawns are not very advanced or if the black king has an unusually favourable position. In the following we try to indicate the factors by which a position can be evaluated.

Let us start by examining positions with the pawns on the a- and b-files. At the same time we shall consider how far advanced the pawns are, and in this way cover all types of position.

24

Diagram 24 is a key position in this ending. As it does not matter whose move it is, we shall make White's task a little more difficult by giving Black the move.

1 ... ♔c5
2 ♔d3 ♔d5
3 ♔e3 ♔e5
4 ♔f3!

We immediately realize the tremendous advantage of a protected passed pawn which does not need the white king to remain near it and yet greatly restricts the enemy king's activity. In this example the black king dare not leave the quadrant represented by the b5-b8-e8-e5 squares, or else the b-pawn queens. This means that 4 ... ♔f5 cannot be played, so Black is forced to relinquish the opposition.

4 ... ♔d5
5 ♔f4 ♔d6
6 ♔e4

White would make no progress with 6 ♔f5 ♔d5, when he would have to return to the 4th rank.

6 ... ♔e6
7 ♔d4 ♔d6
8 ♔c4 ♔c7

So Black has been compelled to concede White the 5th rank, but he has various defensive possibilities.

9 ♔c5

A simpler win is 9 ♔d5 ♔b6 10 ♔d6 ♔b7 11 ♔c5 etc, but we shall give the longer win in order to show one or two instructive points.

9 ... ♔b7
10 ♔d5!

White would spoil everything with 10 b6? ♔a6! 11 ♔c6, giving stalemate, and after 10 ♔d6 ♔b6 11 ♔d7 ♔b7 Black keeps the opposition.

10 ... ♔c7
11 ♔e6 ♔b6

If 11 ... ♔b7 12 ♔d7 ♔b6 12 ♔c8 wins.

12 ♔d6 ♔b7
13 ♔c5 (d7)

with an easy win.

If the position in diagram 24 is moved one rank up (white pawns on a5 and b6 etc), it can no longer be won. Although the white king reaches c6, the b-pawn cannot be advanced because of the stalemate we have already seen. Equally drawn is the position one rank further up (White's pawns on a6 and b7 etc), for the black king can clearly not be driven from the b8 and c7 squares.

If this position in diagram 24 is moved one rank down (white pawns on a3 and b4 etc), it is still won, but two ranks lower (white pawns on a2 and b3 etc) brings about a change. White to move still wins, 1 ♔c2 ♔c5 2 ♔d3! ♔b4 3 ♔d4 ♔b5 4 ♔c3! ♔c5 5 b4+ etc, but Black to move can draw by counterattacking the pawn with 1 ... ♔c3 2 ♔d1 ♔b2!, when White must force stalemate.

Let us now turn to positions where the white pawns are on the b- and c-files. Move the position in diagram 24 one file to the right (white pawns on b4 and c5 etc) and it is even easier for White to win, as is the same position one rank further down (white pawns on b3 and c4 etc). Further explanation seems unnecessary.

It is equally clear that this position moved two ranks down (white pawns on b2 and c3 etc) or two ranks up (white pawns on b6 and c7 etc) cannot be won for White, just as in the corresponding positions already examined. There is, however, a difference if the position in diagram 24 is moved one file to the right and one rank up, giving us diagram 25.

25

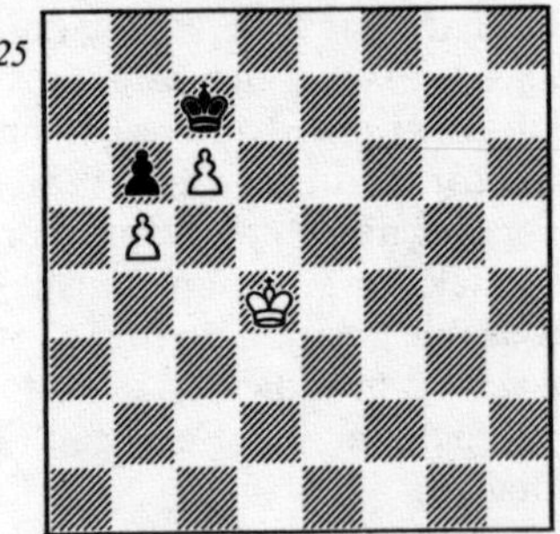

This position is won for White as follows:

1 ... ♔d6
2 ♔e4 ♔e6
3 ♔f4 ♔d6

The passed pawn severely restricts the black king's movements, so that White can immediately advance his king.

4 ♔f5 ♔c7
5 ♔e6 ♔c8

White is now suddenly faced with a problem. If 6 ♔d6 ♔d8 7 c7+ ♔c8 8 ♔c6?, Black is stalemated, so a sacrifice is called for.

6 c7! ♔xc7
7 ♔e7! and wins.

The black pawn will be captured and White obtains the winning position given in diagram 7.

We shall now turn to positions resulting from moving diagram 24 two files to the right. It is easy to see that this position and its counterpart one rank further up (white pawns on c5 and d6 etc) are won for White. Equally the same position moved two ranks up (white pawns on c6 and d7 etc) is won, because White has the possibility of penetrating to the queenside via a6. The position one rank further down (with a slightly different placing of the kings) gives us diagram 26.

26

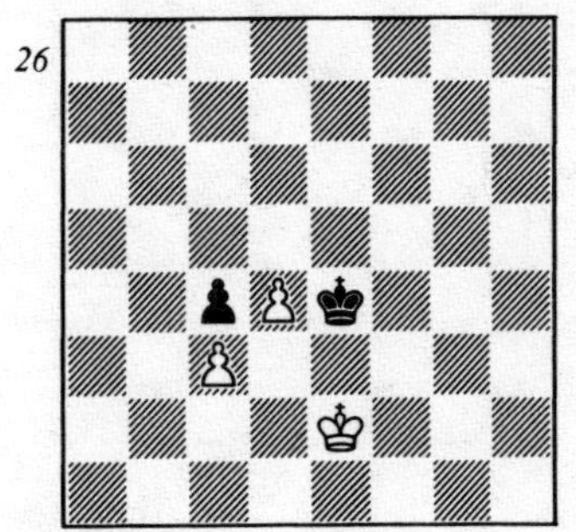

Compared with the similar positions we have seen, this one contains an interesting new possibility. In order to give Black the most favourable defensive position we have placed his king on e4 and given him the move, but this does not change the basic characteristics of the position. Let us first see how Black copes with White's usual winning method:

1 ... ♔f4
2 ♔f2? ♔e4
3 ♔e2!

White must admit the error of his previous move, because the normal 3 ♔g3 will not work here. Black replies 3 ... ♔d3! 4 d5 ♔xc3 5 d6 ♔b2 6 d7 c3 7 d8♕ c2 and draws, as we saw in our analysis of diagram 19. This means that White's usual win does not suffice, but he does have a chance to penetrate via the queen's wing.

3 ... ♔f4
4 ♔d2 ♔e4
5 ♔c2 ♔d5

Black must be ready to answer ♔d2 with ... ♔e4 and ♔a3 with ... ♔b5, and it seems he can succeed, as 6 ♔b2 ♔c6 7 ♔a3 ♔b5, and 6 ♔d2 ♔e4 both get White nowhere. However, there is one possibility.

6 ♔c1!

This waiting move zugzwangs Black. If he plays 6 ... ♔e4 then 7 ♔b2 ♔d5 8 ♔a3 wins, whereas 6 ... ♔c6 fails to 7 ♔d2 and 8 ♔e3. So Black is lost.

Having seen this winning method, we should be able to evaluate correctly the same position one rank further down (white pawns on c2 and d3 etc). White to move wins by 1 ♔d1 ♔f3 (preventing 2 ♔e2) 2 ♔c1 ♔e3 3 ♔b1 etc. However, Black to move can draw by 1 ... ♔f3! 2 ♔d1 ♔e3 3 ♔c1 ♔d4, when White has no space for the tempo move we saw in diagram 26 (6 ♔c1!), his king being already on the back rank. After 4 ♔b1 ♔c5 5 ♔a2 ♔b4, or 4 ♔d1 ♔e3 the game is drawn.

If we move the position in diagram 26 one file to the right, with the white pawns now both on the centre files, White's winning chances are increased, the trickiest position being the one with White's d-pawn on d2, as in diagram 27:

27

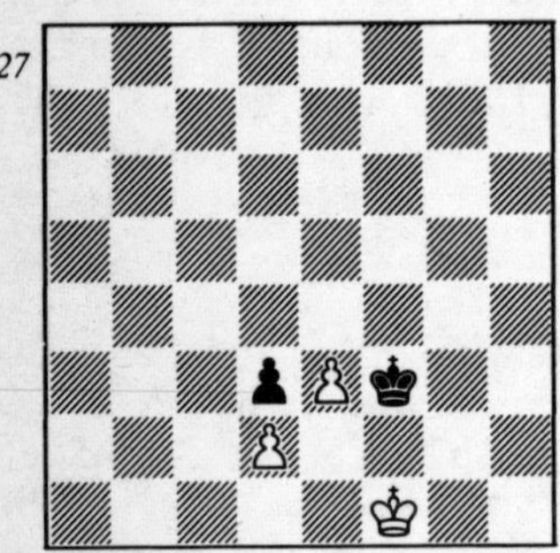

White to move wins easily with 1 ♔e1 ♔g3 2 ♔d1 etc, but even with Black to move, White wins because his king now has the use of the a-file to penetrate down the queenside!

1	**...**	**♔g3**
2	**♔e1**	**♔f3**
3	**♔d1**	**♔e4**

One file to the left, as we have seen, this position could not be won, but here matters are different.

4	**♔c1**	**♔d5**
5	**♔b2**	**♔c4**
6	**♔a3!** wins.	

As a result of the above example, we can state that with the pawns on the centre files (as in diagram 27) all positions are won for White, however advanced the pawns may be. It does not matter where the kings are placed for the black king cannot stop White's king from penetrating via a3 or f2. The other attempt, to counter-attack in the centre, equally fails. For example, in the position with white pawns on d2 and e3 and king on c1, and black pawn on d3 and king on c4, Black can try **1 ... ♔b3 2 ♔d1 ♔b4 3 ♔e1 ♔b3**, in order to answer 4 ♔f2 with 4 ... ♔c2!, but White wins by **4 e4! ♔c4 5 ♔f2 ♔d4 6 ♔f3 ♔e5 7 ♔e3** etc.

Matters become a little more complicated again if we push the position further over to the right, as seen in diagram 28:

28

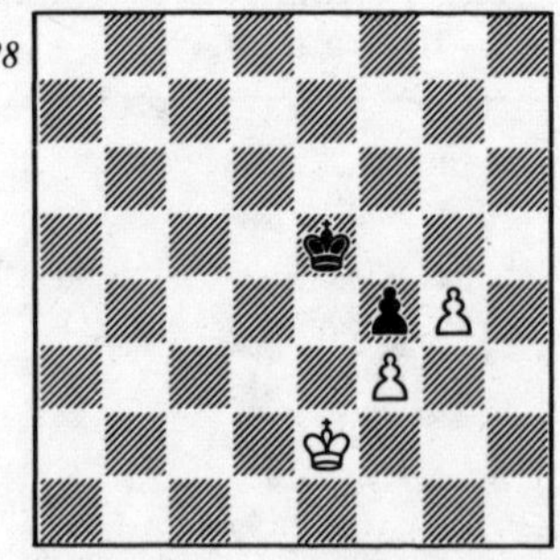

It hardly needs stating that

White's chances are vastly reduced here. He must try to penetrate via the queen's wing, as the h-file is hopeless for this purpose. However, to advance on the queenside, he must gain the opposition, and the distant opposition will not do. It is easy to see that he cannot succeed in doing this from the diagram, if Black defends correctly by using the distant opposition.

White can of course try to utilize the fact that the black king is tied down within the c4-c8-g8-g4 quadrant, and penetrate down the a-file. But Black can use the opposition to defend successfully against this plan also, and White must in this case take into account a possible attack on his f-pawn. Let us see what might happen:

1 ... ♔d4

The simplest, but 1 ... ♔e6 or 1 ... ♔d6 are also possible. Black must play so that he can always answer ♔d3 with ... ♔d5 and ♔c3 with ... ♔c5. There is no point at the moment gaining the distant opposition, as the white king cannot be prevented from using the a-file.

2 ♔d2

If 2 ♔f2 ♔e5 3 ♔g2 ♔f6 4 ♔h3 ♔g5 etc draws.

2 ... ♔c4
3 ♔c2 ♔d4
4 ♔b3 ♔d5!

Black must quickly take the diagonal opposition, as 4 ... ♔d3 fails to 5 g5, and 4 ... ♔c5? allows 5 ♔c3! gaining the opposition. But what about the counter-attack by 4 ... ♔e3 5 g5 ♔xe3 6 g6 ♔e2 7 g7 f3 8 g8♕ f2 reaching an ending similar to the one in our analysis of diagram 26? In fact the position is different, and the white king's position gives him a neat win with 9 ♕g2+ ♔e1 10 ♔c2! f1♕ 11 ♕d2 mate.

5 ♔b4 ♔d4

White can make no further progress. If 6 ♔b5 Black can choose between 6 ... ♔e3, which now works, or 6 ... ♔d5. If 6 ♔b3 ♔d5 7 ♔a3 ♔c5 etc, and finally 6 g5 ♔e5 7 ♔c5 ♔f5 8 ♔d5 ♔xg5 9 ♔e5 ♔g6 10 ♔xf4 ♔f6! gives us the standard drawing position.

From the above, it is clear that White's winning chances are even less if diagram 28 is moved down a rank, but White wins with the position moved up, as the passed pawn restricts the black king's activity too much. For example, with White's pawns on f4 and g5 and king on e3, and Black's pawn on f5 and king on e6, the black king is tied to the d5-h5-h8-d8 quadrant and cannot prevent the entry of White's king via c5, e.g. **1 ... ♔d5 2 ♔d3 ♔e6** if 2 ... ♔c5 3 g6 wins **3 ♔d4 ♔d6 4 ♔c4 ♔e6 5 ♔c5** and White soon wins the pawn.

And now we must examine the case when the passed pawn is on the h-file, as in diagram 29.

Following our analysis of diagram 28 we can in all justice claim that this position is also drawn, but as there are one or two differences in the defensive play,

29

let us look at it a little more closely.

1 ♔e3 ♔e5
2 ♔d3 ♔d5

As in the previous example, Black must keep the opposition, or else White will occupy the key square d4.

3 ♔c3 ♔e5!

Black must defend even more accurately than in diagram 28, as he cannot attack the pawn here (it is not a bishop's pawn). He cannot leave the d4-h4-h8-d8 quadrant and he must never lose the opposition. For instance, after 3 ... ♔e4? 4 ♔c4 ♔e5 5 ♔c5 the white king penetrates via d4 or d6.

4 ♔c4 ♔e4
5 ♔c5 ♔e5
6 ♔b6 ♔d6
7 ♔a7 ♔e7!

Maintaining the distant opposition!

8 ♔b8 ♔d8

Once again, White can make no further progress and the game is drawn. The continuation might be 9 **♔b7 ♔d7 10 ♔a6 ♔e6 11 ♔b6 ♔d6!** but not 11 ... ♔f6 12 ♔b5 ♔f5 13 ♔b4! ♔e6 14 ♔c4 ♔e5 15 ♔c5 and White reaches d4 **12 ♔a5 ♔e5 13 ♔a4 ♔e4 14 ♔a3 ♔e5! 15 ♔b3 ♔d5!** and we are back where we started.

Moving the position in diagram 29 one rank down can only reduce White's chances, but the position one rank further up is won for White. For example, with White's pawns on g4 and h5 and king on f3, and Black's pawn on g5 and king on f6, Black's king is again tied down and cannot stop the entry of White's king, e.g. **1 ... ♔e5 2 ♔e3 ♔f6 3 ♔e4 ♔e6 4 ♔d4 ♔f6 5 ♔d5** with an easy win. Equally, White wins with pawns on g5 and h6, or g6 and h7, unless in the latter case the black king is on h8 when the position is stalemate!

D: CONNECTED PAWNS WITHOUT A PASSED PAWN

a) When one Pawn is Blocked

An example of such a position is diagram 30.

30
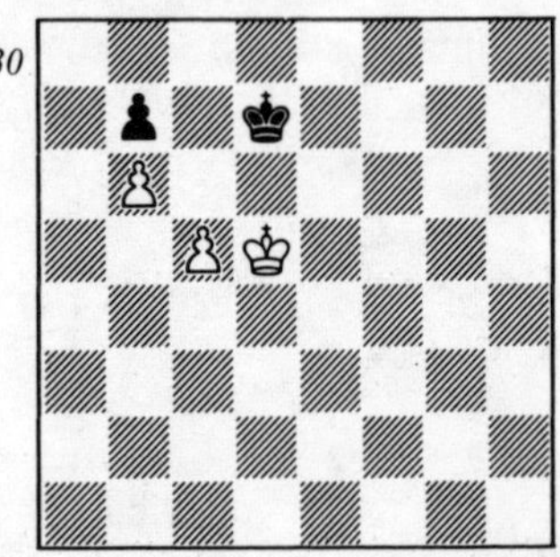

It is clear that, with no passed pawn, White's winning chances are lessened, as he can only win by advancing his king. To do this, however, he needs to gain the opposition, so in most cases it is the opposition which decides one way or the other.

If White's pawns are as advanced as in diagram 30, he can often win even without the opposition. The black king is tied within the d5-a5-a8-d8 quadrant, so White wins as follows:

1 ♔e5!

1 c6+ looks tempting, as 1 ... bc+ fails to 2 ♔c5 ♔d8 3 ♔d6! ♔c8 4 ♔xc6 winning, but in fact 1 c6+ is an instructive mistake. Black draws with 1 ... ♔c8! 2 ♔d6 ♔b8 (threatening 3 ... bc) 3 c7+ ♔c8 etc.

1 ... ♔c6

He cannot maintain the opposition with 1 ... ♔e7, as 2 c6 wins.

2 ♔d4 ♔d7
3 ♔d5

Reaching diagram 30 again, but with Black to move.

3 ... ♔c8
4 ♔e6

Care is still required, as 4 c6? ♔b8! draws. Also possible, however, is 4 ♔d6 ♔d8 5 ♔e6 (5 c6? ♔c8!) 5 ... ♔c8 6 ♔e7 etc.

4 ... ♔d8
5 ♔d6 ♔c8
6 ♔e7 ♔b8
7 ♔d7 ♔a8

And only now does the pawn advance win.

8 c6! bc
9 ♔c7 and mate in 3.

If the position in diagram 30 is moved one rank down, it cannot be won for White, assuming of course that Black has the opposition. For example, with White's pawns on b5 and c4 and king on d4, and Black's pawn on b6 and king on d6, Black can answer **1 ♔e4** with **1 ... ♔e6** 2 c5 is no threat **2 ♔f4 ♔d6!** (not 2 ... ♔f6? 3 c5) and the threat of 3 ... ♔c5 forces the white king back. However, after **3 ♔e3** Black must avoid 3 ... ♔e5? 4 ♔d3 ♔e6 5 ♔e4; or 3 ... ♔c5? 4 ♔d3 ♔d6 5 ♔d4. Instead, **3 ... ♔e7!** with the distant opposition, gives him the draw. If Black were to move in the original position, he is lost after **1 ... ♔e6 2 c5!** or **1 ... ♔c7 2 ♔e5 ♔d7 3 ♔d5 ♔c7 4 ♔e6** etc.

Moving the position in diagram 30 further to the right does not alter the result which is always a win for White, whoever has the move. However, with White's pawns on f6 and g5 and king on h5, and Black's pawn on f7 and king on h7, when the white king can no longer penetrate on the right, another winning method must be used. The continuation might be: **1 ... ♔h8 2 g5 fg+ 3 ♔h6! ♔g8 4 ♔xg6** winning, or with White to move **1 g6+ fg+ 2 ♔g5 ♔h8 3 ♔h6!** winning in the same way. However, with white pawns on g6 and h5 Black can draw by simply playing his king to g8, when there is nothing White can do.

Nor does White have any winning chances if the opposing pawns are on the rook's file. For example, with White's pawns on a5 and b4 and king on c4, and Black's pawn on a6 and king on c6, the opposition gives White nothing, for after **1 ... ♔d6 2 b5 ab+ 3 ♔xb5 ♔c7** the a-pawn cannot queen. White would win only if he could capture the c5 square with his king along with the opposition, clearly an impossibility.

We have now considered all cases similar to diagram 30, but let us finally see an example of correct defence by means of the distant opposition. *(31)*

31

As already mentioned, if Black has to move he loses quickly after 1 ... ♔g6 2 e5, or 1 ... ♔e7 2 ♔g5 ♔f7 3 ♔f5 ♔e7 4 ♔g6 etc. With White to move, the position is drawn, although Black must defend very carefully.

Consider the dangers which threaten Black. First of all he must never allow the white king to reach the 6th rank. In other words, he must maintain the opposition whilst keeping his king on the same file as White's king. For example, with the white king on f1, Black must not play his king to the g-file, for then White wins by **1 ♔e2 ♔f7 2 ♔d3 ♔e7** or 2 ... ♔f6 3 ♔d4 **3 ♔c4 ♔d7 4 ♔b5 ♔c7 5 ♔a6!** etc. Secondly, Black must always be alert to a possible e5, so must never place his king on the h-file.

Futhermore, as far as the opposition is concerned, Black only has to worry about the a-, b-, f- and g-files. This is because the white king cannot penetrate on the c-, d- and e-files so Black can forget about the opposition on these files, as long as he is ready to regain it as soon as he leaves them. With these points in mind, the reader should easily follow our analysis:

1 ♔g4 ♔g6

Not 1 ... ♔e5? 2 ♔f3 ♔f6 3 ♔f4 gaining the opposition and winning.

2 ♔h4 ♔f6

As we have stated, Black dare not play 2 ... ♔h6 because of 3 e5!, but he could well play 2 ... ♔f7, then later take up the opposition again on the g-file.

3 ♔g3 ♔g7!

Again 3 ... ♔e5? loses, as does 3 ... ♔g5? 4 ♔f3! when Black cannot go to f5 and 4 ... ♔f6 5 ♔f4 wins for White.

4 ♔g2 ♔g8

It is safest to keep the distant opposition, although 4 ... ♔g6 is also possible; after 5 ♔f2 ♔f6 6 ♔e2 Black does not need to worry about the opposition on the e-file, so 6 ... ♔e7 7 ♔e3 ♔e8! 8 ♔f4 ♔f8! 9 ♔f5 ♔f7 etc. holds the draw.

5 ♔g1 ♔g7

The only move. If 5 ... ♔f7 6 ♔f1! ♔f8 7 ♔f2 ♔f7 8 ♔f3 ♔f8 9 ♔f4 ♔e8 10 ♔g5 ♔f7 11 ♔f5 wins, or here 6 ... ♔e7 (if 6 ... ♔g7, the white king heads for a6, as the black king cannot reach b7 in time) 7 ♔g2 ♔f8 8 ♔f2! ♔e7 9 ♔g3 ♔f7 10 ♔f3 ♔e7 11 ♔g4 wins.

6 ♔f1 ♔f7

Again the only move, as should now be clear.

7 ♔e2 ♔e7
8 ♔d2 ♔d7
9 ♔c2 ♔c7

Black could have chosen any squares on the files for his last three moves, as the white king cannot approach, but he must now be accurate again.

10 ♔b2 ♔b8

10 ... ♔b6 was also possible, but not 10 ... ♔b7? 11 ♔b3! and White wins, as the reader can check for himself.

11 ♔b3 ♔b7
12 ♔a3 ♔a7

Our analysis ends here, as White cannot strengthen his position further, if Black keeps the opposition. White can try other squares, but the correct defence for Black can be found without great difficulty by applying the given principles.

It could also happen that White's unblocked pawn is further back and has tempo moves. This circumstance of course greatly favours White whose winning chances are vastly increased. All positions which up to now depended on the opposition are won for White because he can always gain a tempo. Further elucidation of this point seems superfluous.

However, it is interesting to note that such a pawn sometimes wins positions so far considered hopeless, such as diagram 32.

32

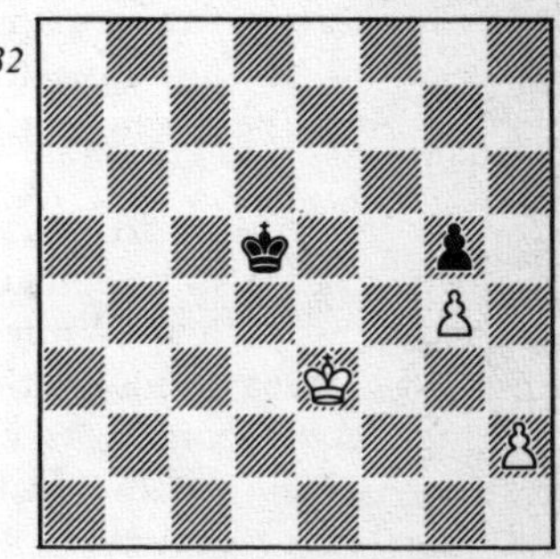

J.Kling 1848

If White's h-pawn were on h3, there would be no doubt about the draw, whoever is to move. Has this extra pawn move, then, such significance that it can alter our evaluation of the position? After all, as the opposition does not matter in diagram 32, why should a reserve move by the h-pawn be of any importance?

This would normally be the case, but we must examine whether White can first improve his king's position, before using his extra pawn move. The first thing that springs to mind is for White to occupy the 4th rank with his king. He could then use his tempo move to gain the opposition, when

Black cannot prevent an entry via f5. This means that White wins if his king reaches e4 before h3 has been played.

Furthermore, White has an additional threat of playing h4 if the black king goes too far away. As Black could not allow h5, he would have to take the pawn, when his king must be ready to occupy g6 as soon as White's king captures on h4. In that case, the black king must be on f6 or the ending is lost.

Now that we have progressed so far, we can look for some pairs of related squares. When White's king is on g3, threatening h4, the black king must be on f6, as we have seen. As White's king on f3 would threaten to occupy e4 as well as g3, the only square for Black's king is then e5, controlling f6 and e4 and finally, the white king on e3 would control both e4 and f3, giving the black king again one square only: d5. This gives us three squares corresponding to Black's f6, e5 and d5.

Continuing the process, what happens when White plays ♔f2? This controls e3, f3 and g3, so Black must be ready to occupy d5, e5 and f6, giving us e6 as the related square. As for the white king on g2, controlling f3 and g3, the related square must again be e6, controlling e5 and f6. This gives us the solution to our problem: as soon as the black king occupies e6, White must play ♔g2 (or ♔f2), whereupon Black cannot remain on the related square e6, and he loses. Let us see what happens in practice:

1 ♔f2!

Also correct is the sequence originally given by Kling: 1 ♔f3 ♚e5 2 ♔g3 ♚f6 3 ♔g2 ♚e6 4 ♔f2 etc. The text line is one move faster.

1 ... ♚e6

As White threatens 2 ♔g3 and 3 h4, the black king must quickly aim for f6. If 1 ... ♚e5 2 ♔f3 wins.

2 ♔g2! ♚f6

Or 2 ... ♚e5 3 ♔f3 ♚d5 (to prevent 4 ♔e4) 4 ♔g3 ♚e6 5 h4 gh+ 6 ♔xh4 ♚f6 (too late) 7 ♔h5 ♚g7 8 ♔g5! wins. Other king moves lose to ♔f3-e4 or ♔g3 and h4.

3 ♔g3!

Black is now in zugzwang.

3 ... ♚g6

If 3 ... ♚e6 4 h4 etc, and other moves lead into the main line.

4 ♔f3 ♚f6
5 ♔e4 ♚e6
6 h3!

At last, the decisive reserve tempo is used! White now wins the opposition and the game after 6 ... ♚f6 7 ♔d5 etc. A most instructive example.

b) Without Blocked Pawns

We shall now turn to the group of positions in which White has no passed pawn but neither is one of his pawns blocked by a black pawn, giving him a backward pawn. Such positions are usually favourable for him. Consider diagram 33.

33

This position is a win for White, if he has the move, but Black to move has the tactical possibility **1 ... f5+! 2 ef ♔f6** which draws for him. If the white king were anywhere else, such as h4, the position would be a win even with Black to move.

General principles tell that White should obtain the best position for his king before moving his pawns. Here, for instance, both 1 e5 fe and 1 f5+ ♔g7 only draw, so White must first manoeuvre with his king as follows:

1	**♔f3**	**♔f7**

If 1 ... ♔h5 2 ♔e3 ♔g4 3 f5 wins, but not here 2 e5 ♔g6! 3 ♔e4 ♔f7 and Black draws.

2	**♔e3**	**♔e6**
3	**♔d4**	**♔d6**
4	**f5!**	

The white king is well-placed, so the time has come to move a pawn. We have now reached a well-known winning position in which both 4 ... ♔c6 5 e5 and 4 ... ♔e7 5 ♔c5 ♔d7 6 ♔d5 win quickly. A useful rule to remember is that the white king should be positioned on the side of his unopposed pawn.

Our evaluation of diagram 33 does not change if the position is moved up or down, or one or two files to the left. However, if it is moved three files to the left, with the white pawns on b4 and c4, it is drawn even if White has the move. The continuation might be: **1 ♔e4** after 1 ♔c3 ♔c7 2 ♔b3 ♔b6 3 ♔a4 ♔a6 4 c5 ♔b7, the white king cannot penetrate on the left **1 ... ♔e6 2 ♔f4 ♔f6 3 c5 ♔e6 4 ♔e4 ♔f6! 5 ♔d4 ♔e6 6 ♔c4 ♔d7** and White can make no progress. The same applies if this position is moved further down, but if placed one rank further up, with white pawns on b5 and c5, White can win by **1 c6+ ♔e7 2 ♔e5 ♔e8 3 ♔e6 ♔d8 4 ♔f7** etc.

If the position in diagram 33 is moved four files to the left, it is equally drawn, as we shall see later when we look at positions with a white rook's pawn.

At this stage we must consider an exception which occurs with the black pawn on the bishop's file, as in diagram 34.

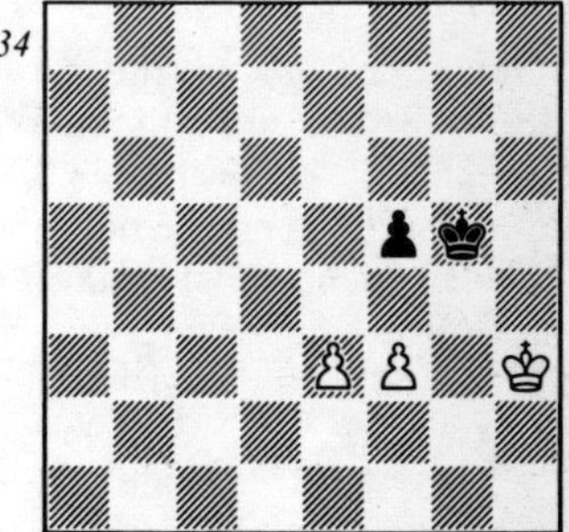

34

This is the same as the position in diagram 33 moved one rank down and the white king on h3 instead of g3. This small difference, which would usually be unimportant, gives Black a draw, whoever has the move, because of the special nature of the bishop's pawn. Let us examine the position thoroughly, beginning with White to move:

A

1 ♔g2

Not of course 1 ♔g3 f4+! with an immediate draw, and 1 ♔h2 ♔f6 would change nothing.

1 ... ♔f6!

Otherwise White wins by playing his king over to the queen's wing, e.g. 1 ... ♔g6 2 ♔f2 ♔f6 3 ♔e2 ♔e5 (if 3 ... ♔e6 4 ♔d3 ♔e5 5 ♔c4 ♔d6 6 ♔d4 ♔e6 7 e4! wins) 4 ♔d3 ♔d5 5 f4! as we saw in our analysis to diagram 33. Equally insufficient is 1 ... f4 2 e4 ♔f6 3 ♔f2 ♔e5 4 ♔f1! and wins, as we saw with diagram 26.

2 ♔g3

2 ♔f2 ♔e5 (e6) would lead to the main line.

2 ... ♔f7!

Once again, the only move. The king must not go to the g-file because of 3 ♔f2, nor to the e-file because of 3 ♔h4. Now both 3 ♔f4 ♔f6 and 3 ♔h4 ♔g6 are no good for White, so he must make an attempt on the queenside.

3 ♔f2 ♔e6
4 ♔e2 ♔d5
5 ♔d2 ♔d6

Not 5 ... ♔e5 (or c5) 6 ♔d3 ♔d5 7 f4 and wins. Black must be able to answer ♔d3 with ... ♔c5.

6 ♔d3 ♔c5!
7 ♔c3

The only try for a win. After 7 e4 ♔d6! 8 ♔d4 fe 9 ♔xe4 ♔e6 or 7 f4 ♔d5 Black draws.

7 ... ♔d5
8 ♔b4

If 8 f4 ♔c5 draws, but not 8 ... ♔e4? 9 ♔d2 ♔d5 10 ♔d3 wins.

8 ... f4!

This is the point. Black uses the peculiar nature of the bishop's pawn, as we saw in diagrams 19 and 26.

9 e4+ ♔d4
10 ♔b3 ♔e3!
11 e5 ♔xf3
12 e6 ♔g2
13 e7 f3
14 e8♕ f2

and White cannot win as his king is too far away, as we shall see later in our section on queen endings.

Now with Black to move:

B

1 ... ♔f6!

The only move to draw. If the black king plays to the rook's file, then White wins by ♔g3-f2-e2-d3 etc, and if 1 ... ♔g6 2 ♔h4 would force the above line. Now 2 ♔h4 ♔g6! or 2 ♔g3 ♔f7! draw for Black.

2 ♔g2 ♔e6

If 2 ... ♔f7 3 ♔g3! and Black is in zugzwang, e.g. 3 ... ♔f6 4 ♔f4, or 3 ... ♔g6 4 ♔f2 or finally 3 ... ♔e6 4 ♔h4 etc. However, 2 ... ♔e7 is also playable.

3 ♔g3 ♔f7!

and we have reached the same position as in line A.

Clearly the attack against White's bishop's pawn is not possible if the position in diagram 34 is moved up one rank, but it is most remarkable to find that, one rank further down, giving us diagram 35, the position is lost for Black if he is to move!

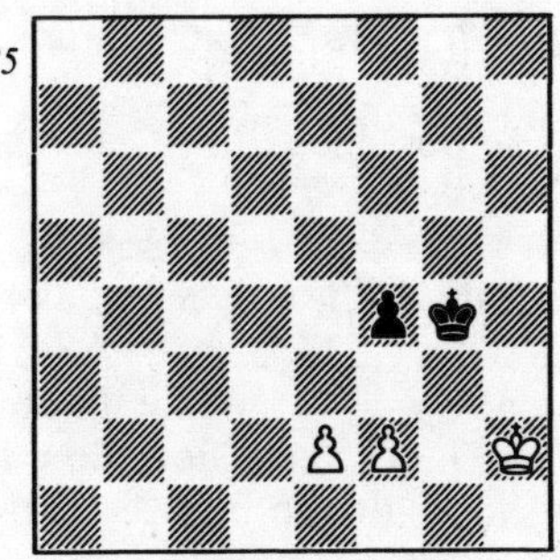

P.Keres 1942

White to move cannot win, for if 1 ♔g2 f3+, or 1 f3+ ♔h4, whereas after 1 ♔h1 f3! 2 e3 ♔g5 would follow, or 1 ♔g1 f3! 2 e3 ♔f5!, both giving us known drawing positions.

However, although in diagram 34 it did not matter whose move it was, this is not the case here. Black to move is surprisingly in zugzwang and loses as follows:

1 ... ♔f5

We already know that 1 ... ♔g5 loses after 2 ♔h3 ♔h5 3 ♔g2 ♔g4 4 ♔f1 ♔f5 5 ♔e1 ♔e5 6 ♔d2 ♔d4 7 f3 etc. White also wins after 1 ... f3 2 e3 ♔h4 3 ♔g1 ♔g4 4 ♔f1 ♔f5 5 ♔e1 ♔e4 6 ♔d2 etc.

2 ♔g2 ♔f6!
3 ♔f1 ♔e5
4 ♔e1 ♔d4
5 ♔d2 ♔c4

If 5 ... ♔e4 6 ♔c3 ♔d5 7 ♔d3 ♔e5 8 e4! etc wins. So far our analysis has followed that of diagram 34, but now we see the subtle differences between the two positions; White's e-pawn has the option of moving two squares!

6 e4! ♔d4

If 6 ... fe+ 7 ♔xe3 ♔d5 8 ♔f4 wins.

7 f3 ♔c4

He cannot allow the white king to d3.

8 ♔e2 ♔d4
9 ♔f2 ♔e5
10 ♔f1!

The winning manoeuvre we saw in diagram 26. Black is now in zugzwang and cannot prevent White's king from pentrating via d3 or h3.

Going back to diagram 33, if we move the position one file to the right and place the kings to the left of the pawns, we arrive at diagram 36.

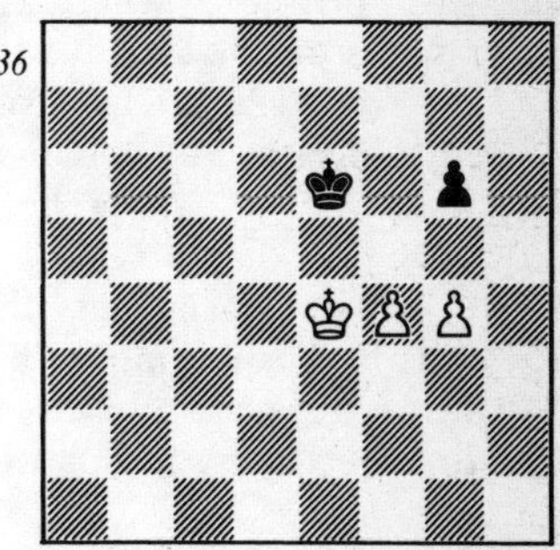

The white king is on the correct

side of the pawns, alongside his unopposed pawn, so the win is easy. With White to move, he plays **1 g5 ♔d6 2 f5**, or here **1 ... ♔f7 2 ♔d5 ♔e7 3 ♔e5** etc. With Black to move, play goes **1 ... ♔d6 2 ♔d4!** again not 2 f5 ♔e7! drawing, nor 2 g5 ♔e6 etc **2 ... ♔e6 3 ♔c5 g5** otherwise the white king breaks through **4 f5+ ♔e5 5 ♔c6** and wins.

Moving this position up or down changes nothing, even with the white pawns on f2 and g2, when Black admaittedly draws by **1 ... ♔d4 2 ♔d2? ♔e4 3 ♔c3 g3! 4 f3+ ♔e3** with a counterattack against White's g-pawn, but **2 f4!** wins. The same position moved to the right, however, would be drawn, as we shall see later.

We have not yet discussed positions arising from diagram 33 which contain a white rook's pawn. Clearly this fact increases Black's drawing chances, although as it is difficult to give general rules here, each case has to considered individually. Let us begin with positions where the black pawn is on the knight's file and the white king has not managed to occupy any square in front of his pawns. As a basic position we give diagram 37.

Black draws easily in this position. If he has the move, 1 ... g6+! draws immediately. With White to move, the continuation might be:

1 ♔e5 ♔e7
2 ♔d5 ♔f7

37

Not 2 ... ♔d7? 3 h6 winning.

3 ♔d6 ♔f8

Also possible is 3 ... ♔e8 4 ♔e6 ♔f8 5 ♔d7 ♔f7 etc.

4 ♔e6 ♔e8

But this is the only move, as 4 ... ♔g8 5 ♔e7 ♔h8 6 ♔f7 ♔h7 7 h6 gh 8 g6+ wins for White. In other words, Black must not allow his king to be driven into the corner before White has played g6.

5 ♔f5 ♔f7

We are back to the original position.

6 g6+ ♔g8

and Black easily draws by keeping his king on g8 or h8.

Moving the position in diagram 37 one rank down changes nothing, as far as the result is concerned. White has winning chances only if his king succeeds in occupying the square in front of his pawns. For instance, if in diagram 37 we move the black king to h7, White wins, whoever has the move. White to move plays **1 ♔e6 ♔g8 2 ♔e7 ♔h7 3 ♔f7 ♔h8 4 ♔g6!** but not 4 h6? ♔h7! drawing **4 ... ♔g1 5 h6 gh 6 ♔xh6** winning. Black to move equally loses after **1 ... ♔g8** 1 ...

♔h8 2 ♔g6 ♔g8 3 h6 leads to the previous variation, and 1 ... g6+ 2 ♔f6 gh 3 ♔f7 wins **2 ♔g6 ♔h8 3 ♔f7** not 3 h6? ♔g8! drawing **3 ... ♔h7 4 h6 gh 5 g6+** and White wins.

If White's pawns are further back, allowing the white king to move in front of them, Black's drawing chances with a knight's pawn are minimal. Take diagram 38 as an example.

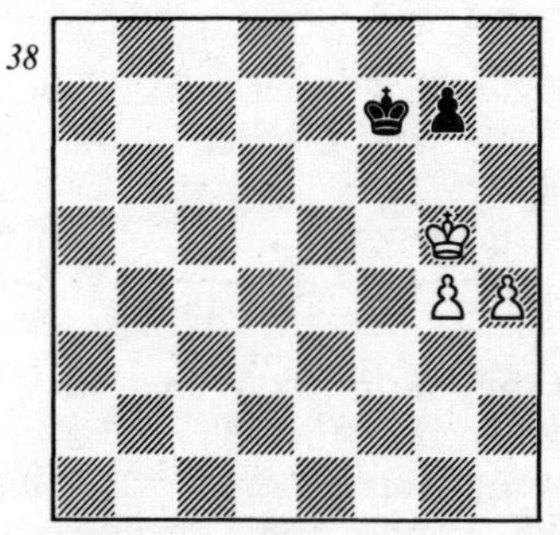

White wins comfortably, whoever has the move.

1 ♔f5

With Black to move, play might go 1 ... ♔f8 2 ♔g6 ♔g8 3 h5 ♔h8 4 h6 ♔g8 5 g5 winning.

1 ... g6+

Otherwise the white king reaches g6 with a win, as seen above.

2 ♔e5

But not 2 ♔g5? ♔g7 2 ♔f4 ♔f6 drawing.

2 ... ♔e7

3 g5 ♔f7

4 ♔d6 and wins.

If Black has a rook's pawn instead of a knight's pawn, his drawing chances are much greater. Our basic position is diagram 39.

White can win here only if he has the move, as Black to move draws easily with 1 ... ♔f4 2 ♔e2 ♔e4 3 ♔d2 ♔d4 (3 ... h3 4 g3 ♔f3 is also playable here, but not with White's pawns further up the board) 4 ♔e2 (or 4 ♔c2 ♔e3 etc) 4 ... ♔e4 5 h3 ♔f4 6 ♔f2 ♔e4 and White can make no progress.

1 ♔e3 h3

No better is 1 ... ♔f5 (1 ... ♔g5 2 h3 ♔f5 3 ♔f3 wins) 2 ♔f3 ♔g5 3 ♔e4! ♔g4 4 h3+! (but not 4 ♔e5? h6! 5 g3 ♔f3 etc) 4 ... ♔g3 5 ♔f5 ♔xg2 6 ♔g4 winning.

2 g3 ♔f5

Or 2 ... ♔g5 3 ♔f3 ♔f5 4 g4+ etc.

3 ♔d4!

No good is 3 ♔f3 ♔g5, as now 4 g4? ♔h4! gives Black a draw (5 ♔f4 is stalemate). The text move gains the opposition.

3 ... ♔g5

4 ♔e5 ♔g4

5 ♔e4 ♔g5

6 ♔f3!

Black is now in zugzwang and loses after both 6 ... ♔f5 7 g4+ and 6 ... ♔h5 7 ♔f4.

Moving the position in diagram

39 one or two ranks further up changes nothing. Black to move draws and White to move wins. But the position three ranks up, with White's pawns on g5 and h5, is drawn, whoever has the move. Black would of course continue **1 ... ♔f7**, whereas White to move can only stalemate Black after **1 ♔e6 h6** king moves are also playable **2 g6 ♔g8 3 ♔f6 ♔f8 4 g7+ ♔g8 5 ♔g6**.

We already know that all positions similar to diagram 39 are drawn if Black has the move. But what happens if we change the position slightly, giving us diagram 40?

40

White to move can only draw, as we have seen, but with Black to move, the opposition wins for White as follows:

1	**...**	**♔e5**

1 ... ♔g5 2 ♔e4 transposes to a win we have already seen, and 1 ... h4 2 g4+ ♔e5 3 ♔e3 wins even more easily.

2	**♔e3**	**♔f5**
3	**♔d4**	**h4**

The only chance, otherwise his pawn falls eventually.

4	**g4+**	**♔f4**
5	**♔d5**	**♔g5**

The counterattack 5 ... ♔g3, which would be good if the position were one rank further down, fails here. Consequently we can state that diagram 40, a rank lower, would be drawn, whoever had the move.

6	**♔e5**	**♔g6**
7	**♔f4**	**♔f6**
8	**g5+** and wins.	

Diagram 40, one rank higher, gives the same result, but is drawn if two ranks higher, whoever has the move, as we saw when diagram 39 was moved three ranks up.

From our previous analysis, we can conclude that Black has the best drawing chances when his pawn is on its original square. In this case Black can draw even when White's king is in front of his pawns, as we can see if we take diagram 41 (diagram 38 with a black rook's pawn instead of a knight's pawn, and his king on g7).

41

First of all, with White to move:

A

1 ♔f5

If 1 h5 h6+ 2 ♔f5 ♔f7 is a known draw.

1 ... ♔f7

2 ♔e5

Or 2 g5 ♔e7 (or 2 ... ♔g7) 3 h5 ♔f7 etc.

2 ... ♔e7

3 g5 ♔f7

and White can make no progress. This position, with White to move, is drawn even if moved further down the board.

Now, with Black to move:

B

1 ... ♔f7

The most natural defence, although 1 ... ♔h8 or 1 ... ♔f8 are also playable, as we know that Black is not worried about the advance of White's pawns. Only 1 ... ♔g8? would be an error, as 2 ♔h6 ♔h8 3 g5 ♔g8 4 h5 ♔h8 5 g6 hg 6 hg wins for White. Black must always play to answer ♔h6 with ... ♔g8. Another mistake is 1 ... h6+? 2 ♔f5 ♔f7 3 h5 winning.

2 ♔h6

No better is 2 ♔f5 ♔e7 3 ♔e5 ♔f7 4 ♔d6 ♔f6 or here 4 h5 ♔e7 etc. If Black had originally played his king to h8, White would now have played 2 ♔f6 ♔g8 3 g5 ♔f8! (not 3 ... ♔h8? 4 ♔f7!) 4 g5 ♔g8, but this too is drawn.

2 ... ♔g8

3 g5 ♔h8

4 h5 ♔g8

5 g6 hg

6 hg ♔h8

with a draw.

The same position, with Black to move, cannot be drawn if moved further down the board. For example, with white pawns on g2 and h2 and king on g3, and black pawn on g5 and king on g5, Black loses after **1 ... ♔f5** if 1 ... h4+ 2 ♔f3 ♔f5 3 h3, or here 2 ... h3 3 g3 ♔f5 4 g4+ White wins also **2 ♔f3 ♔e5 3 g3 ♔f5 4 h3** as in diagram 40.

This systematically covers the most important aspects of endings of two pawns against one, giving the reader a comprehensive picture of this type of ending. Of course there are many other interesting and instructive examples which we have had to omit, as they would have led us too far astray. Readers who are interested enough can always look these up in reference works on the endgame.

King and two Pawns against King

This kind of ending needs a little comment, as it is usually won for White without difficulty. There are, however, a few exceptions which players should know. For instance, two or even more pawns on the rook's file do not win. The game is also drawn if Black can manage to win one of the pawns in a favourable position.

From our previous analyses we also know that White cannot win if he has doubled pawns on the 5th or 6th rank. For example, in diagram 42, even with Black to move, the position is drawn after **1 ... ♔c8! 2 ♔d6 ♔d8 3 c7+**

otherwise the black king returns to f7 **3 ... ♔c8** when both **4 c6** and **4 ♔c6** give **stalemate**.

An interesting draw is to be seen in diagram 43:

Despite his seemingly hopeless situation, Black to move can draw here by **1 ... ♔g7 2 ♔e6 ♔f8**, as both **3 h6** and **3 ♔f6** give **stalemate**, and the h-pawn cannot win on its own.

Finally, let us mention another typical drawn position, diagram 44. White to move cannot win, as 1 ♔h8 ♔f8 2 h7 ♔f7 is stalemate.

King and two Pawns against King and two Pawns

We cannot give specific rules about this type of ending, because we have here equality of material usually leading to a draw. However, apart from material advantages a position can also have other advantages which can have a decisive effect on the result. We are referring to positional advantages, some of the most important of which will now be illustrated by simple examples. Of course, these positional elements also occur in more complex endings which are beyond the scope of the book.

A: CREATION OF A PASSED PAWN

This is achieved by a pawn breakthrough which usually occurs when both kings are in another part of the board and as a result cannot stop or support the resulting passed pawn. The pawn breakthrough is usually connected with a pawn sacrifice, giving both sides a passed pawn. This means that the attacker must accurately calculate that the enemy pawn cannot become more dangerous than his own. Consider diagram 45.

45

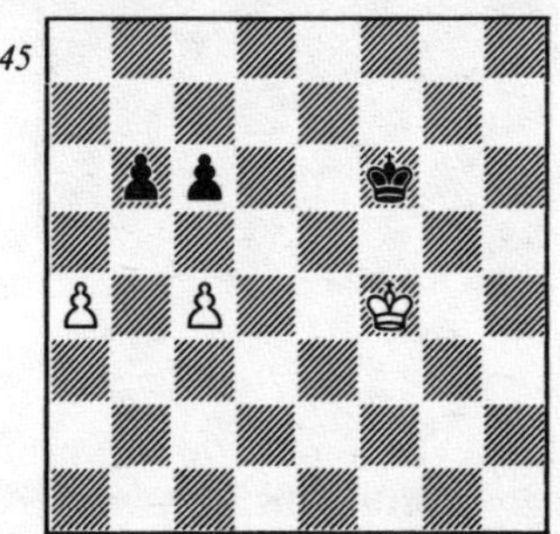

Following the usual principle of bringing the white king nearer, White achieves nothing, as after 1 ♔e4 ♔e6 the draw is unavoidable. However, a pawn sacrifice gives White a win:

1 c5!

In calculating such a break-through White must consider the following points. Firstly, that after 1 ... bc 2 a5 the black king cannot stop the passed pawn. Secondly, that the newly created black passed pawn can be stopped by White, and thirdly, that the pawn sacrifice cannot be profitably declined.

1 ... b5

We select the third possibility as Black's defence. The first two conditions are fulfilled, as after 1 ... bc 2 a5 this pawn cannot be caught, whereas after 2 ... c4 3 a6 c3 4 ♔e3 the black c-pawn is stopped. If Black declines the offer by 1 ... ♔e6, then 2 cb ♔d7 3 a5 wins easily.

2 a5!

But not 2 ab cb 3 c6 ♔e6 and Black draws. After the text move Black obtains a passed b-pawn but the white king is near enough.

2 ... b4
3 ♔e4 b3
4 ♔d3 and wins.

The white a-pawn cannot be prevented from queening.

B: THE DISTANT PASSED PAWN

One of the most common and important positional advantages in pawn endings lies in the possession of a distant passed pawn. By 'distant' we mean how far the pawn is away from the main scene of action. The principal advantage of such a pawn is that it can lure the enemy king away, leaving the attacking king free to create an advantage on the other side. The distant passed pawn is so strong that it often more than compensates for other, even material, advantages.

46

Without his passed pawn White would lose, as the black king

would penetrate via c4 or e4. The passed pawn, however, reverses this result.

1 f5

Even though this pawn is now lost, it takes the black king away from the main scene of action (the b-pawns), allowing White to win quickly.

1	**...**	**♔e5**
2	**f6**	**♔xf6**
3	**♔xd4**	**♔e6**
4	**♔c5**	**♔d7**
5	**♔xb5**	**♔c7**
6	**♔a6** wins	

It is clear from this example that the passed pawn gains in value the further it is away from the main scene of action. For instance, if the white pawn were on h4 instead of f4, White would win even if Black had an extra pawn on a6. The reader can test this for himself!

C: THE PROTECTED PASSED PAWN

When a passed pawn is also protected by another pawn, it becomes a very strong weapon indeed, even stronger than the distant passed pawn (unless this can queen of course). Its main strength lies in the fact that it limits the activity of the enemy king, at the same time allowing its own king complete freedom. Diagram 47 illustrates these characteristics:

White's protected passed pawn on b5 here proves stronger than Black's h-pawn, giving White a win as follows:

47

1	**...**	**h5**
2	**♔d3**	**♔d5**

Black tries to stop the white king capturing his h-pawn.

3	**♔e3**	**♔e5**
4	**♔f3**	**♔d5**

The black king can go no further without allowing the b-pawn to queen.

5 ♔b3 and wins.

White simply captures the h-pawn, then returns to the queen-side, while Black looks on helplessly.

48

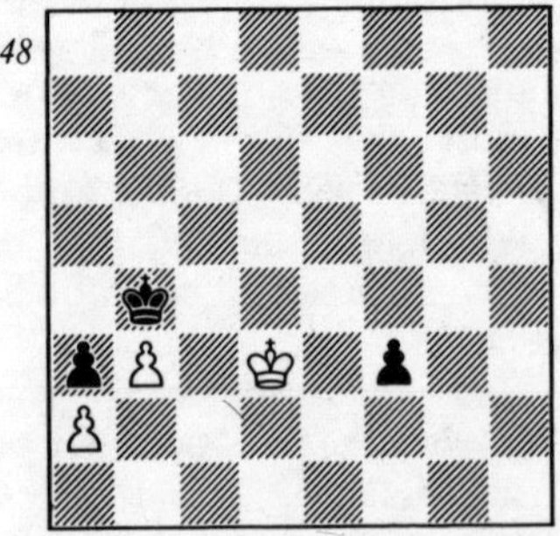

It is worth mentioning that in such cases, White must always check that Black cannot draw by attacking the base pawn. To prevent this, the protected pawn must be at least on the fourth rank. For example, in diagram 48, White cannot win. After **1 ♔e3 ♔c3 2 ♔xf3 ♔b2 3 b4 ♔xa2 4 b5 ♔b2 5 b6 a2** draws.

However, even a protected passed pawn on the fourth rank is not always sufficient to prevent a counterattack.

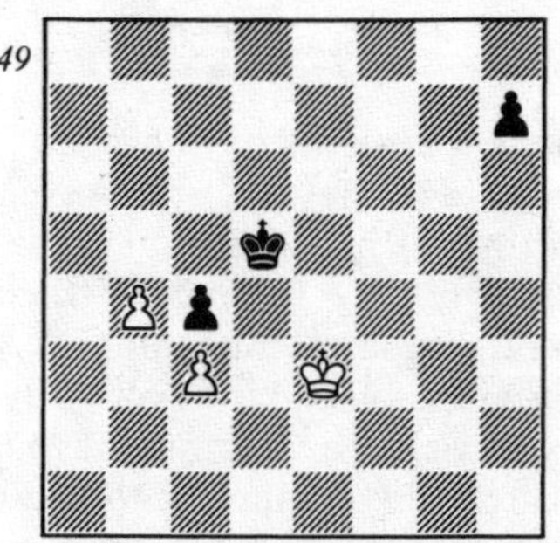

49

In diagram 49, White again cannot win. Play might go **1 ♔f4 h5 2 ♔g5 ♔e4 3 ♔xh5** or 3 b5 ♔d5 4 ♔xh5 ♔c5 draws **3 ... ♔d3! 4 b5 ♔xc3 5 b6 ♔d2 6 b7 c3 7 b8♕ c2** with a theoretical draw, as we again arrive at the peculiar case of the bishop's pawn.

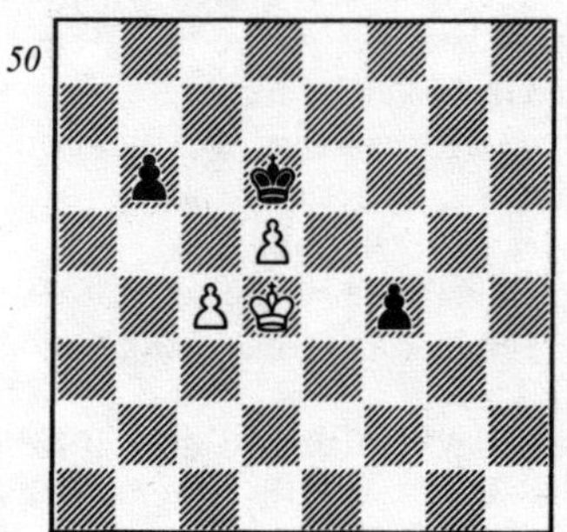

50

Finally we must point out that the defence can sometimes draw by attacking the base pawn with a pawn. For example, in diagram 50, Black draws by **1 ♔e4 f3 2 ♔xf3 b5 3 cb ♔xd5**.

D: THE BLOCKADE OF ENEMY PAWNS

Positions often arise in which a single pawn can blockade (i.e. render immobile) two or even three enemy pawns. This clearly represents a tangible advantage, as the following example shows:

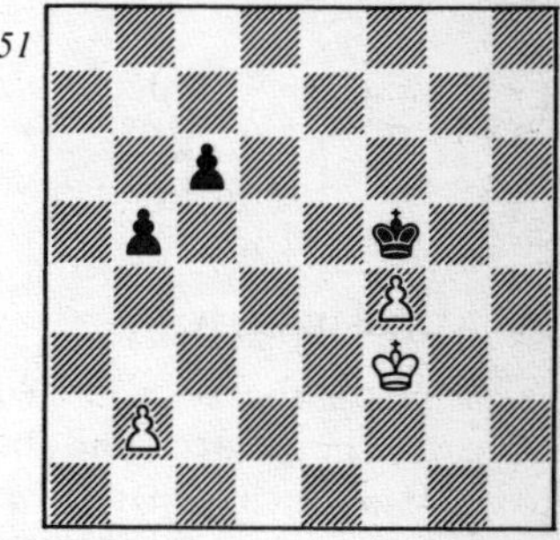

51

White has the advantage of a distant passed pawn, but this alone is insufficient to win because his king is too far away from Black's pawns. Black to move would easily draw by 1 ... c5 2 ♔e3 c4 3 ♔d4 ♔xf4 4 ♔c5 ♔e4 5 ♔xb5 ♔d3. White can, however, first blockade the enemy pawns, which is equivalent to giving himself an extra pawn.

1 b4! c5

The only counterchance, as 1 ... ♔e6 2 ♔e4 ♔d6 3 ♔d4, followed by the advance of the f-pawn, is hopeless for Black.

2 bc b4

Or 2 ... ♔e6 3 ♔e4 b4 4 f5+ etc.

3 c6

White must play exactly, as the apparently simpler 3 ♔e3 would throw away the win, after 3 ... b3 4 ♔d3 b2 5 ♔c2 ♔e6! and Black captures one of the pawns, with a draw. Try it for yourself!

3 ... ♔e6

After 3 ... b3 4 c7 White would queen with check.

4 f5+!

The white pawns are so advanced that they can win even without the help of the king.

4 ... ♔d6
5 f6 b3
6 f7 ♔e7
7 c7 and wins.

E: OTHER POSSIBILITIES

Apart from the above-mentioned advantages, there are various other elements which help in pawn endings, such as the better king position, pawns which are further advanced, connected pawns as against doubled pawns, and so on. To examine all these elements individually would lead us too far astray, so we shall restrict ourselves to a couple of examples, beginning with diagram 52.

At first sight this position seems to offer both sides equal prospects, as they have two connected passed pawns each, with both kings able to stop them. It also appears impossible to advance the pawns further without allowing the opponent's pawns to queen.

52

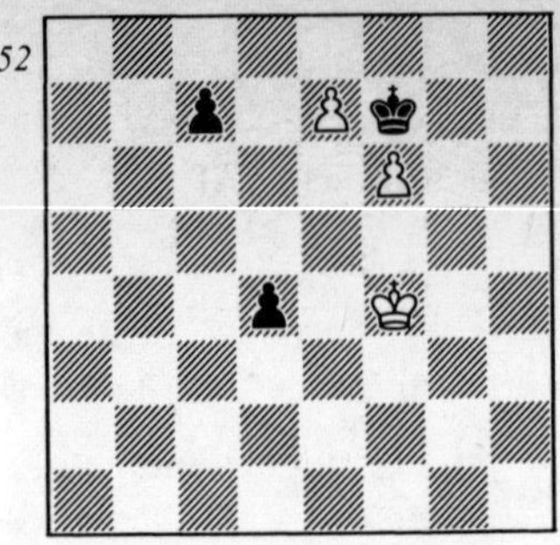

J.Behting 1900

In spite of these facts, however, White has a vital advantage in that his pawns are nearer to their queening squares, thus completely limiting the black king's mobility. As will be seen, this means that Black can be compelled to make weakening pawn moves once his king is in zugzwang. We shall even demonstrate that Black is already in zugzwang in the given position and would lose at once if were not White's move.

Let us first then consider a few possibilities from diagram 52 with Black to move. King moves fail for after 1 ... ♔e8 2 ♔e5 wins the d-pawn because of the threatened 3 ♔e6 followed by mate. As 1 ... d3 2 ♔e3 loses the d-pawn immediately, there remain only moves with the c-pawn.

In the course of the solution we shall see Black is also in zugzwang after 1 ... c5 2 ♔e4, and if 1 ... c6 2 ♔f3 ♔e8 (or 2 ... c5 3 ♔e4) 3 ♔e4 c5 4 ♔d5 White reaches the winning position that will also appear in the solution.

Having demonstrated that Black is in zugzwang in the original position, we now have the task of manoeuvring him into one of the above losing variations. Here is how it is achieved:

1 ♔f3! c6

The most testing defence. Both 1 ... c5 2 ♔e4 and 1 ... ♔e8 2 ♔e4 c5 3 ♔d5 lead to the main line.

2 ♔f4

But not 2 ♔e4? c5, when White himself is in zugzwang and only draws.

2 ... c5
3 ♔e4!

And now Black is in zugzwang and must give way to the white king. His next move is forced.

3 ... ♔e8
4 ♔d5 ♔d7

Again the only move, for 4 ... d3 5 ♔e6 gives mate next move, and 4 ... ♔f7 5 ♔d6 d3 6 ♔d7 allows White to queen with check.

5 ♔c4 ♔e8
6 ♔xc5! d3
7 ♔d6 ♔f7

Or 7 ... d2 8 ♔e6 d1♕ 9 f7 mate.

8 ♔d7 and wins.

A better king position can sometimes be enough to convert a draw into a win, as we see in diagram 53.

This position is completely symmetrical and it seems improbable that White can achieve any advantage. However, having first move gives him the chance to set up a favourable king position and win as follows:

53

C.Salvioli 1887

1 ♔f3

Of course 1 ♔e3 is an alternative, as White is aiming for the e4 square. Black to move would win by a similar manoeuvre.

1 ... ♔f6

1 ... ♔e6 transposes into the main line, and 1 ... e5 2 ♔e4 ♔e6 3 e3 wins for White. Finally, 1 ... e6 2 ♔e4 ♔f6 3 e3 ♔f7 4 ♔e5 ♔e7 5 e4 wins in the same way.

2 ♔e4 ♔e6
3 e3

Putting Black into zugzwang and so forcing an entry for the white king.

3 ... ♔f6
4 ♔d5 ♔f7

4 ... e6+ 5 ♔d6 ♔f7 6 e4 transposes.

5 ♔e5 e6
6 ♔d6 ♔f6
7 e4 wins.

Black's e-pawn is lost whatever he plays.

Endings with more Pawns

We have not yet examined any

endings in which one side has more than two pawns. This type of ending does not really belong to the purely theoretical positions we have been discussing so far, taking on more and more the character of a practical example. For this reason we shall restrict ourselves here to a few positions only, selecting those which illustrate some aspect not yet dealt with.

Firstly, let us consider a position which has practical value in assessing those endings where one side has a pawn majority on the wing.

54

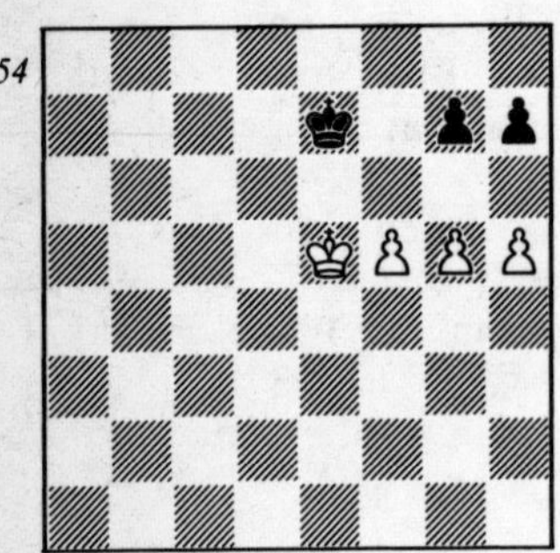

G.Lolli 1763

We shall show that White's 3:2 pawn majority is much easier to utilize than the 2:1 majority we have fully examined in previous examples. First with White to move:

A

1 g6

The simplest. 1 ♔d5 wins too, but not 1 h6 gh 2 gh ♔f7 or 1 f6+? gf+ 2 gf+ ♔f7 3 ♔f5 ♔e8 (or g8) 4 ♔e6 ♔f8, both of which draw for Black.

1 ... h6

White wins easily after 1 ... hg 2 hg etc.

2 ♔d5

Again White must avoid 2 f6+? gf+ 3 ♔f5 ♔f8 with a drawn result.

2 ... ♔f6

3 ♔e4

Or 3 ♔d6 ♔xf5 4 ♔e7 and 5 ♔f7 winning also.

3 ... ♔e7

4 ♔e5 ♔f8

5 ♔e6 ♔e8

6 ♔d6

But not 6 f6? ♔f8 drawing.

6 ... ♔f8

7 ♔d7 ♔g8

8 ♔e7 ♔h8

9 f6 gf

10 ♔f7 wins.

And now with Black to move:

B

1 ... ♔f7

Pawn moves would lose more quickly, e.g. 1 ... h6 2 g6 (or 2 gh gh 3 f6+ winning, but not 2 f6+? ♔f7 with a draw) as in line A, 1 ... g6 2 hg hg 3 fg ♔e8 4 ♔d6 etc winning.

2 g6+

Or 2 ♔d6 which also wins.

2 ... ♔g8

3 ♔e6 ♔h8

3 ... hg would transpose into line A.

4 ♔f7 hg

5 h6 gh

6 fg and mate in 3.

In diagram 55 we see a problem-like finish which everyone should know thoroughly, as it can easily occur in practice. The pawn breakthrough is much more subtle than the one we saw in diagram 45.

Black is threatening to take his king over to the queenside, when the most White can hope for is a draw. At first sight it looks as though nothing works, as both 1 c6 bc 2 bc and 1 b6 ab 2 cb cb lead to nothing. There is, however, a fine breakthrough combination which wins in a few moves.

1 b6 cb

Or 1 ... ab 2 c6 cb 3 a6 wins.

2 a6 ba

3 c6 and wins.

In playing such a combination, the reader must of course make sure that all the given elements are present. If the pawns were all one rank further down the board, the whole plan would be pointless as Black would be able to accept both pawn sacrifices, queen his own pawn and remain with material advantage. Equally, the black king must be far enough away from the c-pawn, otherwise he could stop it queening. For instance, with the black king on f6 instead of g6, White's combination would lose after 1 b6? cb 2 a6 ba 3 c6 ♔e6 etc. In other words, a player must weigh up all factors before plunging into such a sharp combination.

Finally, let us give the reader some practical advice about such positions as diagram 56.

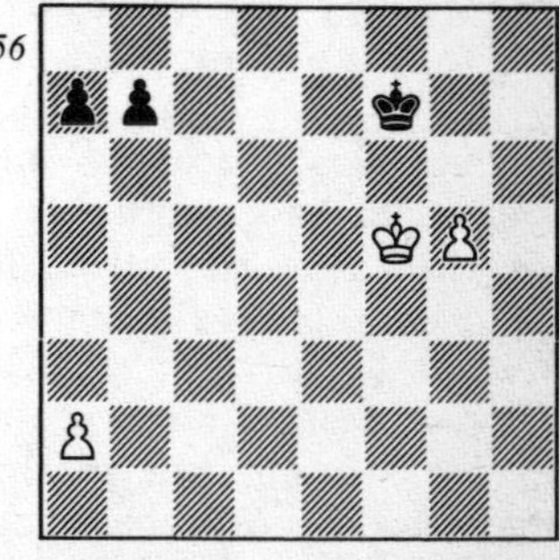

A drawn result springs immediately to mind. Admittedly White has a distant passed pawn, but this has little significance, as his king is so far away from Black's pawns, and Black is threatening to advance these and eliminate White's a-pawn. However, which pawn does Black advance first to make sure of the draw?

It may seem that it does not matter in which order the pawns are advanced, but if the reader remembers what we said about the blockade of pawns, he will realize the importance of choosing the correct pawn here. A good general rule is to **advance the pawn which is unopposed by an enemy pawn.** In this position it is the b-pawn. We shall even show that the advance of the a-pawn is quite wrong and leads to a loss for Black.

So the correct plan is **1 ... b5! 2 g6+** or 2 ♔e5 ♔g6 3 ♔d5 ♔xg5 4 ♔c5 ♔f5 5 ♔xb5 ♔e6 6 ♔a6 ♔d7 7 ♔xa7 ♔c7 drawing **2 ... ♔g7 3 ♔g5 a5 4 ♔f5 b4** and White must now force the draw by **5 ♔e4 a4 6 ♔d4 b3 7 ab ab 8 ♔c3**. Let us see what happens, then, if Black selects the faulty 1 ... a5? instead of 1 ... b5! (or the waiting 1 ... ♔g7).

1	**...**	**a5**

This move loses because White can now blockade both black pawns, which is equivalent to being a pawn up. As Black has a pawn on the fourth rank, he can of course sacrifice his b-pawn and queen his a-pawn, but in this situation this too proves unavailing.

2	**a4!**	**b5**

Black cannot wait either, as White wins after 2 ... b6 3 g6+ ♔g7 4 ♔g5 b5 (4 ... ♔g8 5 ♔f6 ♔f8 6 g7+ ♔g8 7 ♔g6 wins even more quickly) 5 ab a4 6 b6 a3 7 b7 a2 8 b8♕ and 9 ♕c7+ followed by mate in two moves.

3	**ab**	**a4**
4	**g6+!**	**♔g7**

Or 4 ... ♔e7 5 g7 ♔f7 6 g8♕+ ♔xg8 7 b7 and White queens with check, a useful tactical point to remember.

5	**b6**	**a3**
6	**b7**	**a2**
7	**b8♕**	**a1♕**
8	**♕c7+** and mate in 2.	

Practical examples

We have now dealt with the most important basic elements of pawn endings, all of which must be thoroughly mastered by the chessplayer. In this section we examine which illustrate how the above principles can be applied in more difficult endings.

57
B

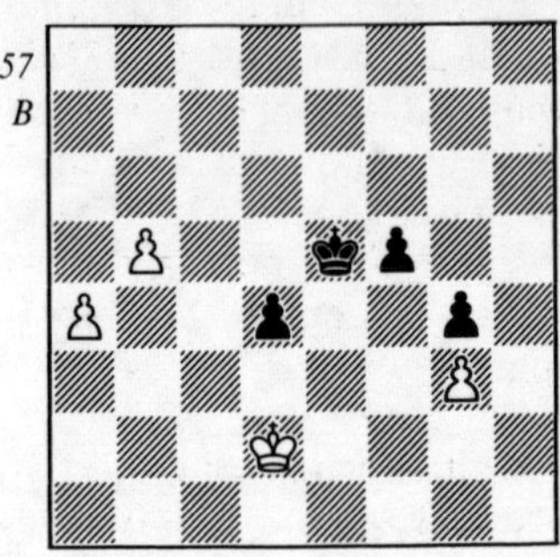

Stoltz-Nimzowitsch 1928

A cursory glance at this position might give us the impression that White stands better. He has two strong connected passed pawns on the queenside, is blocking the advance of the d-pawn with his king and is holding up Black's kingside pawns. What has he to worry about? Upon closer examination, however, Black's advantages become clear. By advancing his f-pawn he can create two passed pawns on the g- and d-files, and these cannot be stopped by the white king, whereas White's queenside pawns are not far enough advanced to be dangerous. So both sides have important advantages and our task is to decide which of these prevail. As is often the case in such situations, the player with the first move has a vital tempo, as Nimzowitsch demonstrated in the following instructive play:

1 ... f4!

It is clear that Black has no time to lose. If White had the move here, he would win by **1 ♔d3!** not 1 b6 ♔d6 2 ♔d3 f4 3 ♔xd4 f3! etc, drawing **1 ... f4 2 gf+ ♔d5** or 2 ... ♔xf4 3 b6 and queens with check **3 b6 g3 4 b7 g2 5 b8♕ g1♕ 6 ♕e5+** and White picks up the d-pawn with a won queen and pawn ending.

2 gf+

If White declines the offer by 2 b6 or 2 a5, then 2 ... ♔d6! gives play similar to the main line.

2 ... ♔d6!

Black does not recapture the f-pawn not only because White would then queen with check, but because the black king's role is to hold up White's queenside pawns. Equally good is 2 ... ♔d5 3 a5 ♔c5 4 a6 ♔b6 or here 4 b6 ♔c6, as the white king cannot stop both of Black's pawns.

3 a5 g3
4 a6 ♔c7!

Now everything is clear. White's pawns are stopped, whereas one of the black pawns must queen.

5 ♔e2 d3+

Or 5 ... g2 6 ♔f2 d3+ etc.

6 ♔xd3 g2
7 ♔e4 g1♕

and Stoltz soon resigned.

This instructive example shows us how complicated a pawn breakthrough can be and how exactly all variations must be calculated.

Equally subtle is our next example which occurred in a game between two grandmasters of world class.

58
B

Flohr-Capablanca 1935

It is immediately clear that White has important positional advantages, as Black's pawn position is badly weakened by his doubled pawns. If White's king reaches f4, Black must sooner or later lose a pawn and the game. To reach f4, the white king must first occupy f3, when he has tempo moves with his h-pawn which ensures that his king reaches f4. What can Black do to counter this plan?

If he plays passively, then White will carry out the above plan with an easy win. This means that Black's only chance lies in playing ... h4 at the moment when he can answer gh by ... f4, eliminating the white e-pawn. But this would not work with the white king on e2 and black king on e5, as White would capture the h-pawn and answer 1 ... f4 with 2 h5! ♔f5 3 ef, keeping all his pawns and winning. To draw, Black must be able to capture the e-pawn *with check*, i.e. the white king must be on d2 or f2. In other words, with the white king on e2 and black king on e4, White to move would have to place his king on d2 or f2, allowing ... h4! drawing. On the other hand, the same position with Black to move is a win for White, as ... h4 does not work, and so the white king occupies f3, the winning square.

Black must obviously plan his defence most carefully and it is interesting to see how Capablanca tackles the problem:

A

1 ... ♔e5!

Showing complete understanding of the subtleties of the position. The obvious gain of the opposition by **1 ... ♔d5?** would lose instructively to **2 ♔d2 ♔e5** 2 ... ♔e4 3 ♔e2 puts Black in zugzwang, and 2 ... h4 3 gh f4 4 ef ♔e4 5 h5 wins for White, which is why the black king needs to be on e5 **3 ♔e1! ♔d5 4 ♔f2 ♔e4** forced, as White was threatening 5 ♔f3 **5 ♔e2 ♔d5** or 5 ... h4 6 gh f4 7 h5 ♔f5 8 ef wins **6 ♔f3 ♔e5 7 h3 ♔d5 8 ♔f4 ♔e6 9 h4** winning the front f-pawn and the game.

Strangely enough, Black has another means of defending successfully, by playing his king over to g5, equally guarding the f4 square and preparing ... h4. We shall examine this later under B.

2 ♔e2

As already mentioned, 2 ♔d2 h4! 3 gh f4! 4 h5 fe+ 5 ♔xe3 ♔f5 draws.

2 ... ♔e4!

Black has now attained his objective and White is in zugzwang. As a king move allow ... h4, he must use up an important tempo by advancing his h-pawn.

3 h3 ♔d5

Not of course 3 ... ♔e5? 4 ♔f3 winning.

4 ♔f3 ♔e5

and both players agreed to a draw. After 5 h4 ♔d5 6 ♔f4 ♔e6, White no longer has the vital tempo move with his h-pawn.

B

1 ... ♔f7!

This move leads to an alternative but riskier draw, with the king reaching g5 just in time.

2 ♔e2

Other king moves are no better, e.g. 2 ♔d4 ♔e6 3 ♔c3 ♔f7 4 ♔d3 ♔g6! (not 4 ... ♔e6 5 ♔e2 and 6 ♔f3) 5 ♔d4 ♔g5 6 ♔d5 ♔g4 7 ♔e6 ♔h3 draws.

2 ... ♔g6

3 ♔f2 ♔h6!

The black king must not occupy g5 until the white king is on f3. For instance, 3 ... ♔g5? 4 ♔f3 h4 5 gh+ ♔xh4 6 ♔f4 ♔h3 wins for White.

4 ♔f3 ♔g5

5 h3

Or 5 h4+ ♔h6 6 ♔f4 ♔g6 7 e4 fe 8 ♔xe4 ♔f7 9 ♔f5 ♔g7 10 ♔e6 ♔g6 11 ♔e7 ♔g7! drawing. The text move looks dangerous for Black, as 5 ... ♔h6 6 ♔f4 ♔g6 7 h4!

wins for White, but another resource saves him.

5	...	**h4!**
6	**♔g2**	

Or 6 gh+ ♔xh4 7 ♔f4 ♔xh3 (the point!) 8 ♔xf5 ♔g3 9 ♔xf6 ♔f3 drawing.

6	...	**♔h5**

Black can also draw with 6 ... hg 7 ♔xg3 f4+ 8 ef+ ♔h5.

7	**♔f2**	**hg+**
8	**♔xg3**	**♔g5**
9	**h4+**	**♔h5**
10	**♔h3**	**f4**
11	**ef**	**f5**

and the position is clearly drawn.

Our next example shows us a clever king manoeuvre such as we saw in diagram 13.

59
W

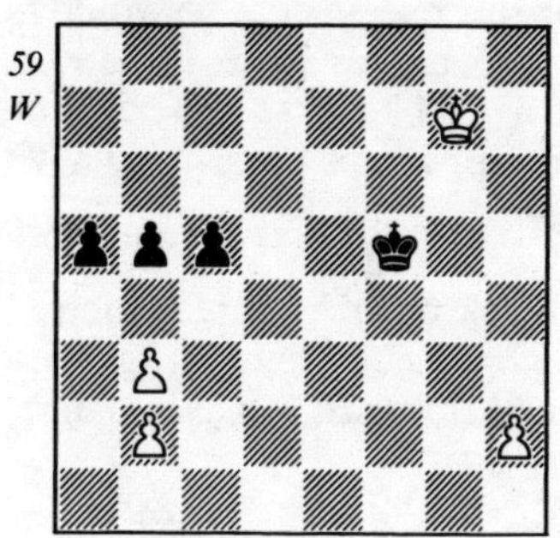

Lasker-Tarrasch 1914

Tarrasch had brought about this position on the assumption that White could now resign. Black in fact threatens to win on the queenside, even without the help of his king, by 1 ... c4 2 bc bc followed by 3 ... a4 and 4 ... c3. It looks as though the white king can do little about this, and the white h-pawn can easily be stopped. However, to the great surprise of Tarrasch, the World Champion produced the following imaginative drawing manoeuvre:

1	**h4**	**♔g4**
2	**♔g6!**	

The point. Tarrasch had only considered 2 ♔f6 c4 3 bc bc 4 ♔e5 c3! 5 bc a4 and this pawn cannot be stopped. Lasker's move gains a vital tempo as he threatens 3 h5 and Black is forced to waste a move by capturing the pawn. This means that the white king can retreat along the light-squared diagonal (b1-h7) instead of the dark one (a1-h8) which is blocked by a pawn, a vast difference as we shall see.

2	...	**♔xh4**
3	**♔f5**	**♔g3**

It must have been about here that Tarrasch awoke from his dream of victory, for if he now continues with his original plan he loses as follows: 3 ... c4 4 bc bc 5 ♔e4 c3 6 bc a4? (he could still draw by 6 ... ♔g5 7 ♔d5 ♔f6) 7 ♔d3! as the white pawn on c3 no longer forces the white king to waste a move in order to reach b2.

4	**♔e4**	**♔f2**
5	**♔d5**	**♔e3**

Now Black must be careful not to lose the game.

6	**♔xc5**	**♔d3**
7	**♔xb5**	**♔c2**
8	**♔xa5**	**♔xb3**

½-½

We have already talked a great deal about the opposition and its importance, with special emphasis on the distant opposition and related squares. However, the reader may well feel that such ideas belong to the realm of endgame studies rather than practical play. The following extremely interesting example from the 1937 Kemeri international tournament may help to disprove this fallacy.

60
B

Berg-Petrov 1937

Once again, appearances can be deceptive, for although material is evenly balanced, with both kings holding the enemy pawns, it is Black who has a winning advantage. This is mainly because he can immediately set up a protected passed pawn, whereas White cannot achieve this.

The advantage of a protected passed pawn lies in the fact that it severely limits the freedom of the enemy king whilst allowing one's own king to wander at will. In this case, the white king must constantly keep an eye on Black's b-pawn, whereas the black king can always attack the white pawns.

However, the win is by no means easy for Black, for White's king can go as far as e4 and still keep an eye on the b-pawn, and the white pawns on h4 and g4 form a barrier which cannot be broken by ... g5, allowing White a protected passed pawn himself after h5. As the game was adjourned here, both players had time to make a thorough analysis of the position and White resigned without continuing! Let us now see why:

1 ... a5!

Clearly an essential move, as Black must protect his b-pawn before White isolates it by 2 a5. For this reason, 1 ... g5 would fail to 2 h5, and as Black has no time for 2 ... g4 because of 3 a5, White can support his passed pawn with 3 g4.

2 g4

Black was now threatening 2 ... g5 3 hg ♔g7, or here 3 h5 g4 with a straightforward win as in diagram 24.

2 ... ♔g8
3 ♔c2 ♔f7
4 ♔d3 ♔e6

As can easily be seen, the opposition plays the main part here. For example, with the black king on d4 and the black king on d6, if White has to move, then Black can immediately penetrate via c5 or e5. As we shall show later, we can discount the fact that White has pawn moves available on the kingside.

Black cannot gain the opposition directly, because White has e4, d4 or c4 for his king, as soon as the black king plays to e6, d6 or c6. So Black has to make sure of the distant opposition. With the black king on e7 or d7, the related squares for the white king are e3 and d3 but as c3 is not available to the king, he cannot take the opposition if the black king plays to c7.

All that remains is to find the best way of carrying out Black's plan, without allowing White tactical chances. The most economical method would be 4 ... ♔e7 5 ♔e3 ♔d7 6 ♔d3 ♔c7! but we select a longer way so that we can indicate some additional points about the position.

5 ♔e4 *(61)*

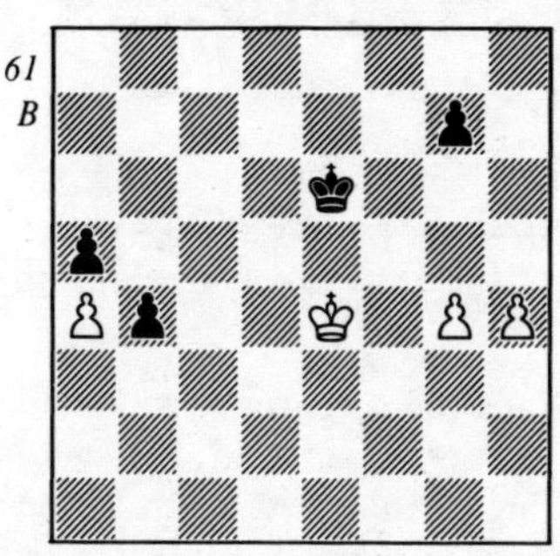

61
B

Let us take this position as the starting point of our analysis, as it best illustrates the various possibilities open to both sides.

It is first worth noting that if White tries to maintain the distant opposition by 5 ♔e2, in order to answer a later ... ♔c7 by ♔c1, this allows the black king to reach c5 by 5 ... ♔d5 6 ♔d3 ♔c5!. As c3 is not available for the white king, he loses after 7 ♔e4 (7 h5 ♔d5) 7 ... ♔c4 8 ♔e3 ♔c3! and the b-pawn queens.

5 ... ♔d6

Again a quicker way would be **5 ... ♔d7 6 ♔d3** or 6 h5 ♔e7! 7 g5 ♔e6! wins by zugzwang **6 ... ♔c7** etc, but we wish to point out an interesting trap.

Note also the important variation 5 ... b3 6 ♔d3 ♔e5 7 ♔c3 ♔f4 when 8 g5! cleverly draws for White after 8 ... ♔g4 9 ♔xb3 ♔xh4 10 ♔c4 ♔xg5 11 ♔b5 ♔f5 12 ♔xa5 g5 13 ♔xb5 g4 and both sides obtain a queen.

6 ♔d4 ♔d7!

Black must play exactly and not place his king on c7 until the white king is on the third rank. This is to make sure that his king can reach e5 if the white pawns advance.

An instructive error, for instance, is an immediate 6 ... ♔c7? which admittedly gains the opposition but allows White to save himself by 7 h5! ♔d6 8 g5 when the threat of h6 forces 8 ... ♔e7 9 ♔e3 ♔e6 10 ♔e4, and White's has regained the opposition thus preventing ... ♔f5.

7 ♔d3

7 ♔e4 ♔e6 gives Black the opposition, and both 7 g5 ♔e6 8 ♔e4 g6, and 7 h5 ♔e6 lose at once.

7 ... ♔c7!

Only now can this move be played without danger, as 8 h5

would fail to 8 ... ♔d6 9 g5 ♔e5!, or here 9 ♔e4 ♔e7! 10 g5 ♔e6! etc. After the text move White is compelled to give up the opposition.

8 ♔e4

Neither 8 ♔c4 ♔c6 nor 8 ♔d4 ♔d6 would change anything, and 8 h5 ♔d6! 9 ♔e4 ♔e7! 10 g5 ♔e6! gives us the zugzwang position we now know.

Black also wins after **8 g5 ♔d6!** not 8 ... ♔d7? 9 h5 drawing **9 ♔e4 ♔e7!** again 9 ... ♔e6? 10 h5 draws **10 ♔e3 ♔e6!** both 10 ... ♔f7 11 h5 and 10 ... g6 11 ♔d3 lead to a draw **11 ♔e4 g6**, and Black wins because his king obtains the f5 square.

8 ... ♔c6!

Gaining the diagonal opposition.

9 ♔d4

Black also wins after 9 g5 ♔d6 10 ♔d4 ♔e6 11 ♔e4 g6, or 9 h5 ♔d6 10 g5 ♔e6.

As a general rule, with the white pawns on g5 and h5, Black must always take the opposition on e6 when White plays ♔e4.

9 ... ♔d6

Black has achieved his objective and wins comfortably.

10 ♔e4

Pawn moves would be answered by 10 ... ♔e6.

10 ... ♔c5

11 h5

We choose the pawn advance as our main line which could, of course, occurred earlier. Equally hopeless is 11 ♔d3 ♔d5 12 ♔e3 ♔e5! (simplest), and 11 g5 ♔d6 12 h5 ♔e6 transposes into the text continuation.

11 ... ♔d6

Or 11 ... ♔c5 12 ♔e3 ♔d5 winning.

12 g5 ♔e6!

13 ♔d4 ♔f5

14 h6 gh

15 gh ♔g6

and Black captures the h-pawn after which he wins as shown in diagram 24. An unusually interesting and instructive example.

Finally we give a position illustrating the importance of the opposition and tempo moves with pawns.

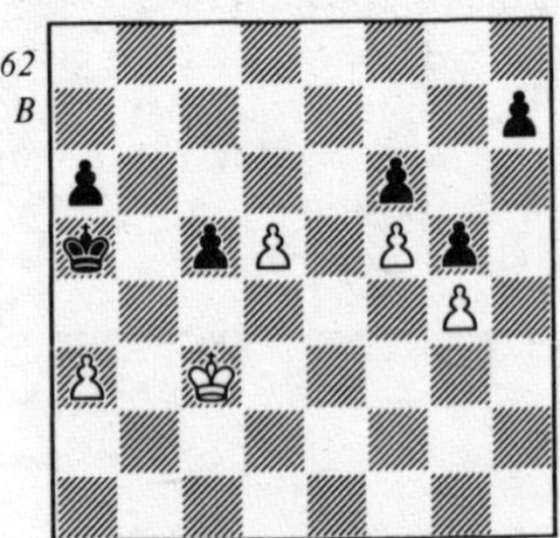

Randviir-Keres 1947

Black has an extra pawn but has difficulties owing to the better placing of the white king, White's dangerous passed central pawn and the backward pawn on h7. However, a pawn is a pawn, and one of its uses might be to play ... h5 to force the g-pawn. A more important use of this h-pawn is as a tempo move (... h6) at a critical moment, to gain the opposition, which may prove vital in forcing the win. As we shall demonstrate later, Black wins this ending only because he has this tempo move at his disposal – with the pawn on h6 the ending is drawn!

1 ... ♔b5

The only way. White draws after 1 ... ♔b6? 2 ♔c4 a5 3 a4, as 3 ... h6 is then forced.

2 a4+

This check is forced, as Black wins quickly after 2 ♔d3 c4+ 3 ♔d4 c3! 4 ♔xc3 ♔c5 etc. Black cannot now take the pawn because of 3 d6 winning.

2 ... ♔b6
3 ♔c4 a5!

In this way Black reaches the position we have seen, without having to use up his precious tempo move ... h6.

4 d6

Or 4 ♔c3 ♔c7 5 ♔d3 ♔d6 6 ♔c4 h6 7 ♔b5 ♔xd5 8 ♔xa5 ♔c6! 9 ♔a6 c4 winning.

4 ... ♔c6
5 d7 ♔xd7
6 ♔xc5 ♔e7

Black can achieve nothing in the centre or on the queenside, as the white king is too active, but he can threaten a breakthrough by ... h5 now that the resulting white h-pawn can be stopped. For instance, he neednot fear 7 ♔b5, when 7 ... h5! 8 gh g4 9 h6 ♔f7 wins at once. In other words the white king dare not leave the square c1-c5-g5-g8.

7 ♔d5 ♔f7
8 ♔e4

White must bring his king over to prevent the threatened 8 ... h5 9 gh ♔g7 followed by 10 ... ♔h6, which he could now answer with 10 ♔f3 ♔h6 11 ♔g4. Black would win easily after 8 ♔d4 h5 9 gh ♔g7 10 ♔d5 g4 11 ♔e4 ♔h6 12 ♔f4 ♔xh5.

8 ... ♔f8!

The winning move which recalls the winning method of diagram 26. White is now in zugzwang. His king dare not leave the e-file by 9 ♔d4 because of 9 ... h5!, nor can he retreat as this allows the black king to reach d6. He must choose between the two evils.

9 ♔e3 ♔e7
10 ♔e4 ♔d6
11 ♔d4 h6!

Only now does Black play his trump card, with his king one rank further up and on the d-file. He gains the opposition and thus manages to advance his king even more. It is clear that without this tempo move Black could not win despite his extra pawn.

12 ♔e4

White has no time to counter-attack on the queen's wing, as after 12 ♔c4 ♔e5 13 ♔b5 h6 14 gh ♔xf5 Black wins quickly.

12 ... ♔c5
13 ♔e3 ♔d5!

Much simpler than the alternative winning plan of 13 ... ♔b4 14 ♔d4 ♔xa4 15 ♔d5 ♔b3 16 ♔e6 a4 etc.

14 ♔d3 ♔e5
15 ♔e3 h5!
16 gh ♔xf5
17 ♔f3 ♔e6

Again simpler than 17 ... g4+ 18 ♔g3 ♔g5 19 h6 etc.

18	**♔g4**	**♔f7**
19	**♔f7**	**♔g7**

0-1

With this example we end our discussion of pawn endings. The reader has been provided with the most important basic positions illustrating the essential principles of pawn endgames. There are of course many positions which cannot be dealt with in this book. As already stated, however, we intend our material to be instructive rather than exhaustive. If the reader studies this material carefully, he will have enough information to steer him through the most complex endings. Let us now turn to queen endings.

3 Queen Endings

We began with pawn endings because to a certain extent they form the basis of endgame theory. Now we shall examine the individual pieces in descending order of strength, starting with the queen.

It is far more difficult to systematize queen endings than was the case with pawn endings, as there are so many possibilities. For instance, it is well known that the queen usually wins against one of the other pieces, or against two minor pieces, whereas it only draws against two rooks or one rook plus a minor piece. We shall therefore refrain from examining such positions in detail.

We are primarily interested in positions or groups of positions in which a win or a draw can be demonstrated from general principles, with few exceptions. And in these endings we shall first consider those which have the most practical value. There is neither the space nor the necessity for examining here all possible ramifications of queen endings.

Queen against Pawn

At first sight it may seem strange for us to consider endings with such material disparity, as the queen usually wins easily. However, complications do arise when the pawn has reached the seventh rank. This situation is common enough in practical play, as we have already seen, so the reader must know exactly how to handle such positions. Let us begin with diagram 63.

63

When Black has a centre pawn on the seventh, White always wins, however far away his king is, apart from the exceptional cases when the pawn cannot be prevented from queening next move because of unfavourable placing of the white pieces. (For example, with the white king on e6, queen on d8, and the black king on e2, pawn on d2, the white king blocks off the queen's checking possibilities, so that 1 ... d1♛ cannot be stopped.)

White wins from the diagram by forcing the black king onto the square in front of his pawn, thus giving him a tempo in which to bring his king nearer. Play might proceed as follows:

1 ♕b2 ♔e1

No better is 1 ... ♔e3 2 ♕c2.

2 ♕b4 ♔e2
3 ♕e4+ ♔f2
4 ♕d3 ♔e1
5 ♕e3+ ♔d1

White has achieved his aim and can now gradually bring up his king by repeating the above manoeuvre.

6 ♔b7 ♔c2
7 ♕e2 ♔c1
8 ♕c4+ ♔b2
9 ♕d3 ♔c1
10 ♕c3+ ♔d1

Again the black king has to block his pawn and White can play 11 ♔c6, followed by the same tempo-gaining line we have already seen. There seems little point in continuing the play, as the reader can check for himself that the position is easily won.

It is clear that White can also use the same method against the knight's pawn, but the situation changes with a rook's pawn or bishop's pawn. Consider diagram 64:

First of all, let us try the same winning plan as from diagram 63:

1 ♕g2+ ♔b1
2 ♕f1+ ♔b2
3 ♕b5+ ♔c2
4 ♕a4+ ♔b2
5 ♕b4+ ♔c2

64

6 ♕a3 ♔b1
7 ♕b3 ♔a1

and we now realise the vital difference; White dare not touch his king, because Black is stalemated, and 8 ♕c2, threatening mate, also gives stalemate. This means that White can make no progress, so the position is drawn.

And yet there are positions in which White wins if his king is near enough. To be more precise, the king must be within the area represented by a1-a5-d5-e4-e1 as indicated on diagram 64. For example, let us see what happens with the king on d5 (diagram 65).

65

White wins by **1 ♕g2+ ♔b1** if

1 ... ♔b3 2 ♕g7! ♔c2 3 ♕a1 wins at once **2 ♔c4! a1♕ 3 ♔b3!** when, despite equality of material, Black cannot prevent mate.

Now let us try the king on e4 (diagram 66). The win is achieved here in a different way by **1 ♕g2+ ♔b1 2 ♔d3! a1♕ 3 ♕c2 mate**.

66

If Black has a bishop's pawn, the outcome again depends on the white king's position, but in addition it is important to take into consideration the placing of the black king. Diagram 67 shows the black king on a central file.

67

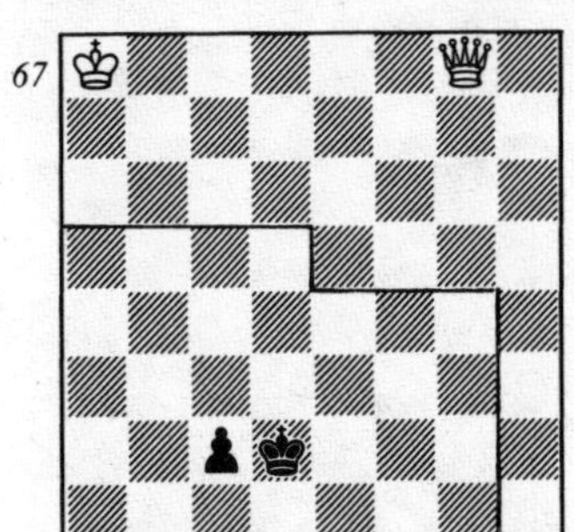

This position is drawn, as the white king is too far away. Play might proceed:

1	**♕a2**	**♔d1**
2	**♕a4**	**♔d2**
3	**♕d4+**	**♔e2**
4	**♕c3**	**♔d1**
5	**♕d3+**	**♔c1**

White can only force the black king to block his pawn once, so must immediately bring his king nearer.

6	**♔b7**	**♔b2**
7	**♕d2**	**♔b1**
8	**♕b4+**	**♔a2**
9	**♕c3**	**♔b1**
10	**♕b3+**	**♔a1!**

The point! Black is not compelled to return to c1, as 11 ♕xc2 gives stalemate. White cannot strengthen his position any further and the game is drawn.

We have again indicated in diagram 67 the area within which the white king must be to force a win. A few examples will make this clear. With the king on d5, White wins by **1 ♕g5+ ♔d1 2 ♕g1+ ♔d2 3 ♕d4+ ♔e2 4 ♕c3 ♔d1 5 ♕d3+ ♔c1 6 ♔c4 ♔b2 7 ♕d2** but not 7 ♕e2 ♔b1 8 ♔b3? c1♘+ drawing, although here 8 ♔c3 c1♕+ 9 ♔b3 still wins **7 ... ♔b1 8 ♔b3 c1♕ 9 ♕a2 mate**.

68

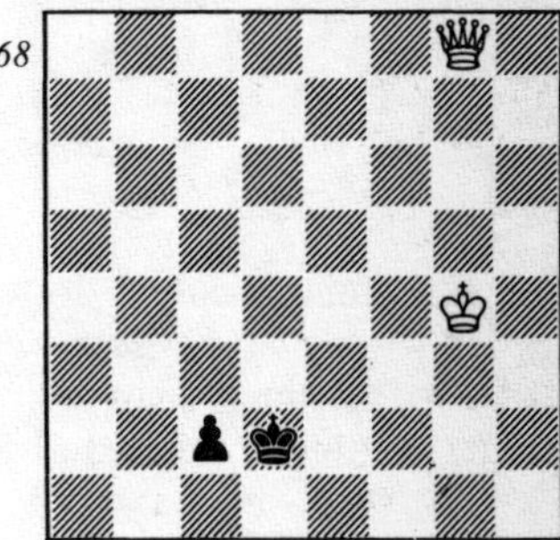

Placing the white king over on g4 (diagram 68), the winning method is **1 ♕a2 ♔c3** 1 ... ♔d1 2 ♔f3 **2 ♕a3+ ♔d2 3 ♕b2 ♔d1 4 ♔f3! c1♕ 5 ♕e2 mate**. Finally, with the king on e5, outside the given zone, White seems to win by **1 ♕a2** ♔d1 2 ♔e4 c1♕ 3 ♔d3! forcing mate. Black has a better defence, however, in **1 ... ♔c3! 2 ♕a3+ ♔d2 3 ♕b2 ♔d1** when White cannot strengthen his position.

From the above analysis we see that in certain cases White can win only because the black king is unfavourably placed on d1 and must lose a tempo when he is forced to go to c1. If we now place the king on the other side of the pawn, on the knight's file, the white king needs to be much nearer to force a win, as shown in diagram 69:

69

This position is of course drawn. In order to win, the white king must be within the indicated area (a4-c4-d3-e3-e1). On e3 and e1 he can easily stop the pawn by a subsequent ♔d2. On a4, he equally has no trouble, as 1 ♕g2 ♔b1 2 ♔b3! c1♕ 3 ♕a2 is mate.

Once again we must mention a position in which the white king stands outside the winning zone but can still cause Black problems. With his king on b5, White plays **1 ♕g2 ♔b1 2 ♕e4 ♔b2 3 ♕e2** and after 3 ... ♔b1? 4 ♔b4! c1♕ 5 ♔b3 wins as already seen. Black must defend more precisely with **3 ... ♔a1!** when 4 ♕xc2 is stalemate, and 4 ♕d2 ♔b1! 5 ♔b4 c1♕ draws because the white queen is attacked.

We have now covered all endings with a queen against an advanced pawn on the 7th rank. The given rules apply in all cases except when the white pieces are so unfavourably placed that the pawn cannot be stopped from queening.

Against a pawn on the 6th rank, the queen always wins, except when the pawn cannot be prevented from playing to the 7th rank, as seen in diagram 70.

70
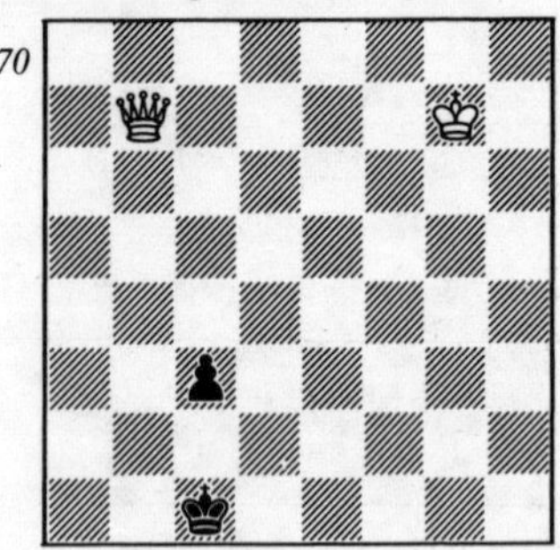

Chess World 1865

White would win easily if his

king were not so unfortunately placed on the long black diagonal. For example, with the king on b8, **1 ♕h1+ ♔b2 2 ♕h8! ♔b3 3 ♕d4 c2 4 ♔a1** wins. As it is however, as White cannot prevent the further advance of the pawn, Black draws by:

1	**♕h1+**	**♔b2**
2	**♕b7+**	**♔c1**
3	**♔f6**	

It is interesting to note that even now White would win if his king were on h6, as after 3 ♔g5! c2 4 ♔f4 he would be within the winning zone (see diagram 67).

3	**...**	**c2**
4	**♔e5**	**♔d2**

As we saw in diagram 67, the position is now drawn, but we shall again give the correct defence.

5	**♕b2**	**♔d1**
6	**♕b3**	**♔d2**
7	**♕a2**	**♔c3**

And now 7 ... ♔d1? 8 ♔d4! c1♕ 9 ♔d3 with a win for White, whereas now, after 8 ♕a3+ ♔d2 White can make no progress.

There are one or two further exceptional positions where White cannnot force a win. For instance, with the white king on c6, queen on d8 and the black king on e2, pawn on f3, after **1 ♕e8(e7)+ ♔f1** White cannot prevent the advance of the pawn, so the position is drawn (2 ♔d5 f2 3 ♔e4 ♔g2, as in diagram 69).

If Black has pawns in addition to one on the 7th rank, the possibilities are various. In general the queen has good winning chances, but the second pawn sometimes saves an otherwise lost position.

For example, if Black possesses two pawns on the 7th rank, White can win only if his king is fairly near the pawns, as is the case when the second pawn is on the 6th. We do not intend to examine the numerous possibilities here, but any interested reader can always look them up in a more specialised book on the endgame. Let us make do with one example, diagram 71, which reveals Black's defensive resources.

71

Without Black's a-pawn, the position would clearly be drawn, but strangely enough White cannot profit from the fact that there is now no danger of stalemate. With the white king on a4, for instance, victory is easily attained by **1 ♕g7+ ♔f2 2 ♕h6 ♔g2 3 ♕g5+ ♔f2 4 ♕h4+ ♔g2 5 ♕g4+ ♔f2 6 ♕h3 ♔g1 7 ♕g3+ ♔h1 8 ♔b5! a4 9 ♕f2 and 10 ♕f1 mate**. However, as in diagram 71 the a-pawn is not blockaded, White cannot carry out this manoeuvre against correct defence.

1 ♕g8+ ♔f2!

Black must never allow the white queen to reach g4. For this reason, he loses after 1 ... ♔f1 2 ♕c4+ ♔g2 3 ♕g4+ ♔f2 4 ♕h3 ♔g1 5 ♕g3+ ♔h1 6 ♕f2, or after 1 ... ♔f3 2 ♕g5! a4 3 ♕h4 ♔g2 4 ♕g4+ etc. However, Black can also draw by 1 ... ♔h3 2 ♕d5 ♔g3! as in the main line.

2 ♕h7 ♔g3
3 ♕d3+ ♔g2
4 ♕e4+ ♔g3!

The only move to draw. As already mentioned, Black must not let the queen reach g4, when his king would be forced to h1. This means that both 4 ... ♔g1 5 ♕g4+ followed by 6 ♕h3, and 4 ... ♔f2 5 ♕h1 ♔g3 6 ♔b7 would lose for Black, as White gains an important tempo on the main line.

5 ♔b7 a4
6 ♔c6 a3
7 ♔d5 a2
8 ♕h1 a1♕!

The extra black pawn completes his mission by sacrificing himself and giving the black king the g2 square.

9 ♕xa1 ♔g2

and the game is drawn as we saw in diagram 64. Strangely enough, White would win from diagram 71 if his king were on any other square than a8!

Finally, let us consider a hidden defensive possibility which occurs with a knight's pawn supported by a rook's pawn. In the position with the white king on a8, queen on b7, and the black king on h1, pawns on g2 and h4, White cannot win. After the plausible continuation **1 ♕f3** Black was threatening 1 ... h3 and 2 ... ♔h2 **1 ... ♔h2 2 ♕f4+ ♔h3 3 ♕f2 g1♕+! 4 ♕xg1 is stalemate**. White wins here if his king is no further away than f6, when 1 ♕f3 ♔h2 2 ♕f2 h3 3 ♔g5 ♔h1 4 ♕f3 ♔h2 5 ♔h4! g1♕ 6 ♕xh3 mate is possible.

Queen against Rook (and Pawn)

A: QUEEN AGAINST ROOK

The ending of queen against rook and pawn will involve us in some complex analysis, but before we go into this, let us briefly consider how the queen forces a win against a rook alone.

72

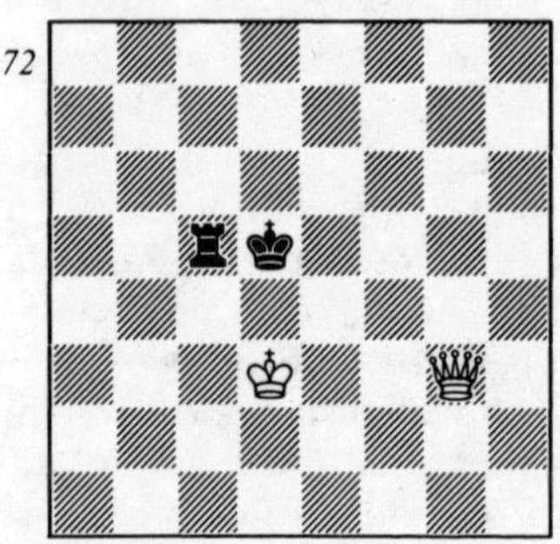

In general, apart from a few special cases, the queen wins against a rook, but this win is not easily achieved, as the following analysis shows:

1 ♕f3+ ♔e5
2 ♕e4+ ♔d6
3 ♔d4

In order to win, White must use both his king and queen to drive the black king to the edge of the board.

3 ... ♖c6

We are not claiming that this is Black's best defence, but no matter where the rook goes, White will eventually manage to drive the black king to the edge of the board by advancing his own king. Let us assume, for instance, that Black tries to prevent the king's advance by **3 ... ♖a5**. White would then proceed **4 ♕g6+ ♔d7** after 4 ... ♔e7 5 ♕b6 ♖h5 6 ♔e4 a position is reached which is symmetrical to the text position **5 ♕f6 ♖b5** or 5 ... ♔c7 6 ♕e6 ♔b7 7 ♔c4 ♔c7 8 ♔b4 and the rook must retreat **6 ♕f7+ ♔d6** 6 ... ♔c6 7 ♕e6+ ♔c7 8 ♔c4 is quicker **7 ♕f8+ ♔d7 8 ♕f6! ♖a5 9 ♔c4 ♔c7 10 ♕e7+ ♔c6 11 ♕e6+ ♔c7 12 ♔b4** and the black rook is forced back.

4 ♕e5+ ♔d7
5 ♔d5 ♖c7

After 5 ... ♖a6 6 ♕g7+ ♔d8 (or 6 ... ♔e8 7 ♕c7) 7 ♕f8+ ♔d7 8 ♕f7+ ♔d8 9 ♔c5 wins. Or 5 ... ♖c1 6 ♕f5+ ♔e8 7 ♕h5+ ♔d7 8 ♕g4+ ♔e8 9 ♔d6 wins.

6 ♕e6+ ♔d8
7 ♕g8+

It is important to avoid the trap 7 ♔d6 ♖c6+! 8 ♔xc6 stalemate.

7 ... ♔e7
8 ♕g7+ ♔d8
9 ♕f8+ ♔d7 *(73)*

73

10 ♕f4

This is probably the simplest of several winning moves. Also possible is 10 ♕h8 ♔e7 11 ♕g8! ♖d7+ (or 11 ... ♔d7 12 ♕f8 etc) 12 ♔e5 ♖c7 13 ♕g7+ ♔d8 14 ♕f8+ ♔d7 15 ♔d5! ♖b7 16 ♕f7+ ♔c8 17 ♕e8+ ♔c7 18 ♔c5! and wins easily, as after 18 ... ♖a7 19 ♕e7+ ♔b8 20 ♕d8+ ♔b7 21 ♔b5 Black will soon lose the rook. White equally wins after 10 ♕b8 but Black can set up a stiff resistance by 10 ... ♖c2!

10 ... ♔c8

If 10 ... ♖b7 White continues 11 ♕f7+ ♔c8 12 ♕e8+ ♔c7 13 ♔c5 and wins as in the last note.

11 ♔d6 ♔b8

11 ... ♖a7 loses immediately to 12 ♕f8+ ♔b7 13 ♕f7+ ♔b8 14 ♕e8+ ♔b7 15 ♕d7+ ♔b8 16 ♕d8+ ♔b7 17 ♕c7+ etc, as does 11 ... ♔b7 12 ♕b4+ ♔c8 13 ♕a5 etc.

12 ♕e5! ♖b7

After other moves Black loses even more quickly, as can easily be seen.

13 ♔c6+ ♔a8
14 ♕a1+ ♔b8

15 ♕a5

Philidor demonstrated that this position is a forced win, as long ago as 1777!

15 ... ♖b1

After 15 ... ♖h7 16 ♕e5+ ♔a8 17 ♕a1+ ♔b8 18 ♕b1+ wins; or 15 ... ♖b3 16 ♕d8+ ♔a7 17 ♕d4+ ♔b8 18 ♕f4+ and the rook is lost. Equally insufficient is 15 ... ♖f7 16 ♕e5+ ♔a7 17 ♕e3+ etc.

16 ♕d8+ ♔a7
17 ♕d4+ ♔a8
18 ♕h8+ ♔a7
19 ♕h7+ wins the rook.

We feel that this example gives an accurate picture of how to play with a queen against a rook, but it is worth mentioning one of the exceptional cases:

74

Black to move draws because the white king cannot escape perpetual check. Play might go **1 ... ♖h7+ 2 ♔g2 ♖g7+ 3 ♔f3 ♖f7+ 4 ♔g4 ♖g7+** 5 **♔f5 ♖f7+ 6 ♔g6 ♖g7+** 7 **♔h6 ♖h7+!** when **8 ♔xh7** gives **stalemate**. Of course, White to move would win from such a position.

B: QUEEN AGAINST ROOK AND PAWN

The situation is much more complicated now that Black has a pawn. Sometimes the analysis is so tricky that the assessment of a given position has changed over the years. From the many possible endings we intend to consider only those in which the pawn protects the rook and is itself protected by the king. Other positions can always be examined by the reader in more specialized endgame books.

Let us begin with positions in which the pawn is on its original square, as in diagram 75.

75

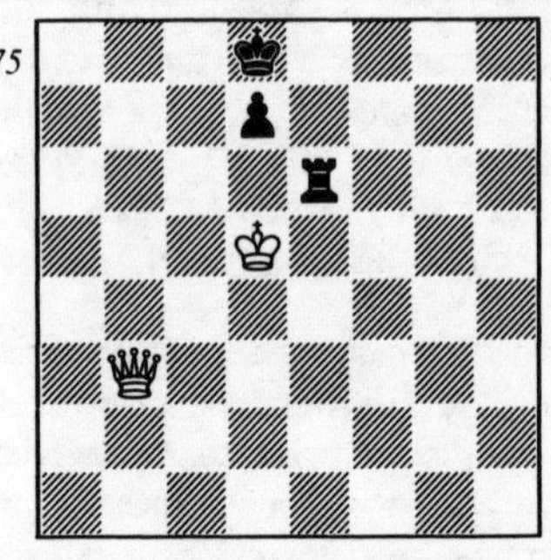

A.Philidor 1803

As Philidor demonstrated years ago, White cannot win in this position. Black cannot be zugzwanged, as his rook can always play from c6 to e6 and back. This means that the white king cannot cross the sixth rank, nor the black king be driven away from the protection of his pawn.

1 ♕b8+ ♔e7
2 ♕g8 ♖c6
3 ♕g7+ ♔d8
4 ♕f8+ ♔c7
5 ♕a8 ♖e6

White can make no further progress and the game is drawn. The game is equally drawn if the position is moved to the right or left, except in the case of a rook's pawn, when Black loses, as in diagram 76.

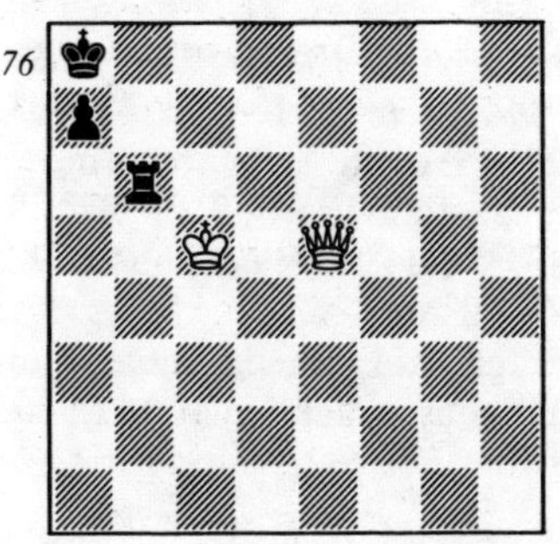

J.Berger 1922

The difference here lies mainly in the fact that the rook no longer has an extra square available where he can be protected by the pawn. As he has only one square (b6), this means that once his king is stalemated, the rook must move away, allowing the white king to penetrate.

1 ... ♔b7

White to move would win at once by 1 ♕c7!, e.g. 1 ... ♖b1 2 ♕c8+ ♖b8 3 ♕c6+ ♖b7 4 ♔d6 and Black must give up his pawn.

2 ♕e7+ ♔a6

After 2 ... ♔b8 3 ♕d7 places Black in zugzwang, e.g. 3 ... ♖h6 (if 3 ... ♖b1 4 ♕e8+ ♔c7 5 ♕f7+ followed by 6 ♕g8+ and 7 ♕h7+ wins, and if 3 ... ♖b2 4 ♕e8+ ♔b7 5 ♕e4+ ♔a6 6 ♕d3+ ♔b7 7 ♕f3+ ♔b8 8 ♕f8+ followed by 9 ♕g7+ equally wins the vulnerable rook) 4 ♕e8+ ♔b7 5 ♕e7+ ♔a6 6 ♕f7! ♖b6 7 ♕d7! transposes to the main line; or 3 ... ♖a6 4 ♔b5 ♖b6+ 5 ♔a5 and Black loses either his pawn or his rook.

3 ♕d7!

Now Black is in zugzwang and must soon lose the rook, e.g. **3 ... ♖b2** if 3 ... ♖b1 4 ♕a4+ and 5 ♕e4+ wins **4 ♕d3+ ♔b7 5 ♕f3+ ♔c7 6 ♕f7+** followed by **7 ♕f8+** and **8 ♕g7+** wins.

White's task is usually easier, however, if the black pawn has left its original square. Let us begin with diagram 77, with the black pawn on its third rank.

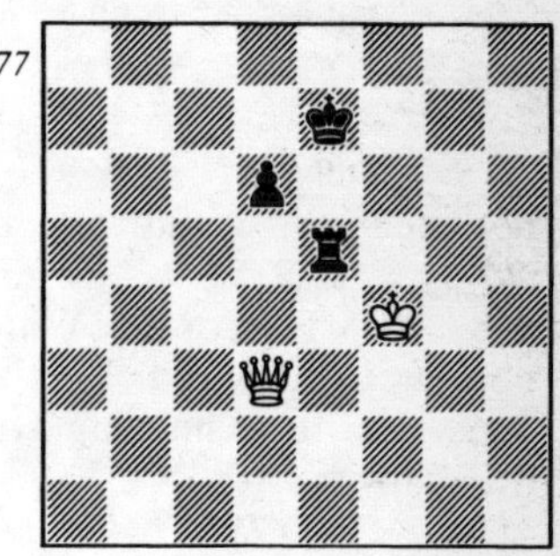

A.Philidor 1777

Philidor has proved that this position is won for White, albeit with some difficulty. Compared with diagram 75, White's queen now has an extra rank from which he can drive the black king into a less favourable position. In order to win, White must firstly drive the black king to d5, secondly force his own king over the fifth rank, and thirdly penetrate with his king over the king's file. Black then loses his pawn. All this is brought about by the use of the zugzwang weapon.

1 ♕h7+ ♔d8

Not of course 1 ... ♔f8 2 ♕d7, and 1 ... ♔e8 2 ♕c7 would make White's task easier. 1 ... ♔e6 2 ♕c7 ♖c5 3 ♕d8 ♖e5 4 ♕e8+ ♔d5 5 ♕c8 leads to the main line.

2 ♕f7! ♔c8

Again 2 ... ♖c5 3 ♕e6 ♔c7 4 ♕e7+ ♔c6 5 ♕d8 transposes to the main line.

3 ♕a7 ♔d8

Or 3 ... ♖c5 4 ♕e7 etc.

4 ♕b8+ ♔d7
5 ♕b7+ ♔d8
6 ♕c6 ♔e7
7 ♕c7+ ♔e6
8 ♕d8 ♔d5

The situation would not be altered by 8 ... ♖f5+ 9 ♔g4 ♖e5 10 ♕e8+ ♔d5 11 ♕c8 etc. White has now attained his first objective and must next force his king over the fifth rank.

9 ♕c8! *(78)*

78
B

A.Philidor 1777

We have reached the first important zugzwang position, as indicated by Philidor. Black cannot prevent the advance of White's king.

9 ... ♖e4+

If 9 ... ♔d4 10 ♕c6 ♖d5 White wins by 11 ♔f3 ♖f5+ 12 ♔g4 ♖d5 13 ♔f4!, or here 11 ... ♔e5 12 ♕c3+ ♔f5 13 ♕c4 etc. Other rook moves lose as follows: if 9 ... ♖h5 10 ♕a8+! ♔d4 11 ♕a4+, and if 9 ... ♖e7 10 ♔f5 ♖f7+ 11 ♔g5! (if 11 ♔g6 ♖f4 can be played) and Black must quickly play 11 ... ♖e7 in order not to lose his rook.

10 ♔f5 ♖e5+

If 10 ... ♔d4 11 ♕c6 d5 12 ♕c2! ♖e5+ 13 ♔f6 ♖e4 14 ♔f7! and Black must allow the white king to cross the king's file.

11 ♔f6 ♖e4

The only move, as otherwise 12 ♕b7+ wins material.

12 ♕c3

Suggested by Guretzky-Cornitz and simpler than Philidor's 12 ♕f5+ which equally wins.

12 ... ♖e6+

Or 12 ... ♖e5 13 ♔f7 etc.

13 ♔f7 ♖e5
14 ♔f8! *(79)*

Bringing about a zugzwang position to attain his third objective, crossing the king's file with his king.

79
B

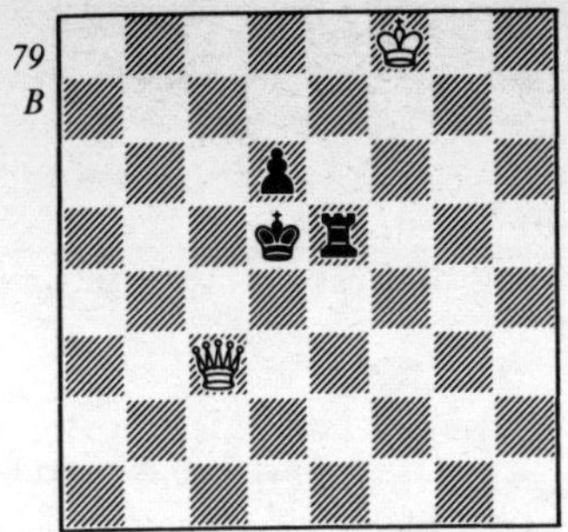

14 ... ♖e4

Nor would 14 ... ♖e6 help, after 15 ♕b3+ ♔e5 16 ♔f7; or 14 ... ♔e4 15 ♕c4+ ♔f5 16 ♕d3+ ♔e6 17 ♔e8 and White's king penetrates.

15 ♕d3+ ♖d4

Or 15 ... ♔e5 16 ♔e7 d5 17 ♕g3+ followed by 18 ♔d6 with an easy win.

16 ♕f5+ ♔c4
17 ♕c2+ ♔d5
18 ♔e7 ♖e4+

Or 18 ... ♔e5 19 ♕c3! d5 20 ♕e3+ ♖e4 21 ♕g5+ ♔d4+ 22 ♔d6 wins.

19 ♔d7

and White wins easily. If now 19 ... ♖d4 20 ♕c6+ ♔e5 21 ♕f3 wins at least the pawn.

If Black's pawn stands on the fourth rank, the winning method is the same, but problems arise if the pawn has reached the fifth rank, as in diagram 80.

We have left out the preliminary moves and come straight to the critical position. For almost a hundred years it was thought that this position was won for White only with Black to move, as follows:

80

B.Guretzky-Cornitz 1864

1 ... ♖e8

After **1 ... ♖e2** White can play 2 ♕a3+ and bring about variations which arise from diagram 80 with White to move, or he can continue **2 ♕d1+ ♖d2** 2 ... ♔e3 3 ♔e5 d3 4 ♕g1+ ♔f3+ 5 ♔d4 d2 6 ♕d1 wins; or here 4 ... ♔d2+ 5 ♔d4 ♔c2 6 ♕b6 ♖d2 7 ♕c6+wins **3 ♕b3+ ♔e2 4 ♔e4 ♔e1** after 4 ... d3 5 ♕g8! wins quickly **5 ♕f3! ♖d1 6 ♔d5 ♖d2 7 ♔c5!** losing a tempo **7 ... ♖d1 8 ♔c4 ♖d2 9 ♔b3** and wins after 9 ... ♖d1 10 ♕e4+ followed by 11 ♔f2, or 9 ... ♖e2 10 ♕g3+! etc.

1 ... ♔e2 also loses quickly after 2 ♕c2+ ♔e1 3 ♔f4 etc.

2 ♕a3+ ♔e2

Or 2 ... ♔d2 3 ♕b4+ winning the pawn.

3 ♕a4 ♖d8

If 3 ... ♖f8+ 4 ♔e4 d3 5 ♕b5 ♖d8 6 ♕h5+ ♔f1 7 ♔e3 etc wins.

4 ♕a5

and after **4 ... ♖f8+ 5 ♔e4 d3 6 ♕h5+** Black loses either the pawn or the rook (6 ... ♔d2 7 ♕h6+).

However, with White to move, diagram 80 was long considered a draw, because no way could be found of bringing about the same position with Black to move. Finally in 1949 Chéron succeeded in demonstrating the win, as follows:

1 ♕c5 ♖e2

If 1 ... ♖e1 2 ♕b5+ wins the pawn or the rook.

2 ♕a3+ ♔d2

Or 2 ... ♔c2 3 ♕a2+ ♔d3 4 ♕b3+ ♔d2 5 ♔f4 etc.

3 ♔f4 ♔c2

If 3 ... d3 4 ♕b3 brings about the main line, whereas after 3 ... ♖e1 (e8) 4 ♕b4+ wins, or 3 ... ♖e3 4 ♕b2+ ♔d3 5 ♕b3+ ♔d2 (or 5 ... ♔e2 6 ♕c2+ ♔e1 7 ♕c4 etc) 6 ♕c4 ♖d3 7 ♔e4 wins.

4 ♕a2+ ♔d3
5 ♕b3+ ♔d2
6 ♕c4 d3 *(81)*

81

B.Guretzky-Cornitz 1864

For a long time this position was assumed to be drawn on the basis of analysis by Guretzky-Cornitz which went 7 ♕c5 ♔d1 8 ♕c3 d2 9 ♕f3 ♔c1! 10 ♕c3+ ♔b1 11 ♕b3+ ♔c1 12 ♕c4+ ♔d1 13 ♔f3 ♖e7 14 ♔f2 ♖e8 and White cannot win. However, White has in fact several ways of winning and we quote Chéron's method:

7 ♕b3

Averbakh and Lisitsin later suggested the alternatives 7 ♕d4 and 7 ♕b4+ ♔c2 8 ♔f3 which lead to variations similar to the main line.

7 ... ♖e1

Not of course 7 ... ♖f2+ 8 ♔e4 ♖e2+ 9 ♔d4 winning, but 7 ... ♖e8 8 ♕b2+ also wins after 8 ... ♔e1 9 ♕b5! ♖d8 10 ♔e3 ♔f1 11 ♕f5+, or 8 ... ♔d1 9 ♕b5 ♖d8 10 ♔e3 ♔c1 (c2) 11 ♕c5+ ♔d1 12 ♕b6.

8 ♕b2+ ♔d1
9 ♔f3 ♖e2

After 9 ... ♖e7 (or e8) 10 ♕b1+ ♔d2 11 ♕b4+ wins.

10 ♕c3 ♖d2
11 ♕c4

But not 11 ♔e3 ♖e2+ 12 ♔xd3? ♖e3+! 13 ♔xe3 giving stalemate. Black must now lose the pawn.

This example proves that Black cannot draw even with a central pawn on the sixth rank, so we can now state that Black can draw only if his central pawn is on its original square.

His drawing chances are increased with a bishop's pawn. In fact it was thought for a long time that Black always draws with a bishop's pawn, on whichever rank this is placed. New analyses by Halberstadt and Chéron have, however, demonstrated that this generalization is faulty, at least with the pawn on the second or third rank. Let us examine one of the possibilities more closely.

82

V.Halberstadt 1931

1 ♕b6!

Halberstadt proved in 1931 that Black would be in zugzwang if he had to move in the original position. White can easily bring about this situation.

1 ... ♔d7

Or 1 ... ♖e5+ 2 ♔d4 ♖d5+ 3 ♔c4 winning easily.

2 ♕b7+ ♔d6
3 ♕a7!

White has now attained his first objective and Black must allow the white king to cross the d-file.

3 ... ♖e5+

Black cannot maintain his rook on the d-file, as 3 ... ♖d2 4 ♔f5 ♖d5+ 5 ♔f6 or 3 ... ♖d1 4 ♕a3+ ♔d7 5 ♕h3+! ♔c7 6 ♕g3+ ♖d6 7 ♕e5 ♔d7 8 ♕g7+ followed by 9 ♔e5 both allow the white king to penetrate.

4 ♔d4 ♖d5+
5 ♔c4 ♖b5
6 ♕f7 ♖c5+

If 6 ... ♖d5 7 ♔b4 wins, or 6 ... ♖b6 7 ♕e8! wins.

7 ♔b4 ♖d5
8 ♔a4 ♖b5
9 ♕g7

This is the position White has been angling for, as Black cannot now prevent the manoeuvre ♕b7-c8.

9 ... ♖d5
10 ♕b7 ♖b5

If 10 ... ♖d1 11 ♕b4+ ♔c7 12 ♕f4+ ♔b6 (or 12 ... ♔b7 13 ♕f7+ ♔c8 14 ♔a5 etc) 13 ♕e3+ ♔c7 14 ♕g3+ ♔d8 15 ♔a5 wins easily.

11 ♕c8 ♔d5

Or 11 ... ♖d5 12 ♕d8+ ♔c5 13 ♕c7 ♖d1 (if 13 ... ♖d3 14 ♕a5+ ♔c4 15 ♕a6+) 14 ♕a5+ ♔c4 15 ♕b4+ wins.

12 ♕d7+ ♔c5
13 ♕d8!

Again placing Black in zugzwang.

13 ... ♔c4

Or 13 ... ♖b4+ 14 ♔a5 ♖b5+ 15 ♔a6 ♖b4 16 ♕d3! and wins as we saw in our analysis of diagram 78.

14 ♕d6 ♖c5

If Black now had the move he would be forced to give up the pawn, but it is not easy for White to bring about this situation.

14 ♕e6+ ♔d3

If 15 ... ♔c3 16 ♕e3+ ♔c4 17 ♕e4+ ♔c3 18 ♕b4+ wins, and 15 ... ♔d4 16 ♕g4+ leads to the main line.

16 ♕h3+ ♔d4

Or 16 ... ♔c4. If the king goes to the seventh rank, then 17 ♔b4 wins.

17 ♕g4+ ♔d3

If 17 ... ♔d5 18 ♕d7+ either forces the king to the e-file, when 19 ♔b4 wins, or leads to zugzwang after 18 ... ♔c4 19 ♕d6! If 17 ... ♔e5 18 ♕d7 also wins.

18 ♕d1+ ♔c3

Again both 18 ... ♔c4 19 ♕d6 or 18 ... ♔e4 19 ♕d7 win for White.

19 ♕c1+ ♔d4

20 ♕d2+ wins.

Black can choose between 20 ... ♔c4 21 ♕d6 or 20 ... ♔e4 (e5) 21 ♕d7, which both lead to an easy win for White.

There are many more interesting positions involving the bishop's pawn, but they do not come within the scope of this volume and should be studied in more specialized endgame books.

Black's best drawing chances are found in positions containing a knight's pawn, wherever this pawn may be, as long as his pieces are favourably placed. Let us consider diagram 83 as an example of this.

83

B.Guretzky-Cornitz 1864

1 ♕f7+ ♔b8

Black must not allow the white queen to occupy a7 after 1 ... ♔c8, or even after 1 ... ♔c6 2 ♕a7 ♖a5 3 ♕b8 when latest analysis proves that Black cannot hold the position.

2 ♕e6 ♔b7

3 ♕d7+ ♔b8

4 ♔e4 ♔a8

5 ♕a4+ ♔b7

6 ♔d4 ♖c7!

Allowing the white king past the fifth rank, but this has no significance here. Again latest research gives a win for White after 6 ... ♔b8 7 ♕a6 ♔c7 8 ♕a7+ ♔c6 9 ♕b8 or 6 ... ♖a5 7 ♕d7+ ♔b8 8 ♕c6 ♔a7 9 ♕c7+ ♔a6 10 ♕b8 etc.

7 ♔d5 ♖c5+

8 ♔d6 ♖c7

9 ♕b5 ♖c5

10 ♕d7+ ♔b8

11 ♕g4 ♖c7

Black must not permit ♔d7-d8.

12 ♕e2 ♔b7

White cannot strengthen his position any more, so Black draws.

84

Even when the b-pawn is further advanced, Black usually draws, as can be seen from the basic position in diagram 84.

After **1 ... ♖c5+ 2 ♔d6 ♖c8! 3 ♔d7 ♖c4 4 ♔d8 ♖c5 5 ♕b2+ ♔a4! 6 ♔d7 ♖c4** the white king cannot cross the c-file, as it is impossible to drive the rook away from the file.

Now let us consider the case of the rook's pawn, and in particular a position, diagram 85, in which the pawn is on the third rank.

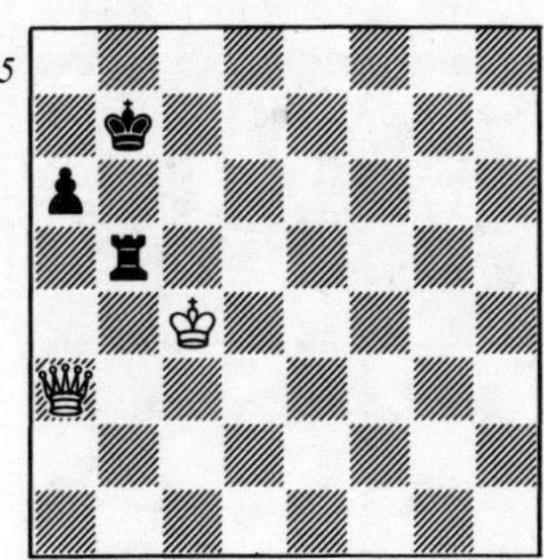

B.Guretzky-Cornitz 1864

This is drawn unless the white king can cross the b-file or reach c8. Equally, the black king must remain on the corner squares. Play might go:

1	**♕e7+**	**♔b8**
2	**♕e8+**	**♔b7**
3	**♕d8**	**♔a7**
4	**♕c8**	

White has obtained some success and Black must now allow the white king past the fifth rank. However, this has no real significance.

4	**...**	**♖b7!**

But not 4 ... ♔b6 5 ♕b8+ ♔c6 (or 5 ... ♔a5 6 ♕d8+ ♔a4 7 ♕d2+ etc) 6 ♕a7 ♖b6 7 ♔d4 ♔b5 8 ♕d7+ ♔b4 9 ♕c7 ♖h6 10 ♕e7+ ♔a4 11 ♕e8+ ♔a5 12 ♔c5 wins.

5	**♕c5+**	

5 ♔c5 leads to nothing after 5 ... ♖b5+ 6 ♔c6 ♖b6+ 7 ♔c7 ♖b5 for the white king will now be checked back to c4.

5	**...**	**♔b8**
6	**♕d6+**	**♔a7**
7	**♕d4+**	**♔a8**
8	**♔c5**	**♖b5+**

Or 8 ... ♔a7 9 ♔c6+ ♔a8 with the same position.

9	**♔c6**	**♖b7** *(86)*

86
W

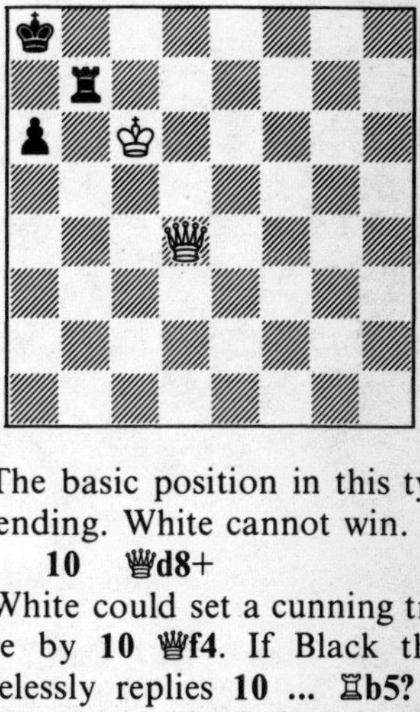

The basic position in this type of ending. White cannot win.

10	**♕d8+**	

White could set a cunning trap here by **10 ♕f4**. If Black then carelessly replies **10 ... ♖b5?** he loses after **11 ♔c7! ♔a7** or 11 ... ♖b7+ 12 ♔c8 ♖b5 13 ♕c7 wins **12 ♕d6 ♖b8 13 ♕c5+ ♔a8 14 ♕c6+ ♔a7 15 ♕d6! ♖b7! 16 ♔c8 ♖b5 17 ♕d7+ ♔a8 18 ♕c7** and Black will soon lose his rook.

However, Black should simply play **10 ... ♔a7!** when White can make no progress.

10 ... ♖b8

Or 10 ... ♔a7 11 ♕c8 ♖b6+ 12 ♔c7 ♖b5 can also be played.

11 ♕d5

If 11 ♕a5 ♔a7 12 ♕c7+ ♔a8 13 ♕f4 ♖b7! again brings about the required position.

11 ... ♖b7!

Not of course 11 ... ♔a7? 12 ♔c7 etc, whereas now Black can always check the white king away from c8 and White has no way of strengthening his position. The game is drawn.

From the above analysis it is now clear why White would win with his king on the a-file.

87

For example, in diagram 87, White would win as follows: **1 ♕e7+ ♔b8 2 ♕d7 ♔a8 3 ♕c7 ♖b1** or 3 ... ♖b7 4 ♕d8+ ♔a7 5 ♕d4+ followed by ♔a5 **4 ♕d8+ ♔a7 5 ♕d4+ ♔a8 6 ♔a5** wins.

White would also win with the black pawn on a5 or a4. For example, in diagram 88, play might go: **1 ♕d5 ♔a6 2 ♕c6+ ♔a7**

88

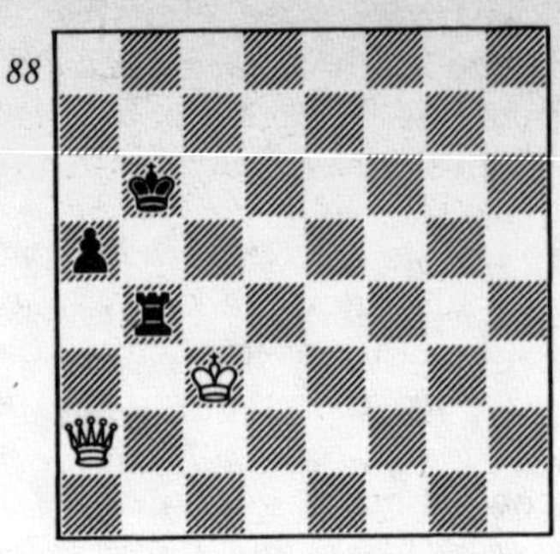

or 2 ... ♖b6 3 ♕a8+ ♔b5 4 ♔b3 etc. **3 ♔d3! ♖b6** Black is in zugzwang and must allow the white king over the fourth rank. If 3 ... a4 4 ♔c3 is the simplest way to win **4 ♕c7+ ♔a6 5 ♕c8+ ♔a7 6 ♔c4 ♖b7 7 ♕d8 ♔a6 8 ♔c5 ♖b5+ 9 ♔c6** winning.

89

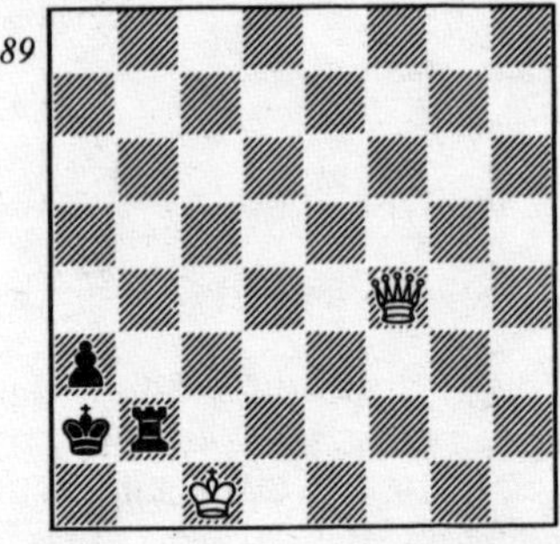

However, Black draws if his pawn has reached the sixth rank with his king in front of it. For example, in diagram 89, White can make no progress. Play might go: **1 ♕f3 ♖b4 2 ♕d5+ ♔a1 3 ♕a5 ♖b1+ 4 ♔c2 ♖b2+ 5 ♔c3 ♔a2 6 ♕a4 ♖b1** and Black draws.

Finally, let us examine positions in which the black rook supports the pawn from behind. Everything depends upon how far advanced the pawn is. In general, White wins against a pawn on the fourth rank, whereas with the pawn on the fifth rank the placing of the pieces decides matters. If the pawn has reached the sixth rank, however, Black usually manages to draw. Only in exceptional cases can White force a win, as in diagram 90.

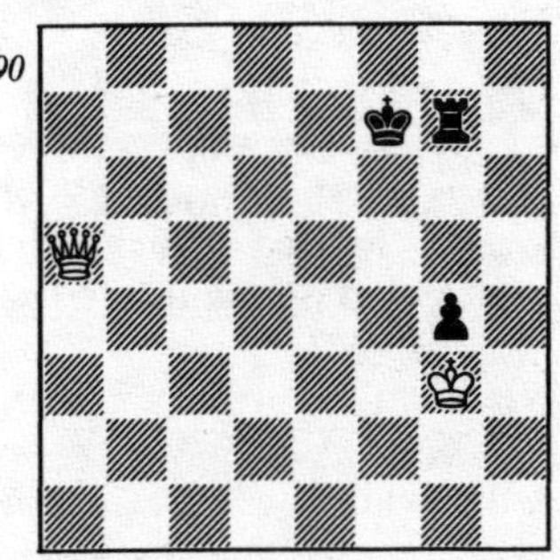

Kling and Horwitz 1851

The pawn is blockaded by the white king, but at first sight it seems difficult for White to strengthen his position. He achieves a win by the following subtle play:

1 ♕f5+

The composers began their solution with 1 ♕d5+ ♔f6 2 ♕c6+ and demonstrated the win after complicated variations. They apparently did not wish the black king to go to g8, but there is no need to fear this and the text move is the shortest way to victory.

1 ... ♔e7

If 1 ... ♔g8 2 ♕f6 ♔h7 3 ♕f8 Black is in zugzwang and loses after 3 ... ♖g6 4 ♕f7+ ♖g7 5 ♕e8! ♖g6 6 ♔h4 g3 7 ♔h5 and the mating threats force at least the win of Black's pawn.

Also 1 ... ♔e8 loses to 2 ♕f6 ♖g8 3 ♔h2! g3+ 4 ♔g2 and the pawn is again lost.

2 ♕f2

With this clever tempo move, White manages to drive back the black pieces. 2 ♕f1 is also possible, but not 2 ♕f4 ♖g6! and it is White who is in zugzwang.

2 ... ♖g6

White also wins easily after 2 ... ♖g5 3 ♕e3+ ♔f6 4 ♕f4+ ♔g6 5 ♔h4, or 2 ... ♔e6 3 ♕f8 ♖g6 4 ♔h4! g3 5 ♔h5 etc.

If 2 ... ♖g8 3 ♕c5+ ♔f6 4 ♕d6+ ♔f7 5 ♕d5+ ♔f8 6 ♕e6 we arrive at the main line.

3 ♕f4! ♖g7

We have already seen 3 ... ♔e6 4 ♕f8 and 3 ... ♖g8 4 ♕e5+ would shorten the solution by one move.

4 ♕f5! ♖g8
5 ♕e5+ ♔f7
6 ♕d5+ ♔f8
7 ♕e6!

Again Black is placed in zugzwang and is reduced to moving his rook between g8 and g7. White now wins by using the same tempo-losing manoeuvre twice.

7 ... ♖g7
8 ♔h2

White could also win by 8 ♕f6+ ♔g8 9 ♕f5 ♔h8 10 ♕f8+ ♔h7 11 ♕e8! as we saw in our notes to the first move.

8 ... g3+
9 ♔g2 ♖g8

The trap 9 ... ♖f7 would lose to 10 ♕c8+ followed by 11 ♔xg3 but not 10 ♔xg3? ♖g7+ 11 ♔h4 ♖h7+ 12 ♔g5 ♖g7+ 13 ♔h6 ♖h7+! when 14 ♔xh7 is stalemate.

10 ♕f6+ ♔e8
11 ♔h1! g2+
12 ♔g1 wins.

Black is forced to relinquish his pawn by 12 ... ♖f8. With this example we conclude our examination of queen v rook and pawn.

We have only been able to discuss a small part of all the possible positions and have not touched at all upon endings with more than one pawn. However, we feel that the reader has been given sufficient basic positions to enable him to deal with this type of ending.

Queen against Queen (and Pawns)

Endgames with queen and pawns on both sides are among the most difficult in chess. Even in the most clear-cut example of queen and pawn on the seventh against queen alone, it is by no means easy to formulate general principles. In the following pages, we hope to offer the reader an overall picture of queen endings, along with the conclusions reached by present-day theory.

A: QUEEN AGAINST QUEEN

It may seem a little mad to mention such an ending, for there is apparently no win unless the opponent's queen is immediately captured. However, victory can in fact be achieved in certain positions which must be known thoroughly.

91

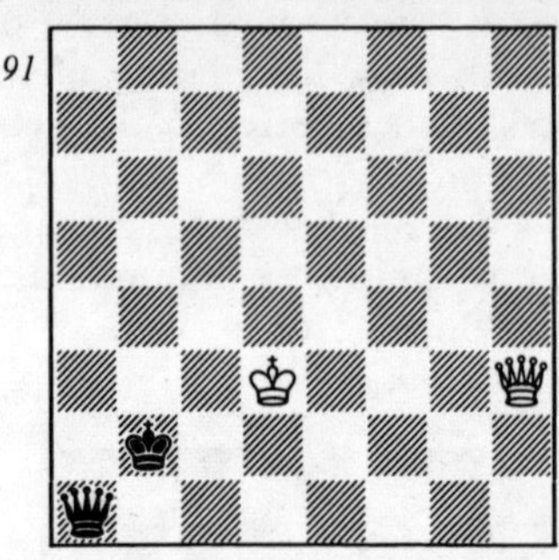

This is a typical example of a successful mating attack which White carried out as follows:

1 ♕g2+

White cannot win by 1 ♕h8+? ♔b1 2 ♕h1+ ♔a2 3 ♕d5+ ♔b1! and the white queen cannot get any nearer to the black king. Equally 1 ♕h2+? fails to 1 ... ♔a3! 2 ♕d6+ ♔a2 3 ♕e6+ ♔b1! 4 ♕e1+ ♔a2 etc. In such positions White must always be ready to give check on the a-and b-files to prevent the black king from clinging to the a2 and b1 squares.

1 ... ♔a3
2 ♕a8+ ♔b2
3 ♕b7+ ♔c1

We now see the point of White's play in checking on the b-file. Black's king cannot go to a2 as 4 ♔c2! would immediately win for White. However, the text move proves just as unsuccessful.

4 ♕c6+ ♔b2

5	**♕b5+**	**♔a3**
6	**♕a5+**	**♔b2**
7	**♕b4+**	**♔a2**

Now forced, as after 7 ... ♔c1 8 ♕d2+ ♔b1 9 ♕c2 Black is mated.

8 **♔c2!** forces mate.

If the white queen is near enough, the win can sometimes be achieved even if the black king occupies a2. For example, diagram 92:

92

White wins by **1 ♕c5+ ♔a2 2 ♕c4+!** not 2 ♕a5+? ♔b1! drawing **2 ... ♔a3** if 2 ... ♔b1 3 ♕c2 mate **3 ♕a6+** etc, as we have already seen.

However, if we were to change diagram 91 by placing White's king on the more favourable square d2, he almost always wins irrespective of the placing of his queen.

There are one or two other positions in which White can win. For instance, the enemy queen can occasionally be captured after a series of checks, or an unusual mating attack is possible. A most surprising example comes from a study by Kantorowitsch:

93

Although Black has the move he cannot avoid a loss. White threatens ♔f2 (g3)+ followed by mate. If **1 ... ♕h4 2 ♕a1+** leads to mate, as do **1 ... ♔g1 2 ♕a7+ ♔h1 3 ♕h7+ ♔g1 4 ♕g7+**, or **1 ... ♕f1+ 2 ♔g3+ ♔g1 3 ♕a7+ ♔h1 4 ♕h7+** etc. What a queen!

B: QUEEN AGAINST QUEEN AND PAWN

This ending is not only difficult to conduct but even trickier to analyse. We usually arrive at positions in which both kings are subject to checking by the enemy queen, making it virtually impossible to analyse every variation fully. We must therefore restrict ourselves to guiding principles which can be illustrated by one or two concrete examples.

Because there are so many possibilities, we shall deal only with positions containing a pawn on the seventh rank. Despite this limitation, there still remain a number of complex situations which we cannot hope to investigate fully in a volume such as this.

For a long time it was thought that this type of ending was usually drawn because the side with the pawn could rarely succeed in promoting it. Only the bishop's pawn was considered to give winning chances. In recent times, however, as great deal of exact analysis has shown that all positions containing a pawn on the seventh rank offer good winning chances. The rook's pawn is an exception to this, although even in this case some chances have been discovered.

In order to give the reader an idea of the difficulties faced by both defender and attacker in such positions, we intend to discuss one or two examples in some depth. In this way we can pinpoint several winning methods which can be applied generally to similar positions.

94

This position could have occurred in the game Alekhine-Stoltz (1942) and is a reasonably favourable example of the type of situation which can arise when the attacker has a central pawn. Such a pawn offers White good winning chances, mainly because the white king can take refuge from checks by using both sides of the pawn.

As White to move could win at once by 1 ♕c2+ ♔a3 (a5) 2 ♕c3+ followed by 3 ♔f8, let us see how Black, to move, defends such a position. He has not a great deal of choice which means that we can analyse the position out to a clear win.

A

1 ... ♕b3+

1 ... ♕a7 2 ♔f8 loses at once and we shall examine 1 ... ♔a3 and 1 ... ♕c7 in variations B and C.

2 ♔f8

The simplest, although White can also win by 2 ♕e6 ♕f3+ 3 ♕f6 ♕h5+ (or 3 ... ♕d5+ 4 ♔g7 ♕g2+ 5 ♔f8 wins) 4 ♔g7 ♕g4+ 5 ♔f8 ♕b4 6 ♕a6+ ♔b3 7 ♕e6+ followed by 8 ♔g8.

2 ... ♕b4

White exchanges queens after 2 ... ♕a3 3 ♕d7+.

3 ♕e5!

The reader should note that well-calculated quiet moves often achieve more in such endings than the seemingly more forceful checks. This move places Black in zugzwang.

2 ... ♔b3

If 3 ... ♕a3 4 ♔g7 wins, and if 3 ... ♔a3 4 ♕a1+ forces the exchange of queens.

4 ♕e6+ wins.

After 5 ♔g8 the pawn queens.

B

1 ... ♔a3

In this way Black stops the white queen gaining the important central squares d4 or e4 without loss of time.

2 ♕f4!

There are obviously other winning methods, but the text move threatens 3 ♔f8, so Black must move his queen.

2 ... ♕a7

Both 2 ... ♕b3+ and 2 ... ♕d7 lose to 3 ♔f8, and if 2 ... ♕d5+ 3 ♔g7 ♕g2+ (or 3 ... ♕b7 or d7 4 ♔f8 wins.

3 ♔e6 ♕a8

The only move, for 3 ... ♕b6 (a6)+ allows 4 ♕d6+.

4 ♕d6+ ♔b2

If 4 ... ♔a4 5 ♕d7+, or 4 ... ♔a2 (b3) 5 ♕d5+.

5 ♕e5+ ♔c2 (c1)

Again 5 ... ♔a2 (b3) allows 6 ♕d5+ and 5 ... ♔b1 fails to 6 ♕b5+ followed by 7 e8♕.

6 ♕c5+ wins.

White either exchanges queens on d5 or else queens his pawn after 7 ♕b5+.

C

1 ... ♕c7

2 ♕e4+

White is aiming to place his queen on d4 when ♔f8 will win at once, so Black must try to prevent this.

2 ... ♔b3

The only move. After 2 ... ♔a3 3 ♕d4 wins at once, as 4 ♔f8 is threatened and 3 ... ♕b7 fails to 4 ♕a1+. Or if 2 ... ♔a5 (b5) 3 ♔f6 ♕b6 (d6)+ 4 ♕e6! and Black has no more checks.

3 ♕e3+

There are of course other winning methods, but the text move illustrates an important idea which is well worth learning as it often occurs in these endings.

3 ... ♔c2

If 3 ... ♔a2 4 ♔f6 wins, or 3 ... ♔c4 4 ♕c1+ wins. Other king moves allow the white queen to reach d4 with check.

4 ♔g6

The white king begins a journey back to the first rank and Black cannot prevent this, however much he checks.

4 ... ♕c6+

Or 4 ... ♕d6+ 5 ♔g5 ♕d5+ 6 ♔h4! ♕c4+ (if 6 ... ♕h1+ 7 ♔g3) 7 ♔g3 ♕g8+ 8 ♔f2 ♕f7+ 9 ♔e1 etc, as in the main line.

5 ♔g5 ♕g2+

6 ♔f4 ♕h2+

Or 6 ... ♕f1+ 7 ♔g3 and Black has no more checks.

7 ♔f3 ♕h5+

If 7 ... ♕h3 (h1)+ 8 ♔f2 ♕h2+ 9 ♔f1 ♕h1+ 10 ♕g1! etc, as in the main line.

8 ♔g2 ♕g6+

After 8 ... ♕g4+ 9 ♔f1 ♕d1+ 10 ♕e1! or 8 ... ♕d5+ 9 ♔f1 ♕h1+ 10 ♕g1! Black has no more checks which do not allow the exchange of queens. Nor is he saved by 10 ... ♕h5 11 ♕f2+ ♔d3 12 ♕g3+ and the white queen eventually gains control of the e8 square. This is the manoeuvre we were talking about; the white king retreats to the first rank when Black's king is on the seventh rank, and this means that Black's checking possibilities are restricted because of the threat to exchange queens by interposing with check. It is clear that the same method will work, for example, on the a-file when Black's king is on the b-file (White's king on a8, queen on a7 and Black's king on b2).

9 ♔f1 ♛e8

Check allows the exchange of queens.

10 ♔e1! wins.

Whatever Black plays, he cannot prevent 11 ♕e6 followed by 12 ♕d6 and 13 ♕d8.

As we can see from the above example, a central pawn offers White very good winning chances, but what about the other pawns? Diagram 95 illustrates the case of a bishop's pawn.

95

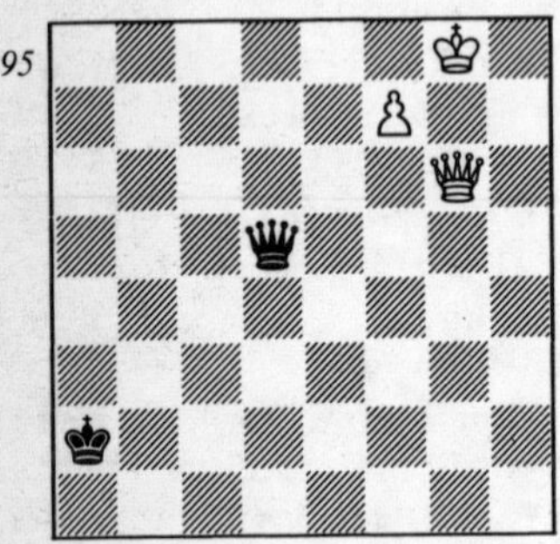

In order to avoid a host of complex variations involving checks by the black queen, we have chosen a relatively favourable position. The object of the exercise is to demonstrate how the win is achieved in such positions.

1 ♕g3!

White's plan is simple but effective, and we have already seen the basis of it. He intends to place his queen on f2, then proceed according to the position of the black king. If the latter occupies the sixth rank, then the white king will head for g2, and if the black king goes to the eighth rank, then White checks on f1 and plays his king to g1. In both cases Black would have no more checks and could not stop the pawn queening. There is no defence to this plan.

1 ... ♚a1

White would win in the same way after queen moves.

2 ♔g7

White must make a few preparations before beginning his plan. An immediate 2 ♕g1+ ♚b2 3 ♕f2+ ♚a3 4 ♔g7 would not do, as Black can stop the white king's advance by playing 4 ... ♛g5+ 5 ♔h7 ♛h5+.

2 ... ♛d4+
3 ♔h7 ♛e4+
4 ♔h6 ♛c6+

After 4 ... ♛e6+ 5 ♔g7 ♛e7 (d7) 6 ♕g1+ followed by 7 ♕f2+ wins as in the main line.

5 ♔g7 ♛b7 (d7)
6 ♕g1+ ♚b2
7 ♕f2+ ♚a1

Or 7 ... ♚a3 (b3,c3) 8 ♔h6 and the king returns to g2.

8 ♕f1+ ♚b2
9 ♔h6 wins.

Play might go **9 ... ♛c6+ 10 ♔g5 ♛d5+ 11 ♔g4 ♛e4+ 12 ♔g3 ♛g6+ 13 ♔h2 ♛h6+ 14 ♔g1 ♛f8** there are no more useful checks! **15 ♕f6+ ♔a2 16 ♔f1!** followed by ♕e6-e8. There are other winning methods from the diagrammed position but the one we have given is the most instructive.

Extensive analysis has shown that White has very good winning chances with the bishop's pawn, but there are more difficulties to be overcome than with the centre pawns. Let us now consider positions containing a knight's pawn. Black's defensive possibilities are greater here, but White still wins in most cases. One example, diagram 96, should suffice.

96

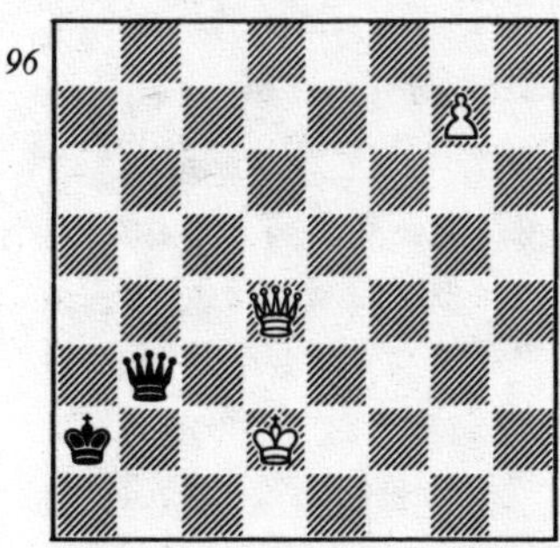

Again we have selected a reasonably favourable position, having omitted the lengthy manoeuvre required for the king to reach d2. White to move would win at once by 1 ♕f2, so let us look at Black to move.

1 ... ♕f7

1 ... ♕e6 loses to 2 ♕a7+ ♔b2 3 ♕b8+ ♔a1 4 ♕a8+ (but not 4 g8♕? ♕e3+! with stalemate) followed by 5 g8♕. Nor would 1 ... ♕g8 improve on the text move, as after 2 ♕g4 Black would have to transpose to the main line by 2 ... ♕d5+. White could also answer 1 ... ♕g8 with 2 ♕d7 winning.

2 ♕g4!

The most clear-cut winning method. White now threatens to play his king to g1, so Black must seek salvation in checks.

2 ... ♕d5+

If 2 ... ♕f2+ 3 ♔d3 and Black has no more checks, and if 2 ... ♕g8 3 ♔e1 etc wins.

3 ♔e1!

White must play precisely in order to escape the many checks. For example, 3 ♔e2 ♕b5+ 4 ♔f2 ♕b6+ 5 ♔g2 ♕c6+ 6 ♔h2 ♕h6+ and the king cannot escape perpetual check.

White must play his king to the g-file in such a way that Black has no effective diagonal checks.

3 ... ♕h1+

If 3 ... ♕e5+ 4 ♕e2+; or 3 ... ♕a5+ 4 ♔f1, or 3 ... ♕g8 4 ♔f2 (threatening 5 ♔g1) 4 ... ♕f7+ 5 ♔g1 ♕a7+ 6 ♔h1 etc.

4 ♔f2 ♕h2+

5 ♕g2 wins.

We shall not examine positions involving the rook's pawn, which only offer slender winning chances. The reason for this is clear: White's king has difficulty escaping the checks. The examples we have chosen are relatively few in number, but we can nevertheless draw some important conclusions from them. We first see that both queens must strive to occupy a commanding central position from where they can quickly switch to any part of the board. Secondly, we have shown that White can seldom make any progress without using his king out in the open. Thirdly, in order to check most effectively, Black must place his king as far away as possible from the pawn. For this reason, his king usually stands best at the edge of the board or in the corners. The reader should try out similar endgame positions so as to become familiar with both attacking and defensive possibilities.

Before concluding this section, we must point out one further idea which can occur in queen endings with knight's pawn. *(97)*

97

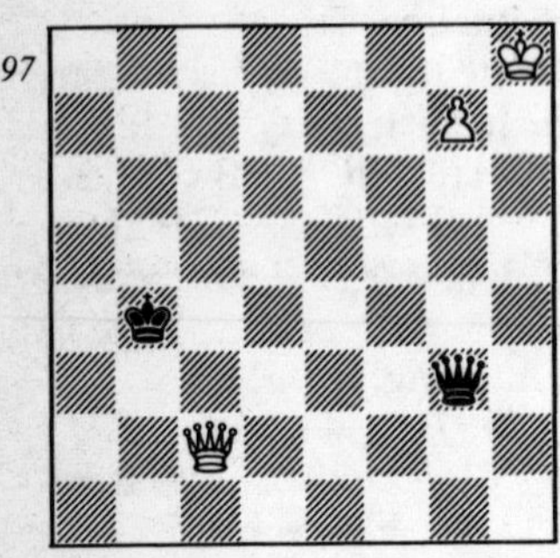

Black can force an immediate draw, as was demonstrated long ago by Lolli. He plays **1 ... ♕h4+ 2 ♕h7** or 2 ♔g8 ♕d8+ 3 ♔f7 ♕d7+ 4 ♔f6 ♕d4+! 5 ♔g6 ♕g4+ etc. **2 ... ♕d8+ 3 g8♕** or 3 ♕g8 ♕h4+ etc **3 ... ♕f6+ 4 ♕gg7 ♕d8+ 5 ♕hg8 ♕h4+ 6 ♕7h8 ♕f6+** when despite his two queens White cannot escape perpetual check.

If White has more than one pawn, the win is usually easy, so we shall next consider positions in which both sides have pawns.

C: QUEEN AND PAWN(S) AGAINST QUEEN AND PAWN(S)

Here again there are a wealth of possible positions which can hardly be systematized. Moreover, as in practice both sides usually have pawns left on the board, these positions mostly belong to the practical endings section. So we will restrict ourselves to analysing an interesting position with two pawns against one.

98
W

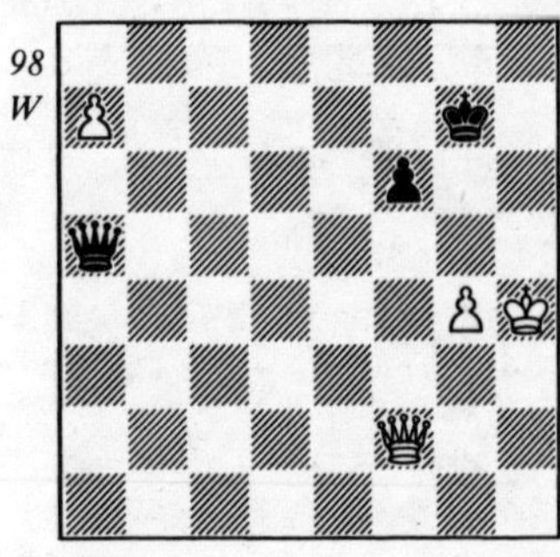

H.Friedmann-Gilg 1936

White has a stong passed pawn which is, however, held by the black queen. The presence of pawns on the kingside gives both kings better protection from checks, but White wins by the following subtle play:

1 ♕e3

Threatening 2 ♕e7+ ♔g6 3 ♕e8+ followed by 4 a8♕, and at the same time providing the white king with a safe retreat square on g3.

1 ... ♕a2

An imaginative defence. White's threat is prevented because at the end Black's queen mates on h2. If instead 1 ... ♔f8 2 ♕h6+ wins the pawn with check, and 1 ... ♔f7 allows 2 ♕b3+ and the pawn soon queens. However, White's task is not so easy after **1 ... ♕a4** (which controls e8) when 2 ♕e7+ ♔g6 3 ♕b7 ♕a2 , or 2 ♕b6 ♕e4! both give Black good counterplay. White wins by **2 ♔h5! ♔f7** 2 ... ♕a5 3 g5 **3 ♕d3! ♔e7** 3 ... ♕a5+ 4 ♕f5 ♕d2 5 ♕h7+ ♔e6 6 ♕g8+ and 7 a8♕ **4 ♕h7+ ♔d6 5 ♕b7 ♕a5+ 6 ♔g6 ♕g5+ 7 ♔f7** etc.

2 ♔g3 ♔f7

Preventing 3 ♕e7+ followed by 4 ♕e8+.

3 ♕d3!

An alternative is **3 ♕e4! ♕a3+ 4 ♔h4 ♕b2** or 4 ... ♕a2 5 ♕h7+ ♔f8 6 a8♕+!, or 4 ... ♕d6 5 ♕h7+ ♔e6 6 ♕c2 **5 ♕c4+ ♔g6** or 5 ... ♔g7 6 ♕c7+ and 7 a8♕ **6 ♕d3+** followed by **7 a8♕** winning.

3 ... ♔g7
4 ♕d7+ ♔h6

Seemingly setting up a successful defence.

5 g5+! ♔xg5

If 5 ... fg 6 ♕c6+ or 5 ... ♔g6 6 ♕e8+, both followed by 7 a8♕.

6 ♕g7+ ♔f5

Or 6 ... ♔h5 7 ♕h8+ etc.

7 ♕g4+ wins.

After 7 ... ♔e5 8 ♕f4+ the white queen checks on f3 or e4, then promotes his pawn.

As we have already mentioned, we shall examine other endings, with pawns on both sides, in our practical endings section.

Queen against other pieces

We have already dealt with endings of queen against rook, against pawn, and against rook and pawn. In general a queen and minor piece cannot win against a queen alone, although exceptions are possible. Equally, endings with queen against rook and minor piece are usually drawn. On the other hand, a queen wins easily against a single minor piece, but a minor piece in conjunction with a far advanced passed pawn can sometimes draw.

However, with two rooks, or two bishops, or two knights, or bishop and knight, against a queen, the result depends on the placing of the pieces. Let us examine these four possibilities in turn.

A: QUEEN AGAINST TWO ROOKS

This ending is usually drawn, so we will just analyse an exceptional. position in which the two rooks win because of an unfavourably placed black king. *(99)*

1 ♖h7+ ♔g8
2 ♖he7

White's first move took away g8 from Black's queen and also prevented the black queen from escaping (1 ♖f7 ♕d6!). He must constantly be on the watch for the latter threat which would give

99

H.Rinck 1916

Black perpetual check, and the following rook moves can be understood in this context.

2 ... ♔h8

Queen moves along the rank fail to 3 ♖g7+ ♔h8 4 ♖h7+ ♔g8 5 ♖bg7+ ♔f8 6 ♖h8+ winning the queen.

3 ♖bc7!

Why this square? The idea is to answer 3 ... ♛g8 with 4 ♔f1! when c4 is denied to Black's queen and after 4 ... ♛f8+ 5 ♖f7 ♛g8 6 ♔f2! would lead to zugzwang, winning the queen or mating. So Black must continue to play waiting moves.

3 ... ♔g8

4 ♖a7

4 ♖cd7 would also win, as in the main line, but not 4 ♔e1 ♔h8 5 ♖f7 because of 5 ... ♛b4+, whereas 4 ♖b7 ♔h8 would give us the same position as after Black's second move.

4 ... ♔h8

5 ♖f7 ♛e8+

If 5 ... ♛g8 any king move to the f-file wins.

6 ♔f2!

But not 6 ♔f3? ♛c6+ or 6 ♔f1? ♛b5+. Note that 4 ♖cd7 would have allowed both these king moves.

6 ... ♔g8

7 ♖g7+ ♔f8

Or else the queen is lost as we have seen.

8 ♖h7! ♔g8

Black has no checks and his queen cannot simultaneously prevent the mates on a8 and h8.

9 ♖ag7+ ♔f8

10 ♖h8+ wins the queen.

It may even be possible for the queen to win against two rooks, but only if the latter are loose, i.e. not guarding one another or guarded by the king. If either side has a minor piece as well this is usually sufficient to ensure the win. Even the ending of queen against rook and two minor pieces is worse for the side with the queen, but should usually be drawn.

B: QUEEN AGAINST TWO BISHOPS

With a queen against minor pieces, the result usually depends on the placing of the pieces. Four minor pieces usually win, three minor pieces do no more than draw, and two minor pieces can be disadvantageous. Let us begin by examining diagram 100 in which the two bishops manage to hold their own.

Diagram 100 shows the set-up Black must aim for. Both bishops

100

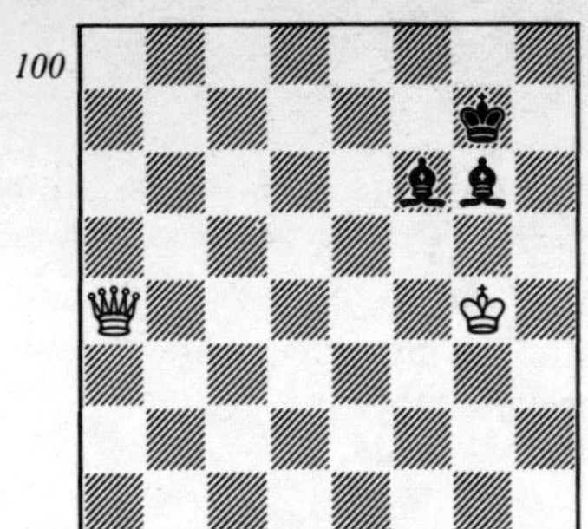

G.Lolli 1763

stand best next to each other to prevent the advance of the enemy king and the king is best placed near the corner, next to the two bishops, on the second rank. This means that he has sufficient room to manoeuvre whilst being well protected from attacks on both sides. The defence goes as follows:

1 ♕d7+ ♔g8!

But not **1 ... ♗f7?** which allows the white king to approach by **2 ♔f5!** giving the winning variations: a) **2 ... ♗c3 3 ♕a7 ♗b2** the bishop has no other moves, and 3 ... ♔g8 loses to 4 ♕a8+ **4 ♕b6 ♗a3** if 4 ... ♗c3 5 ♕g1+ ♔h7 6 ♕h2+ ♔g8 7 ♕b8+ ♔h7 8 ♕c7 wins a bishop **5 ♕d4+ ♔f8** or 5 ... ♔g8 6 ♔f6 ♔f8 7 ♕d8+ ♗e8 8 ♔e6 wins **6 ♕a1** or the composer's solution 6 ♕h8+ ♔e7 7 ♕e5+ ♔f8 8 ♔f6 etc. **6 ... ♗b4** or 6 ... ♗e7 7 ♕h8+ ♗g8 8 ♔g6 etc, or 6 ... ♗d6 7 ♕h8+ ♔e7 8 ♕f6+ wins **7 ♕h8+ ♔e7** or 7 ... ♗g8 8 ♔g6 **8 ♕e5+** and Black loses his bishop on b4. b) **2 ... ♗b2** 2 ... ♗a1 3 ♕a7 ♗b2 4 ♕b6 etc transposes to variation a **3 ♕a7 ♗c3 4 ♕g1+ ♔h7 5 ♕h2+ ♔g8 6 ♕b8+ ♔h7 7 ♕c7** wins a bishop.

2 ♕e6+ ♔g7
3 ♔f4 ♗h7

Black must of course keep his bishops near his king, but at the same time prevent ♔f5. If 3 ... ♗f7 4 ♕d7 ♔g6 5 ♕g4+ followed by 6 ♔f5 wins for White.

4 ♕d7+ ♔g6

Even safer is 4 ... ♔g8, but the text move draws.

5 ♔g4 ♗g8
6 ♕e8+ ♔g7

Or 6 ... ♗f7 7 ♕d7 ♗g8 etc.

7 ♔f5 ♗h7+
8 ♔e6 ♗g8+
9 ♔d7 ♗f7

and we have now reached approximately the same position as in diagram 100, with the board turned 90 degrees. White has made no progress and we cannot see what else he can do. After 10 ♕e4 ♗g8 11 ♕g4+ ♔f7 12 ♕h5+ ♔g7 13 ♔e8 the simplest is 13 ... ♗e6 14 ♕f3 ♗f7+ 15 ♔d7 ♗g8 and so on. The position is drawn.

Even in the middle of the board, the two bishops can often draw against a queen, but play is much more complex and is of little practical interest to us here.

C: QUEEN AGAINST TWO KNIGHTS

Rather surprisingly, the two knights offer even better chances than the two bishops, and this ending is considered a draw. Black must of course post his pieces correctly. At first sight, the knights might appear to be best placed defending each other, but this is not the case. Such a set-up would allow the enemy king to slip in through the gaps created, when the queen would drive the defending king away from the knights. As with the two bishops, the main task of the defence is to prevent the approach of the enemy king, so the knights are best placed as in diagram 101. At all events they must stay close to the king and must not cling to the edge of the board.

101

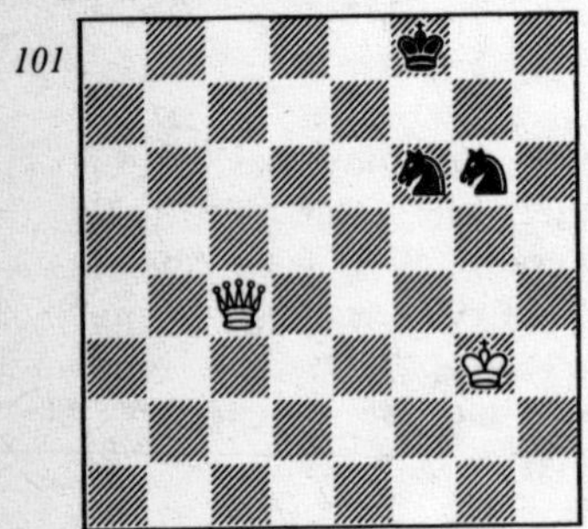

T.von der Lasa

1 ♕e6 ♔g7
2 ♔f3 ♘h7

2 ... ♘h8 3 ♔f4 ♘f7 would create more difficulties for Black, as after 4 ♕c6! threatening 5 ♕g2+ it would not be easy to prevent the advance of White's king.

3 ♔g4

If 3 ♕d7+ ♔g8 4 ♕d8+ ♔f7 5 ♕c7+ ♘e7 and 6 ... ♘f6 when the black pieces also work well together. Black can bring his pieces towards the centre whenever he likes, as there is little to fear.

3 ... ♘hf8

3 ... ♘f6+ would be risky after 4 ♔f5 ♘h4+ 5 ♔g5 ♘f3+ 6 ♔f4 ♘h4 7 ♕h3 ♘g6+ 8 ♔f5 and White's king gives him some winning chances.

4 ♕d6 ♔f7
5 ♕d5+

If 5 ♔h5 ♘e6 and Black aims for a position with his knights on e6 and e5 and king on f6. There is little White can do to prevent this.

5 ... ♔g7

White has been able to make hardly any progress. As he cannot play 6 ♔g5? ♘h7+ and his queen is lost, he must play **6 ♕d4+ ♔f7 7 ♔f5 ♘e7+ 8 ♔e4 ♘fg6** when he has achieved nothing.

In such endings it is difficult to quote definite drawing positions, but it is just as difficult to prove how White can win against correct defence. For this reason, queen against two knights is, with reason, held to be drawn.

D: QUEEN AGAINST BISHOP AND KNIGHT

Unlike the other two combinations of minor pieces, bishop and knight offer only slight drawing chances, mainly because these two pieces have difficulty in holding back the advance of the enemy king. Diagram 102 shows us that the defence cannot even survive from a relatively favourable position.

102

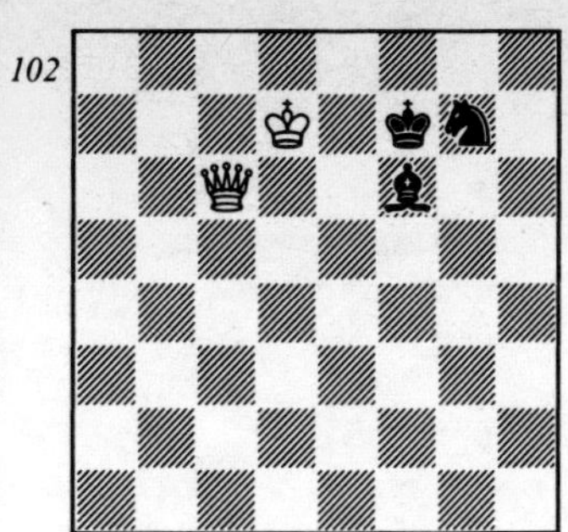

P.Bilguer 1843

Bilguer himself gave this position as drawn, a verdict accepted by his contemporaries. Berger was the first to demonstrate that Black cannot defend the position. It would take us too far to present a complete analysis here, so we will just examine one fairly clear variation:

1 ♕g2

Simpler than Bilguer's 1 ♕d5+ ♔g6 2 ♕g2+ which gives Black the option of playing 2 ... ♔h7 (h6).

1 ... ♗e5

The other possibility 1 ... ♔g8 (1 ... ♔f8 2 ♕g6 is even better for White) 2 ♕g6 ♗a1 (2 ... ♗h4 3 ♕h6) 3 ♕a6 ♗e5 4 ♔e7 followed by 5 ♕c4+ and 6 ♔f7 wins easily for White, as does 1 ... ♘f5 (or 1 ... ♘h5 2 ♕d5+ ♔g6 3 ♕e4+ and 4 ♔e6 etc) 2 ♕d5+ ♔g6 3 ♕e4 followed by 4 ♔e6, or 1 ... ♗h4 2 ♕d5+ ♔g6 3 ♕e4+ winning a piece.

2 ♕g5

If 2 ♕d5+ ♔f6 and White has no good waiting move.

2 ... ♗f6

3 ♕g4

White also wins after Karstedt's suggested 3 ♕g3 ♗d4 4 ♕b3+ ♔f6 5 ♔c6, but the text move seems simpler.

3 ... ♗e5

4 ♕c4+ ♔g6

5 ♕e4+ ♔f6

6 ♕d5!

Much stronger than Bilguer's 6 ♔c6 ♘f5 7 ♕f3 ♔e6 8 ♕b3+ ♔f6 9 ♕d5, as Black could vary with 6 ... ♔e6! posing problems for White. Black is now in zugzwang.

103
B

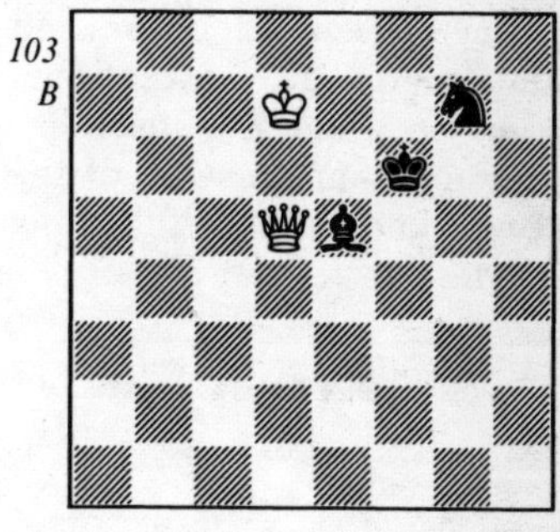

6 ... ♗f4

Black cannot prevent the approach of the white king. Black loses after 6 ... ♗a1 (or 6 ... ♗b2 7 ♕f3+ ♘f5 8 ♕c6+ ♔g7 9 ♕b5 etc) 7 ♕c6+ ♔f7 8 ♕c4+ ♔g6 9 ♕c2+ ♔f6 10 ♕f2+ ♘f5 11 ♕b6+ ♔g7 12 ♕a5, and his pieces are very badly placed after 6 ... ♗g3 (or 6 ... ♗h2 7 ♕c6+ ♔f7 8 ♕f3+ ♔g8 9 ♔e7 etc) 7 ♕c6+ ♔g5 8 ♕c3 ♘h5 9 ♕f3, or 6 ... ♗b8 7 ♕c6+ ♔f7 8 ♕b5 ♗h2 9 ♕f1+ ♔g8 10 ♔e7, or 6 ... ♔f5 7 ♔e7 ♔f4 8 ♔f7 etc.

7 ♕c6+ ♔g5

If 7 ... ♔f5 8 ♔e7 which would also be good after the text move.

8 ♕e4 ♘f5

9 ♔e6 ♘g3

After 9 ... ♘g7+ 10 ♔f7 ♘f5? 11 ♕d5 ♔g4 12 ♕e6 wins the knight.

10 ♕f3

and White has disturbed the co-ordination of Black's pieces, so that the ending can now be asssessed as won for him. If the reader wishes to pursue this analysis, he can check it in a more specialized book on endings.

However, even with bishop and knight there are exceptional positions in which the queen has no winning chances. One of the most well-known is the following position.

104

M.Karstedt 1903

The black pieces are ideally posted for defence, with the bishop protecting the knight, and the king the bishop, whilst allowing enough space for manoeuvring without being driven into zugzwang. White can make no progress.

1 ♔e7 ♗h8

2 ♔e6 ♗g7

3 ♔f5 ♗h8

4 ♔g5 ♗g7

The position remains practically unchanged.

5 ♕e8+ ♔h7

6 ♔h5 ♗h8

7 ♕e7+ ♗g7

8 ♔g5 ♔g8

and White can neither advance his king nor bring about zugzwang. The game is clearly drawn.

We might also mention the position in diagram 105. White cannot free his king from the stalemate position. However, these are exceptions and do not alter our general assessment of a win for the queen against knight and bishop.

105

With this, we finish our survey of the basic positions arising from queen endings. Such endings cannot be so easily classified as pawn endings, and we often have to base our judgement on general positional considerations.

However, we have indicated many key ideas for the handling of the various positions.

In conclusion, let us now see how this knowledge can be applied to a few endings from practical play.

Practical examples

Our first example, diagram 106, comes from a tournament game Lisitsin-Capablanca, Moscow 1935.

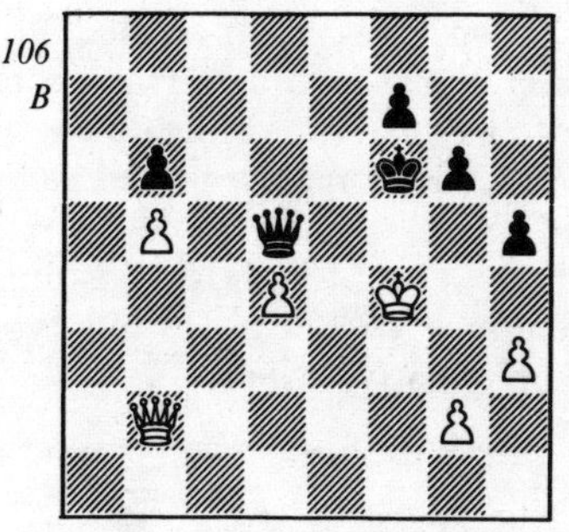

Lisitsin-Capablanca 1935

As material is even and Black has neither real threats nor a mating attack, the position might at first sight seem equal. However, closer examination reveals several small advantages for Black. Firstly, his queen is powerfully centralized on d5, secondly, his pawn position is more compact, thirdly White's pawns are weak, reducing the white queen to a passive role, and fourthly the black king is better protected from checks than is White's.

Viewed individually, the above advantages are minimal, but together they give Black a clear positional superiority. It is extremely instructive to see how Capablanca uses these elements to bring about a win.

1 ... ♔e6

Although the white queen is passively placed, it is defending the b-, d- and g-pawns, so Black can make no progress without the help of his king which is now heading for d5.

2 h4 f6

3 ♔e3

If White tries to use his passed d-pawn by playing 3 ♕e2+ ♔d6 4 ♕e4, Black replies 4 ... g5+ 5 hg ♕xg5+ 6 ♔f3 ♕xb5 7 ♕f4+ ♔d7! when 8 ♕xh6 ♕d3+ 9 ♕e3 ♕xe3+ 10 ♔xe3 gives him a won pawn ending.

3 ... ♕c4

4 g3

Black was threatening to increase his pressure by 4 ... ♔d5 which would now be countered with 5 ♕g2+. However, this pawn move entails a further weakening of the king's wing, and in particular of the f3 square. In the following play Capablanca exploits in masterly fashion the weakness of this square.

Bondarevsky has recommended a more active defence for White by means of 4 ♕b1!, certainly giving White better prospects than the game continuation. After 4 ... ♕c3+ 5 ♕d3 ♕xd3+ 6 ♔xd3 ♔d5 Black wins the ending (7 ♔e3 g5! 8 hg fg 9 ♔d3 h4 10 ♔e3 g4, or here 8 g3 g4! 9 ♔d3 f5 10 ♔e3 ♔c4 etc),but White can instead play

5 ♔e2! with counterplay, for even though Black wins a pawn by 5 ... ♕xd4 6 ♕xg6 ♕e5+ 7 ♔f3 ♕xb5, White has some drawing chances after 8 ♕g8+ ♔e5 9 ♕b8+ etc. A good general rule in queen endings is not to use the queen as a passive defender but always be on the look-out for active counterplay.

4	**...**	**g5**
5	**hg**	**fg**
6	**♕h2**	

Surprisingly, White has been forced into a kind of zugzwang position, a rare situation indeed in queen endings. The pawn ending after 6 ♕e2 would clearly be lost, and 6 ♔e4 g4 7 ♔f4 ♔f6 8 ♔e4 ♕e6+ 9 ♔d3 ♕d5! seems unattractive for White.

Relatively best is 6 ♕b1 ♕c3+ 7 ♔e2 losing a pawn after 7 ... ♕xd4 but giving White some drawing chances with 8 ♕g6+ ♕f6 9 ♕xh5.

The counterattack begun by the text move is a desperation measure which quickly loses.

6	**...**	**♕b3+**
7	**♔e4**	**g4!**

Threatening 8 ... ♕f3 mate, so forcing the white queen back to defence.

8	**♕e2**	

Or 8 ♕f2 ♕d5+ 9 ♔e3 ♕xb5 etc.

8	**...**	**♕xg3**
9	**♕c4+**	**♔e7**
10	**♕c8**	

At last White looks like obtaining some counterplay but it is all too late.

10	**...**	**♕f3+**
11	**♔e5**	**♕f6+**
12	**♔d5**	**♕d6+**

0-1

Black forces the exchange of queens next move and easily wins the pawn ending.

In queen endings, passed pawns are vitally important. It is clear that a passed pawn supported by the queen is a force to be reckoned with, and many a time such a pawn has compensated for material disadvantage. This means that pawns can sometimes be sacrificed to create a passed pawn and save what would would otherwise be a totally lost position. Diagram 107 illustrates this type of imaginative defence.

107
B

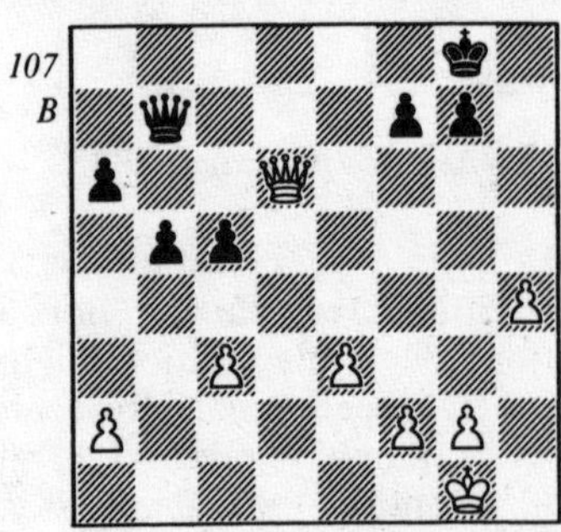

Rubinstein-Capablanca 1914

White is a pawn up and has a more actively posted queen. The black queen on the other hand is tied to the defence of his queenside pawns. If Black defends passively White will advance his pawn majority and soon obtain a winning position.

What can Black do? His c-pawn is attacked and after 1 ... c4 2 a3 the black queen would be permanently tied to the protection of the a-pawn. Nor would 1 ... ♕c8 change the situation much, as the queen would still be tied down to passive defence. Finally, there is the counterattack by 1 ... ♕e4, but this is ineffective after 2 ♕xa6, when White is two pawns up and has a secure king's position. Capablanca finds another way of creating excellent counterchances.

1 ... b4!

The object is to create a passed pawn as quickly as possible.

2 ♕xc5?

This makes Black's task relatively easy. No better is 2 cb ♕xb4 but 2 c4! would pose more problems for Black, as both 2 ... ♕c8 3 ♕b6 and 2 ... ♕a7 3 ♕d8+ followed by ♕a5 are no good for him. As soon as White fixes Black's queenside pawns, he can proceed with the advance of his pawns.

However, Black has one interesting possibility at his disposal. He can counterattack by 2 ... ♕e4! when 3 ♕xc5 ♕b1+ 4 ♔h2 ♕xa2 5 ♕xb4 ♕xf2 gives White no chances. So best is 3 ♕xa6 when Black coolly replies 3 ... ♔h7! leaving White with difficult problems to solve. His queen is tied to the defence of his a- and c-pawns, and the capture of either would give Black a strong passed pawn. If White guards his h-pawn with 4 g3, Black forces repetition of moves after 4 ... ♕b1+ 5 ♔g2 ♕e4+ 6 ♔h2 ♕c2 etc. Despite his two extra pawns, there may be no way for White to utilize his advantage, but he should at least have tried this line.

2 ... bc
3 ♕xc3 ♕b1+
4 ♔h2 ♕xa2

We can now see the first results of Black's play on the queen's wing. He has created a passed a-pawn which threatens to march on to the queening square. Moreover White must lose time defending his f-pawn, after which he himself has to start an action on the kingside. His winning chances have gone.

5 ♕c8+ ♔h7
6 ♕f5+ g6

Of course 6 ... ♔g8 was also possible, but the text move gains an important tempo, even though it slightly weakens his kingside.

7 ♕f6+ a5
8 g4 a4
9 h5 gh!

Black must be careful, as 9 ... a3? 10 h6! ♔xh6 11 ♕h8+ ♔g5 12 ♔g3! gives a mating attack. Similarly 9 ... ♕e6 loses to 10 hg+.

10 ♕f5+

Rubinstein decides not to play with fire. Indeed 10 gh ♕e6! would give Black winning chances.

10 ♔g7
11 ♕g5+ ♔h7

Or 11 ... ♔f8 12 ♕d8+ etc.

12 ♕xh5+ ♔g7
13 ♕g5+ ♔h7

½-½

Black cannot escape perpetual

check and White has nothing better than to take the draw. In queen endings, as we have said, passed pawns are more important than material considerations.

It might be thought that purely theoretical endings have little application to practical play, but this is hardly the case with queen endings, many of which arise after pawn promotion on both sides. Diagram 108 is such an example, also illustrating the inexact play which often occurs in endgames.

108
W

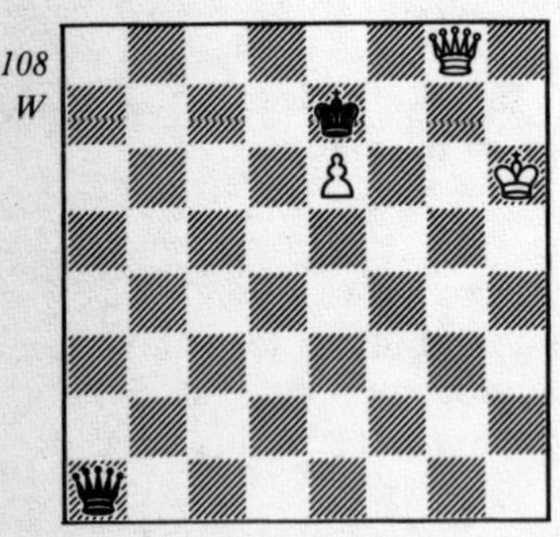

Alekhine-Stoltz 1942

In general such positions offer White good winning chances, or are even theoretically won, but one circumstance favours Black here. His king is near the pawn and prevents the white queen from taking up a dominating position in the centre where it would be able to protect the white king from checks. Let us see the game proceeded:

1 Qf7+ Kd6
2 Qd7+ Kc5

Black loses his queen after 2 ... Ke5 3 Qg7+. White cannot now play 3 e7 because there is perpetual check after 3 ... Qf6+.

3 Kg6 Qg1+

We pointed out many times that ill-considered, purposeless checks often have disastrous consequences. The text move in no way improves the position of Black's queen but gives White a useful tempo by forcing his king to go where it wants to go! Such checks should always be avoided. We already know that active centralized queens are called for in this kind of ending, and as White has not been able to centralize his own queen, it is up to Black to take his chance of playing **3 ... Qe5!**

As Alekhine himself admitted after the game, this move would have given Black a draw. 4 Qc8+ or 4 Qa7+ get nowhere after 4 ... Kd6, and 4 Kf7 gives Black perpetual check by 4 ... Qh5+ 5 Ke7 Qh4+ 6 Ke8 Qh8+ etc, as does 4 e7 Qg3+ 5 Kf7 Qf4+ 6 Ke8 Qb8+ 7 Qd8 Qb5+ 8 Kf7 Qf1+ etc.

4 Kf7 Qh1

Black can no longer prevent the advance of the pawn, nor has he any chances of perpetual check. For instance, after 4 ... Qf2+ 5 Ke8 Qg3 6 Qe7+ Kc6 7 Qf6 Kg8+ 8 Ke7 Qh7+ 9 Kf8 Black could resign. Or 4 ... Qf1+ 5 Ke8 Qa1 (to prevent White's Qe7+ and Qf6) 6 Qc7+ Kb5 7 e7 and White's king soon escapes the checks.

Black most stubborn defence is **4 ... Qf2+ 5 Ke8 Qh2** but after

6 ♕e7+ and 7 ♕f6. White can advance his pawn when Black would hardly be able to hold the position.

5 ♕c7+ ♔b5

Stoltz defends badly and makes White's task fairly easy. But even 5 ... ♔b4 would not save the game after 6 ♕f4+ ♔a3 7 e7 ♕h7+ (or 7 ... ♕d5+ 8 ♔g7 ♕d7 9 ♔f8 wins) 8 ♔e6 ♕h3+ 9 ♔d6 ♕d3+ 10 ♔c7 ♕c3+ 11 ♔b7 ♕b2+ 12 ♔a7 ♕g7 13 ♕d6+ and 14 ♔a6 wins.

6 ♕e5+ ♔a4 *(109)*

If the king goes to the third rank then 7 e7 ♕h7+ 8 ♕g7 wins at once, and 6 ... ♔b4 is certainly no improvement on the text line.

109
W

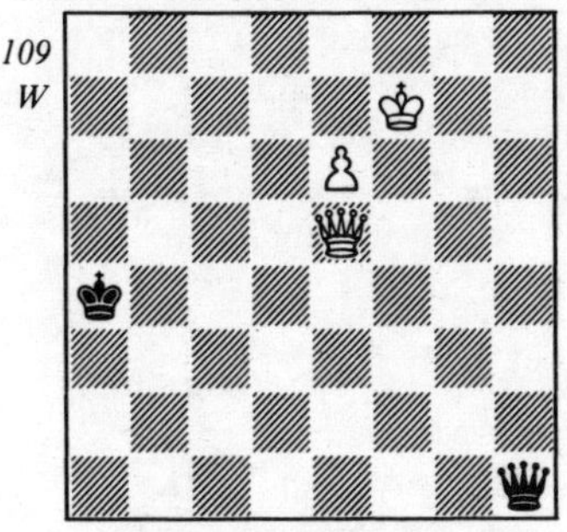

Alekhine-Stoltz 1942

7 ♕d4+

Alekhine here makes the same mistake as his opponent did earlier, by needlessly checking the black king into a better position whilst in no way improving the position of his queen. White has two simple ways of winning. Either **7 e7 ♕h7+** if 7 ... ♕f3+ or 7 ... ♕f1+, then 8 ♕f6 and 9 ♔f8 wins **8 ♔e6 ♕h3+ 9 ♔d6 ♕d3+ 10 ♔c7 ♕c4+ 11 ♔b8 ♕b3+ 12 ♔a7 ♕f7 13 ♕d6!** wins. Or **7 ♕f5! ♕b7+ 8 e7** winning as we showed in our analysis of diagram 94.

Of course, the text move does not spoil anything, unlike Stoltz's error, but unnecessarily complicates matters.

7 ... ♔a3
8 ♕d3+ ♔b4

This loses immediately but even the better 8 ... ♔b2 would eventually lose. White could play either 8 e7 ♕h5+ 9 ♔e6 ♕g4+ 10 ♔d6 (or 10 ♕f5), or 8 ♕f5 followed by 9 e7, as in the analysis to diagram 94.

9 ♕f5!

Now even simpler than 9 e7 etc.

9 ... ♕c6

Black would have more choice after 9 ... ♕b7+ 10 e7 but would still lose. 10 ... ♕c7 transposes into the main line, 10 ... ♕a7 11 ♔f8 loses at once, and 10 ... ♔a3 11 ♕f4! ♕a7 12 ♔e6 wins, as we saw from diagram 94.

10 e7 ♕c7
11 ♕e4+ ♔a3
12 ♕d4!

Now the threat of 13 ♔f8 cannot be prevented, as 12 ... ♕b7 fails to 13 ♕a1+ and 14 ♕b1+. Black could resign but hopes for one last trap.

12 ... ♕h2
13 ♕c5+ ♔a2
14 e8♕ ♕f4+
15 ♔g7 ♕g3+
16 ♔f8!

Careful to the end. After 16 ♕g6? ♕c3+! would produce a surprising stalemate. Black now finally resigned.

Diagram 110 provides us with an interesting example of queen against rook and knight.

110
W

Sämisch-Prins 1938

White has a clear material advantage which is, however, difficult to convert into a win. All the pawns are on the same wing, White has no passed pawn yet, there are no points of attack in Black's camp and as the rook can oscillate between d4 and f4, zugzwang is out of the question. Nevertheless White has a clear winning plan: play g3 and create a passed pawn which he can then queen. He could prepare this with 1 ♕h8 but instead endangers his chances of victory by playing overhastily:

1 g4 hg
2 fg ♘g5

A clever defensive move which almost saves Black. He eliminates the passed pawn and brings about a queen versus rook ending with a pawn on either side. An interesting position arises.

3 ♕f5 ♘xh3+
4 ♕xh3 ♖c6

White was now ostensibly so shaken by the knight sacrifice that he continued planlessly and finally agreed to a draw with White's king on f5, queen on c3, pawn on g4, and Black's king on g8, rook on e6, pawn on f7. White can in fact make no progress in this position, for the black king cannot be driven from g8 or g7, nor the black rook from the third rank.

However, let us forget about the game continuation and devote our attention to the position reached after the sacrifice. It turns out that White threw his chances away by allowing Black's king to reach g8. The king had to be kept on the e-file when we shall prove that White could force a win:

5 ♕h4+ ♔e8

As we have seen in our analysis of queen versus rook endings, 5 ... f6 would only help White.

6 ♕h8+ ♔e7
7 ♔f2

Now that Black's king has been restricted, White plans to play his pawn to g5 and his king to f5 or h5. Black can only wait.

7 ... ♖g6
8 ♔f3 ♖e6
9 ♔g4 ♖g6
10 ♔h5 ♖e6

Not of course 10 ... ♖xg3? 11 ♕e5+ etc.

11 g4 ♖g6

12 g5 ♖e6 *(111)*

Sämisch-Prins 1938 (variation)

White can now proceed to more active measures in this theoretically won position.

13 ♕b8! ♖g6

The only move, as 13 ... ♔d7 fails to 14 ♕f8, and 13 ... ♖d6 14 ♕c7+ would allow the exchange of pawns.

14 ♕b4+ ♔e8

Black cannot let the queen reach f8 and 14 ... ♖d6 fails to 15 ♕b7+ and 16 ♕b8+ exchanging the pawns, as we have seen.

15 ♕e4+ ♖e6

Or 15 ... ♔f8 16 ♕xg6 fg+ 17 ♔xg6 ♔g8 18 ♔h6 ♔h8 19 g6 wins.

16 ♕xe6+ fe

17 ♔h6 and wins.

The pawn cannot be stopped. A most instructive winning method and not at all obvious, for even after the game both players were convinced that g4 was the decisive mistake that threw away the win.

Diagram 112 presents us with a rare situation in which White's material advantage has to be geared to stopping a strong passed pawn.

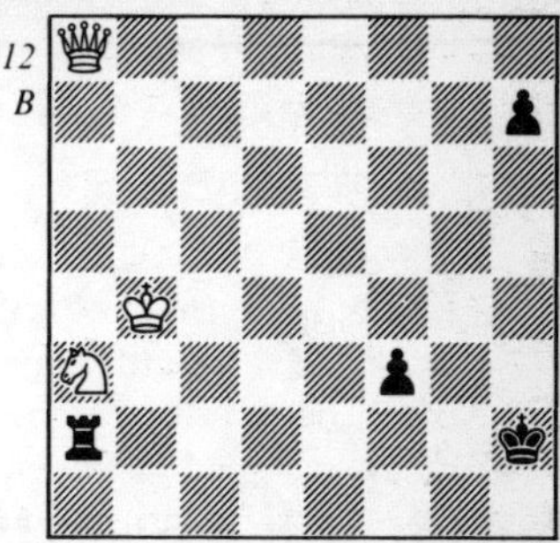

Flohr-Ozols 1937

At first sight it seems that White wins easily, but on closer examination certain difficulties emerge. Black has the move and can immediately advance his pawn to the seventh rank. Indeed, if it were not for the h-pawn, Black could draw at once by giving up his rook for the knight, then advancing his pawn. In addition, the win is not always guaranteed even if White wins the rook, for his knight is far away from the scene of action.

First of all, let us briefly examine the game continuatin:

1 ... ♖b2+

The idea behind this move is to drive the white king to the third rank so that the rook can later pin pieces along this rank. However, the plan cannot be executed and quickly leads to a loss. By 1 ... f2! Black could have set White difficult problems, as we shall see later.

2 ♔c3 ♖g2

Now 2 ... f2 would be answered by 3 ♕f3 ♔g1 4 ♕g4+ ♔h2 5 ♕d1 ♔g2 6 ♘c4! winning.

3 ♘c4

Not of course 3 ♕xf3? ♖g3 pinning the queen.

3 ... f2

4 ♘d2!

Black had hoped for 4 ♘e3? when 4 ... ♖g3! would have drawn. Now, however, the game is lost and Black resigned after **4 ... h5 5 ♔d3 h4 6 ♘f1+ ♔g1 7 ♕a1 ♔h1 8 ♔e3 h3 9 ♔f3 ♖g1 10 ♕b1 ♖xf1 11 ♕xf1+ ♔h2 12 ♕xf2+ ♔h1 13 ♔g3** with mate next move.

So far so good, but could White have won against the better move 1 ... f2! given by the tournament book as drawing for Black? Let us analyse:

1 ... f2!

2 ♕f3!

The tournament book continues with 2 ♕b8+ ♔h1 3 ♕b7+ ♔h2 4 ♕xh7+? ♔g2 5 ♕e4+ ♔h2 leading to a draw after 6 ♕f3 ♔g1 7 ♕g4+ ♔h2 8 ♕d1 ♖xa3! 9 ♔xa3 ♔g2 etc.

However, this variation contains a gross error. White should not capture the h-pawn, for we have already shown that an extra pawn is a hindrance to the defence in such endings, preventing the stalemate resource.

2 ... ♔g1

3 ♕g4+

Even here White must be careful. For instance, 3 ♕e3? allows Black to draw by 3 ... ♖xa3! 4 ♔xa3 h5! 5 ♕g3+ ♔f1 6 ♔b2 h4 etc.

3 ... ♔h2

4 ♕d1!

The winning move, threatening 5 ♕f1 followed by 6 ♘c4. As Black cannot play 4 ... ♔g2 5 ♘c4! he must eliminate the knight.

4 ... ♖xa3

5 ♔xa3 ♔g2

If the black pawn had already advanced to h5 or h4, the game would be drawn, whereas now White wins without great difficulty.

6 ♕g4+ ♔h2

7 ♕f3 ♔g1

8 ♕g3+ ♔f1

9 ♔b3 h5

If 9 ... ♔e2 10 ♕g2 ♔e1 11 ♔c2! wins.

10 ♔c2 h4

11 ♕g4 h3

12 ♔d2 h2

13 ♕f3 ♔g1

14 ♔e2! wins.

With this example we conclude our discussion of queen endings. Once again we have only been able to consider a few among many possibilities, but hope that we have indicated the basic essentials of such endings. If the reader wishes to study these further, he should turn to specialized books on the endgame or play through games containing instructive endgames. Only through this kind of intensive study can he hope to understand fully the many ramifications of this difficult aspect of endgame play.

4 Rook Endings

Of all endings there is no doubt that rook endings are by far the most common. For this reason they are probably the best analysed, with most examples coming from practical play. In spite of all this, however, they form the most difficult part of endgame theory, and amongst leading specialists only a few have a thorough grasp of them. Even the best grandmasters in the world have had to work hard to acquire the technique of rook endings. It is said of Capablanca that in his early years he exhaustively analysed more than a thousand such endings, before he attained his splendid mastery in this field.

In view of the above, one can hardly exaggerate the importance of a good understanding of this type of ending. As in queen endings, there is a vast range of possibilities, but these are easier to classify and assess. In the following section we intend to give the reader a limited selection of positions which are basic to rook endings.

Rook against Pawn(s)

The rook usually wins against a pawn but there are many exceptions, especially when the king cannot be brought up quickly enough and the rook has to stop the pawn on its own. Occasionally there are exceptions when the pawn proves stronger than the rook, and we shall begin with the classic case of this.

113

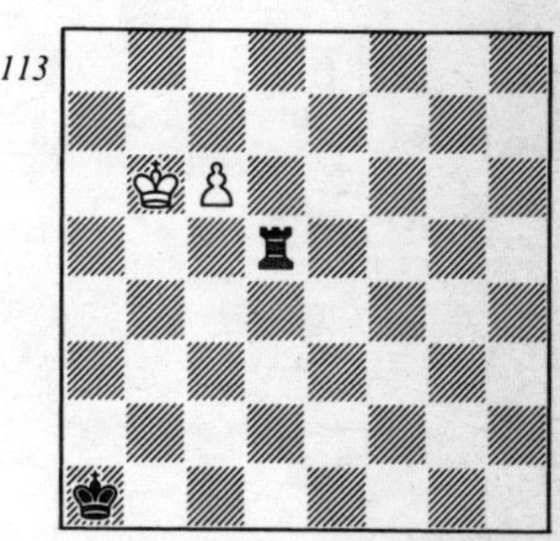

F.Saavedra 1895

This position occurred in a game played in 1895 which ended in a draw. After the game Saavedra demonstrated that White can win in the following imaginative way:

1 c7 ♖d6+

This is forced, as d8 and c5 are inaccessible to the rook. The next few moves can easily be understood in this light.

2 ♔b5 ♖d5+

3 ♔b4 ♖d4+
4 ♔b3 ♖d3+
5 ♔c2!

Only now does White play his king to the c-file, as 5 ... ♖d1 is now impossible. The game seems over, but Black is not finished yet.

5 ... ♖d4
6 c8♖!

6 c8♕ ♖c4+! 7 ♕xc4 is stalemate. White now threatens 7 ♖a8 mate, so Black's reply is forced.

6 ... ♖a4
7 ♔b3

and White wins the rook or forces 8 ♖c1 mate. A glorious position of classical beauty!

The same idea is presented in an even more complicated form in the following study by Selesniev:

114

White wins as follows: **1 f7 ♖c6+ 2 ♔e5!** but not 2 ♔e7 ♖c1! 3 f7♕ ♖e1+ and 4 ... ♖f1+ drawing **2 ... ♖c5+ 3 ♔e4 ♖c4+ 4 ♔e3 ♖c3+ 5 ♔f2! ♖c2+ 6 ♔g3 ♖c3+ 7 ♔g4 ♖c4+ 8 ♔g5 ♖c5+ 9 ♔g6 ♖c6+ 10 ♔g7** and White queens next move.

As already stated, however, these are rare occurrences. More useful to us are those positions in which the rook can stop the pawn, the main question being whether or not they are won. Such positions arise when the pawn is protected by the king and cannot immediately be stopped by the enemy king. Let us begin with a typical set-up:

115

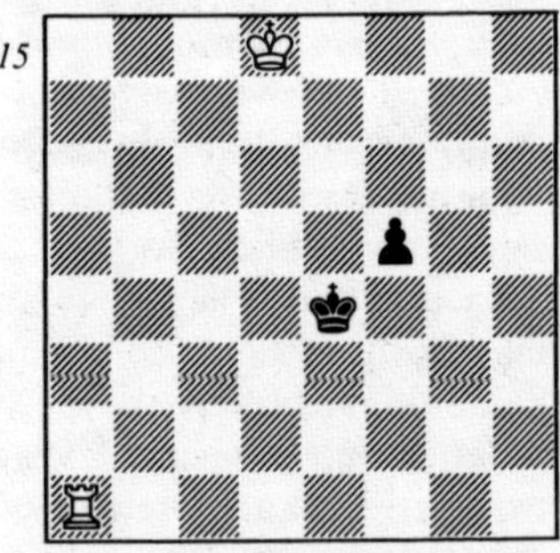

It is clear that the rook on its own cannot win, but can the white king arrive in time to stop the pawn queening? It is fairly easy to answer this question if we count moves. In order to stop the pawn, the white king must reach g2 (or e2 if the black king is on the g-file). He needs 6 moves for this, whereas Black needs only 5 moves to reach a position with his king on e2 and pawn on f2. We can conclude from this that White wins only if he has the move, as follows:

1 ♔e7

Black to move draws by 1 ... f4 2 ♔e7 f3 3 ♔f6 f2 4 ♔g5 ♔e3 5 ♔g4 ♔e2 etc.

1 ... f4

2 ♔f6 f3

It makes no difference whether Black moves his pawn or his king.

3 ♔g5 f2
4 ♔g4 ♚e3
5 ♔g3 ♚e2
6 ♔g2 wins.

Of course, positions are not always so clear-cut. We have seen that the white king has to approach on the opposite side to the enemy king, for his way not to be blocked. Black can sometimes gain valuable time by preventing the king's approach and this can be an effective method of defence.

For example, if we change diagram 115 by placing the white king on c7. White cannot win with the move, even though theoretically his king only needs 5 moves to reach g2. The reason for this is that the black king can force White to waste time, as follows: **1 ♔d6 f4 2 ♖a4+** or 2 ♔e6 f3, or 2 ♔c5 f3 3 ♔c4 f2 4 ♔c3 ♚e3 etc **2 ... ♚e3 3 ♔e5 f3 4 ♖a3+ ♚e2 5 ♔e4 f2 6 ♖a2+ ♚e1 7 ♔e3 f1♘+!** and Black draws. Or **1 ♖e1+ ♚d4 2 ♖f1 ♚e4 3 ♔d6 f4 4 ♔e6** or 4 ♔c5 f3 5 ♔c4 ♚e3 6 ♔c3 f2 etc **4 ... f3 5 ♔f6 ♚e3 6 ♔g5 f2 7 ♔g4 ♚e2** again drawing.

If the white king is on the wrong side, he must be correspondingly nearer the queening square to win. For example, if we place the king on c6 in diagram 115, White wins by **1 ♔c5 f4 2 ♔c4 ♚e3** or 2 ... f3 3 ♖e1+ and 4 ♔d3 **3 ♔c3 ♚e2** or 3 ... f3 4 ♖e1+ ♚f2 5 ♔d2 ♚g2 6 ♔e3 f2 7 ♖e2 **4 ♔d4 f3 5 ♖a2+** followed by 6 ♔e3.

We have not yet exhausted all the possibilities of diagram 115. Instead of moving the white king, let us place the white rook on d1, with White to move. The normal sequence comes up against a difficutly, as after 1 ♔e7 f4 2 ♔f6 f3 3 ♔g5 f2 4 ♔g4 ♚e3 5 ♔g3 ♚e2 the white rook is attacked, so the game is drawn. In order to win from this position, White must first improve the placing of his rook by **1 ♖e1+! ♚d4** or 1 ... ♚f3 2 ♖f1+ ♚g4 3 ♔e7 f4 4 ♔e6 f3 5 ♔e5 ♚g3 6 ♔e4 f2 7 ♔e3 etc **2 ♖f1! ♚e4**, and only now play **3 ♔e7! f4 4 ♔f6 f3 5 ♔g5 ♚e3 6 ♔g4 f2 7 ♔g3** winning.

In practice, positions occur where the rook is not on the first rank but somewhere behind the pawn along with the king. Let us analyse such a position:

116

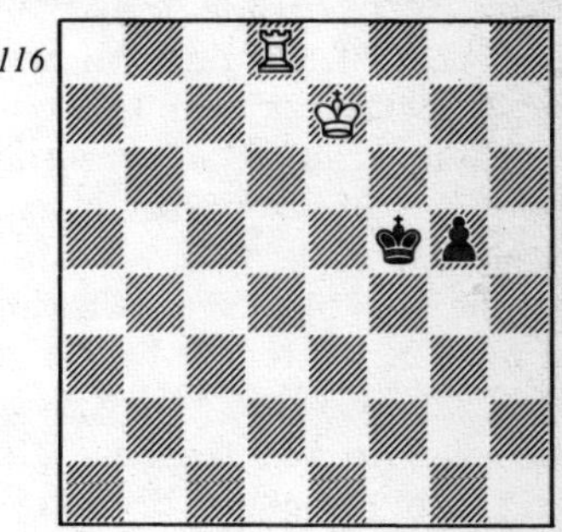

M.Euwe 1934

White has various ways of winning, so we will choose one of them as our main line:

1 ♔d6

Alternatives are **1 ♖f8+ ♔e4 2 ♔f6** or 2 ♖g8 ♔f4 3 ♔f6 g4 4 ♔g6 g3 5 ♔h5 etc **2 ... g4 3 ♔g5 g3 4 ♔h4 g2 5 ♖g8 ♔f3 6 ♔h3** winning, or **1 ♖g8** or first 1 ♔f7 **1 ... g4 2 ♔f7! ♔f4 3 ♔g6 g3 4 ♔h5 ♔f3 5 ♔h4** with an easy win.

1 ... g4

If Black tries to prevent the king's advance by 1 ... ♔e4 White wins after 2 ♖g8 ♔f4 3 ♔d5 etc.

2 ♔d5 ♔f4
3 ♔d4 ♔f3

If 3 ... g3 4 ♖f8+ and 5 ♔e3 wins.

4 ♔d3 g3

Or 4 ... ♔f2 5 ♖f8+ ♔g2 6 ♔e2 etc.

5 ♖f8+ ♔g2
6 ♔e2 ♔g1
7 ♔f3 g2
8 ♖g8 ♔h1
9 ♔f2! wins.

However, if we change the placing of the white rook, our asssessment of this position may alter. For example, with the rook on a6, White can no longer win, as the rook is unfavourably placed on the 6th rank. After **1 ♖f6+ ♔e4!** the rook blocks its own king and must lose a tempo by **2 ♖g6 ♔f4 3 ♔f6** or 3 ♔e6 g4 4 ♔d5 g3 5 ♔d4 ♔f3 draws **3 ... g4** with the rook again blocking his king's approach via g6, or here **2 ♔d6 g4 3 ♔c5 g3 4 ♖g6 ♔f3 5 ♔d4 g2,** both drawing.

If instead **1 ♔f7 g4 2 ♔g7 g3 3 ♔h6 ♔f4 4 ♔h5 g2** and **5 ... ♔f3** draws, or **1 ♔d6 g4 2 ♔d5 g3 3 ♔d4 g2!** (king moves would lose), as the rook cannot go to g6, Black draws after **4 ♖a1 ♔f4 5 ♔d3 ♔f3** etc. One final attempt by White is **1 ♖a5+ ♔f4 2 ♔f6,** but Black still draws by **2 ... g4 3 ♖a4+ ♔f3 4 ♔f5 g3 5 ♖a3+ ♔f2 6 ♔f4 g2 7 ♖a2+ ♔f1 8 ♔f3 g1♘+!** etc. This ending cannot be won as we shall see later.

However, if in the diagrammed position we place the white king on f7, White wins wherever his rook is positioned. The reader can check for himself.

Finally let us look at a most interesting study by Réti:

117

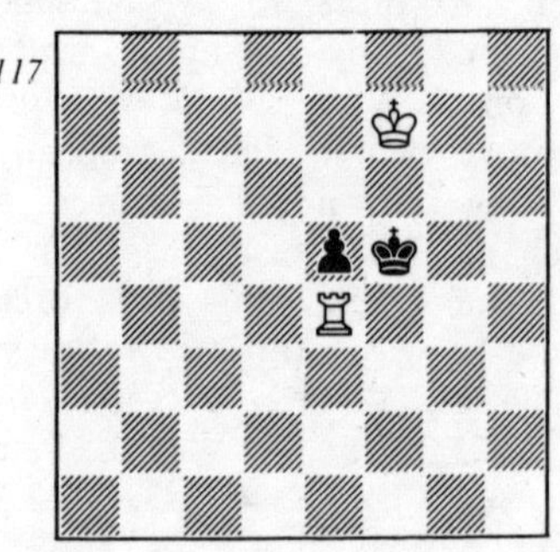

R.Réti 1928

The rook must retreat, because 1 ♖a4 (or h4) fails to 1 ... e4 2 ♖a5+ ♔f4 3 ♔e6 e3 4 ♖e5 ♔f3 5 ♔d5 e2 6 ♔d4 ♔f2 drawing, as White is a tempo too late.

1 ♖e2 (e3)!!

This retreat is not only surprising but even incomprehensible without a thorough analysis of the position. **1 ♖e1** seems more logical, as after **1 ... e4 2 ♔e7 ♔f4** 3 ♔d6 e3 4 ♔d5 ♔f3 5 ♔d4 e2 6 ♔d3 White wins easily. However, Black has a more cunning defence in **2 ... ♔e5!** when both 3 ♔f7 ♔f5! and 3 ♔d7 ♔d5! lead to no progress for White. He must therefore move his rook, and as it dare not leave the e-file because of 3 ... e3 **3 ♖e2** is forced (3 ♖e3 transposes). But now Black can play **3 ... ♔d4** or 3 ... ♔f4 **4 ♔e6 e3 5 ♔f5 ♔d3!** gaining the vital tempo to draw.

In other words, 2 ... ♔e5! would place White in zugzwang, which explains the text move.

1 ... e4

Or 1 ... ♔f4 2 ♖e1 e4 3 ♔e6, or here 2 ... ♔f5 3 ♔e7 etc winning easily.

2 ♖e1!

Only now does the rook go to the first rank.

2 ... ♔e5

3 ♔e7!

Now it is Black who is in zugzwang and he must give way to the white king. 3 ♔g6? would spoil everything, as 3 ... ♔f4! 4 ♔h5 e3 5 ♔h4 ♔f3 draws.

3 ... ♔d4

Or 3 ... ♔f4 4 ♔d6 e3 5 ♔d5 etc.

4 ♔f6 e3

5 ♔f5 ♔d3

6 ♔f4 e2

7 ♔f3 wins.

One of the best studies with this material. It is amazing how much subtlety is contained in such a simple setting.

Before we end this part, let us consider two useful positions given in diagram 118.

In the top position White wins

118

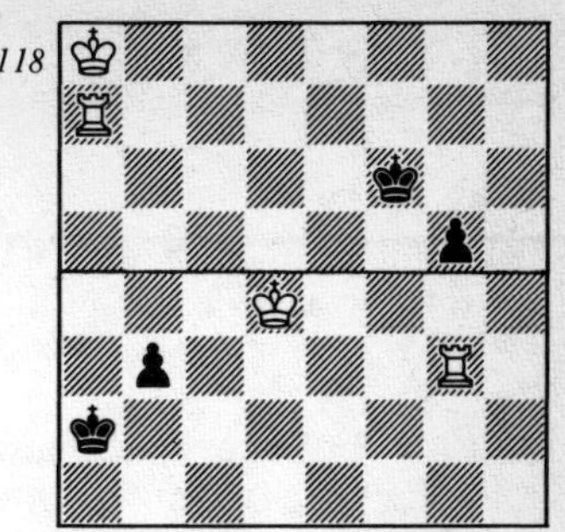

by a noteworthy manoeuvre which often occurs in such endings:

1 ♖a5!

White profits from the fact that the pawn cannot advance to the sixth rank without the help of the king which is now shut off from one side of the pawn. He must not play the alternative **1 ♔b7? ♔e5! 2 ♔c6 g4 3 ♖g7** or 3 ♔c5 g3 4 ♔c4 ♔e4! 5 ♖g7 ♔f3 6 ♔d3 g2 7 ♔d2 ♔f2 8 ♖f7+ ♔g3! **3 ... ♔f4 4 ♔d5 g3 5 ♔d4 ♔f3 6 ♔d3** or 6 ♖f7+ ♔e2! **6 ... g2** and Black draws.

1 ... ♔g6

The pawn cannot advance as after 1 ... g4 2 ♔b7 g3 3 ♖a3! it is lost, and even if the pawn does not go to the sixth the king is permanently cut off.

Black now intends to bring his king up first, but this costs a great deal of time which White uses to advance his own king.

2 ♔b7 ♔h5

3 ♔c6 ♔g4

Black must lose even more time in order to prevent the white king's advance, as 3 ... ♔h4 loses at once to 4 ♔d5 g4 5 ♔e4 g3

6 ♔f3 etc.

4 **♔d5** **♔f3**

Or 4 ... ♔f4 5 ♔d4 g4 6 ♔d3 ♔f3 7 ♖f5+ etc.

5 **♔e5!**

Much simpler than **5 ♔d4 g4** when White must avoid the pitfall **6 ♔d3? g3 7 ♖f5+ ♔g4! 8 ♖f8** or 8 ♖f1 g2 9 ♖a1 ♔f3 etc **8 ... g2 9 ♔e2 g1♘+!** White must play instead **6 ♖a3+ ♔f4** or 6 ... ♔f2 7 ♔e4 **7 ♔d3 ♔f3 8 ♔d2+ ♔f2 9 ♖a8 g3 10 ♖f8+** followed by 11 ♔e2 winning.

5 **...** **g4**

6 **♖a3+**

with an easy win.

The reader should remember this idea of using the rook on the fifth rank to cut off the enemy king.

The bottom position of diagram 118 is drawn, despite the fact that White has the move. The reason for this lies in the unfavourable position of White's rook. For instance, if the rook were on g8, White would win easily by 1 ♔c3 b2 2 ♖a8+ ♔b1 3 ♖b8 ♔a1 4 ♔c2! etc.

Play from the diagram might go as follows:

1 **♔c3** **b2**

2 **♖g2**

Or ♖g8 b1♘+! draws.

2 **...** **♔a1**

3 **♖xb2** stalemate.

If Black has two pawns, then everything depends on the placing of the pieces. If the pawns are advanced and supported by the king, they can often win, but if they are blockaded, the rook wins. Let us consider a few examples:

119
W

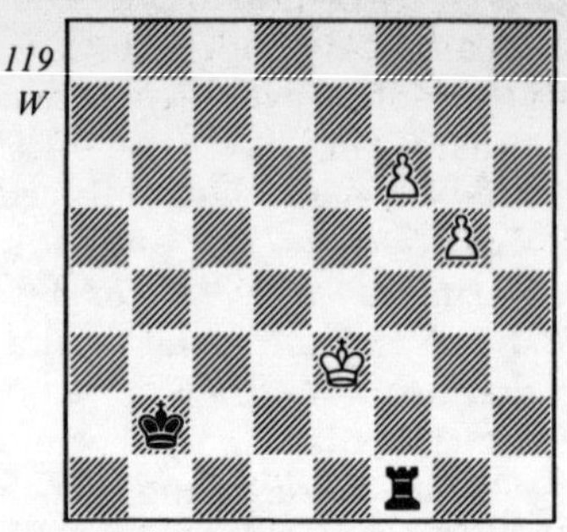

Tarrasch-Janowski 1907

This instructive position occurred in an important tournament game. White has strong passed pawns but they still need the support of the king, as otherwise the rook would simply pick them up by 1 ... ♖f5, 2 ... ♖xg5 and 3 ... ♖f5. As it is, White can support the pawns with his king, but must play exactly.

1 **♔d4!**

Following the principles we have already stated, White advances his king whilst at the same time hindering the black king's approach. Black to move would easily draw by 1 ... ♔c3 2 ♔e4 ♔c4 3 ♔e5 ♖g1 4 f7 (or 4 ♔f5 ♔d5 and Black wins!) 4 ... ♖xg5+ 5 ♔e4 (or 5 ♔e6 ♖g6+) 5 ... ♖g1 6 ♔e5 with a draw.

1 **...** **♔b3**

Black must bring his king nearer the pawns as quickly as possible. Rook moves are useless, for after 1 ... ♖f5 2 ♔e4! ♖xg5 3 f7

♖g4+ 4 ♔e3 ♖g3+ 5 ♔f2 wins.

2 ♔e5

Maizelis subsequently showed that 2 ♔d5! would have made White's task easier. Black's king is kept away from c4, and 2 ... ♖f5+ loses to 3 ♔e6 ♖xg5 4 f7. After 2 ... ♔c3 3 ♔e6 ♔d4 4 f7 wins, or here 3 ... ♖e1+ 4 ♔f7 ♔d4 5 g6 ♔e5 6 ♔g7!

2 ... ♔c4

3 g6

Stronger according to Maizelis is 3 ♔e6! ♖e1+ (as 4 f7 was threatened) 4 ♔f7 ♔d5 5 g6 threatening 6 g7 and after 5 ... ♔e5 or 5 ... ♖g1 6 ♔g7! and 7 f7 wins.

3 ... ♖e1+

4 ♔d6

But not 4 ♔f5 ♔d5! 5 f7 ♖f1+ and 6 ... ♔e6 drawing, or here 5 g7 ♖f1+ 6 ♔g6 ♖g1+ 7 ♔f7 ♔e5 8 ♔e7 ♖g2 etc.

4 ... ♖g1!

In the actual game Janowski played the weaker 4 ... ♖d1+ 5 ♔e7 ♖e1+ 6 ♔f7 and had to resign. On the other hand, the text move poses interesting problems.

5 g7

The only move, as Black draws after 5 f7 ♖xg6+ 6 ♔e5 ♖g5+ 7 ♔e4 ♖g1! etc.

5 ... ♔d4

Preventing 6 f7 when he draws by 6 ... ♖g6+ and 7 ... ♖xg7. Now White cannot win by 6 ♔e6 ♔e4 7 ♔f7 ♔f5, nor by 6 ♔e7 ♔e5 etc.

6 ♔c6!

Threatening 7 f7. If now 6 ... ♖g6 7 ♔b5 wins.

6 ... ♔c4

7 ♔d7!

Profiting from the fact that Black cannot play 7 ... ♔e5. Instead 7 ♔b6 would only draw after 7 ... ♖g6 8 ♔a5 (8 ♔c7 ♔d5 9 ♔d7 ♔e5) 8 ... ♖g5+ 9 ♔a4 ♖g1 10 ♔a3 ♔c3 11 ♔a2 ♖g2+ etc.

7 ... ♔d5

8 ♔e8

And now 9 f7 cannot be stopped.

8 ... ♔e6

9 f7 ♖a1

The last try, threatening mate.

10 f8♘+!

followed by 11 g8♕ winning.

This example has shown us that the rook has excellent defensive chances against advanced pawns, sometimes in seemingly hopeless situations. Our next position reinforces this point.

120

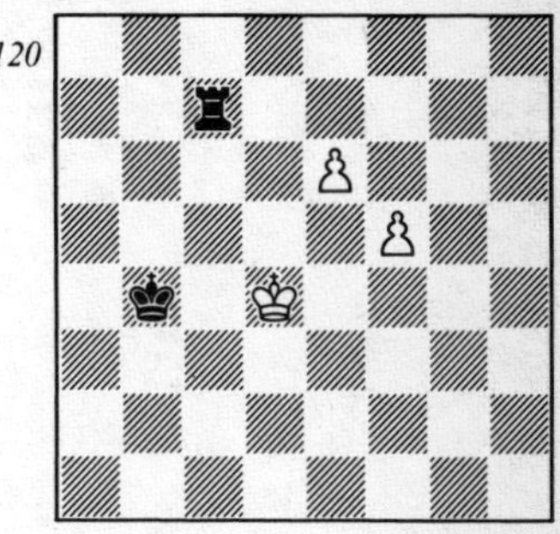

H.Keidanski 1914

Compared to the previous example, the black king is here more favourably placed, whereas the rook is at the moment in rather a passive position, being unable to prevent the threatened f6. Black's first task, therefore, is to improve the position of this rook.

1 ... ♖c1!

Even simpler according to Kopayev is 1 ... ♖c4+! 2 ♔e5 (2 ♔d5 ♖c5+ 3 ♔d6 ♖xf5! or 2 ♔d3 ♖c3+ 3 ♔e2? ♖c8! and 4 ... ♔c5 etc) 2 ... ♔c5 3 e7 ♖c1 giving us the main variation.

2 e7

This move gives the defence the most problems, whereas 2 ♔d5 is harmless after 2 ... ♖f1 3 ♔e5 ♔c5, or here 3 e7 ♖xf5+ 4 ♔d4 ♖f1! etc.

2 f6 is also easier to answer, Black playing 2 ... ♖d1+ 3 ♔e5 ♔c5 4 f7 (or 4 e7 ♖e1+ and 5 ... ♔d6) 4 ... ♖e1+ 5 ♔f6 ♖f1+ 6 ♔e7 ♔d5 7 ♔d7 ♖f6 drawing.

2 ... ♖d1+
3 ♔e5 ♔c5
4 ♔e6

Again 4 f6 ♖e1+ and 5 ... ♔d6 gives an easy draw, or 4 ♔f6 ♖e1 5 ♔f7 ♔d6 6 e8♕ (6 f6 ♔d7 7 ♔f8 ♖e6 etc) 6 ... ♖xe8 7 ♔xe8 ♔e5 draws.

4 ... ♖e1+
5 ♔d7 ♖d1+
6 ♔c7

If 6 ♔e8 ♖f1 and the king must return to the d-file. Or 6 ♔c8 ♖e1 7 f6 ♔d6 8 ♔d8 ♖a1! draws.

6 ... ♖e1
7 f6 ♖e6!

The only move, preventing the threatened 8 ♔d7 ♖d1+ 9 ♔e8 and 10 f7.

8 ♔d7 ♖d6+
9 ♔c8

Not 9 ♔e8 ♖xf6. White now hopes for 9 ... ♖e6 10 f7 winning, but Black has a stronger move.

9 ... ♖c6+
10 ♔b7 ♖b6+
11 ♔a7 ♖e6!

and the draw is clear, for White cannot prevent 12 ... ♔d6 and 13 ... ♖xe7.

We already seen that far advanced pawns can be neutralized or captured by the rook, if they are unsupported by the king. Here is a further example of this:

121

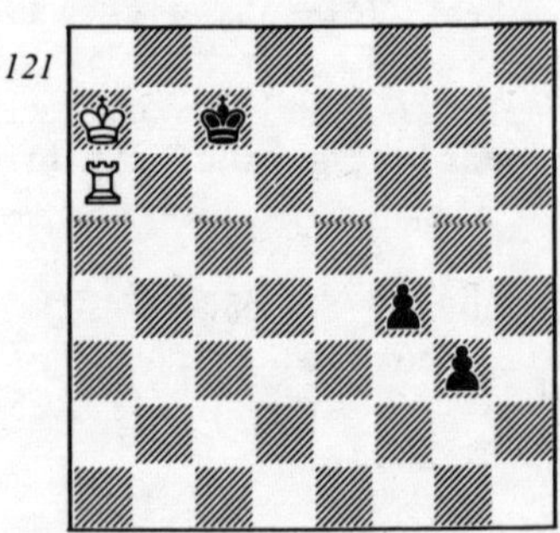

Black to move wins easily by 1 ... f3 or 1 ... g2, but with White to move the rook can destroy the pawns on its own by **1 ♖g6! ♔d7 2 ♖g4 g2** or 2 ... ♔e6 3 ♖xf4 and 4 ♖g4 **3 ♖xg2 ♔e6 4 ♖g5! ♔f6 5 ♖a5** with an easy win, as the pawn can never advance.

Very interesting positions arise when the king is cut off at the side of the board but his pawns are far advanced, as in our next example.

With White to move, the position seems hopeless for Black as the pawns cannot be stopped. However, Black saves himself by using the unfavourable position of

122

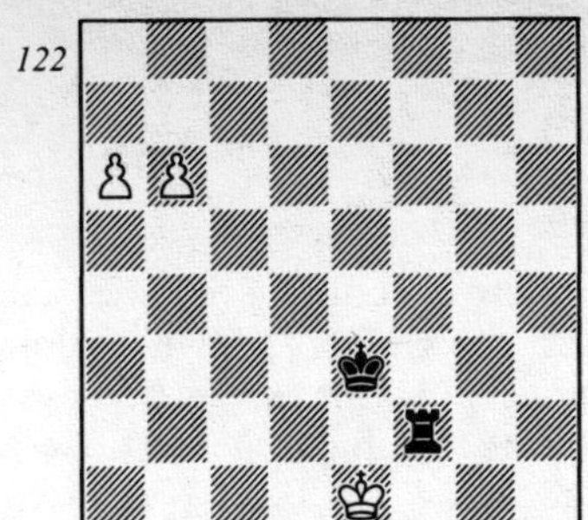

after J.Moravec 1924

White's king which cannot escape the constant mating threats.

1 b7

Similar variations arise after 1 a7 ♖a2! 2 ♔d1 (2 ♔f1 ♔f3) 2 ... ♔d3 3 ♔c1 ♔c3 4 ♔b1 ♖a6 5 b7 ♖b6+ 6 ♔c1 ♖h6! 7 ♔d1 ♔d3 8 ♔e1 ♔e3 9 ♔f1 ♔f3 10 ♔g1 ♖g6+ 11 ♔f1 ♖h6 and White cannot escape the mating threats. An astonishing draw!

1 ... ♖h2!

The only square for the rook. 1 ... ♖b2 loses to 2 ♔d1 ♔d3 3 ♔c1 ♔c3 4 a7 ♖h2 (if 4 ... ♖a2 5 b8♕!) 5 ♔d1 ♔d3 6 ♔e1 ♔e3 7 ♔f1 ♔f3 8 ♔g1 ♖g2+ 9 ♔h1 etc. Or 1 ... ♖a2 2 ♔d1 ♔d3 3 ♔c1 ♔c3 4 b8♕ ♖a1+ 5 ♕b1 wins.

2 ♔f1

If 2 ♔d1 ♔d3 3 ♔c1 ♔c3 4 ♔b1 Black can draw either by 4 ... ♖b2+ 5 ♔a1 ♖b6 6 a7 ♖a6+ 7 ♔b1 ♖b6+ 8 ♔c1 ♖h6! or by 4 ... ♖h1+ 5 ♔a2 ♖h2+ 6 ♔a3 ♖h1 7 ♔a4 ♔c4 8 ♔a5 ♔c5 and the king must return.

2 ... ♔f3

3 ♔g1 ♖g2+

Not 3 ... ♖b2? 4 a7 ♖b1+ 5 ♔h2 ♖b2+ 6 ♔h3 ♖b1 7 b8♕ ♖h1+ 8 ♕h2 winning, but 3 ... ♖h8 is equally possible.

4 ♔h1 ♖g8

5 a7 ♖h8+

6 ♔g1 ♖g8+

7 ♔f1 ♖h8

and White can make no progress, e.g. 8 ♔e1 ♔e3 9 ♔d1 ♔d3 10 ♔c1 ♔c3 11 ♔b1 ♖h1+ 12 ♔a2 ♖h2+ 13 ♔a3 ♖h1 14 ♔a4 ♔c4 15 ♔a5 ♔c5 16 ♔a6 ♖a1 mate, so the king must turn back.

When the pawns are isolated, the rook usually wins, unless they are far advanced. An instructive position from practical play is given in diagram 123.

123
W

Lehner-Rotschild 1881

In the actual game, play went 1 ♖xh7? ♔d5! 2 ♖f7 ♔e4 3 ♔c5 f3 4 ♔c4 ♔e3 5 ♔c3 f2 6 ♔c2 ♔e2 7 ♖e7+ ♔f3! ½-½. White's first move was a serious error for the dangerous pawn is the f-pawn not the h-pawn. He could have won as follows:

1 ♖f8!

Or 1 ♖d8+ ♚e5 2 ♔c5 etc, with the same result.

1 ... ♚e5
2 ♔c5 ♚e4

After 2 ... h5 3 ♖e8+ ♚f5 4 ♔d4 h4 the simplest win is 5 ♔d3 and 6 ♔e2.

3 ♔c4 ♚e3
4 ♔c3 h5

Or 4 ... f3 5 ♖e8+ ♚f2 6 ♔d2 h5 7 ♖h8 ♚g2 8 ♔e3 followed by 9 ♖g8+ with an easy win.

5 ♖e8+ ♚f2
6 ♔d2

6 ♖h8 would waste time after 6 ... ♚e2 when White must play 7 ♖e8+ again, as 7 ♖xh5 f3 draws.

6 ... h4
7 ♖h8 ♚g3
8 ♔e2 h3
9 ♖g8+ and
10 ♔f2

with an easy win.

Endgames with rook against three or more pawns belong to the sphere of the practical ending. Of some interest to us here is the case when the rook is up against three connected pawns, as in our next diagram.

124

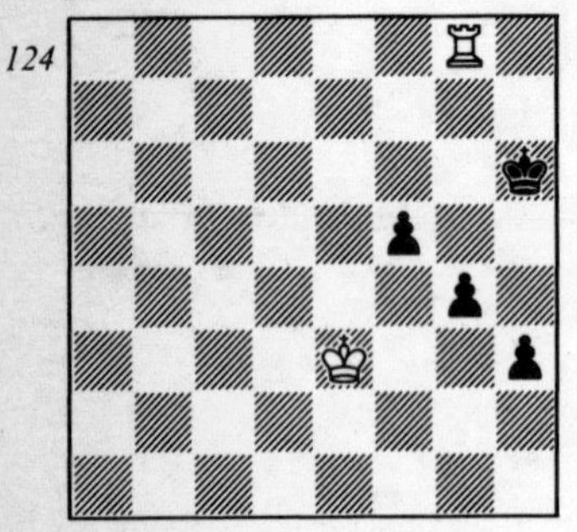

H.Lehner 1887

In this position Black to move is in zugzwang and loses quickly, e.g. **1 ... ♚h7** or 1 ... ♚h5 2 ♔f4 ♚h6 3 ♔xf5 **2 ♖g5 ♚h6 3 ♖xf5 h2 4 ♖f1 g3 5 ♔f3.**

However, White to move can seemingly do nothing decisive, as after **1 ♔f4 ♚h7 2 ♖g5 ♚h6** White cannot capture the f-pawn because of 3 ... h2 winning. If he continues **3 ♖g8 ♚h7 4 ♖a8** Black plays **4 ... ♚g7!** but not 4 ... ♚g6 5 ♖f8! ♚h6 6 ♖f6+ and 7 ♖xf5 winning **5 ♖a6 ♚f7!** not 5 ... ♚h7 6 ♔g5! ♚g7 7 ♖a7+ followed by 8 ♔f4 and 9 ♖a5; 5 ... ♚g8 or 5 ... ♚f8 also lose to 6 ♖a5 **6 ♖h6 ♚g7 7 ♖h5 ♚g6 8 ♖g5+** if 8 ♖xf5 h2 9 ♖g5+ ♚h6 10 ♖g8 ♚h7 wins **8 ... ♚h6 9 ♖g8 ♚h7 10 ♖a8 ♚g7** and we are back where we started. Black must watch that the rook does not reach f8 or, as we shall see later, in some lines g8.

Yet despite all this, White to move can still force a win, as Kopayev has shown in the following fine analysis:

1 ♔e2

White intends to lose a tempo and bring about the same diagram with Black to move. As we shall see, Black cannot prevent this, so diagram 124 must now be assessed as won for White, whoever has the move.

1 ... ♚h5

There is no pawn move available.

2 ♔f2 ♚h4

If 2 ... ♚h6 3 ♔e3 gives us diagram 124 with Black to move, and 2 ... f4 3 ♖h8+ leads to the main line.

3 Rg7 f4

Or 3 ... Kh5 4 Ke3 Kh6 5 Rg8 and again White has achieved his aim. Even the present position was long thought to be drawn, but the following winning plan of Kopayev is convincing enough.

4 Rh7+ Kg5
5 Kg1!

This is the subtle point. White's king heads for h2 to prevent for ever the advance of the pawns. Black will then be forced to play ... f3 when Kg3 proves decisive.

5 ... Kf5

Even easier for White is 5 ... f3 6 Kf2 Kf4 7 Rf7+ and 8 Kg3.

6 Kh2 Ke4

Nor would previous play be any better. After 6 ... Kg5 7 Rf7! or 6 ... Ke5 7 Rg7 Kf5 8 Rg8! White forces 8 ... f3 when 9 Kg3 wins easily.

7 Rg7 Kf3
8 Rg8!

Zugzwang! Black must give up a pawn.

8 ... Ke2

Or 8 ... g3+ 9 Kxh3 Kf2 10 Ra8 etc.

9 Rxg4 f3
10 Re4+ Kf1
11 Kg3

But not 11 Kxh3 f2 with a draw.

11 ... f2

Or 11 ... h2 12 Kxh2 f2 13 Rf4 and 14 Kg2.

12 Rf4 wins.

We can draw various conclusions from this fine piece of analysis. Against three connected pawns, White wins if his king is near and the pawns are no further advanced than the fourth rank. With a pawn on the sixth, Black has good drawing chances, and a pawn on the seventh usually forces White to look for a draw.

125

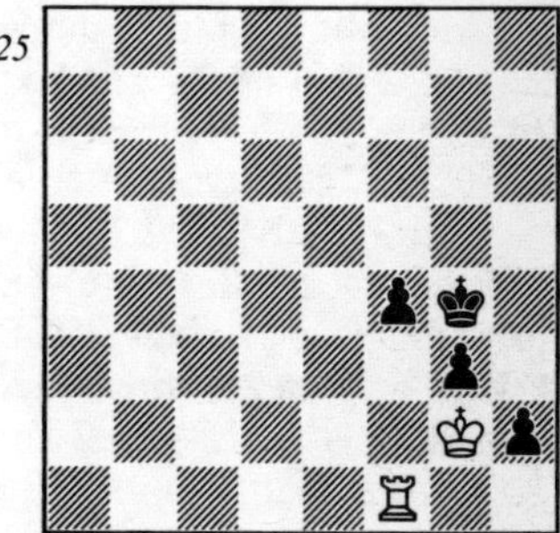

For example in diagram 125 Black to move wins by **1 ...f3+! 2 Rxf3 h1Q+ 3 Kxh1 Kxf3 4 Kg1 g2**. White to move can draw by **1 Kh1!** as **1 ... f3** or 1 ... Kh3 2 Rf3 **2 Rxf3 Kxf3** gives stalemate.

Finally, another interesting study by Réti:

126

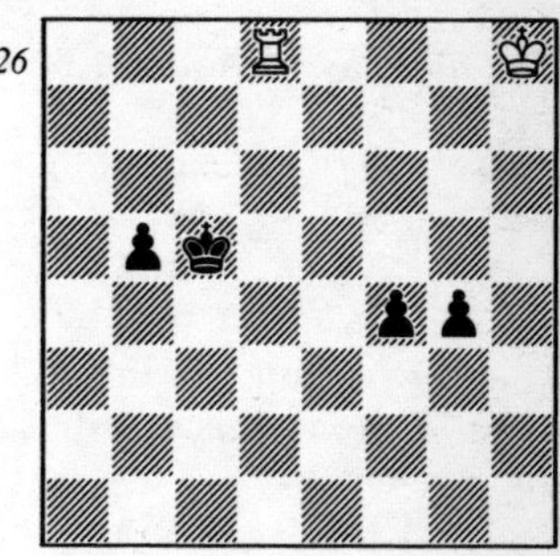

R.Réti 1929

As the white king is far away from the scene of action, his only hope is to draw. To do this he must eliminate at least one of the dangerous connected pawns, but which one is the all-important question. Réti's solution gives us the answer:

1 ♖g8!

The alternative 1 ♖f8 would lose in the following instructive way: 1 ... f3 2 ♖f4 b4 3 ♖xg4 b3 4 ♖g1 (4 ♖g5+ ♔d4 5 ♖g4+ fails to 5 ... ♔e5! 6 ♖g5+ ♔f4, but not here 5 ... ♔d3 6 ♖b4 ♔c2 7 ♖c4+ ♔d2 8 ♖d4+ ♔e2 9 ♖e4+ etc) 4 ... f2 5 ♖f1 b2 6 ♔g7 ♔d4 7 ♔f6 ♔d3! wins. 8 ... ♔e2 is threatened and 8 ♖b1 fails to 8 ... ♔c2 and 9 ... b1♕. We shall soon see the difference between this and the main line.

1 ... g3

The only chance, as 1 ... f3 2 ♖xg4 and 3 ♖f4 wins the f-pawn, and 1 ... ♔d4 2 ♖xg4 ♔e3 3 ♖g5 leads to the capture of the b-pawn.

2 ♖g4 b4
3 ♖xf4 b3
4 ♖f1

The only way of holding both pawns.

4 ... g2
5 ♖g1 b2
6 ♔g7 ♔d4
7 ♔f6 ♔e3

Again threatening to win by 8 ... ♔f2, but White in this case has a satisfactory defence.

8 ♖b1! ♔d3
9 ♖g1! draw.

Black can bring his king no nearer. For White to draw like this, there must be at least four files between the pawns.

We could show many more interesting positions in which the rook has to fight against several pawns, but this would take us too far afield. Let us instead turn to perhaps the most important part of the simpler rook endings, rook and pawn against rook.

Rook and Pawn against Rook

We have already mentioned that rook endings are in practice the most common of all endings and therefore represent an especially important part of endgame theory. For this reason the reader must devote special attention to the following section. In spite of their apparent simplicity, rook endings are in reality very difficult to play well and often contain subtleties which one would hardly suspect at first glance.

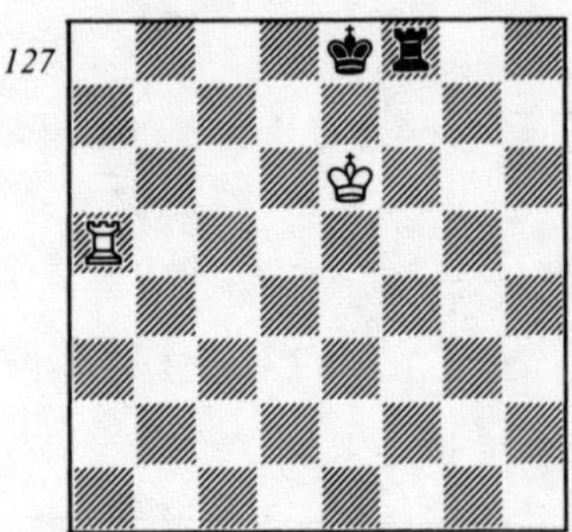
127

Before we proceed to a thorough examination of basic positions, let us briefly consider the few exceptional situations in which rook against rook can win, even without pawns on the board. Of course, this can only happen when a king is in a mating net or when there is a forced win of a rook. For example, in diagram 127, Black loses even with the move, for he must give up his rook to prevent mate. Black equally loses in the position with White's king on e6, rook on a6, and Black's king on e8, rook on f5.

128

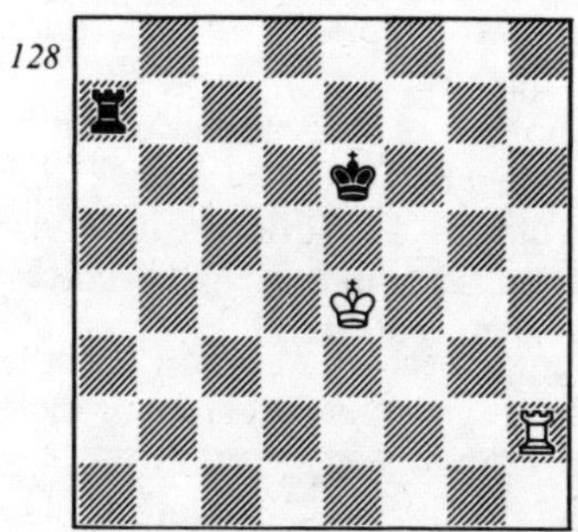

Finally, in diagram 128, White to move wins the rook by 1 ♖h6+ and 2 ♖h7+. Naturally, these exceptional positions usually occur during a more complicated ending rather than on their own (see the Saavedra position), but are worth learning.

The reader will soon see how complicated even the simplest looking ending can be, but these basic positions must be fully understood before more complex positions can be attempted.

This is why a relatively large part of this book is devoted to these endings. Many chessplayers may find it a little dull to study such basic elements but this knowledge is indispensable if any progress is to be made.

We can usually talk of a win only when the defending king is not in front of the pawn and the attacking king is near the pawn. Apart from this, it is difficult to give any general indications about a win or a draw, as the result of each position can often be changed by a slightly different placing of the pieces. This makes it all the more vital for the reader to learn the basic positions thoroughly, so that he understands the various nuances.

Finally, before we look at particular positions, there are one or two general considerations which apply to most rook endings.

Firstly, **the passed pawn should be supported by the king and the enemy king kept as far away as possible, usually by cutting it off by use of the rook along a rank or file.**

Secondly, **the rook is best placed behind the pawn, either to support its advance most effectively, or to prevent its advance whilst maintaining maximum mobility**. These important rules in rook endings will often be applied in the following pages.

Let us begin our examination by considering a classic example, the Lucena position, known almost 500 years ago.

This is a typical winning position when the pawn is on the seventh rank with its own king in front of it and the enemy king cut off. The win is forced by the following characteristic manoeuvre:

129 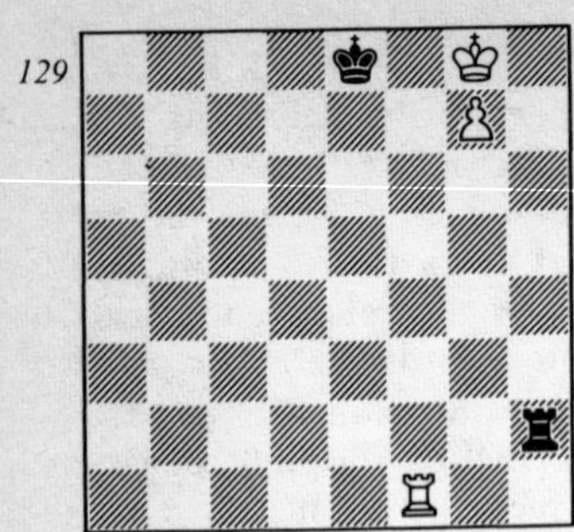

Lucena (?) 1497 (?)

1 ... ♔e7
2 ♖e1+

It is clear the black rook must not leave the rook's file, when the white rook would take it over, allowing ♔h8. White would get nowhere by 2 ♖f7+ ♔e8 3 ♖f8+ ♔e7, as his own king is still tied in.

2 ... ♔d7

A quicker way to lose is 2 ... ♔f6 3 ♔f8, or 2 ... ♔d6 3 ♔f8 ♖f2+ 4 ♔e8 ♖g2 5 ♖e7 followed by 6 ♔f8.

3 ♖e4!

We shall soon see why the rook plays here. Instead 3 ♔f7 would be pointless, for after 3 ... ♖f2+ 4 ♔g6 ♖g2+ 5 ♔f6 ♖f2+ 6 ♔e5 ♖g2 the king must go back to f6.

3 ♖e5 would also win, although the ending after 3 ... ♔d6 4 ♔f7 ♖f2+ 5 ♔e8 ♔xe5 6 g8♕ would offer White more difficulties than the text continuation.

3 ... ♖h1

Black must wait, as 3 ... ♖f2 loses to both 4 ♔h7 and also 4 ♖h4 followed by 5 ♔h8.

4 ♔f7 ♖f1+
5 ♔g6 ♖g1+
6 ♔f6 ♖f1+

White was threatening 7 ♖e5 and 8 ♖g5, and 6 ... ♔d6 loses to 7 ♖d4+ followed by 8 ♖d8 or 8 ♖d5.

7 ♔g5 ♖g1+
8 ♖g4!

Here is the reason for playing this rook to the fourth rank. All checks are stopped and the pawn now queens.

Another classic position must be known before we can move on, the famous Philidor position in diagram 130, in which the black king is placed directly in front of the pawn.

130 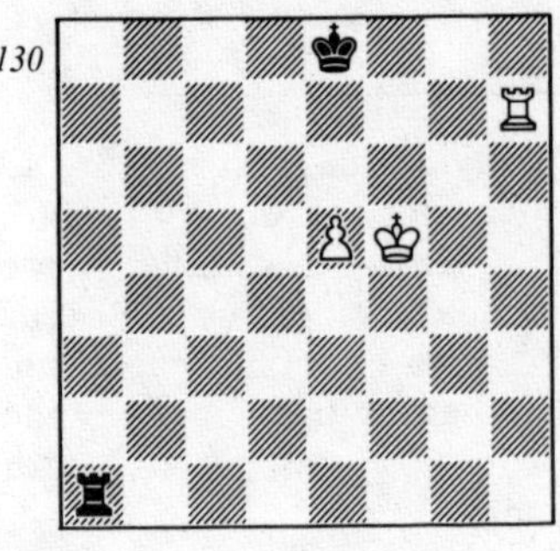

A.Philidor 1777

Such positions are usually drawn but there are one or two exceptions. Philidor demonstrated how the defence should handle this type of ending:

1 ... ♖a6!

Black's plan is simple. He first stops the king's advance so that he can answer checks by playing his king between e7 and e8. If White plays his rook to g6, Black exchanges rooks and draws the pawn ending. To make any progress White must advance his pawn, when Black immediately plays his rook up the board so as to check the white king away from behind.

2	**♖b7**	**♖c6**
3	**♖a7**	**♖b6**
4	**e6**	

Forced sooner or later. White now threatens 5 ♔f6.

4	**...**	**♖b1!**

Now that the e6 square has been denied to the white king, Black's rook can calmly move away. The draw is clear for the white king cannot defend effectively against the coming checks.

White to move could try to win by 1 ♔f6 but does not succeed against best defence which is 1 ... ♖e1! Even Philidor's continuation 1 ... ♖f1+ 2 ♔e6 ♔f8! does not lose, as the composer wrongly assumed. We shall be returning to these possibilities later, after we have looked at some other basic positions.

It seems best to classify these endings according to the placing of the pawn, assuming that the black king is never in front of the pawn.

A: ROOK AND ROOK'S PAWN

With a rook's pawn, White's winning chances are restricted is in front of the pawn. The reason is clear: the king can support the pawn from one side only. However, as many different positions are possible which are difficult to assess, we intend to examine this type of ending in more detail.

131

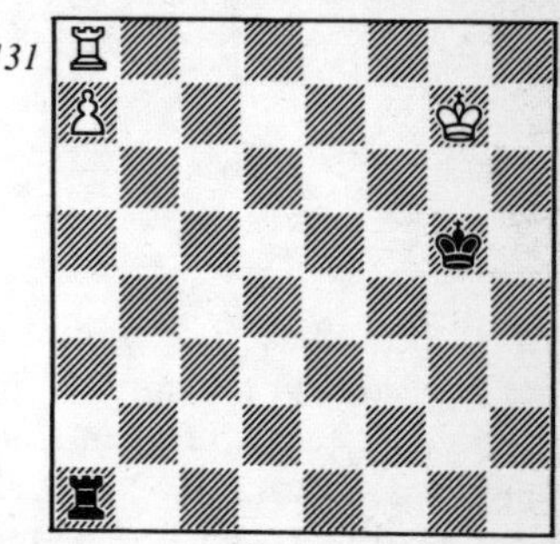

J.Berger 1922

This is perhaps the most unfavourable position for White, with his pawn on the seventh rank and his rook tied to the defence of it, with no freedom of movement at all. White can hope to win only if the black king is badly placed, but even this factor is insufficient here. Play might go:

1	**♔f7**	**♔f5**

Black has little choice, as 2 ♖g8+ was threatened.

2	**♔e7**	**♔e5**
3	**♔d7**	**♔d5**
4	**♔c7**	**♔c5**
5	**♖c8**	

The last attempt, as 5 ♔b7 ♖b1+ followed by 6 ... ♖a1 (+) gets him no further.

5	**...**	**♖xa7+**
6	**♔b8+**	**♔b6** draw.

In such positions Black's king is best placed on g7 or h7, after

132

which White has no winning chances at all. For example, in diagram 132, White can do nothing, e.g. **1 ♔f5 ♖a2 2 ♔e5 ♖a1 3 ♔d5 ♖a2 4 ♔c5 ♖a1 5 ♔b6 ♖b1+ 6 ♔c6 ♖a1** etc. The king cannot guard the pawn without being driven away immediately.

However, if the black king were in a worse position in diagram 131, White could win, as in the following study by Troitsky.

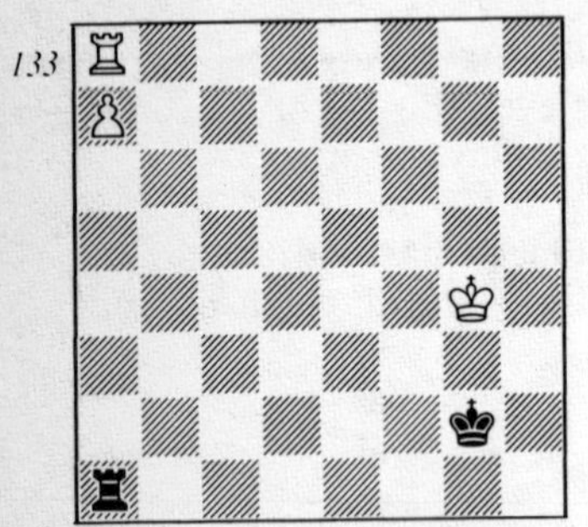

133

White wins by **1 ♔f4 ♔f2 2 ♔e4 ♔e2 3 ♔d4 ♔d2 4 ♔c5 ♔c3** or 4 ... ♖c1+ 5 ♔b4 ♖b1+ 6 ♔a3 and Black has no defence against 7 ♖d8+ **5 ♖c8! ♖xa7 6 ♔b6+**.

If the black rook is placed less actively on the second rank instead of at a1, then White usually has good winning prospects. Here is an example of how to handle such positions:

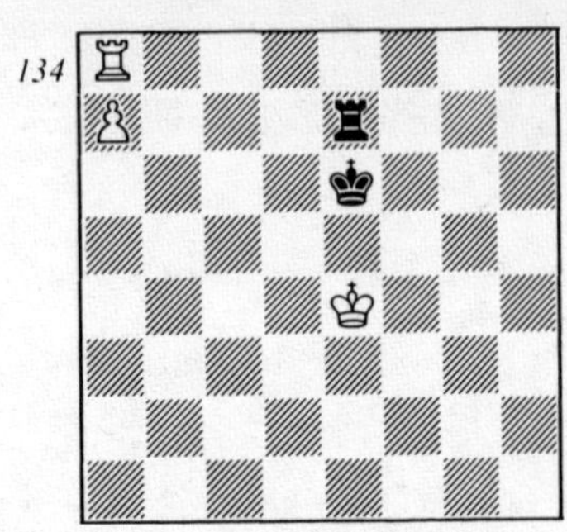

134

A.Chéron 1923

White to move would of course win easily by 1 ♔d4 ♖d7+ 2 ♔c5 ♖e7 3 ♔b6 etc. However, Black to move draws in the following interesting way:

1 ... ♔f6+

Surprisingly enough, the black king has to move away from the pawn; as **1 ... ♔d6+** loses to **2 ♔d4 ♔e6** or 2 ... ♖d7 3 ♔c4 ♖c7+ 4 ♔b5 ♖d7 5 ♔b6, or here 4 ... ♖c5+ 5 ♔b4 winning **3 ♔c5 ♔e5 4 ♔c6!** when Black is in zugzwang, e.g. 4 ... ♔e6 5 ♔b6, or 4 ... ♔e4 5 ♔d6, or finally 4 ... ♖e6+ 5 ♔d7 ♖d6+ 6 ♔c7.

2 ♔d4 ♖f7!

Thus setting up a new defensive position on the f-file. We shall soon see that this file offers him certain advantages compared to the e-file. We have already seen that 2 ... ♔e6 loses to 3 ♔c5, and 2 ...

♖d7+ to 3 ♔c5 ♖f7 4 ♔b6 etc.

3 ♔d5

Or 3 ♔c5 ♔f5 4 ♔b6 ♖f6+ and 5 ... ♖f7 draws. Black cannot be brought into zugzwang.

3 ... ♔f5
4 ♔d6 ♔f6!

Black must careful, as 4 ... ♖f6+ loses to 5 ♔e7.

5 ♔c6 ♔f5
6 ♔c5 ♔f4!

The only move. If 6 ... ♔f6 or 6 ... ♖c7+ then 7 ♔b6 wins at once.

7 ♔b6 ♖f6+
8 ♔c7 ♖f7+
9 ♔c6 ♔f5

White cannot make any progress, as his king cannot simultaneously threaten the critical squares b6 and e6, when he could zugzwang Black. The position is drawn.

These examples have demonstrated how badly placed White's rook is on a8, cutting down his winning chances. Let us now examine positions in which the white king is in front of the pawn.

135

M.Karstedt 1909

This is a typical drawing position. White's king can get out only if his rook reaches b7 or b8, but this gives Black's king time to reach c7 with a drawn result.

1 ♖h2 ♔d7
2 ♖h8 ♔c7
3 ♖b8 ♖c1

Simplest, although 3 ... ♖d1 4 ♖b7+ ♔c6 5 ♖b2 ♖d8+ 6 ♖b8 ♖d1 7 ♖c8+ ♔d7 8 ♖c2 ♖b1 etc, also draws.

4 ♖b2 ♔c8

The position is drawn, as White can make no further progress if Black keeps his rook on the c-file and plays his king to c7 and c8. Leaving this file could be dangerous, e.g. 5 ♖b4 ♖h1? 6 ♖c4+ ♔d7 7 ♔b7 ♖b1+ 8 ♔a6 ♖a1+ 9 ♔b6 ♖b1+ 10 ♔a5 ♖a1+ 11 ♖a4 wins.

White can win only if the black king is at least as far away as the f-file, as in our next example.

136

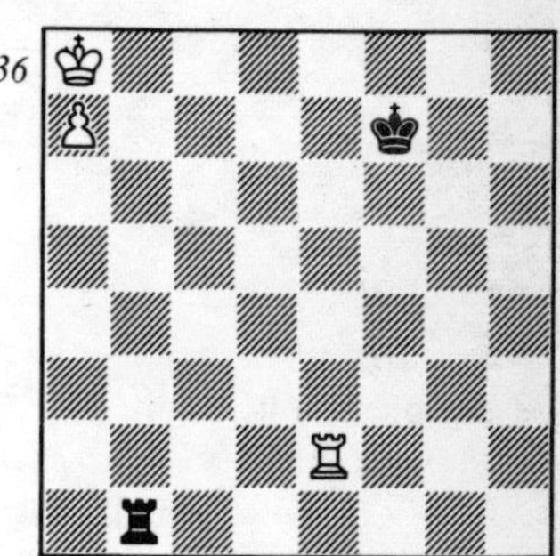

M.Karstedt 1909

The white rook can reach b8 without the black king having time to occupy c7. The winning method is very instructive:

1 ♖c2 ♔e7

2 ♖c8

But not 2 ♖c7+? ♔d8 3 ♖b7 ♖c1! when 4 ♔b8 allows 4 ... ♖c8 mate, so Black draws.

2 ... ♔d6

White wins more easily after 2 ... ♔d7 3 ♖b8 ♖a1 4 ♔b7 ♖b1+ 5 ♔a6 ♖a1+ 6 ♔b6 ♖b1+ 7 ♔c5 ♖c1+ 8 ♔d4 and so on.

3 ♖b8 ♖a1
4 ♔b7 ♖b1+
5 ♔c8!

Now 5 ♔a6 would be waste of time after 5 ... ♖a1 6 ♔b6 ♖b1+ 7 ♔a5 ♖a1+ etc.

5 ... ♖c1+
6 ♔d8 ♖h1
7 ♖b6+ ♔c5 *(137)*

137
W

8 ♖c6+!

The simplest, although 8 ♖b1 would also win after 8 ... ♖h7 (or 8 ... ♖h8+ 9 ♔c7 ♖h7+ 10 ♔b8 ♖h8+ 11 ♔b7 ♖h7+ 12 ♔a6 ♖h6+ 13 ♔a5 ♖h8 14 ♖b8 ♖h1 15 ♖c8+ wins) 9 ♖a1 ♖h8+ 10 ♔d7 ♖h1 (or 10 ... ♖h7+ 11 ♔e6 etc) 11 ♔c7 wins. Not, however, 8 ♖a6? ♖h8+ 9 ♔e7 ♖h7+ 10 ♔e8 ♖h8+ 11 ♔f7 ♖a8 12 ♔e7 ♔b5 13 ♖a1 ♔b6 14 ♔d6 ♖xa7 15 ♖b1+ ♔a5! drawing.

8 ... ♔d5

Or 8 ... ♔b5 9 ♖c8 ♖h8+ 10 ♔c7 ♖h7+ 11 ♔b8 wins, whereas now 9 ♖c8 is answered by 9 ... ♔d6.

9 ♖a6 ♖h8+
10 ♔c7 wins.

Let us now turn to positions in which the pawn is on the sixth rank, and begin with the white rook in front of the pawn.

138

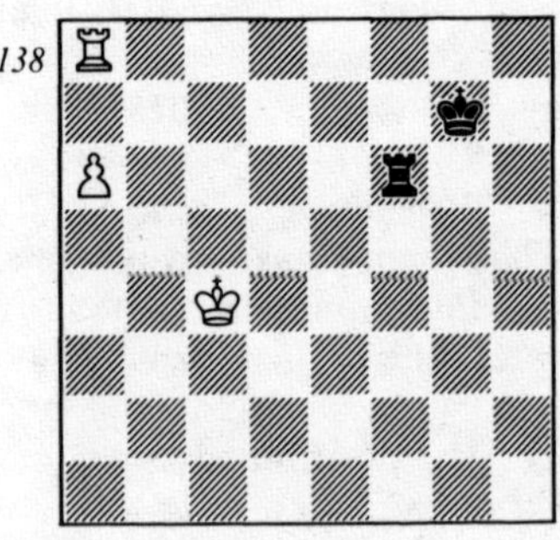

J.Vancura 1924

This is one of the most important drawing positions in this type of ending (the pawn could be further back). It is characterised by the placing of the white rook in front of the pawn, the black king on g7 or h7 and the black rook attacking the pawn from the side. White can make no progress and the position is drawn.

1 ♔b5 ♖f5+

The king must be driven from defence of the pawn, as 2 ♖c8 was threatened.

2 ♔c6 ♖f6+

3 ♔d5 ♖b6

No further checks are required, but the rook must maintain the attack on the pawn.

4 ♔e5 ♖c6

Or 4 ... ♖b5+ and 5 ... ♖b6, but not 4 ... ♖f6? 5 ♖g8+!

5 ♖a7+ ♔g6

Or 5 ... ♔g8. It is clear that White cannot strengthen his position, if Black sticks to his drawing plan. As soon as White plays a7, Black plays ... ♖a6 and draws as in diagram 131.

Now that we are acquainted with this basic drawing position, we can consider a more general set-up in which the win or the draw depend upon the placing of White's king.

139 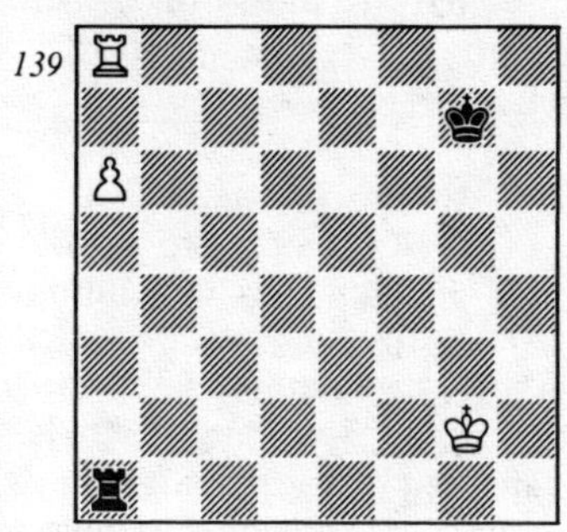

S.Tarrasch 1908

Over the years the assessment of this position has changed. In 1908, Tarrasch gave analysis proving a win for White (in the book of the Lasker-Tarrasch match). Vancura's drawing position (diagram 138) changed all this, and we now know that Black draws with best defence. Let us first ascertain the plans to be followed by both sides.

The first point is whether White has to bring his king across to the pawn quickly to prevent the approach of the black king. As Black must always bear in mind the possibility of a7, his king has to be ready to return to g7 or h7, which means it can to to f7 or f6 but dare not move onto the e-file. For example, **1 ... ♔f7 2 ♔f2 ♔e7 (e6)? 3 a7!** ♔**d7** 4 ♖h8 was the threat 4 **♖h8 ♖xa7 5 ♖h7+** wins. So there is no danger of the black king approaching the pawn.

The second point of interest is whether Black can play passively and allow White's king to reach a7. He cannot, for White wins as follows: **1 ♔f2 ♔h7? 2 ♔e2 ♔g7? 3 ♔d3 ♖a4 4 ♔c3 ♔f7 5 ♔b3 ♖a1 6 ♔b4 ♖b1+ 7 ♔c5 ♖c1+ 8 ♔b6 ♖b1+ 9 ♔a7 ♔e7 10 ♖b8 ♖c1 11 ♔b7 ♖b1+ 12 ♔a8 ♖a1 13 a7**, continuing as in our analysis of diagram 136.

All this means that Black must take active measures if he is to draw. His aim is to reach the drawing position shown in diagram 138, as follows:

1 ♔f2 ♖a5!

2 ♔e3

2 ♖a7+ changes nothing, as Black simply plays 2 ... ♔g6, although 2 ... ♔g8 is possible.

2 ... ♖e5+

3 ♔d4 ♖e6!

and we have reached Vancura's position which we know is drawn.

It would, however, be wrong to

assume from this that all positions similar to diagram 139 are drawn. As we have said, everything depends on the placing of White's king. For example, with the king on the fourth rank, the rook can obviously not use the same method to arrive at Vancura's position.

Is it then essential for Black's rook to gain a tempo to reach the third rank? Why cannot Black leave his king on g7 and play his rook away from the a-file, then back to the third rank? Play might go, from diagram 139, **1 ♔f2 ♖c1**, and as Black is threatening 2 ... ♖c6, White must move his rook. **2 ♖b8 ♖a1 3 ♖b6 ♔f7 4 ♔e3 ♔e7 5 ♔d4 ♔d7 6 ♔c5 ♔c7 7 ♖b7+ ♔c8 8 ♔b6 ♖b1+ 9 ♔a7 ♖c1** gives White nothing (even simpler here 3 ... ♖a3!) so he must try **2 ♖a7+**

Where does Black now play his king? Black loses after 2 ... ♔f8 3 ♖b7 and 4 a7, but draws with **2 ... ♔g6 3 ♖b7 ♖a1 4 a7 ♖a3 5 ♔e2 ♔f6** etc. This means that Black has a second way of reaching Vancura's position, so long as the white king is far enough away. How far must this be then, if Black is to draw? Before defining these limits, let us examine a further position, as seen in diagram 140.

The white king is just near enough to his pawn to achieve the win in the following instructive fashion:

1 ♔d3

The only winning move, as

140

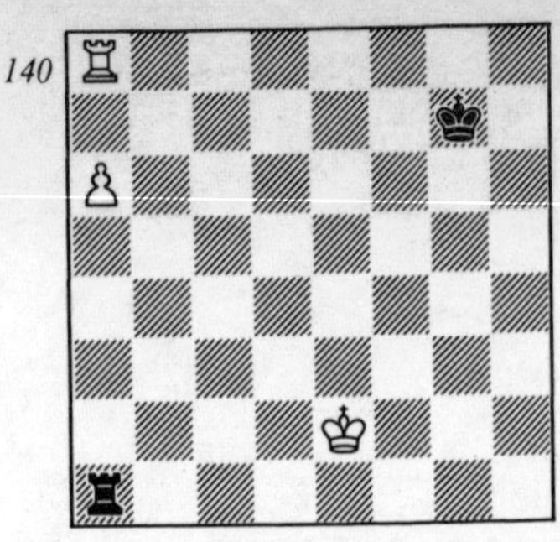

1 ♔e3 fails to 1 ... ♖e1+ and 2 ... ♖e6, and 1 ♔d2 ♖b1 2 ♖a7+ ♔g6 draws for Black, e.g. 3 ♖b7 ♖a1 4 ♖b6+ (or 4 a7 ♔f6 5 ♔c3 ♔e6 6 ♔c4 ♔d6) 4 ... ♔f7 5 ♔c3 ♔e7 drawing. Equally ineffective is 1 ♖a7+ ♔f6 2 ♔d3? ♔e6 3 ♔c4 ♔d6 and Black draws.

This analysis shows that, with Black to move, the position is drawn after 1 ... ♖c1 or 1 ... ♖a5.

1 ... ♖a4

The alternative method 1 ... ♖d1+ 2 ♔c4 ♖d6 fails to 3 ♔b5! ♖d5+ 4 ♔c6 ♖a5 5 ♔b6 winning.

Or **1 ... ♖f1 2 ♖a7+!** not 2 ♖c8 ♖a1 3 ♖c6? ♔f7 4 ♔c4 ♔e7 5 ♔b5 ♔d7 6 ♖c4 ♖b1+ 7 ♔a5 ♖a1+ 8 ♔b6 ♖b1+ 9 ♔a7 ♖b2 etc. **2 ... ♔g6** or 2 ... ♔f6 3 ♖h7! ♔g6 4 ♖b7 transposing; or here 3 ... ♖a1 4 a7 ♔e6 5 ♔c4 ♔d6 6 ♔b5 winning **3 ♖b7 ♖a1 4 a7 ♔f6**, or 4 ... ♖a4 5 ♔c3 ♔f6 6 ♔b3 ♖a1 7 ♔c4 ♔e6 8 ♔c5 or 8 ♖h7 wins **5 ♔c4 ♔e6 6 ♔c5** or **6 ♖h7** with an easy win.

Finally, Black can try 1 ... ♖h1 to prevent 3 ♖h7 after 2 ♖a7+ ♔f6! and to draw after 3 ♖b7 ♖a1 4 a7 ♔e6 5 ♔c4 ♔d6.

However, the rook is badly placed on the h-file and allows White to win by 2 ♔c4! ♖h6 3 ♔b5 ♖h5+ 4 ♔b6 ♖h6+ 5 ♔b7, as the black king now interferes with the rook's action.

2 ♔c3 ♖h4

Black cannot wait, because 3 ♔b3 and 4 ♔b4 is threatened.

If 2 ... ♖f4 3 ♖a7+ ♔f6 4 ♖h7 ♔g6 5 ♖b7 wins as we have already seen.

3 ♖a7+ ♔f6

The point of his previous move. White wins after 3 ... ♔g6 4 ♖b7, whereas now 4 ♖b7 ♖a4 5 a7 ♔e6 6 ♔b3 ♖a1 draws for Black.

4 ♔b3! ♖h1

The black king dare not play to the e-file because of 5 ♖a8 followed by 6 a7, and if 4 ... ♖h8 5 ♖b7 ♔e6 6 a7 ♖a8 7 ♔c4 ♔d6 8 ♔b5 wins.

5 ♖a8 ♖a1

The threat is 6 a7, and 5 ... ♔g7 6 ♔c4 wins, as we saw in our note to move 1.

6 ♔b4

and White wins by playing his king to a7. Black cannot play 6 ... ♔e7 (or e6) because of 7 a7. We have already demonstrated this winning method.

We can now define the zone within which the white king must be situated for Black to draw with the move. Diagram 141 illustrates this.

In order to give an example of correct defence by Black, let us assume that the white king is on f4.

141

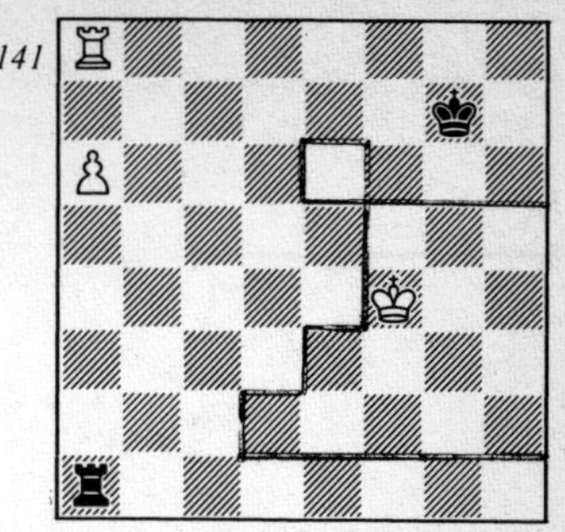

P.Romanovsky 1950

1 ... ♖c1

Black has an alternative and perhaps even simpler drawing method in **1 ... ♖a5! 2 ♔e4 ♖c5 3 ♖a7+** Black threatened 3 ... ♖c6, and 3 ♖b8 ♖a5 4 ♖b6 ♔f7 5 ♔d4 ♔e7 6 ♔c4 ♔d7 also draws **3 ... ♔g6!** but not 3 ... ♔f6? 4 ♔d4 ♖c6 5 ♖h7 ♔g6 6 a7 ♖a6 7 ♖b7 winning **4 ♖b7 ♖a5 5 a7** or 5 ♖b6+ ♔f7 6 ♔d4 ♔e7 etc **5 ... ♔f6 6 ♔d4 ♔e6 7 ♔c4 ♔d6 8 ♔b4 ♖a1** and Black draws comfortably.

However, other moves lose for Black. 1 ... ♖b1 fails to 2 ♖a7+ ♔g6 (or 2 ... ♔f6 3 ♔e4 ♖b6 4 ♖h7 etc) 3 ♖b7 ♖a1 4 ♖b6+! ♔f7 5 ♔e5 as Black is forced into 5 .. ♔e7 6 ♖b7+ and 7 a7 winning.

Or 1 ... ♖h1 2 ♖a7+ ♔f6 3 ♔e4! ♔e6 4 ♖a8! and 5 a7 wins.

Or 1 ... ♖f1+ 2 ♔e5 ♖f6 3 ♖g8+ wins.

2 ♖a7+

As already mentioned, White only draws after 2 ♖b8 ♖a1 3 ♖b6 ♖a5! 4 ♔e4 ♔f7 5 ♔d4 ♔e7 etc. Meanwhile, Black is threatening 2 ... ♖c6.

2 ... ♔g6

The only move. After 2 ... ♔f6? (or 2 ... ♔f8? 3 ♖b7 and 4 a7 wins) 3 ♔e4! ♖c6 (3 ... ♔e6 4 ♖a8! and 5 a7) 4 ♖h7 ♔g6 5 a7 ♖a6 6 ♖b7 ♖a5 7 ♔d4 ♔f6 8 ♔c4 ♔e6 9 ♔b4 and 10 ♔b5 wins.

After the text move, Black again threatens to play 3 ... ♖c6.

3 ♖b7 ♖c5

An alternative drawing line is 3 ... ♔f6! as 4 ♔e4 can be answered by 4 ... ♖a1 5 ♖a7 ♔e6 6 ♖a8 ♔d6 7 a7 ♔c7 etc. After 4 ♖b8 ♖a1 5 ♖a8 ♖a4+! 6 ♔e3 ♔g7 7 ♔d3 ♖f4 8 ♖a7+ ♔g6! 9 ♖b7 ♖a4 10 a7 ♔f6 11 ♔c3 ♔e6 12 ♔b3 ♖a1 13 ♔c4 ♔d6 Black draws.

Notice that this variation does not disprove our indicated drawing zone for the position of the white king, as diagram 141 is only valid with the black king on g7, not e6 as here, after White's 6th move.

4 a7

After 4 ♔e4 ♖a5 5 ♖a7 ♖c5! again threatens 6 ... ♖c6.

Or 4 ♖b8 ♖a5 5 ♖a8 ♔g7 followed by 6 ... ♖c5, and White can make no progress.

4 ... ♖a5

5 ♔e4 ♔f6

and draws after 6 ♔d4 ♔e6 7 ♔c4 ♔d6 8 ♔b4 ♖a1 etc.

Now let us see how White to move can win from diagram 141:

1 ♔e5

Or 1 ♔e4, as illustrated by our zone, with play similar to the main line.

1 ... ♖a5+

Black has no choice, as 1 ... ♖e1+ only helps the white king to reach a7 and 1 ... ♖b1 2 ♖a7+ ♔g6 3 ♖b7 ♖a1 4 a7 wins.

2 ♔d4

We give this continuation because it could also arise from the 1 ♔e4 line. White can also win by 2 ♔d6 ♖f5 3 ♖a7+ ♔f8 (or 3 ... ♔g8 or 3 ... ♔g6 4 ♖e7 wins, whereas now 4 ♖e7 fails to 4 ... ♖a5 5 a7 ♖a6+) 4 ♔e6 ♖a5 5 ♖a8+ ♔g7 6 ♔d7 ♖f5 7 ♖e8 winning.

2 ... ♖b5

3 ♖a7+ ♔f6

Or 3 ... ♔g6 4 ♖b7 ♖a5 5 a7 ♔f6 6 ♔c4 ♔e6 7 ♔b4 ♖a1 8 ♔c5 wins.

4 ♔c4

4 ♖h7 also wins after 4 ... ♖a5 (or 4 ... ♔g6 5 ♖b7) 5 a7 ♔e6 6 ♔c4 ♔d6 7 ♔b4 ♖a1 8 ♔b5 etc. Not, however, 4 ♖b7 ♖a5 5 a7 ♔e6 6 ♔c4 ♔d6 7 ♔b4 ♖a1 drawing.

4 ... ♖b6

Or 4 ... ♖a5 5 ♖a8 and the white king reaches a7.

5 ♔c5 ♖e6

6 ♖h7

and wins easily after 6 ... ♔g6 7 a7 ♖a6 8 ♖b7 etc.

In order to complete our discussion of diagram 141, let us finally examine what happens with the white king on f5. Black draws by **1 ... ♖a5+!** but not 1 ... ♖f1+ 2 ♔e5! ♖f6? 3 ♖g8+, or 1 ... ♖b1 2 ♖a7+ ♔h6 3 ♖b7 and 4 a7 **2 ♔e6** or 2 ♔e4 ♖c5, as already analysed **2 ... ♖h5!** if 2 ... ♖g5, then White wins by 3 ♖a7+ ♔g8

4 ♔f6 ♖a5 5 ♔g6 ♔f8 6 ♖a8+ ♔e7 7 a7 **3 ♖a7+** or 3 ♔d7 ♖h6 4 ♔c7 ♖f6! with Vancura's position **3 ... ♔g8 4 ♖f7 ♖a5!** and now **5 a7?** fails to **5 ... ♖a6+**.

This analysis points to the correct defence with the white king on e6. Black draws by **1 ... ♖h1!** (not 1 ... ♖g1? 2 ♔f5! or 1 ... ♖f1? 2 ♔e5!) transposing to our indicated drawing line.

We can now turn to positions in which the white king has been driven in front of his pawn, beginning with diagram 142.

142

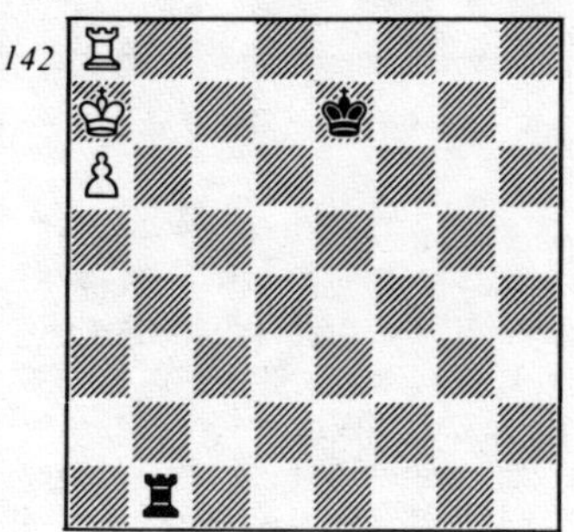

This typical set-up is won for White, if he has the move, as follows:

1 ♖b8! ♖d1

Or 1 ... ♖a1 2 ♔b7 with play similar to our main line.

2 ♔b7 ♖b1+

Or 2 ... ♖d7+ 3 ♔b6 ♖d6+ 4 ♔a5 ♖d5+ 5 ♔b4 ♖d1 6 a7 wins.

3 ♔a8 ♖a1

4 a7

and we have arrived at the main variation arising from diagram 136. White wins easily after 4 ... ♔d7 5 ♔b7 ♖b1+ 6 ♔a6 ♖a1+ 7 ♔b6 ♖b1+ 8 ♔c5, or after 4 ... ♔d6 5 ♔b7 ♖b1+ 6 ♔c8 ♖c1+ 7 ♔d8 ♖h1 8 ♖b6+ ♔c5 9 ♖c6+!

If Black has the move, he draws by 1 ... ♔d7 2 ♖b8 ♖c1 3 ♔b7 ♖b1+ 4 ♔a8 ♖c1 followed by 5 ... ♔c7.

In the same way we can state that the following position is drawn:

143

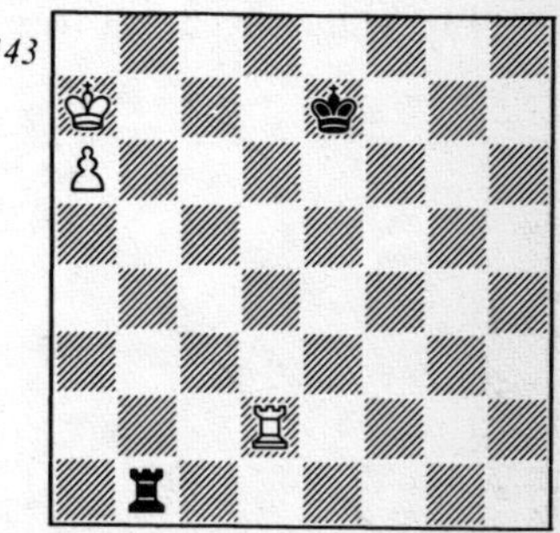

White can do no better than reach diagram 135 by playing ♔a8 and a7. However, if the black king is on f7, with White's rook on e2, then White wins easily by ♔a8 and a7 followed by ♖c2-c8-b8 (see diagram 136).

To complete our examination of positions with a white pawn on a6, let us consider diagram 144.

144

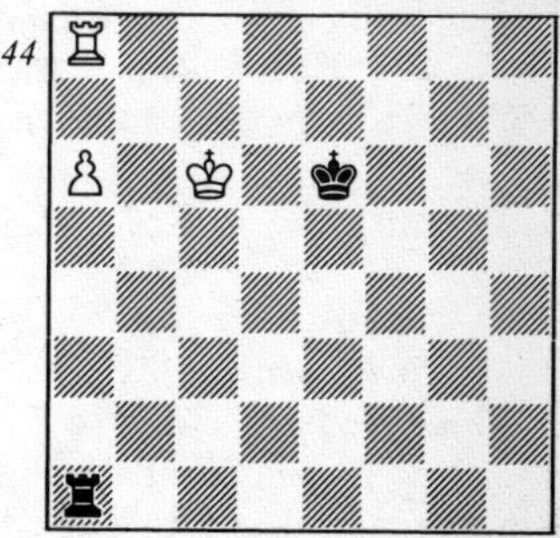

N.Grigoriev 1936

White to move wins at once by 1 a7, but Black cannot save the game even if he has the move.

Play might go:

1 ... ♖c1+

If Black tries 1 ... ♔f7 in order to answer 2 a7 with 2 ... ♔g7! White plays 2 ♔b7 ♖b1+ 3 ♔a7 ♔e7 4 ♖b8, giving us diagram 142, so Black must seek salvation in checks.

2 ♔b5

After 2 ♔b7 ♖b1+ 3 ♔a7? Black draws by 3 ... ♔d7! (diagram 142).

2 ... ♖b1+

The threat was 3 a7.

3 ♔c4

An alternative is 3 ♔a4 ♖a1+ (or 3 ... ♔f7 4 ♔a5 ♖a1+ 5 ♔b6 ♖b1+ 6 ♔a7 ♔e7 7 ♖b8) 4 ♔b3 ♔f7 5 ♔b4, the black king dare not play to the e-file because of a7.

3 ... ♖c1+

4 ♔b3

White wins equally by **4 ♔d3 ♖d1+ 5 ♔e3! ♖d7 6 ♔e4!** not 6 a7? ♔d5! drawing **6 ... ♔d6** or 6 ... ♔f6 7 ♖b8 ♖a7 8 ♖b6+ **7 a7! ♖e7+ 8 ♔d4 ♖d7 9 ♔c4** etc, but an even simpler winning method is **4 ♔b4! ♖b1+** or 4 ... ♖c7 5 ♖h8 **5 ♔a3 ♔f7** 5 ... ♖a1+ 6 ♔b2 and 7 a7 **6 ♔a4** etc.

4 ... ♖c7

5 a7 ♖e7

6 ♔c4 ♔e5

7 ♔c5 wins easily.

If White's pawn is not so far advanced, it is clear that Black's drawing prospects are increased. In general, however, the defensive methods remain the same, except for the fact that Black can sometimes advantageously post his rook in front of the pawn, as shown in diagram 145.

145

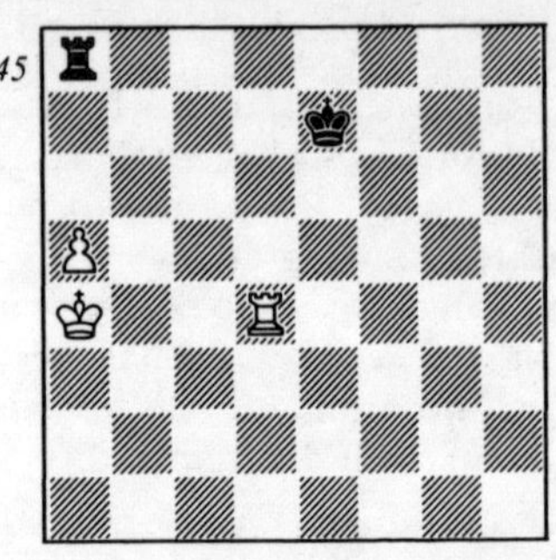

A.Chéron 1927

To all appearances White has all factors in his favour. The black king is cut off and his rook alone cannot prevent the combined advance of White's king and pawn. Despite all these advantages, however, Black can save himself by an extremely subtle defence:

1 ♔b5 ♖d8!

We here see one advantage of the rook being in front of the pawn. Black can offer exchange of rooks, as he would draw the ending after 2 ♖xd8 ♔xd8 3 ♔b6 ♔c8. This means that White's rook is driven from the d-file, which allows Black to bring his king nearer to the pawn.

Note that the careless 1 ... ♖b8+ loses 2 ♔c6 ♖b1 (or 2 ... ♖a8 3 ♖a4 ♖c8+ 4 ♔b7 ♖c1 5 a6 ♖b1+ 6 ♔c7 ♖c1+ 7 ♔b6 ♖b1+ 8 ♔a5 wins) 3 a6 ♖a1 4 ♔b5 ♖b1+ 5 ♔a5

♖a1+ 6 ♖a4.

2 ♖c4

Or 2 ♖a4 ♔d7 3 a6 ♔c7 drawing.

2 ... ♖b8+!

Black must play exactly. After 2 ... ♔d7 3 a6 ♖a8 (or 3 ... ♖c8 4 a7!) 4 ♔b6 ♖b8+ 5 ♔a5 ♖a8 6 ♖h4! ♖g8 7 a7 ♔c7 8 ♖h7+ and 9 ♔a6 wins.

3 ♔a4

Or 3 ♔a6 ♔d7 or 3 ♔c6 ♖c8+ 4 ♔d5 ♔d7, both drawing.

3 ... ♔d7

4 a6 ♖c8

Even simpler is 4 ... ♖b1 5 ♔a5 ♖a1+ 6 ♔b6 ♖b1+ 7 ♔a7 ♖b2 etc.

5 ♖b4 ♔c6

We select the most complicated defensive method for Black in order to show that he draws even this way. There was again a simpler line in **5 ... ♖h8 6 ♔a5** or 6 a7 ♖a8 7 ♖b7+ ♔c6 **6 ... ♔c7 7 ♖b7+** or 7 a7 ♖h5+ 8 ♔a4 ♖h8 etc **7 ... ♔c8!** not 7 ... ♔c6? 8 ♖b6+ ♔c7 9 a7 ♖h1 10 ♖a6! winning, or here 9 ... ♖h5+ 10 ♔a6 ♖h2 11 ♖c6+! **8 ♖b5** or 8 ♔b6 ♖h6+ 9 ♔a7 ♖c6 **8 ... ♖h7** and White cannot make any progress.

6 ♔a5 ♖c7!

7 ♖b6+ ♔c5

The black king cannot now be driven from the c-file, so Black draws. For example **8 ♖b7 ♔c6 9 ♖b1 ♔c5 10 ♖b6 ♔d5** or 10 ... ♖h7 11 ♖b7 ♖h1 12 ♖c7+ ♔d6 13 ♖c4 ♖a1+ 14 ♔b6 ♖b1+ draws **11 ♖h6** 11 ♔b5 ♖c5+ 12 ♔b4 ♖c4+ 13 ♔b3 ♖c7 draws **11 ... ♔c5 12 ♖g6 ♖f7 13 ♖g5+ ♔c6 14 ♖g6+ ♔c5 15 ♖g1 ♖c7 16 ♖c1+ ♔d6** followed by **17 ... ♔c6**, and White is back where he started.

146

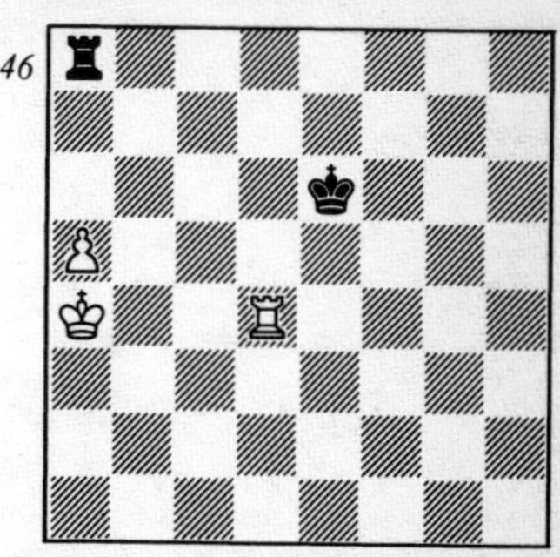

It must be stressed that Black's defence is only possible because of the favourable position of his pieces.

147

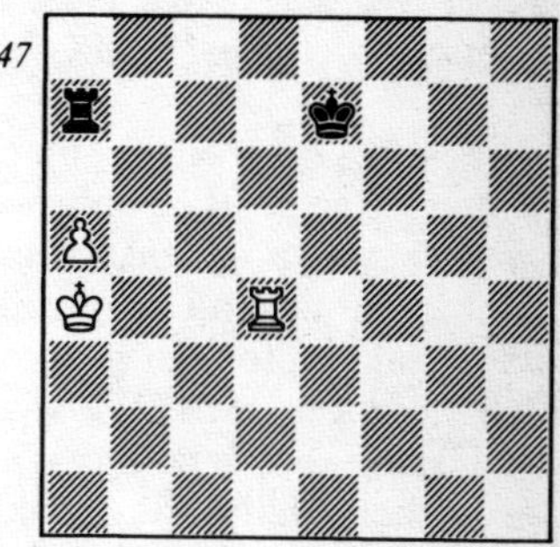

Even slight alterations would allow White to win. For example, in diagram 146, White wins by 1 1 ♔b5. Black no longer has the 1 ... ♖d8 resource. Equally, in diagram 147, White wins by 1 ♔b5 ♖d7 2 ♖a4! since the black king cannot stop the pawn.

If White's rook is, for example, on d2 (diagram 148) his winning

148

chances disappear, even though Black cannot play 1 ... ♖d8. Play might go: **1 ♔b5 ♖b8+ 2 ♔c6 ♖c8+ 3 ♔b7 ♖c1! 4 a6** both 4 ♖b2 and 4 ♖a2 are answered by 4 ... ♔d7 **4 ... ♖b1+ 5 ♔c7** 5 ♔a7 ♔e7 draws **5 ... ♖c1+ 6 ♔d8 ♖a1 7 ♖h2 ♖d1+! 8 ♔e8 ♖g1 9 ♖h6+ ♔d5 10 a7** or 10 ♔d7 ♔c5 11 ♔c7 ♖g7+ etc **10 ... ♖g8+ 11 ♔f7 ♖a8** draws.

There are of course many more interesting positions of rook and rook's pawn against rook, containing subtle and surprising points. However, for our purpose enough has been seen. We shall now consider rook endings with pawns other than the rook's pawn, and shall discover that they offer even more interesting and complex possibilities.

B: ROOK AND PAWN OTHER THAN ROOK'S PAWN

It is clear that these endings offer White more winning chances than was the case with the rook's pawn. Firstly, Black can hardly ever exchange rooks. Secondly, the white king can now support his pawn from both sides, and thirdly, the white rook has more freedom of action, with space on both sides of the pawn. Black thus finds it much harder to draw such positions, and sometimes fails to draw even if his king occupies the pawn's queening square.

We shall systematically examine the most important positions in this type of ending, beginning with the cases where the white pawn has already reached the 7th rank.

a) Pawn on the Seventh Rank

We have already discussed an example of this in Lucena's position (diagram 129), where we showed how White converted his advantage into a win. Let us now consider further basic positions.

149

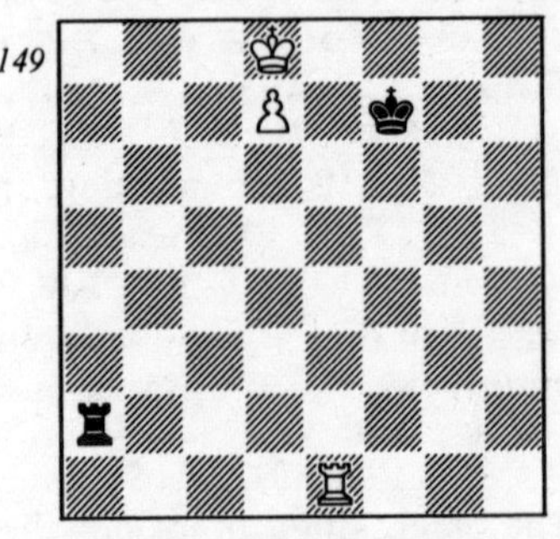

S.Tarrasch 1906

This is a win for White, even with Black to move. As 1 ♖f1+ ♔e6 2 ♔e8 is threatened, Black must immediately begin checking the white king, but this proves insufficient.

1 ... **♖a8+**
2 **♔c7** **♖a7+**
3 **♔c8**

White can also win by 3 ♔c6 ♖a6+ (or 3 ... ♖a8) 4 ♔b7 etc.

3 ... **♖a8+**
4 **♔b7** and
5 **♔c7** wins.

This example demonstrates that Black lost only because his rook was not far enough away from the pawn and this allowed the white king to gain a vital tempo by attacking the rook. If we move every piece, except the black rook, one square to the right (diagram 150), then Black can draw.

150

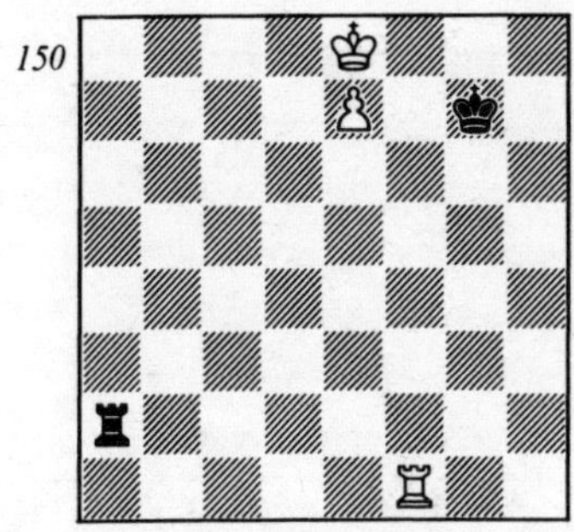

S.Tarrasch 1906

1 ... **♖a8+**
2 **♔d7** **♖a7+**
3 **♔d6** **♖a6+**
4 **♔d5**

Or 4 ♔c7 ♖a7+. Or 4 ♔c5 ♖a5+, or even 4 ... ♖e6.

4 ... **♖a5+**

and the game is drawn, for the white king cannot escape the checks without forsaking his pawn which is then captured by the black rook.

Both these examples show us how Black must defend, but what happens if the position of the pieces is slightly changed? In diagram 149 White wins no matter where his rook is, except on b7.

151

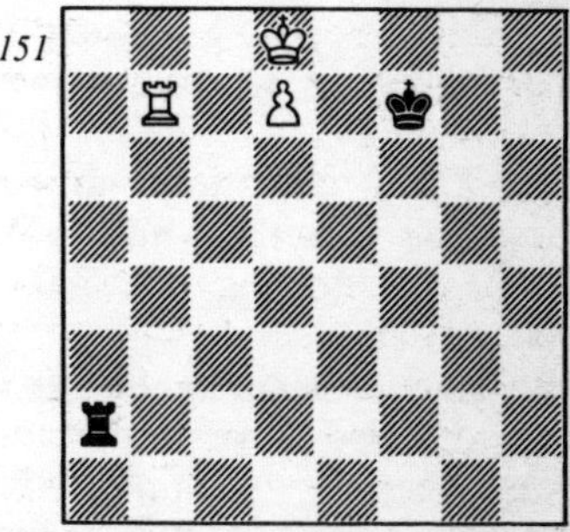

In diagram 151 Black draws by **1 ... ♖a8+ 2 ♔c7 ♔e7!** as the white rook cannot check on the e-file. One might imagine that the same would apply with the rook on b6, but White wins after **1 ... ♖a8+ 2 ♔c7 ♔e7** by playing **3 ♖a6! ♖h8** 3 ... ♖d8 4 ♖e6+! **4 ♖a1!**

Even here, however, Black would draw if he had an extra file for his rook on the queenside.

In diagram 150, matters are not so simple. Admittedly, if the white rook were on the h-file, nothing would be changed, but with his rook on the d- or c-file White would win easily. For example, placing the white rook on c3, we have: **1 ... ♖a8+ 2 ♔d7 ♖a7+ 3 ♖c7** winning, and the white rook on the d-file can interpose either on d8 or, after ♔d7-e6, on d6. The b-file is no good for the rook, as an exchange of rooks would lose the pawn. An exception to this is if the rook is on b8, preventing 1 ... ♖a8+. White wins after **1 ... ♖d2** the threat was 2 ♔d7 ♖d2+ 3 ♔c6, and 1 ... ♖a7 fails to 2 ♔d8 **2 ♖d8** followed by **3 ♔d7.**

White also wins with his rook on the e-file, as his king can simply escape the checks, when the pawn must queen.

Once again, exceptional draws are possible with the white rook on c6 or c7, allowing **1 ... ♖a8+ 2 ♔d7 ♔f7** etc.

Changing the position of Black's pieces can also have important consequences. For example, with the black rook on the b-file (say, b2) White wins after **1 ... ♖b8+ 2 ♔d7 ♖b7+ 3 ♔d8 ♖b8+ 4 ♔c7 ♖a8 5 ♖a1!** followed by **6 ♔d7** wins.

152

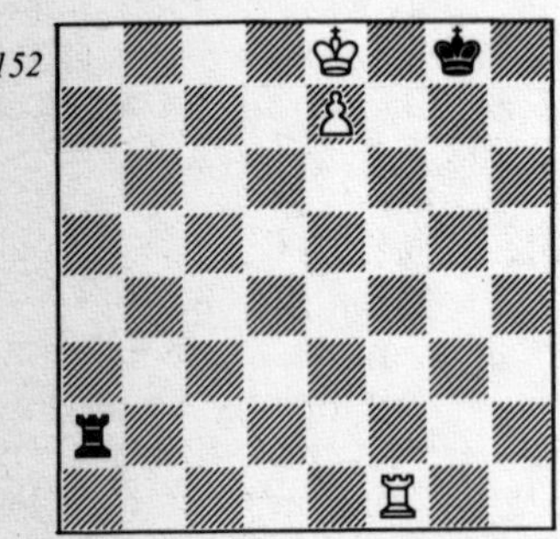

Black is also lost if his king is on g8, e.g. **1 ... ♖a8+ 2 ♔d7 ♖a7+ 3 ♔d6** or 3 ♔e6 ♖a6+ 4 ♔e5 ♖a5+ 5 ♔f6! ♖a6+ 6 ♔g5 ♖a5+ 7 ♔g6 and 8 ♖f6-d6 wins **3 ... ♖a6+ 4 ♔c5 ♖a8** or 4 ... ♖a5+ 5 ♔c6! **5 ♔c6! ♔g7** or 5 ... ♖a6+ 6 ♔b7 ♖e6 7 ♖f8+ – the point! **6 ♖a1! ♖b8 7 ♔c7** followed by **8 ♔d7** wins.

We can generalize about such positions by stating that Black can draw if:

1) his king is on the shorter side of the pawn and not more than one file away,

2) his rook is at least three squares away and can check horizontally, and

3) the white rook stands relatively passively (see notes to diagram 150).

In conclusion, the reader may be interested in the following exceptional position:

153

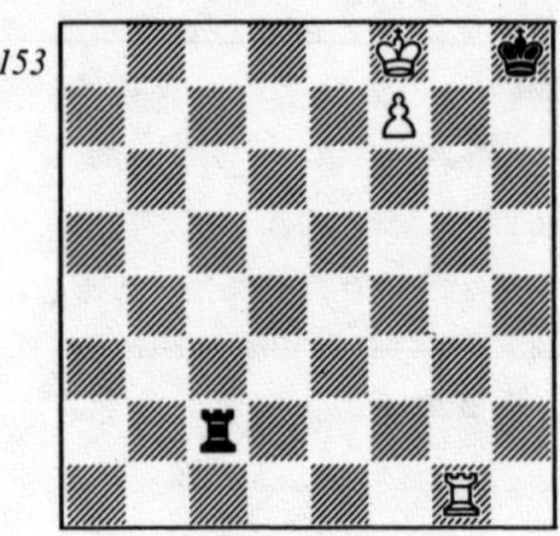

N.Kopayev 1953

At first it would seem that Black can draw this position for, as will be seen, White cannot use the same winning method as in the corresponding position of diagram 150 (black king on g8). However, White can win in the following instructive fashion, by using the fact that the black rook is only two files away from the pawn:

1 ... Rc8+
2 Ke7 Rc7+
3 Kf6

If 3 Ke6 Rc8, White has nothing better than to transpose to the main line with 4 Kf6, as 4 Kd7 Ra8 5 Ra1 fails 5 ... Rb8! (the extra square!)

3 ... Rc6+
4 Ke5!

Our previous winning method does not work here, as after 4 Kf5 Rc5+ 5 Kg6 Rc6+ 6 Kh5 Rc5+ 7 Kh6 Rc6+ 8 Rg6 Rxg6+ 9 Kxg6 Black is stalemated.

4 ... Rc8

Or 4 ... Rc5+ 5 Kd6 Rc8 6 Re1! Kg7 7 Re8 wins. Note that if Black's rook were now on the b-file, he would draw here by 4 ... Rb5+ 5 Kd6 Rb8 6 Re1 Kg7 7 Re8 Rb6+ 8 Kc5 Rf6.

5 Rg6!

The winning move, made possible only because the white king has left the sixth rank.

5 ... Kh7

If 5 ... Ra8 6 Ra6 and 7 Kf6 wins.

6 Rc6 Ra8
7 Kf6 Rb8
8 Re6 and
9 Re8 wins.

b) Pawn on the Sixth Rank

With the pawn on the 6th rank, Black's drawing chances are increased. Although his king must still be no more than a file away from the pawn and on the short side, the position of his rook is not so critical.

Before we examine systematically this type of ending, let us consider an important basic set-up.

154

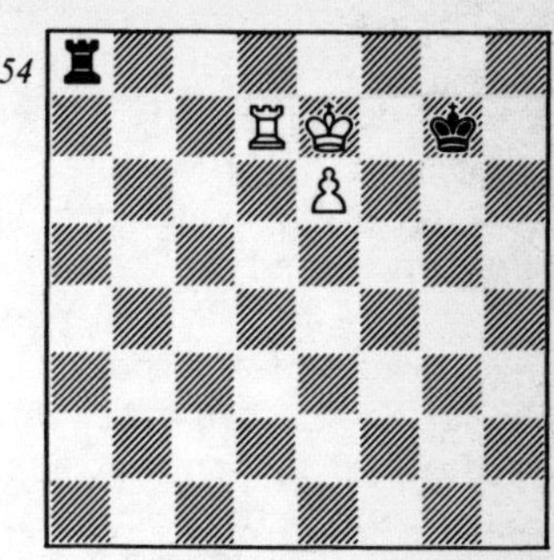

S.Tarrasch 1906

This position is drawn and has three distinguishing factors:
1) the pawn is on the sixth rank,
2) the black king is one file away from the pawn,
3) the black rook is three files away from the pawn.

Play might go:

1 Rd8

After 1 Kd6+ Kf8 or 1 ... Kf6 2 Rf7+ Kg6 Black draws comfortably. Other moves transpose into the main line.

1 ... Ra7+

Black dare not play 1 ... Ra1? 2 Ke8! Kf6 3 e7 Ke6 4 Rb8 Ra6 5 Kf8 winning, but 1 ... Ra6 2 Rd6 Ra8! etc is possible.

2 Rd7

There is nothing better, as 2 Ke8 Kf6 is an immediate draw, and 2 Kd6 Ra6+ 3 Ke5 Ra5+ 4 Rd5 Ra1 5 Kd6 Kf8 gives Black equality.

2 ... Ra8

The rook can play to other squares, except a6, as we shall see later.

3 ♖d6

A crafty move against which Black must defend exactly. Other rook moves on the d-file allow 3 ... ♖a7+ 4 ♔e8 ♔f6 which would now be answered by 5 e7+ winning. Nor can White play waiting moves with the rook, e.g. **3 ♖b7 ♖a1** or 3 ... ♔g6 **4 ♔e8+** or 4 ♔d7 ♖a8 5 e7 ♔f7 transposing, or 4 ♔d6+ ♔f6 5 ♖f7+ ♔g6 **4 ... ♔f6 5 e7 ♖a8+ 6 ♔d7 ♔f7 7 ♖b1** ♖a7+ with a clear draw.

3 ... ♔g6!

The only move to save Black. He would lose after 3 ... ♖a7+ (or 3 ... ♖a1) 4 ♔e8 ♔f6 5 e7+, or here 4 ... ♖a8+ 5 ♖d8, and 3 ... ♖b8 fails to 4 ♖d8 ♖b7+ 5 ♔d6 ♖b6+ 6 ♔d7! ♖b7+ (or 6 ... ♔f6 7 ♖f8+ and 8 e7) 7 ♔c6 winning.

4 ♖d7

Or 4 ♔d7 ♔f6. Or 4 ♖d8 (d1) ♖a7+ 5 ♔e8 ♔f6. White can make no progress.

4 ... ♔g7
5 ♖c7 ♖a1
6 ♖d7 ♖a2

The last moves are played so as to prove that Black does not need to play his rook to a8. Only 6 ... ♖a6? would lose after 7 ♔e8+ ♔f6 8 e7 ♔e6 9 ♔f8!, as Black cannot now check on the f-file.

7 ♔e8+

After 7 ♖d6, threatening 8 ♔e8, Black's only move is 7 ... ♖a8! drawing.

7 ... ♔f6
8 e7 ♔e6!
9 ♔f8

Strangely enough, White cannot win. 9 ♖d1 ♖a8+ 10 ♖d8 ♖a7 gives him nothing.

9 ... ♖f2+
10 ♔e8 ♖a2

½-½

We can now turn to further examples, beginning with diagram 155.

155
B

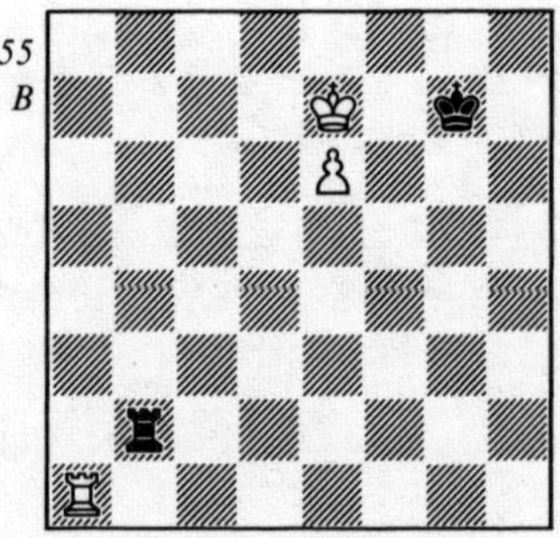

N.Grigoriev 1937

The remaining positions are all with Black to move, as otherwise the white rook would check the king away from the g-file, with a decisive advantage. Despite the fact that Black's rook is not far enough from the pawn, he draws in the following way:

1 ... ♖b7+
2 ♔d6 ♖b6+

Not of course 2 ... ♔f8 3 ♖a8+ or 2 ... ♔f6 3 ♖f1+ etc.

3 ♔d7 ♖b7+
4 ♔d8 ♖b8+

Black checks the king until it leaves the d-file.

5 ♔c7 ♖b2

6 ♖f1

To prevent the threatened 6 ... ♔f8 which Black would play after 6 ♖e1.

6 ... ♖a2!

and Black has obtained the drawn position which we saw in our analysis of diagram 150.

Taking diagram 155 as our starting point, we can now discuss the variations which arise if we change the position of White's rook or Black's king. Nothing happens if we place the rook on the f- or h-files, or on a1-a6, as Black would successfully defend in the same way. However, most other positions of the rook win for White. Diagram 156 has the rook on a7.

156

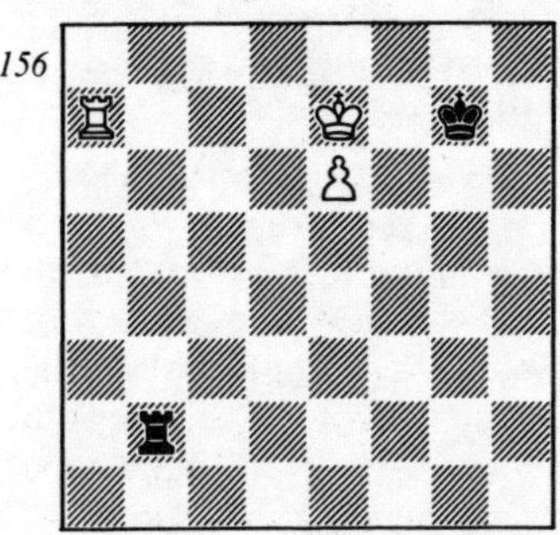

White wins, as Black cannot check on b7, but the winning method is both interesting and instructive. It is worth mentioning that, with the rook on a8, White wins fairly easily. He threatens 2 ♔e8 and 3 e7, and after **1 ... ♖b7+** or 1 ... ♖b1 2 ♔e8 ♖h1 3 ♖a7+ ♔f6 4 e7 ♖h8+ 5 ♔d7 ♔f7 6 ♖a1 wins **2 ♔d6 ♖b6+ 3 ♔d7 ♖b7+ 4 ♔c6 ♖e7 5 ♔d6 ♖b7 6 e7** the pawn queens. Now to our analysis of diagram 156.

1 ... ♖b8!

The best defence. Other waiting moves such as 1 ... ♖b1 or 1 ... ♔g6 would allow White to play 2 ♖a8, transposing to the main variation. The text move prevents this and sets White complex problems.

2 ♔d6+!

The only move. If 2 ♖a1 ♖b7+ draws (diagram 155). If 2 ♖d7 ♖a8 draws (diagram 154), and if 2 ♔d7 both 2 ... ♔f6 and 2 ... ♔f8 draw.

2 ... ♔f6

Black has no choice as the following lines show:

1) **2 ... ♔f8 3 ♔d7! ♖e8** 3 ... ♔g7 4 ♔e7! transposes to the main line, and 3 ... ♔g8 4 ♖a1 ♖b7+ 5 ♔d8 ♖b8+ 6 ♔e7 ♖b7+ 7 ♔f6 wins **4 ♖a1 ♖e7+ 5 ♔d6 ♖b7 6 ♖a8+ ♔g7 7 e7** wins.

2) **2 ... ♔g6 3 ♖a1! ♖b6+** or 3 ... ♖b2 4 ♖e1 **4 ♔d7 ♖b7+ 5 ♔c6 ♖b8 6 ♔c7 ♖b2 7 ♖e1! ♖c2+ 8 ♔d7 ♖d2+** 9 ♔e8 and **10 e7 wins.**

3 ♔d7!

But not 3 ♖f7+ ♔g6 4 ♖f1 ♖a8! etc. The text move brings about a zugzwang position which White wins only because it is Black to move. The reader can check this for himself.

3 ... ♔g7

After 3 ... ♔g6 White wins as in variation 2 in the note to Black's 2nd move, and rook moves quickly lose to 4 e7. However, White now seems to be in difficulties.

4 ♔e7!

Another subtle move, again placing Black in zugzwang. Not of course 4 ♖a1 ♖b7+ drawing (diagram 155).

4 ... ♖b1

After 4 ... ♔g6 5 ♖a1 ♖b7+ 6 ♔d6 we again arrive at variation 2 in the notes to Black's 2nd move, and after 4 ... ♔g8 5 ♔f6 (or 5 ♖a1) 5 ... ♖f8+ 6 ♔g6 ♖b8 7 ♖g7+ ♔h8 8 ♖f7 ♔g8 9 e7 wins. If 4 ... ♖c8 5 ♖a1 ♖c7+ 6 ♔d8 and 7 e7 wins.

5 ♖a8!

and we have finally obtained diagram 156 with the white rook on a8, already analysed as a win. A very fine sequence of moves worthy of an endgame study.

If we place the white rook on c1, we have the position given in diagram 157.

157

This is a win for White, as are all placings of the rook on the c-file, except c4, c5 and c6. We shall see later why these squares only lead to a draw.

1 ... ♖b7+
2 ♔d8

This move would only draw with the white rook on c8 (2 ... ♔f6), but in that case 2 ♔d6 ♖b6+ 3 ♔d7 ♖b7+ 4 ♔c6 wins easily. With the rook on c4 or c5, 2 ♔d8 allows Black to draw by 2 ... ♔f6 3 e7 ♖xe7! 4 ♖f4+ ♔e5 etc.

An alternative winning method is **2 ♔d6 ♖b6+ 3 ♔d7** not 3 ♖c6 ♖b8! 4 ♖c1 ♔f8!, or here ♔f6 drawing in both cases **3 ... ♖b7+** with the white rook on c4 or c5, 3 ... ♔f6! draws **4 ♖c7 ♖b8 5 ♖c8! ♖b7+ 6 ♔c6** winning easily.

2 ... ♔f6

With the white rook on c6, Black could now draw 2 ... ♔f8! and on the previous move, after 2 ♔d6, by 2 ... ♔f6! If instead 2 ... ♖b8+ then 3 ♖c8 wins quickly.

3 e7!

Only this subtle move can win for White.

3 ... ♖b8+
4 ♔d7

Also possible is 4 ♔c7 ♖a8 5 ♖a1! ♖e8 6 ♔d6, or here 4 ... ♖e8 5 ♔d6 ♖a8 6 ♖f1+ ♔g7 7 ♖a1! winning.

4 ... ♖b7+
5 ♔d6 ♖b6+

Or 5 ... ♖b8 6 ♖f1+ ♔g7 7 ♔c7 ♖a8 8 ♖a1! wins.

6 ♔c7! ♖e6
7 ♔d8 ♖d6+
8 ♔e8 and wins easily.

If the white rook in diagram 157 is placed on e1. White wins after **1 ... ♖b7+ 2 ♔d8 ♖b8+ 3 ♔d7!** not 3 ♔c7? ♖a8! drawing **3 ... ♖b7+ 4 ♔c8 ♖e7 5 ♔d8** etc. However, with the white rook on e5, we have an exceptional draw, as in this final position Black could play **5 ... ♔f6!** It is also known that, with the white rook on e8, Black can draw by **1 ... ♖a2!**

Diagram 158 illustrates the white rook on the d-file.

158

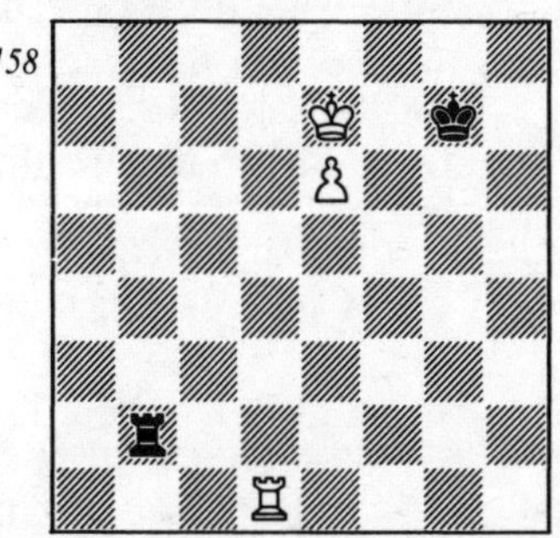

Again this is won for White, on whichever square on the file rook is placed, the only exception being d7 when Black draws by 1 ... ♖a2! (see the analysis to diagram 154).

1 ... ♖b7+

With the white rook on d5, Black could try **1 ... ♔g6** but White still wins by **2 ♖d8** or 2 ♖d1 **2 ... ♖b7+** the threat was 3 ♔e8, and 2 ... ♔f5 loses to 3 ♔f7 **3 ♖d7 ♖b8** or 3 ... ♖b6 4 ♖a7 ♔f5 5 ♖a5+ ♔g6 6 ♖a1! ♖b7+ 7 ♔d8 ♖b8+ 8 ♔c7 ♖b2 9 ♖e1! winning, a position we shall come back to later **4 ♖a7! ♔g7** and White wins, as we saw from diagram 156, with 5 ♔d6+ ♔f6 6 ♔d7! ♔g7 7 ♔e7!

2 ♖d7 ♖b1

Transposition would occur after 2 ... ♖b8 3 ♖d8 ♖b7+ 4 ♔d6, and 2 ... ♖b6 fails to 3 ♔e8+ ♔f6 4 e7 ♔e6 5 ♔f8!

3 ♖d8

Threatening 4 ♔e8 which cannot be played at once because of 3 ... ♔f6 4 e7 ♔e6! drawing.

3 ... ♖b7+

4 ♔d6 ♖b6+

Black is unable to prevent the threatened 5 e7 by 4 ... ♔f6 as 5 ♖f8+ and 6 e7 follows.

5 ♔d7 ♖b7+

6 ♔c6 ♖e7

Or 6 ... ♖a7 7 ♖d7+ wins.

7 ♔d6 wins.

We have now analysed all possible displacements of the white rook in diagram 155. To summarize our conclusions: White wins if his rook stands on the c-, d-, e- or g-files, with the exception of White's c4, c5, c6, e5 and e8 squares. He also wins with his rook placed on a7 or a8. All other positions of the rook give Black a draw with correct defence.

Let us now change diagram 155 by moving the black king to g6. This slight alteration can sometimes be vitally important and lead to different treatment of the position. Diagram 159 can be our starting point for a discussion of this.

159

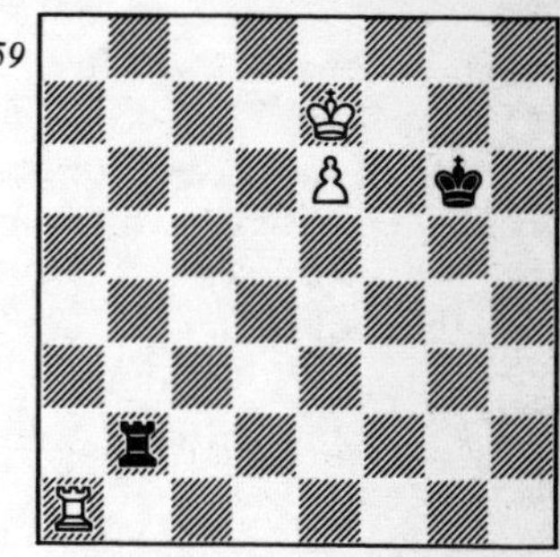

N.Grigoriev 1937

Although with the black king on g7 this position was drawn, it is now a win for White as follows:

1 ... ♖b7+

Forced, as White was threatening 2 ♖g1+ ♔f5 3 ♔f7 winning.

2 ♔d8 ♖b8+

After 2 ... ♔f6 3 e7 ♖b8+ White wins either by 4 ♔c7 ♖e8 5 ♔d6 ♖b8 6 ♖f1+ ♔g7 7 ♔c7 ♖a8 8 ♖a1! or by 4 ♔d7 ♖b7+ 5 ♔d6 ♖b6+ 6 ♔c7 ♖e6 7 ♔d8 ♖d6+ 8 ♔e8 etc.

If the white rook were on a5, Black would draw by 2 ... ♔f6 (even after 2 ♔d6). We shall return later to the drawing position with the rook on a4 and a6.

3 ♔c7 ♖b2

4 ♖e1!

Here lies the difference! With his king on g7, Black could play 4 ... ♔f8, whereas now the pawn cannot be stopped. Not however 4 ♖f1 ♖a2! drawing, as we saw in our analysis of diagram 150.

4 ... ♖c2+

5 ♔d7 ♖d2+

6 ♔e8 and

7 e7 winning easily.

With White's rook on a4 (or a6), the position is drawn after **1 ... ♖b7+ 2 ♔d8** or 2 ♔d6 ♖b6+ 3 ♔d7 ♔f6! 4 ♖f4+ ♔e5, or here 4 ♖a1 ♖b7+! With the white rook on a6, 2 ♔d6 ♔f6! draws **2 ... ♔f6!** or, with the rook on a6, 2 ... ♖b8+ 3 ♔c7 ♖b1 as White cannot play his rook to the e-file. In this position, however, 2 ... ♖b8+ loses to 3 ♔c7 ♖b1 4 ♖e4! **3 ♖e4** or 3 e7 ♖xe7! **3 ... ♖b8+ 4 ♔d7** or 4 ♔c7 ♖a8! **4 ... ♖b7+ 5 ♔d6 ♖b6+** and Black draws, as is clear.

The position is equally drawn with White's rook on the f- or h-files. For instance, with the rook on f1, Black defends by **1 ... ♖b7+ 2 ♔d8 ♖b8+ 3 ♔c7 ♖a8!** drawing as in the play from diagram 150.

With the rook on the c-, d- or e-files, White wins as from diagram 155, but there are two noteworthy differences:

Firstly, White now wins with his rook on c6 after **1 ... ♖b7+** or 1 ... ♖b8 2 ♖c1 ♖b7+ 3 ♔d8 ♖b8+ 4 ♖c8 and 5 e7, or here 3 ... ♔f6 4 e7 ♖b8+ 5 ♔d7 ♖b7+ 6 ♔d6 ♖b6+ 7 ♔c7 ♖e6 8 ♔d8 **2 ♔d8 ♖b8+** Black no longer has the saving 2 ... ♔f8! **3 ♖c8** and **4 e7** winning easily.

Secondly, and this time in Black's favour, White cannot now win if his rook is on e4, as it is too near the pawn. Play might go: **1 ... ♖a2!** This draws equally against the rook on e5, but with the rook on e8 Black draws by 1 ... ♖b7+ 2 ♔d6 ♖b6+ 3 ♔d7 ♖b7+ 4 ♔c6 ♖a7 **2 ♖g4+** otherwise Black reaches the drawing position seen in diagram 154 **2 ... ♔f5 3 ♖d4** if the white rook were not attacked 3 ♔f7 would now win **3 ... ♔e5!** but not 3 ... ♔g6 4 ♔e8! followed by 5 e7, or 3 ... ♖a7+ 4 ♖d7 ♖a6 5 ♖d6 ♖a7+ 6 ♔f8 winning **4 ♖d1 ♖a7+ 5 ♖d7 ♖a6** and Black draws.

With other rook positions, the winning method is the same as against the black king on g7, except with the rook on the d-file. In this case, White has more problems, as we see in diagram 160.

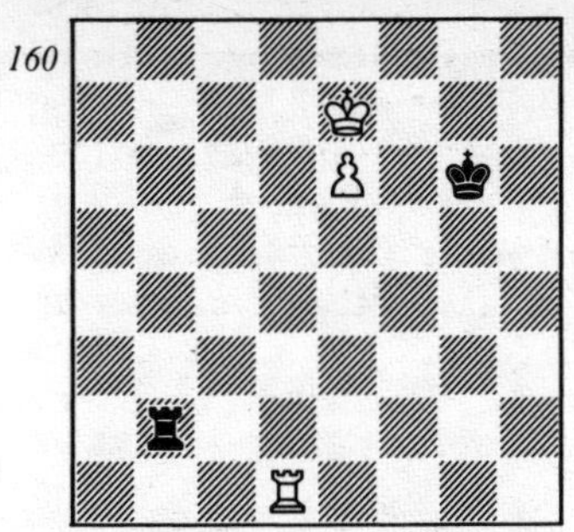

1	...	♖b7+

With the white rook on d5, Black would draw by 1 ... ♖a2! 2 ♔e8 ♔f6 3 e7 ♔e6!, and 1 ... ♖a2! also draws against the rook on d7.

White wins, however, with his rook on d4, after 1 ... ♖a2 2 ♔e8! ♔f6 3 e7 ♔e6 4 ♖e4+ etc.

2 ♖d7 ♖b8

Or 2 ... ♖b6 3 ♖a7 ♔f5 4 ♖a5+ ♔g6 5 ♖a1 winning as in diagram 159. Or 2 ... ♖b1 3 ♖a7 again wins.

3 ♖a7!

In diagram 158 (with Black's king on g7) White could win easily here by 3 ♖d8 ♖b7+ 4 ♔d6 ♖b6+ 5 ♔d7 ♖b7+ 6 ♔c6 etc, but now 6 ... ♖a7! would draw as 7 ♖d7 would no longer be check. This means that White has to choose a longer way.

3 ... ♔g7

and we arrive at diagram 156 (with Black's best defensive move 1 ... ♖b8). As we saw there, White wins by 4 ♔d6+ ♔f6 5 ♔d7! ♔g7 6 ♔e7! ♖b1 7 ♖a8 ♖b7+ 8 ♔d6 ♖b6+ 9 ♔d7 ♖b7+ 10 ♔c6 ♖e7 11 ♔d6 ♖b7 12 e7 etc. The reader must refer back to diagram 156 for detailed analysis of this important line.

To summarize our conclusions: White can win from diagram 159 if his rook is on the a-, c-, d-, e- or g-files, with exception of his a4, a5, a6, c4, c5, d5, d7, e4, e5 and e8 squares. The game is drawn if the rook is on these squares or the f- or h-files.

We have devoted a fair amount of space to endings with the pawn on the sixth rank, but not without good reason. Such positions form the basis of all endings with rook and pawn against rook, and therefore need to be known in some detail, with all their refinements. Time spent on acquiring this knowledge is by no means wasted.

If all these positions were moved one file to the right, it is clear that Black's drawing chances would be increased, as his rook would have more manoeuvring space. However, the basic treatment of such positions remains the same. To complete our discussion, let us consider an example where the black king is situated on the wrong (i.e. the longer) side of the pawn.

The main result is that the black rook is short of space for effective horizontal checking. Black loses, even with the move, as follows:

161

1 ... ♖a1

Black could draw, if he had another move, by 1 ... ♖a7+ 2 ♔c6 ♖a6+ 3 ♔b7 ♖a1! etc. Equally, Black could draw, if his king were on b7, by 1 ... ♖h1! (diagram 154).

2 ♖c8 ♖a7+

White threatened 3 ♔d8 and 4 d7.

3 ♔c6 ♖a6+
4 ♔c7 ♖a7+
5 ♔b6 ♖d7
6 ♔c6 wins.

c) Pawn on the Second to the Fifth Ranks

The further back the pawn is, Black's drawing chances are correspondingly increased. We do not intend to discuss all possible positions sysematically, as this would take us too far, considering the wealth of material available. The main point to remember is that Black continues to use the same defensive resources we have already mentioned, and with a greater chance of success.

With the pawn on the fifth rank, however, new positions arise in which Black's king occupies or threatens to occupy the queening square of the pawn. In this respect diagram 162 is of great practical value.

162

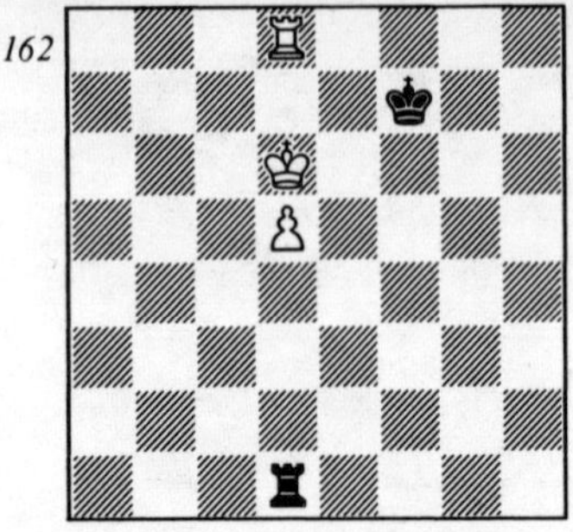

Kling and Horwitz 1851

This position was analysed more than a century ago and was found to contain an important defensive resource. First of all let us see how White, to move, wins:

1 ♔c7!

The only move. After 1 ♖a8 ♖d2 2 ♔c6 ♔e7! Black draws, as we shall show in our analysis of Black to move. An immediate 1 ♔c6 fails to 1 ... ♔e7 2 ♖d7+ ♔e8.

1 ... ♖a1

Or 1... ♖c1+ 2 ♔d7 ♖a1 3 ♖c8 and 4 d6 winning as in diagram 161.

2 ♖b8!

In our analysis to diagram 161 we have already shown that 2 d6? ♖a7+ 3 ♔b6 ♖a1 leads to a draw.

2 ... ♖a7+
3 ♖b7 ♖a8
4 ♔d7!

Not 4 d6? ♔e6 5 d7 ♔e7

drawing. Black can now play only waiting moves.

4 ... ♔f6
5 d6 ♔f7
6 ♖b1

Many roads now lead to Rome. Kling and Horwitz continued 6 ♖c7 ♔f6 7 ♖c1 ♖a7+ 8 ♔c6 ♖a6+ 9 ♔c7 ♖a4 10 ♖d1, whereas Levenfish and Smyslov recommend 6 ♔c6+ ♔e8 (or 6 ... ♔f6 7 ♖e7) 7 ♔c7 ♔f7 8 ♖b8 ♖a7+ 9 ♔b6. However, the text move seems the most logical.

6 ... ♖a7+
7 ♔c8

Or 7 ♔c6 ♖a6+ 8 ♔c7 ♖a7+ 9 ♖b7 ♖a8 10 ♖b8 wins.

7 ... ♔e6
8 d7 ♖a8+
9 ♔b7 ♖d8
10 ♔c6 wins easily.

This winning method shows us nothing new, but the position with Black to move contains an interesting and instructive drawing line:

1 ... ♖a1!

In order to prevent 2 ♔c7. As we saw in our analysis to diagram 161, White cannot allow horizontal checks by the rook.

2 ♖c8

Black now seems lost, for after 2 ... ♖a6+ 3 ♔d7 ♖a7+ 4 ♖c7 White wins as shown above, and otherwise there seems no defence to the threatened ♔d7 followed by d6.

2 ... ♖d1!

The solution! Now that the white rook has left d8, the black rook immediately switches to the d-file to prevent the advance of the pawn. A simple but most effective move, well worth remembering, as it often occurs in more complex positions.

3 ♖c2

The point of Black's plan is that 3 ♔c6 ♔e7! holds up the pawn, and after 4 ♖c7+ ♔d8 5 ♖h7 ♖d2! 6 ♔d6 ♔c8 7 ♖h8+ ♔b7 we have arrived at a position similar to the diagram.

White makes no progress either after 3 ♖c5 ♔e8 4 ♔c7 ♔e7 etc.

3 ... ♔e8!

Just in time to prevent White from cutting him off by 4 ♖e2, with a winning position.

4 ♖a2 ♖d3

Black cannot move his king, when 5 ♖e2 follows, and if the rook leaves the d-file, White wins by 5 ♖a8+ and 6 ♔d7 etc.

5 ♖a8+ ♔f7
6 ♖a7+

Or 6 ♔c6 ♔e7! Or 6 ♖d8 ♖a3!

6 ... ♔e8

and White can make no further progress.

163

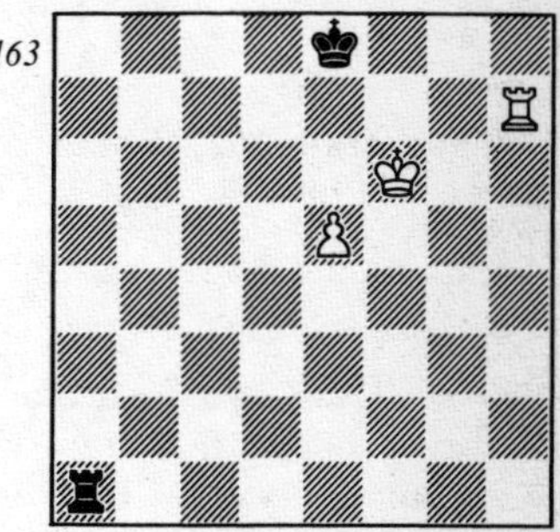

A.Philidor 1777

We can now turn to a version of Philidor's position (diagram 130) and follow his analysis, in which he wrongly evaluates the position as won for White.

Philidor's analysis runs:

1 ... ♖f1+?

The first inexactitude which however does not yet throw away the draw. If White's rook were now on a7 he would win by 2 ♔e6 when both 2 ... ♔f8 3 ♖a8+ ♔g7 4 ♔e7 and 5 e6 (diagram 156), and also 2 ... ♔d8 3 ♖a8+ ♔c7 4 ♔e7 and 5 e6 (diagram 161) give White the win.

We have already indicated the correct defence in our analysis to diagram 162: **1 ... ♖e1! 2 ♔e6 ♔f8** as a general rule, it is best to play the king to the shorter side, but Black also draws by 2 ... ♔d8 3 ♖h8+ ♔c7 4 ♖e8 ♖h1! **3 ♖h8+ ♔g7 4 ♖e8** or 4 ♖a8 ♖e2! **4 ... ♖a1! 5 ♖d8 ♖e1!** and draws.

2 ♔e6 ♔f8!

The only move. After 2 ... ♔d8 3 ♖h8+ ♔c7 4 ♔e7 White wins as in diagram 161.

3 ♖h8+ ♔g7
4 ♖e8 ♖e1

Again not the most exact. As we saw from digram 162, the correct defensive method is 4 ... ♖a1! 5 ♖d8 ♖e1!

5 ♔d7 ♔f7?

The decisive error. By **5 ... ♖d1+ 6 ♔e7 ♖e1 7 e6 ♖a1!** Black could bring about the draw we gave in our analysis to diagram 154. Here 6 ... ♖e1 simplifies Black's defence, for if instead 6 ... ♖a1 7 ♖d8 ♖a7+ 8 ♔e8, Black has to find the subtle 8 ... ♖a6! 9 ♖d7+ ♔g8 10 ♖d6 ♖a8+ 11 ♖d8 ♖a6! drawing. After 8 ... ♔g6 White wins by 9 ♖d6+ ♔f5 10 e6 ♔e5 11 ♖b6 followed by 12 e7.

6 e6+ ♔g7

Or 6 ... ♔f6 7 ♖f8+ and 8 e7 wins.

7 ♔e7?

An incomprehensible error, throwing away the win. Instead 7 ♖a8! ♖d1+ 8 ♔e8 and 9 e7 wins without difficulty.

7 ... ♖e2?

And this finally throws away the draw. Diagram 154 shows us that 7 ... ♖a1! is the only defence, e.g. 8 ♖d8 ♖a7+ 9 ♖d7 ♖a8 (or 9 ... ♖a1) draws.

8 ♖d8 ♖e1

It is too late for 8 ... ♖a2, when 9 ♔e8 and 10 e7 wins.

9 ♖d2

Even quicker is 9 ♔d7 ♖d1+ (or 9 ... ♔f6 10 ♖f8+ and 11 e7) 10 ♔e8 followed by 11 e7 winning.

9 ... ♖e3

There is no longer any defence.

10 ♖g2+ ♔h7
11 ♔f7 ♖f3+
12 ♔e8 ♖e3
13 e7 wins.

An excellent example of the subtleties contained in the simplest looking position, and a suitable ending for trying out our newly acquired knowledge.

If we move the position in diagram 162 one or two files to the left, it is won for White, as the horizontal checks by the black rook are either too short or impossible. In addition, the Philidor position can produce the following after faulty defence by Black:

164

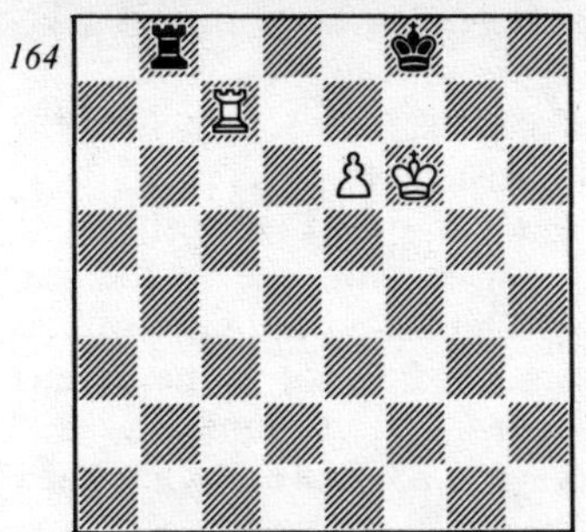

This is easily won for White by **1 ♖h7 ♔g8 2 ♖g7+ ♔f8** or 2 ... ♔h8 3 ♖g1 and 4 ♔f7 **3 e7+ ♔e8 4 ♖g8+**. The result is not changed if the position is moved to the left or right, except for two files to the right, when the white rook has insufficient space to manoeuvre, so that **1 ♖h7+ ♔g8 2 g7? ♖d6+** or **1 ♖e6 ♖a8 2 g7+ ♔g8** both draw for Black.

These positions are fairly simple to understand without further analysis, but a good player must know them off by heart. It is not always possible in the Philidor position to cut off the enemy king from the sixth rank, so we must then use other resources to save the position.

If the position is further back, on the fourth rank at least, then the black rook is often more effectively placed in front of the pawn rather than behind it. For example, in diagram 165 White

165

cannot advance his pawn without the help of the rook. After **1 ♔c4 ♖c8+ 2 ♔b5 ♖d8! 3 ♔c5 ♖c8+ 4 ♔d6 ♖d8+ 5 ♔e5 ♖e8+ 6 ♔f5 ♖d8!** White is back where he started. This method of defence is very important and can often save Black, as for example in diagram 166.

166

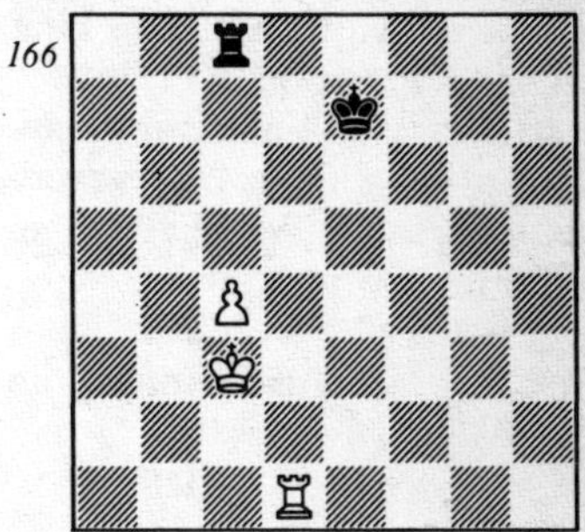

As already mentioned, White must use his rook to help his pawn advance. By exploiting the unfavourable position of Black's king, White wins as follows:

1 ♔b4!

He cannot invert moves with 1 ♖d4 because of 1 ... ♖d8! (one advantage of the rook in front of the pawn!) and the pawn ending is drawn after 2 ♖xd8 ♔xd8 2 ♔b4

♔c8!

1 ... ♖b8+
2 ♔a5 ♖c8!

Black must not check thoughtlessly, as 2 ... ♖a8+? 3 ♔b6 allows White to advance the pawn, or attack the rook after 3 ... ♖b8+ 4 ♔c7 etc.

3 ♔b5 ♖b8+
4 ♔a6 ♖c8
5 ♖d4!

Now that White has pushed his king forward as far as possible, he guards the pawn with his rook and Black cannot stop the pawn advancing.

5 ... ♔e6

If the black king were already here, then 5 ... ♔e5 would draw at once. In other words, diagram 166 would be drawn with Black's king on e6 or e5. However, if the king is on e4 or beyond, White can win by 1 ♖e1+ driving him two files away from the pawn. We shall come back to this point later.

6 ♔b7 ♖c5

Or 6 ... ♔e5 7 ♖d5+ winning the rook.

7 ♔b6 ♖c8
8 c5 wins.

It is now clear that, with Black to move, diagram 166 is drawn either by 1 ... ♖d8 (see note to move 1 above) or by 1 ... ♔e6 (see note to move 5). In other words White's winning chances are minimal if the black king is no more than a file away from the pawn.

We must also point out that White wins from diagram 166 only because the black rook has insufficient space to give horizontal checks from the left. Move the diagram position at least two files to the right, and White cannot win. It is also clear that Black's drawing possibilities would disappear if his rook were behind the pawn instead of in front.

If we move the position in diagram 166 one file to the left, then White can no longer win, as the move 2 ♔a5! is no longer possible. For example, **1 ♔a4 ♖a8+ 2 ♔b5 ♖b8+ 3 ♔a5 ♖a8+ 4 ♔b6 ♖b8+** draws.

Or after **1 ♖c4** Black has either **1 ... ♖c8** or **1 ... ♔d6 2 ♔a4 ♔d5!** but not 2 ... ♖a8+ 3 ♔b5 ♖b8+ 4 ♔a6 ♔d5 5 ♖g4! winning **3 ♖c5+ ♔d6 4 ♔a5 ♖a8+ 5 ♔b5 ♖b8+ 6 ♔c4 ♖h8** etc drawing. This last variation is important, as the 1 ... ♖c8 resource is not always available (i.e. with Black's king on d5).

Matters become even more interesting if the black king is cut off two files away from the pawn, as in the basic position in diagram 167.

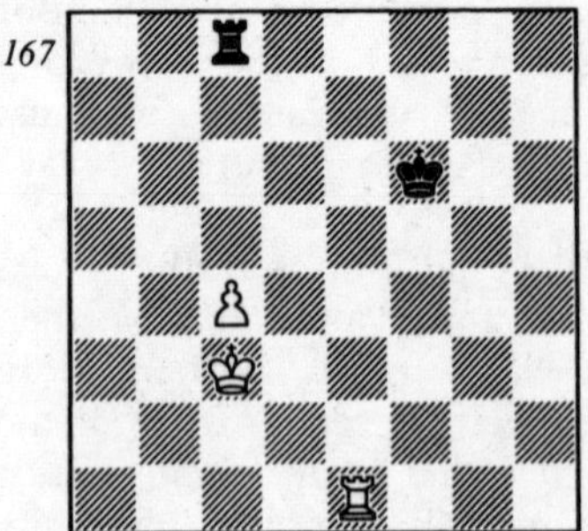
167

The following winning method applies to a central pawn also, and is slightly different from the one arising from diagram 166, although no less instructive:

1 ♔b4

The order of moves is not so important here, as Black could not play 1 ... ♖e8 even with his king on f7. After 2 ♖xe8 ♔xe8 3 ♔b4 ♔d8 4 ♔b5! the pawn ending is a loss for him. The exact position of the black king is unimportant.

1 ... ♖b8+
2 ♔a5 ♖c8
3 ♔b5 ♖b8+
4 ♔a6

Again we see the importance of the extra file, which is why a similar position with a knight's pawn is only drawn.

4 ... ♖c8
5 ♖c1!

In this position White can also win by 5 ♖e4 ♔f5 6 ♖h4 (threatening 7 ♔b7) 6 ... ♖b8 7 c5 when both 7 ... ♔e6 8 ♖d4 and 7 ... ♔e5 8 ♖h6 win. However, this line would be impossible with the black king on f5 or if the whole position were moved one file to the right.

5 ... ♔e7
6 ♔b7 ♖c5

If the position were one file further to the right, Black could now try 6 ... ♖a8 but White would still win by 7 d5 ♖a7+ 8 ♔b6 ♖d7 (or 8 ... ♖a2 9 ♖e1! etc) 9 ♔c6 ♔e7 10 d6+ ♔d8 11 ♖h1 etc.

7 ♔b6 ♖h5

Or 7 ... ♖c8 8 c5 ♖b8+ 9 ♔c7 wins.

8 c5

Or 8 ♖d1 ♖h6+ 9 ♔c7 ♖h5 10 ♖d5 wins.

8 ... ♔d8
9 ♖a1

But not 9 c6? ♖h2 and Black draws. Alternative rook moves such as 9 ♖d1+ or 9 ♖g1 also win.

9 ... ♖h2
10 ♖a8+ and
11 c6 **(+)** wins easily.

168

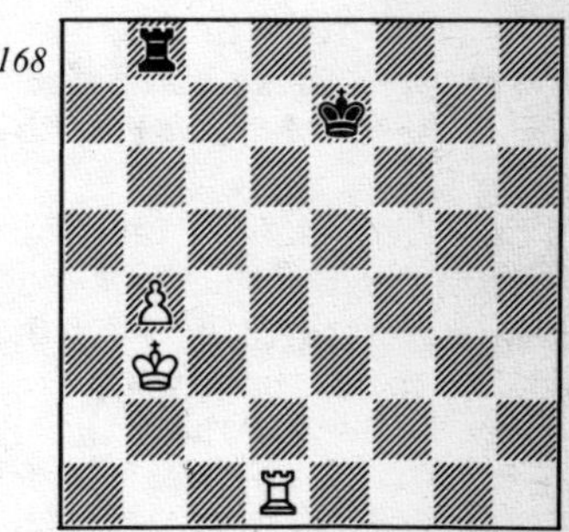

As already stated, a similar position with a knight's pawn is only drawn, but White wins if the black king is further back. For example, in the position in diagram 168, White wins by **1 ♖d4 ♔e6** or 1 ... ♖d8 2 ♖xd8 ♔xd8 3 ♔a4 ♔c8 4 ♔a5! wins **2 ♔c4 ♖c8+** or 2 ... ♔e5 3 ♖d5+ ♔e6 4 b5 ♖c8+ 5 ♖c5 ♔d7 6 b6! wins **3 ♔b5 ♖b8+** or 3 ... ♔e5 4 ♖d7 ♔e6 5 ♖a7 wins **4 ♔c6 ♔e5 5 ♖h4** wins.

Also with the king too far advanced (on e4 for example as in diagram 169), Black loses to **1 ♖d6! ♔e5 2 ♖a6 ♔d5 3 ♔a4** and the pawn advances. Or White can

169

play the more complicated **1 ♖d7 ♔e5 2 ♔c4 ♖c8+** or 2 ... ♔e6 3 ♖d4 as given above **3 ♔b5 ♖b8+ 4 ♔c5 ♖c8+ 5 ♔b6 ♖b8+ 6 ♖b7** winning.

In order to win every time with the knight's pawn, the black king must be at least three files from the pawn, and there is hardly any need to show the reader how this is done. Play is similar to the above analysis and only becomes interesting if the pawn is on the third rank. Possibilities are then extremely complex and demand very exact play, as can be seen from our next example.

170

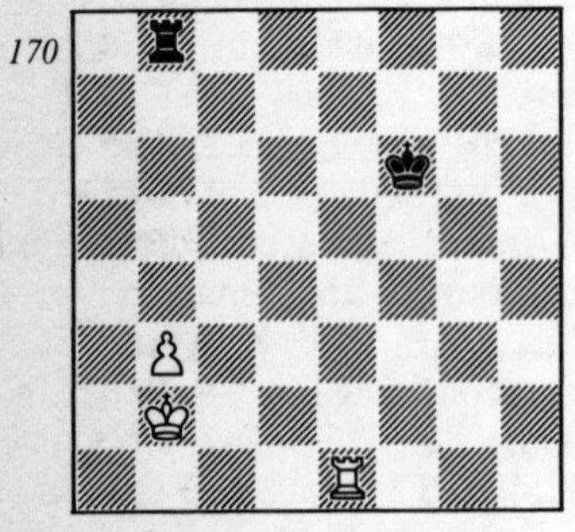

N.Grigoriev 1937

Before we analyse this position in detail, let us clarify one or two points. If White advances his king, play might go: **1 ♔c3 ♖c8+ 2 ♔d4**. It is inadvisable for Black to continue checking now, as after 2 ... ♖d8+ 3 ♔c5 ♖c8+ 4 ♔d6 ♖b8, his king can be driven away by 5 ♖f1+. So play continues **2 ... ♖b8 3 ♔c4 ♖c8+ 4 ♔d5 ♖b8**. Now White must guard his pawn, but 5 ♖b1 allows the king to head for the queenside with 5 ... ♔e7, and after **5 ♖e3 ♔f5 6 ♖f3+ ♔g4**, the rook is forced to give way. So it appears that White must prepare the advance of his king.

The above analysis indicates that the black king is relatively well placed on f6. For instance, if he were on f8, 1 ♖e4 and 2 b4 would win easily. Nor would the king stand well on ... f4. White wins by **1 ♔c3 ♖c8+ 2 ♔d4 ♖b8** or 2 ... ♖d8+ 3 ♔c5 ♖c8+ 4 ♔d6 ♖b8 5 ♖b1! ♔e4 6 b4 ♔d3 7 b5 ♔c2 8 ♔c7! wins **3 ♖b1!** not 3 ♔c4 ♖c8+ 4 ♔d5 ♖b8 5 ♖b1 ♔e3! 6 b4 ♔d3 7 b5 ♔c2 8 ♖b4 ♔c3 drawing. Nor 3 ♖f1+ ♔g5 4 ♖b1 ♔f6 etc. **3 ... ♔f5 4 ♔d5!** winning a vital tempo **4 ... ♔f6 5 b4 ♔e7 6 ♔c6** and **7 b5** winning easily.

Black would lose with his king on f5, after **1 ♔c3 ♖c8+ 2 ♔d4 ♖b8 3 ♔c4 ♖c8+ 4 ♔d5 ♖b8** or 4 ... ♖d8+ 5 ♔c5 ♖c8+ 6 ♔d6 ♖b8 7 ♖b1 ♔e4 8 b4 ♔d3 9 b5 ♔c2 10 ♔c7! wins **5 ♖b1** transposing to the above quoted variation.

When we come to our main analysis, we shall consider the case of the black king on f7. If the king is further up the board, say on f3, White wins comfortably by **1 ♖e6 ♔f4 2 ♔a3 ♔f5** or 2 ... ♖a8+ 3 ♔b4 ♔f5 4 ♖c6 ♔e5 5 ♔c5 and 6 b4 wins **3 ♖a6 ♔e5 4 b4 ♔d5 5 ♔a4 ♔c4 6 ♖c6+ ♔d5 7 b5 ♖a8+ 8 ♔b4** etc. Notice that occasionally we have not continued our analysis beyond a certain point, after driving the black king one more file to the right. We shall demonstrate later that this leads to a win for White.

All the given variations clearly indicate that the black king stands badly anywhere except on f6. This leads to the surprising conclusion that in diagram 170 Black is practically in zugzwang! Now that we are aware of this fact, the clearest winning plan is no longer hard to find:

1 ♖e4

The aim of this and the next move is to bring about diagram 170 with the white rook on e3, and we shall see why this is necessary. At the beginning of our discussion we mentioned the possibility **1 ♔c3 ♖c8+ 2 ♔d4 ♖b8 3 ♔c4 ♖c8+ 4 ♔d5 ♖b8 5 ♖b1 ♔e7** Grigoriev assumed that Black now draws after **6 ♔c6 ♖b4! 7 ♖e1+ ♔d8** 7 ... ♔f6 8 ♖e3 ♖b8 9 ♔c7 ♖b4 10 ♔d6! leads to the main line **8 ♖e3 ♖h4! 9 ♖e5? ♖h6+ 10 ♔b7 ♖h7+ 11 ♔b8 ♔d7! 12 ♖c5 ♖h4 13 ♖b5 ♔c6** etc. However, Kopayev later found the following improvement for White: **9 ♖g3! ♖h6+ 10 ♔b7 ♖h7+ 11 ♔b8 ♖h4** or 11 ... ♔d7 12 ♖g6! ♖h4 13 ♖b6 and 14 b4 wins **12 ♖d3+ ♔e7 13 ♔c7 ♖b4 14 ♖e3+ ♔f6 15 ♔d6** and wins as in the main variation.

However, the winning method is much longer and more complicated than our main variation.

1 ... ♔f5

If 1 ... ♔f7 2 ♔c3 etc wins, as White will force b4.

2 ♖e3 ♔f6

After 2 ... ♔f4 3 ♖e1 we arrive at one of the given positions, with the king on f3, f4 or f5. The text position would also arise if the black king were originally on f7. After 1 ♖e3 Black would have nothing better than 1 ... ♔f6. However, White could also win easily by 1 ♖e4 ♔f6 2 ♔c3 ♖c8+ 3 ♔d4 ♖b8 4 ♔c4 ♖c8+ 5 ♔d5 ♖b8 6 b4 ♔f5 7 ♖h4 etc.

Instead of 2 ... ♔f6 Black has a cunning defence in **2 ... ♖h8 3 b4 ♔f4! 4 ♖e1 ♖h3!** preventing the advance of White's king. White then wins in the following instructive fashion: **5 ♔c2!** not of course 5 b5? ♖h5, but also 5 ♖e8 ♔f5! 6 b5 ♖d3! 7 b6 ♖d6 8 ♖b8 ♔e6, or 5 ♔a2 ♖d3! 6 b5 ♖d5 7 ♖b1 ♔e5 8 ♔a3 ♔d6 9 b6 ♔c6 draws for Black **5 ... ♔f5** the waiting move 5 ... ♖g3 loses to 6 b5 ♖g5 7 b6 ♖c5+ 8 ♔d3 ♖b5 9 ♖e6 etc. **6 b5 ♔f6** or 6 ... ♖g3 7 b6 ♖g7 8 ♔c3 ♖b7 9 ♖b1 ♔e6 10 ♔c4 ♔d7 11 ♔b5 ♔c8 12 ♔a6 ♖d7 13 ♖h1 ♖d8 14 ♔a7 ♖d7+

15 ♔a8 wins **7 b6 ♔f7** or 7 ... ♖h8 8 ♔c3 ♖b8 9 ♖b1 ♔e6 10 ♔c4 ♔d7 11 ♔b5 ♔c8 12 ♖c1+ and 12 ... ♔b7 allows mate in two **8 ♖b1 ♖h8 9 ♔c3 ♔e6 10 ♔b4 ♔d7 11 ♖c1! ♖c8 12 ♖c5** winning (12 ... ♖c6 13 ♔b5).

The above variation not only shows us a new defensive resource but also a subtle winning method for White. It is worth noting that after Black's 4 ... ♖h3!, if his king now stood on f5 instead of f4, he would draw after 5 ♔c2 ♔f6 6 b5 ♖h5 7 b6 ♖c5+ 8 ♔d3 ♖b5 as White could no longer play 9 ♖e6. Or 5 b5 ♖d3! 6 ♔c2 ♖d5 7 ♖b1 ♖c5+ 8 ♔d3 ♔e5 9 b6 ♖c8 draws. Now let us return to our main line:

3 ♔c3

White could play 3 ♖e1 and bring about diagram 170 with Black to move, but we now know that Black can change his defensive plan by 3 ... ♖h8! when White is compelled to play 4 ♖e3, as 4 b4? ♖h3! 5 ♔c2 ♔f7 6 b5 ♖h5 7 ♖b1 ♔e6 draws.

3 ... ♖c8+
4 ♔d4 ♖b8

Or 4 ... ♖d8+ 5 ♔c5 ♖c8+ transposing.

5 ♔c5 ♖c8+
6 ♔d6! ♖b8

Or 6 ... ♖d8+ 7 ♔c7 ♖d4 8 ♔c6 ♖h4 9 ♔b5 ♖h5+ 10 ♔a4 and the pawn advances.

7 ♖f3+!

The point of the whole manoeuvre. The fact that White's pawn was guarded by the rook on e3 allowed 5 ♔c5 and 6 ♔d6 which in turn has forced the black king one file further away.

7 ... ♔g5 *(171)*

171

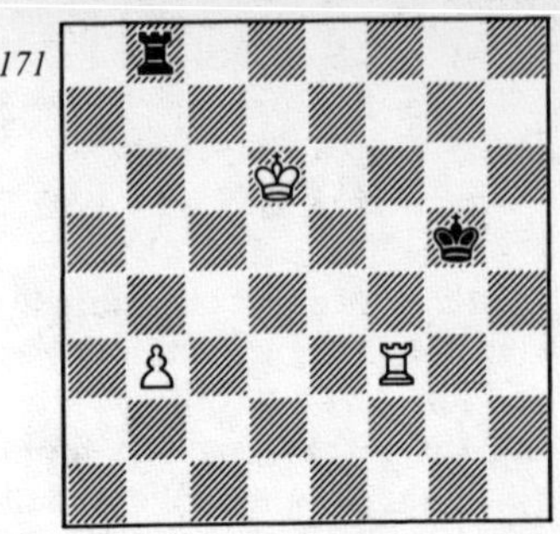

Despite his advantage, White's task is still not easy. If 8 ♔c7 ♖b4 9 ♔c6 ♖b8 and the pawn cannot advance. Rook moves allow the black king to return. In order to win, White has to switch plans back to placing his rook on b8, when he will win because Black's king is just far enough away.

8 ♔c5! ♖c8+

Or 8 ... ♔g4 9 ♖d3! ♖c8+ (to stop 10 b4) 10 ♔b6 ♖b8+ 11 ♔c7 ♖b4 12 ♔c6 ♔f4 (or 12 ... ♖b8 13 ♖d4+ ♔f5 14 b4 ♔e5 15 ♖h4 wins) 13 ♔c5 ♖b8 14 b4 ♖c8+ 15 ♔d5 ♖d8+ 16 ♔c4 ♖c8+ 17 ♔b3 ♔e4 (or 17 ... ♖b8 18 ♖d5, or 17 ... ♔e5 18 b5 etc) 18 ♖d6 ♔e5 19 ♖a6 and wins as we saw in our analysis of diagram 167.

9 ♔d4 ♖b8
10 ♔c3 ♖c8+

Here, or previously, 10 ... ♔g4 11 ♖f1 would only help White.

11 ♔b2 ♖b8

After a great deal of trouble and subtle play, White is now almost back where he started, with the vital difference that the black king is four files away from the pawn instead of three. This is the deciding factor.

12 ♖f1!

Heading for b1. There is no defence to this plan.

12 ... ♔g6
13 ♔c3

Beginning the old dance routine for the last time!

13 ... ♖c8+
14 ♔d4 ♖b8
15 ♔c4 ♖c8+
16 ♔d5 ♖b8
17 ♖b1!

Finally. The black king now arrives too late.

17 ... ♔f7
18 b4 ♔e7
19 ♔c6 and wins easily.

A tremendous piece of analysis by Grigoriev, full of subtle and surprising points. We have brought it to the reader's attention in order to convince him about the difficulties even the simplest looking ending can contain. All the more reason, then, for studying such endings before we are faced with them over the board.

There are many more interesting endgames with the pawn on its original square or with a centre pawn on the third rank, but we shall dispense with these. Instead, let us examine two examples in which the defending king is placed behind the pawn.

In general such positions are won for White, especially if the

172

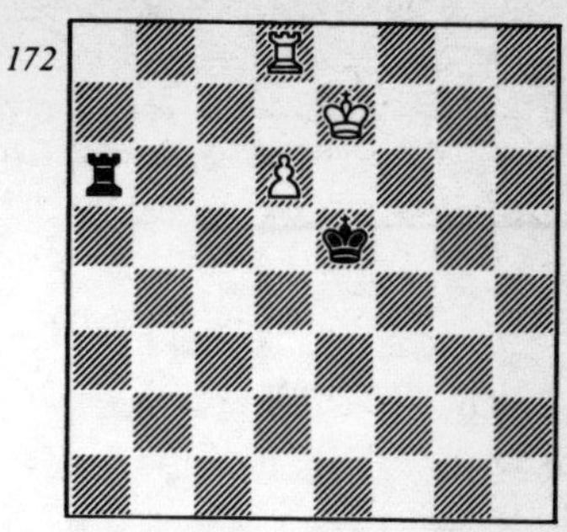

Kling and Horwitz 1851

king is a rank away from the pawn. Black has drawing chances only when the white pieces are awkwardly placed or the pawn has not advanced much. At first sight diagram 172 seems to give Black good drawing chances, for the white pieces are tied to the defence of the pawn. However, White frees his game by the following typical manoeuvre:

1 ♖h8!

But not 1 d7? ♖e6+ 2 ♔f7 which would indeed win after 2 ... ♔d6? 3 ♖e8! but which only draws after 2 ... ♖f6+! 3 ♔g7 ♔e6 4 ♖e8+ ♔xd7.

1 ... ♖xd6
2 ♖h5+ wins.

This position is still won if we move it to the left, but it is clear that, one file to the right, it is drawn after 1 ♖h8 ♖xe6 2 ♖h5+ ♔g4 etc.

Diagram 173 is another position of practical value. White's pieces are more effectively placed than in the preceding example, yet surprisingly enough Black to move can draw.

173

White to move wins by 1 e6, but Black to move draws as follows:

1 ... ♔f5

Black must use this opportunity to bring his king to the fourth rank.

2 e6+ ♔f6
3 ♖a6 ♖e2!

The rook must play a waiting move on the e-file, as both 3 ... ♖d1+? 4 ♔e8 and 5 e7+, and 3 ... ♔g7 4 ♖a2 win for White.

4 ♖d6

After 4 e7+ ♔f7 the draw is clear.

4 ... ♖e1
5 ♖d2 ♖a1!

Again the only move, as White was threatening to win with 6 ♖f2+ and 7 e7. Of course 5 ... ♖xe6 fails to 6 ♖f2+.

6 ♖f2+ ♔g7

and Black has reached a drawn position of the diagram 154 type.

If the position in diagram is moved one file to the left, it is won for White after **1 ... ♔e5 2 d6+ ♔e6 3 ♖a6 ♖d2 4 ♖c6 ♖d1 5 ♖c2 ♖a1 6 ♖e2+ ♔f7 7 d7**, reaching a position of the diagram 149 type.

Moving the position to the right does not change the result, but, two files to the right, Black has to defend differently. After **1 ... ♔h5 2 g6+ ♔h6 3 ♖a6 ♖g2 4 ♖f6 ♖g1? 5 ♖f2 ♖a1 6 ♖h2+** wins, as Black's king must go to g5. However, Black has a stalemate resource in **4 ... ♖g5! 5 ♖f1 ♖f5+! 6 ♖xf5 stalemate**. Note that Black dare not play 3 ... ♖g5? as 4 ♖f6! then places him in zugzwang, and wins for White.

With this, we conclude our treatment of rook and pawn against rook. We make no apology for the size of this section which only serves to indicate the extraordinary importance of this type of ending. More complex rook and pawn endings are usually reduced to one of these basic positions which must therefore be known thoroughly.

Rook and two Pawns against Rook

The ending of rook and two pawns against rook is usually won quite easily for White. Even if he has to lose one of the pawns he can normally use this opportunity to set up a theoretically won position with the remaining pawn. Only in exceptional cases can Black hope for a draw, and it is a few of these cases with the most practical value that we shall examine now.

Our first position is extremely interesting. Despite the fact that his rook protects both pawns and

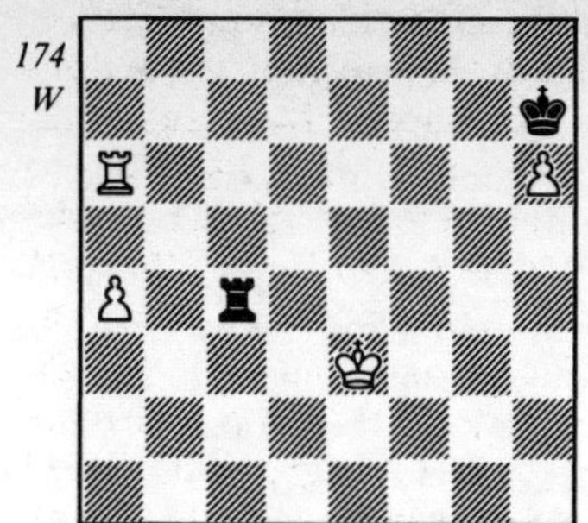

Smyslov-Bondarevsky 1940

that his king has freedom of movement along the rank, White cannot force a win. Black keeps in mind the important Vancura position (diagram 138) and draws, while the pawn on h6 plays no part at all in the proceedings.

1 ♔d3

Rook moves would lose a pawn at once and if the king heads for the h-pawn he can always be checked away from g5 or h5.

1 ... ♖b4
2 ♔c3 ♖f4

Black's plan is simple. His rook maintains a horizontal attack on the a-pawn, then checks away the white king as soon as it approaches the pawn. To do this successfully, the rook must choose a file along which it can check from every square, and as far away as possible from the a-pawn. It is clear that the f-file is ideal for this, although the e-file is far enough from the pawn and 2 ... ♖e4 is also playable. On the other hand 2 ... ♖g4 is not as accurate because the rook would not then be able to check on g7.

3 ♔b3 ♖f3+

Forced, as 4 ♖c6 was threatened.

4 ♔c4 ♖f4+
5 ♔d5 ♖b4

Black only checks until the white king leaves the vicinity of the a-pawn. For example, 5 ... ♖f5+? fails to 6 ♔e6 ♖f4 7 a5 and Black cannot play 7 ... ♖f5.

6 ♔c6 ♖f4

Again 7 a5 was the threat.

7 ♔d7 ♖d4+
8 ♔c7 ♖f4
9 a5 ♖f5!

All according to the Vancura recipe (diagram 138).

10 ♔d7 ♖d5+
11 ♔e7 ♖e5+
12 ♔f6 ♖c5
13 ♖a8 ♖b5
14 a6 ♖b6+

and White can make no progress. After 15 ♔e7 ♖xh6 (15 ... ♖c6 is also possible) 16 ♔f7 ♖b6 17 ♖a7 ♔h6 18 ♔f8 ♖b8+ 19 ♔e7 ♖b6 20 ♔d8 ♖f6 21 ♔c8 a draw was agreed. As can be seen, this defensive method is of great practical value.

There are many other exceptions when two pawns do not guarantee a win. Sometimes the reason for this is the poor position of White's king, or unusually active black pieces, or the fact that one of the pawns is almost worthless. Most of these positions seldom occur in practical play, so we shall devote our attention to those few which will prove of most value to the reader.

When the two pawns are the bishop's pawn and rook's pawn on the same wing, theory states that the game is usually drawn, surprising though this may seem. However, to defend such positions requires the utmost exactitude, because there are many situations which win for White, especially when the pawns are far advanced. In view of the great practical value of this ending, we intend to discuss it in some detail, beginning with diagram 175, our first critical position:

175

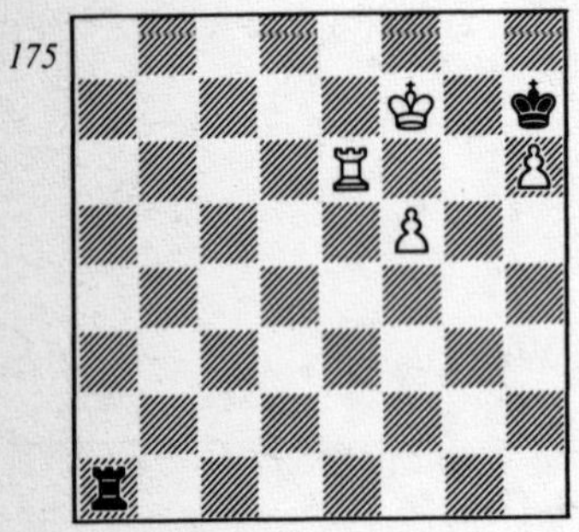

I.Maizelis 1939

Both White's king and rook are actively placed and allow him to win as follows:

1 ... ♖a8

If Black checks, White has an interesting win by 1 ... ♖a7+ 2 ♔f8 ♖a8+ 3 ♖e8 ♖a6 (to prevent 4 f6) 4 ♖e7+ ♚h8 5 ♖e6 ♖a8+ (again 6 f6 was threatened) 6 ♖e8 ♖a6 7 f6! ♖xf6+ 8 ♔e7+.

Nor can Black wait, as 1 ... ♖a2 fails to 2 f6 ♖a8 (or 2 ... ♚xh6 3 ♔f8 etc) 3 ♖e8 ♖a7+ 4 ♔e6! ♖a6+ 5 ♔f5 ♖a5+ 6 ♖e5 ♖a1 7 f7 ♖f1+ 8 ♔e6 ♚g6 9 ♖g5+! ♚xg5 10 h7 winning, as the king will escape the checks by heading for f8.

Just a slight alteration of the position, placing White's rook on d6, would allow Black to draw by **1 ... ♖a7+ 2 ♔e8 ♖a8+ 3 ♔e7** or 3 ♖d8 ♖a6 etc **3 ... ♖a7+ 4 ♖d7 ♖a8 5 ♖d8** if 5 f6 ♚xh6 draws **5 ... ♖a7+ 6 ♔f6 ♖a1 7 ♖e8 ♖a2** when White cannot play 8 ♔f7 because of 8 ... ♚xh6.

2 ♖e8

Not of course 2 f6 ♚xh6 drawing.

2 ... ♖a7+

Or 2 ... ♖a6 3 ♖e1! ♚xh6 4 ♖e6+ or 4 f6 wins, or here 3 ... ♖a7+ 4 ♔f8 wins as given above; or 3 ... ♖b6 4 f6 ♖b8 (or 4 ... ♚xh6 5 ♖h1+ and 6 ♔g7) 5 ♖e8 ♖b6 (or 5 ... ♖b7+ 6 ♔e6 wins as we have seen) 6 ♔e7 ♖b7+ 7 ♔e6 and wins as in our previous note.

3 ♔f8 ♚xh6

Or 3 ... ♖a6 4 ♖e7+ etc.

4 ♖e6+ ♚g5
5 f6 ♚f5
6 ♖b6

Or 6 ♖d6 ♚g6 7 f7+ ♚h7 8 ♔e8 wins.

6 ... ♚g6
7 f7+ ♚h7
8 ♖b8 winning easily.

In this type of ending, the black king must avoid being cut off on the back rank, as such positions are usually lost. Here is an example of this:

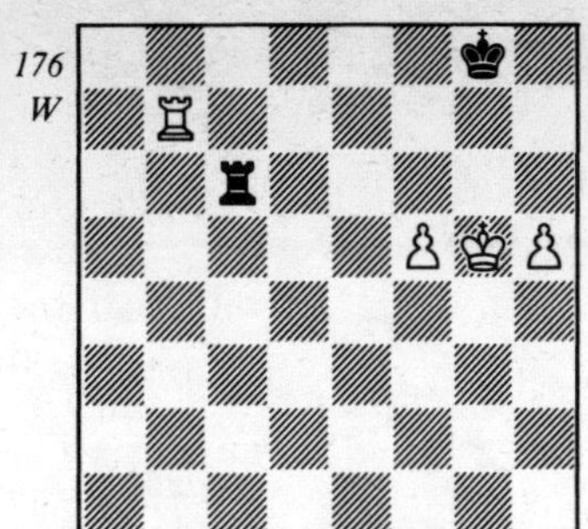

Capablanca-Kostić 1919

White has at least three winning ocntinuations, but we select the longest of these in order to point out various incidental possibilities.

1 h6

In the game Capablanca played 1 f6 ♖c1 2 ♖g7+ and after 2 ... ♔f8 3 h6 Black resigned, for he can do nothing to prevent 4 h7 and 5 ♖g8+. Black could hold out a little longer by 2 ... ♔h8 when 3 ♔g6 (or 3 ♖e7 ♔g8 4 h6 winning) 3 ... ♖g1+ 4 ♔f7 ♖a1 5 ♖g8+ ♔h7 6 ♖e8 ♖a6 7 ♔e7 ♖a7+ 8 ♔f8 wins comfortably.

Kopayev has pointed out another win by 1 ♖b8+ ♔h7 (1 ... ♔f7 2 h6 and 3 h7, or 1 .... ♔g7 2 f6+ ♖xf6 3 h6+ wins) 2 f6 ♖c5+ 3 ♔g4 ♖c4+ 4 ♔f5 ♖c5+ 5 ♔e6 ♖c6+ 6 ♔e7 ♖c7+ 7 ♔f8 winning.

1 ... ♖c1
2 f6

Not the only way to win but perhaps the most instructive one, showing that White always wins with both pawns on the sixth rank whenever Black's king is cut off on the back rank.

2 ... ♖g1+

White threatened 3 ♖b8+ or 3 ♖g7+ when one of the pawns queens.

3 ♔f5 ♖f1+
4 ♔e6 ♖e1+
5 ♔d6

Care is still required, as 5 ♔d7? ♔f7! 6 h7 ♖h1 draws for Black.

5 ... ♖d1+

Or 5 ... ♖f1 6 ♖b8+ ♔h7 7 ♔e7 wins. Or 5 ... ♖h1 6 ♖b8+ ♔f7 7 h7! wins. Black does best to check.

6 ♔e7 ♖e1+
7 ♔d8 ♖f1

The best chance. If 7 ... ♔f8 8 ♖g7 and 9 h7 wins. Or 7 ... ♖d1+ 8 ♔e8 ♖e1+ 9 ♖e7 wins.

8 h7+ ♔h8
9 ♔e7

Not, however, 9 f7 ♖xf7! drawing, whereas now 9 ... ♖xf6 will lose to the zwischenzug 10 ♖b8+.

9 ... ♖e1+
10 ♔f7

Again White could go wrong with 10 ♔f8? ♖e8+ 11 ♔f7 ♖f8+! drawing, whereas after the text move White answers 10 ... ♖e8 with 11 ♔g6 or 11 ♖b1.

10 ... ♖a1
11 ♖b8+ ♔xh7
12 ♔f8 wins.

Here is another position with the black king on the back rank.

White wins, whoever has the move, so let us give Black the move and consider two main variations:

177

A

1 ... ♖a2

Waiting. We shall analyse the more active 1 ... ♖h1 in variation B. After 1 ... ♖a6+ 2 ♔g5 followed by 3 f6, we arrive at a winning position from diagram 176.

2 ♔e5!

After 2 h7+ ♔h8 3 ♔f7 ♔xh7? 4 ♔f8+ ♔h6 5 ♖e6+! ♔h7 (or 5 ... ♔g5 6 f6 etc) 6 f6 ♖a8+ 7 ♖e8 wins, but Black has better with the problem like 3 ... ♖a5! 4 f6 ♔xh7 5 ♔f8+ ♔g6 6 f7 ♔f6! drawing.

2 ... ♖e2+
3 ♔d6 ♖d2+

If 3 ... ♖f2 or 3 ... ♖h2 White still plays 4 ♔e6! (4 ... ♖xh6+ 5 f6 etc).

4 ♔e6 ♖e2+
5 ♔d7 ♖d2+

After 5 ... ♖f2 White plays 6 ♖e8+ ♔h7 7 ♔e6 ♖a2 (or 7 ... ♖e2+ 8 ♔f7 ♖a2 9 ♖e6 arriving at diagram 175) 8 f6 ♖a6+ 9 ♔f5 (9 ♔f7 ♖a7+ 10 ♔f8? allows an interesting draw 10 ... ♔g6! 11 ♔g8 ♔xf6 12 h7 ♖g7+ 13 ♔h8 ♖a7!) 9 ... ♖a5+ 10 ♖e5 winning, as we saw in our analysis to diagram 175 (note to Black's first move).

6 ♔e8 ♖f2
7 ♖e5 ♔h7

If Black's rook leaves the file, then 8 f6 wins. Or 7 ... ♖f1 8 ♔e7 wins.

8 ♔f7!

Not 8 ♔e7? ♔xh6 9 f6 ♔g6 10 ♖e6 ♖f1 drawing.

8 ... ♔xh6

Or 8 ... ♖a2 9 ♖e6 and we have diagram 132.

9 ♖e6+!

Again White only draws after 9 f6 ♖a2 10 ♔f8 ♔g6! 11 f7 ♔f6 etc.

9 ... ♔h7
10 f6 ♖a2

To draw Black would have to be in a position to play 10 ... ♖a8 here.

11 ♔f8 ♖a8+
12 ♖e8 and
13 f7 wins.

B

1 ... ♖h1

The same position could arise with White's rook occupying other squares on the 7th rank, e.g. b7. He would then only draw after 2 ♖b8+ ♔h7 3 ♔f7 ♖a1 4 f6 ♖a7+ 5 ♔e8 ♔g6 6 f7 ♖xf7! 7 ♖b6+ ♖f6, but 2 ♖g7+ is the winning move, as the following main line demonstrates.

2 ♖g7+

Or 2 ♖e8+ ♔h7 3 ♔f7 ♖a1 4 ♖e6 winning, as from diagram 175.

If 2 ♔e6 ♖e1+ (2 ... ♖xh6+ 3 f6) 3 ♔d7 winning, as in variation A above.

2 ... ♔f8

Or 2 ... ♔h8 3 ♖e7 ♔g8 (or 3 ... ♖xh6+ 4 ♔f7 ♖a6 5 f6 ♔h7 6 ♔f8+ ♔g6 7 f7 ♔f6 8 ♔g8! wins) 4 ♖e8+ (or ♔e6) winning as above.

3 ♔g6!

It was once thought that White could win here by **3 ♖g6 ♖h2 4 ♔e6 ♖h1 5 ♔d7** if 5 ♖f6+ ♔e8! 6 ♔d6 ♖d1+ 7 ♔c7 ♖a1 8 ♖d6 ♔f7 draws **5 ... ♖a1** or 5 ... ♖h5 6 ♖e6! ♔f7 7 h7 ♔g7 8 f6+ wins **6 ♖d6 ♔f7 7 h7 ♖h1** or 7 ... ♔g7 8 f6+ ♔xh7 9 ♔e8 etc **8 ♔d8 ♔g7 9 ♖d7+ ♔h8 10 f6 ♖f1 11 ♔e7!** etc.

However, Kopayev has shown that Black can improve by **5 ... ♔f7!** with the continuation **6 ♖e6** or 6 ♖d6 ♖h4! draws **6 ... ♖a1! 7 h7** if 7 ♖e7+ ♔f6 8 h7 ♖a8! draws. Or 7 ♖d6 ♖a7+ 8 ♔d8 ♖a8+ 9 ♔c7 ♖a7+ 10 ♔c6 ♖a1 11 h7 ♔g7 12 ♖d7+ ♔h8 drawing **7 ... ♔g7 8 f6+** or 8 ♖h6 ♖a7+ 9 ♔c8 ♖a8+ 10 ♔b7 ♔xh6 etc **8 ... ♔xh7 9 ♔e7 ♖a8** with a theoretical draw.

3 ... ♖g1+
4 ♔h7 ♖f1

Otherwise White wins by 5 f6 followed by ♔g6 and h7.

5 ♖a7! ♖g1

If 5 ... ♖xf5 6 ♔g6 followed by 7 ♖a8+ and 8 h7 wins.

6 f6 ♖g2
7 ♖g7 ♖f2
8 ♔g6 wins easily.

Very interesting and instructive variations which show the reader the problems faced by both sides.

So far we have considered positions in which the black king is cut off on the back rank or the white king has advanced to f7. In these cases White usually wins, although there are technical difficulties. Let us now turn to the average type of position in which the black king is correctly placed. Against best defence White cannot win.

178
B

Bondarevsky-Keres 1939

In this position Black must guard against three situations. Firstly, he must not allow his king to be driven to the back rank, secondly he must avoid diagram 175 (with White's king on f7), and thirdly, once he has captured the h-pawn, he must not allow White to obtain a winning rook and bishop's pawn ending.

1 ... ♖g2

Black wishes to stop White's king reaching f6 via g5, but this move was not absolutely vital. He could also draw by **1 ... ♖f2+ 2 ♔g5 ♖g2+ 3 ♔f6 ♖f2!** the only defence; after 3 ... ♖a2 4 ♔f7 White obtains diagram 175, and after 3 ... ♔g8 4 ♖e7 diagram 177.

If 3 ... ♔xh6 White does not play 4 ♔f7+? ♔h7 5 f6 ♖g7+ 6 ♔f8 ♖g8+ 7 ♔e7 ♖a8 drawing, but wins by 4 ♔e7+! ♔h7 5 f6 ♖f2 6 ♔f8 etc **4 ♖e8** after 4 ♖d6 the simplest is 4 ... ♖a2 5 ♔e7 ♖a7+ 6 ♖d7 ♖a8, or here 6 ♔e8 ♖a8+ 7 ♖d8 ♖a6 drawing, as we saw in our analysis to diagram 175. If 4 ♖e5, or 4 ♖e7+, then 4 ... ♔xh6 is possible **4 ... ♖a2!** and White can make no progress. King moves allow 5 ... ♔xh6 as do rook moves on the 5th, 6th and 7th ranks. After other rooks moves Black plays a waiting move with his rook on the a-file.

2 ♔e5 ♖a2

Simpler than 2 ... ♖e2+ 3 ♔f6 (or 3 ♔d6) when Black has to find the drawing move 3 ... ♖f2!

3 ♔d6

The only way to cross the sixth rank, as 3 ♔f6 allows 3 ... ♔xh6 4 ♔f7+ ♔h7 5 f6 ♖a8! drawing.

3 ... ♖a5

More forcing than 3 ... ♖f2 which also draws after 4 f6 (or 4 ♖f6 ♖a2) 4 ... ♔xh6 5 ♔e7 ♔g6 6 ♖e2 ♖a2! 7 ♖g2+ ♔h7.

4 f6 ♔g6

We select as our main line the somewhat surprising game continuation. Simpler was 4 ... ♔xh6 5 ♔e7 ♖a8! etc drawing.

5 ♖e8

Or 5 h7 ♔xh7 6 ♔e7 ♖a8 and so on.

5 ... ♖a6+

6 ♔e7 ♖xf6

Or 6 ... ♖a7+ 7 ♔f8 ♔xf6 8 ♔g8 ♔g6 9 ♖e6+ ♔f5 10 ♖d6 ♖a8+ 11 ♔g7 ♖a7+ drawing.

7 ♖g8+ ♔h7

8 ♖g7+ ♔h8

9 ♔xf6 stalemate.

So we see that Black can set up a satisfactory defence if his pieces are effectively posted as in diagram 178.

Otherwise matters are not clear, as our following example shows.

179
B

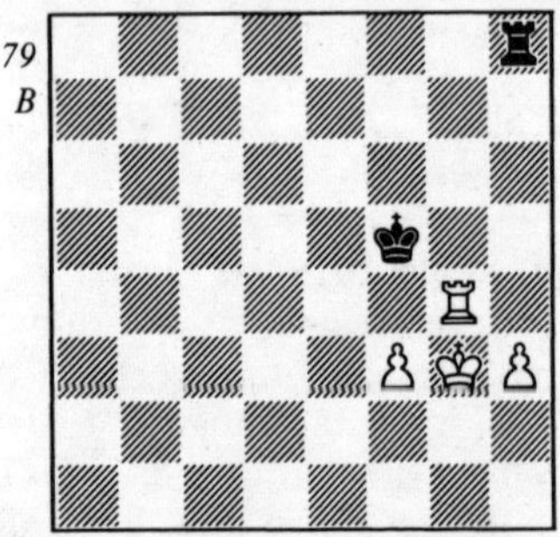

Keres-Sokolsky 1947

We see here a plan by White which forces Black to defend with the utmost care and precision. The black king is cut off from the g-file, and his rook will be tied down by the advance of the h-pawn. White's f-pawn protects his king from horizontal checks and gives the rook a strong post on g4, so that rook checks from behind are not to be feared. Black must watch that White cannot advance his h-pawn under favourable circumstances.

1 ... ♖a8

As the rook will have no effective checks, it should stay where it is. With 1 ... ♔f6 2 h4 ♖h5! Black could have put a satisfactory defence by using his rook along the fourth rank.

2 h4 ♖a1?

It is interesting to note that after this inexact move Black is lost. Botvinnik recommended **2 ... ♖h8! 3 ♖g5+ ♔f6** and only after **4 ♔g4** would Black play **4 ... ♖a8** White would then be unable to carry out the h4-h5-h6 manoeuvre and Black would gain more space for his rook to work in. If we continue this line by **5 h5 ♖a1 6 ♖g6+ ♔f7 7 f4 ♖a5** we arrive at a game position Gligorić-Smyslov, 1947, with the minor difference that the rook was on b5.

180
W

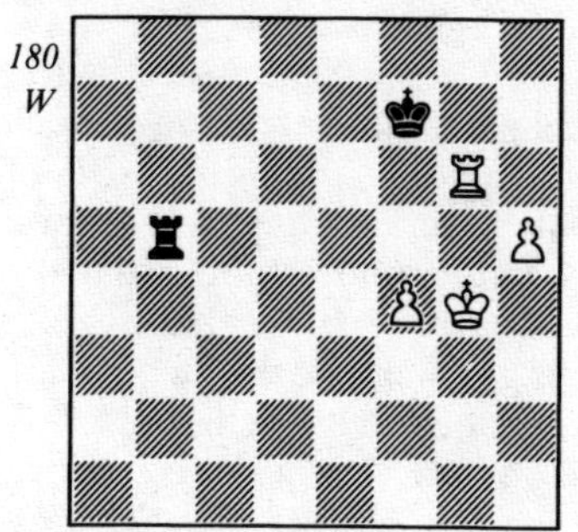

Gligorić-Smyslov 1947

The game continued from diagram 180: **8 ♖g5** if 8 f5 ♖b1 draws, and Kopayev has shown that 8 ♔h4 ♖b1! also draws for Black. His main variations run: 9 ♔g5 ♖g1+ 10 ♔f5 ♖h1 11 ♔g5 ♖g1+ 12 ♔h6 ♖f1 13 ♖g4 ♖h1. Or 9 ♖a6 ♖g1 10 h6 ♖h1+ 11 ♔g5 ♖g1+ 12 ♔f5 ♖h1 13 ♖a7+ ♔g8 14 ♔g6 ♖g1+ 15 ♔f6 ♖h1 16 ♖g7+ ♔h8 17 f5 ♖xh6+ 18 ♖g6 ♖h7! 19 ♖g1 ♖a7 20 ♖e1 ♖a6+ 21 ♔f7 ♖a7+ 22 ♔g6 ♖g7+ 23 ♔f6 ♖g2 and Black draws after both 24 ♔f7 ♖g7+ 25 ♔e8 ♖a7! 26 f6 ♔g8! and 24 ♔e7 ♖g7+ 25 ♔d6 ♖f7! etc. Long and complex variations which are explained in more detail in specialized books on endings. **8 ... ♖b1 9 ♖c5** or 9 h6 ♖a1! 10 ♖h5 ♔g8 11 h7+ ♔h8, or here 11 f5 ♔h7, both drawing **9 ... ♔f6 10 ♖c6+ ♔g7! 11 ♔g5 ♖g1+ 12 ♔f5 ♖a1 13 ♖c7+ ♔h6 14 ♖e7 ♖b1** and we have reached a position similar to diagram 178. After a further 25 moves the game ended in a draw.

3 h5 ♖a6

Admitting his mistake. After 3 ... ♖h1 4 ♖h4 ♖g1+ 5 ♔f2 ♖g7 6 h6 ♖h7 7 ♔g3 wins easily.

4 ♖h4 ♖h6

5 ♖f4+

White must stop the king blockading the h-pawn, so 5 ♖a4 ♖b6 6 ♖a5+? ♔f6 would not be so effective.

5 ... ♔g5

6 ♖g4+ ♔f5

After 6 ... ♔xh5 7 ♖h4+ or 6 ... ♔f6 7 ♖g6+, both pawn endings are lost for Black.

7 ♔h4 ♖h8

The black rook must remain passive, as 7 ... ♖a6 fails to 8 ♖g5+ ♔f4 9 ♖g6 and 10 ♖f6+.

8 ♖g5+ ♔f6

Or 8 ... ♔f4 9 ♖g7 wins.

9 ♔g4 ♔f7

10 ♖f5+

White must not throw away his advantage by playing 10 ♖a5

♖g8+ 11 ♔f5 ♔g7! when the black king reaches the h-file.

10	**...**	**♔g7**
11	**♔g5**	**♖g8**
12	**♖f6**	**♔h7+**

So the king finally manages to blockade the h-pawn, but meanwhile White's pieces are placed so actively that Black cannot save the game.

13	**♖g6**	**♖a8**
14	**f4**	**♖a1**
15	**♖e6**	**♖g1+**
16	**♔f6** *(181)*	

Keres-Sokolsky 1947

It is very important to have left the h-pawn on h5 where it cannot be captured so easily. With this pawn on h6 the game would be drawn, as the reader can verify for himself.

16	**...**	**♖f1**

After 16 ... ♖h1 White wins by 17 f5 ♖xh5 18 ♖e7+ ♔h6 19 ♖e8 ♔h7 20 ♔e6 and 21 f6.

17	**f5**	**♖f2**

Or 17 ... ♔h6 18 ♔f7+ ♔xh5 19 f6 ♔h6 20 ♔f8 wins.

18	**♖e5**	**♖h2**

Or 18 ... ♔h6 19 ♔f7 ♔xh5 20 f6+ ♔h6 21 ♖e1 wins.

19	**♖e7+**	**♔h6**
20	**♖e8**	**♔h7**
21	**♔e6**	**♖e2+**
22	**♔f7**	**♖a2**
23	**f6**	**♖a6**
24	**♔e7**	**♖a7+**
25	**♔f8**	**♖a6**

White's h-pawn prevents the saving move 25 ... ♔g6.

26	**f7**	**♖a7**
27	**♖c8**	**♖a1**
28	**♔e7**	

1-0

This example completes our discussion of rook and bishop's pawn against rook. We have devoted a fair amount of space, perhaps relatively too much space, to this ending but it is of great practical importance and still badly understood by many chessplayers. It is basic rook endings such as this which are mishandled over the board.

If White has two connected pawns, he almost always wins. Consider, for example, how to win with the g- and h-pawns.

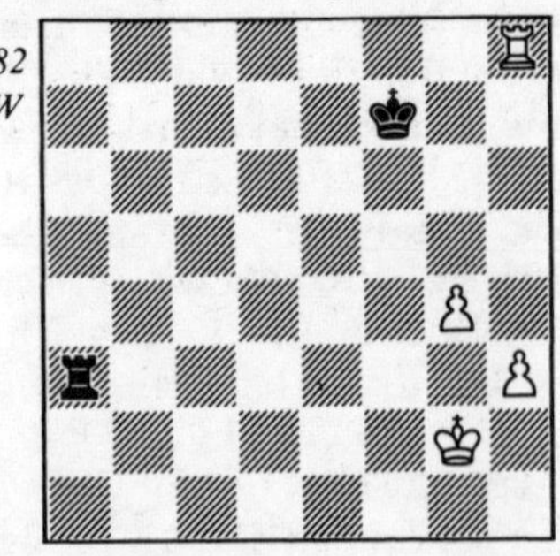

(Zukertort-Steinitz 1883)

A guiding rule in this type of position is to **post the king as advantageously as possible before advancing the pawns**. If the king is too far from the pawns, the defender can often draw by attacking the pawns and driving them to unfavourable squares. In our analysis we shall follow the actual game with its instructive errors, rather than give the strongest continuation.

1 ♖b8

The most logical plan would be ♖h5-f5-f3 followed by ♔g3 and only then begin to advance the pawns. White makes his task much more difficult by ignoring this general principle.

1 ... ♔g6
2 ♖b5 ♖c3
3 ♖e5

He should still play 3 ♖f5 and 4 ♖f3 but not of course 3 h4 when his king would have no protection from horizontal checks after 3 ... ♖f2+.

3 ... ♖a3
4 h4

Advancing his pawns before bringing up his king. Admittedly the position is still won but more logical was 4 ♖f5 ♖b3 5 ♖f3 ♖b1 6 ♔g3 ♖g1+ 7 ♔h4 ♖a1 8 ♖b3 ♖a6 9 ♖b4 followed by 10 g5, 11 ♔g4 and the advance of the h-pawn to h5.

4 ... ♖b3
5 h5+

It was important to avoid 5 g5? which would only draw after 5 ... ♔h5! 6 ♖e4 ♖a3 7 ♖f4 ♖b3 8 ♖f3 ♖b4 etc. **The pawns must never be advanced in such a way that the black king can attack the backward pawn and be sheltered by the other pawn.**

5 ... ♔h6
6 ♖f5 ♖a3
7 ♖f3 ♖a1

Black could set a trap by 7 ... ♖a5 when 8 ♔g3? ♔g5! draws. However, White wins by 8 ♖f6+ ♔g5 (or 8 ... ♔g7 9 ♖g6+ and 10 ♔g3) 9 ♖g6+ ♔f4 10 h6 etc. Note that in this position the pawns can advance without the help of the king, e.g. 10 ... ♖a8 11 g5 ♔f5 12 ♖g7 ♖h8 13 h7 followed by 14 g6 and 15 ♖g8.

8 ♔g3

White creates difficulties for himself. There was an easy win by 8 ♖f6+ ♔g5 9 ♖g6+ ♔f4 10 h6 ♖a2+ 11 ♔f1 (not 11 ♔h1? ♔g3 and Black even wins!) 11 .... ♔f3 12 ♔e1 ♔e3 13 ♔d1 ♔d3 13 ♖d6+ and 15 g5 etc. Or here 8 ... ♔g7 9 ♖g6+ and 10 ♔g3 winning.

8 ... ♖g1+
9 ♔h4 ♖h1+
10 ♖h3 ♖g1 *(183)*

183
W

(Zukertort-Steinitz 1883)

11 ♖h2!

Placing Black in zugzwang and so forcing g5, but White ought not to have to resort to such methods!

11 ... ♖a1
12 g5+ ♔g7
13 ♖f2

White dare not move any of the pawns and he must keep his rook fairly near in case of horizontal checks.

13 ... ♖h1+

Or 13 ... ♖a4+ 14 ♔g3 ♖b4 15 ♖f4 ♖b1 16 ♔g4 etc, as in the game.

14 ♔g4 ♖g1+
15 ♔f5 ♖h1
16 h6+ ♔h7

In the actual game Zukertort now continued 17 ♔f6 and after 17 ... ♖g1! had to change his plan again. After the game (which was played with colours reversed) he gave our text line as an improvement. However, the quickest way to win lies in 17 g6+! ♔xh6 18 ♔f6 and the pawn cannot be stopped. To prevent this line, Black should have played 15 ... ♖a1 instead of 15 ... ♖h1.

17 ♖f4 ♖g1
18 ♖e4 ♖f1+
19 ♔g4 ♖g1+
20 ♔h5 ♖h1+
21 ♖h4 ♖g1
22 ♖h2! ♖g3

Forced, or else White plays 23 g6. However, Black's rook is now too near his king and White can decisively improve the placing of his pieces.

23 ♖e2 ♖h3+
24 ♔g4 ♖a3
25 ♖e7+ ♔g8
26 g6

Clinching matters, although there are now several ways of winning the game.

26 ... ♖a4+
27 ♔f5 ♖a8
28 ♖e5

Also possible is 28 ♖d7 followed by advancing the king to e7 and the exchange of rooks on d8, or after 29 ♔f6 ♔h8 White has the neat finish 30 ♖f7 ♖a6+ 31 ♔g5 ♖a8 32 ♖f8+ ♖xf8 33 g7+ ♔g8 34 ♔g6! winning.

28 ... ♔h8
29 ♔g5

and Black has no defence against 30 h7 and 31 ♔h6. Certainly a very long-winded method of play, but giving us the chance of acquainting the reader with various instructive possibilities in this ending.

Our next example, diagram 184, illustrates the difficulties White faces when he allows the enemy king to occupy a favourable blockading square.

184

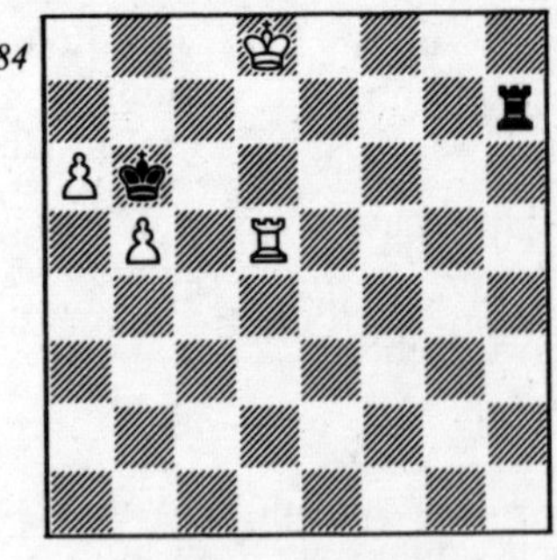

A.Chéron 1926

Although White's pawns are far advanced and the white rook is actively placed, there is no way to win, mainly because of the excellent position of Black's king.

1	**♔c8**	**♖g7**
2	**♖d7**	**♖g8+**
3	**♖d8**	**♖g7**
4	**♔b8**	

Indirectly protecting his pawn, as 4 ... ♔xb5 fails to 5 a7. If 4 ♖d6+ ♔xb5 5 ♔b8 then 5 ... ♖g8+ draws.

4	**...**	**♖h7**
5	**♖d6+**	

Or 5 ♖e8 ♖g7 6 ♖e6+ ♔xb5 7 a7 ♖g8+ 8 ♔b7 ♖g7+ draws.

5	**...**	**♔c5**

And not 5 ... ♔xb5 6 a7 ♖h8+ 7 ♔c7 ♖h7+ 8 ♖d7 winning.

6	**b6**	

If 6 ♖e6 then 6 ... ♔xb5 can be played. Or 6 a7 ♔xd6 7 b6 ♔c5 etc. Or 6 ♖d8 ♔b6! draws.

6	**...**	**♔xd6**

and the game is drawn after both 7 b7 ♖h8+ followed by 8 ... ♔c7 and 7 a7 ♔c5 8 b7 ♔b6! etc.

White's winning chances are far better if the pawns are nearer the centre and there is little point in analysing such positions. However, before leaving the connected knight's pawn and rook's pawn, we must mention the following interesting study by Kling and Horwitz.

White has great difficulties to overcome before he achieves the win: **1 ♔a5 ♖h5+ 2 ♖b5 ♖h8 3 ♖b6!** the only move to win; after 3 ♖c5? ♖h6! draws and other king

185

Kling and Horwitz 1851

moves would be answered by check along the rank followed by ... ♖h8. If the same position occurred further down the board, the text move would not be available, so Black would draw **3 ... ♖h5+ 4 ♔b4 ♖h4+ 5 ♔c5 ♖h5+ 6 ♔d4 ♖h4+ 7 ♔e5 ♖h5+ 8 ♔f4 ♖h4+ 9 ♔g5 ♖h8 10 ♖c6! ♔b8** forced, as White threatened 11 ♖c8 **11 ♔g6 ♖f8 12 ♔g7 ♖d8 13 ♖f6** and **14 ♖f8** winning.

Surprisingly enough, if the white king is far enough away from the connected pawns, there are many drawing positions. Consider our next example:

186

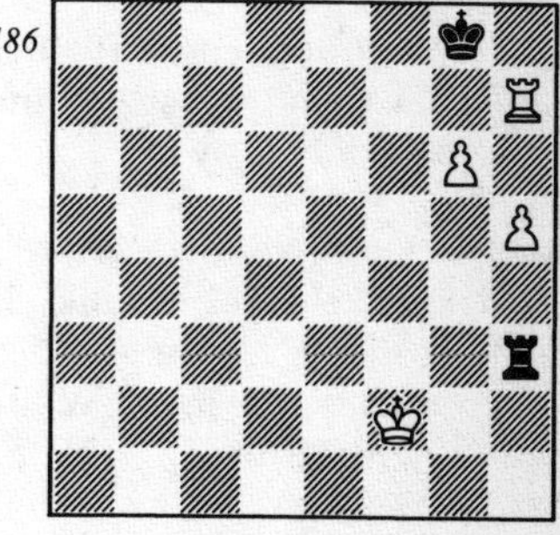

G.Kasparian

At first sight there seems no problem, for White's king has only to reach h6 and Black can resign. However, upon closer examination of Black's hidden resources, we see that White has considerable difficulties. His plan is to drive the black rook away from the attack on the h-pawn so as to activate his own rook. To do this, his king has to go to g2 whereupon Black plays ... ♖a3, and if now ♖b7 then ... ♖a5! follows. The white rook must now go back to h7, because the position of White's king means that h6 allows ... ♖g5+ and ... ♖xg6.

If White plays an immediate h6, Black answers ... ♖h5-g5 forcing ♖g7+ when Black's king nestles into the corner stalemate position by ... ♔h8! and White must lose a pawn or allow perpetual check by Black's rook. So White must free his rook from defence of the h-pawn without placing his king on the g-file. This is indeed possible with Black to move, but White to move is equally in zugzwang and cannot transfer the move to his opponent. In other words, Black to move loses, White to move can only draw.

1 ... ♖a3

Black cannot allow White's king to cross the third rank. If instead 1 ... ♔f8 2 ♖f7+ ♔g8 3 ♖f5 follows. On the other hand, White to move can make no progress, for if 1 ♔f1 ♖f3+ (or 1 ... ♖h2) 2 ♔g2 ♖a3 3 ♔f2 ♖h3 etc, whereas if the king moves away from the kingside, the black rook oscillates between h3 and g3.

2 ♖c7 ♖h3

Now that White's king is not on the g-file, 2 ... ♖a5 loses to 3 h6 etc.

3 ♖c5 ♔g7

4 ♔g2

White now wins fairly easily, as the black rook is forced to give way. Even if White's king were further away, he would still win, but with much more difficulty. For instance, with his king on a2, we have diagram 187.

187

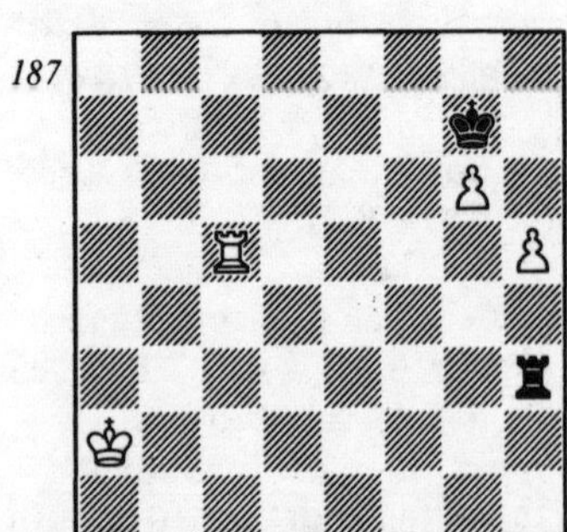

White would proceed as follows: **1 ♖g5** or 1 ♔b2 ♔h6 2 ♖g5! **1 ... ♖h4** the rook dare not leave the file because of 2 h6+ **2 ♔b3 ♖h1 3 ♔c4** no quicker is 3 ♔c2 ♖h4 4 ♔d3 ♖h1 5 ♔e2 ♖h4 6 ♔f2, because Black plays 6 ... ♖h2+! 7 ♔g3 ♖h1 8 ♔g2 ♖h5 and White cannot gain a tempo **3 ... ♖c1+ 4 ♔d5 ♖d1+** or 4 ... ♖c2 5 ♖e5 ♔h6 6 ♔e6 etc **5 ♔e6 ♖e1+ 6 ♔d6 ♖d1+ 7 ♖d5 ♖a1** or 7 ... ♖e1 8 ♔d7 ♔h6 9 ♔d8 threatening 10 ♖d7 **8 ♔e7 ♖a6** or 8 ... ♖e1+ 9 ♔d8! ♔h6 10 ♖d7! ♔xh5 11 g7

♖g1 12 ♔e8 etc **9 ♖d7 ♖c6** if 9 ... ♖b6 White plays 10 ♔d8+ ♔g8 11 ♔c7 ♖a6 12 ♖d6 with h6 to follow **10 ♔d8+ ♔g8 11 ♖e7 ♔f8** or 11 ... ♖d6+ 12 ♔c7 ♖a6 13 ♔d7 threatening 14 ♖e6 **12 ♔d7 ♖a6 13 ♖e6 ♖a7+ 14 ♔d6 ♖a6+ 15 ♔e5** wins.

4 ... ♖h4

5 ♔g3 ♖h1

Or 5 ... ♖h4 6 ♖c7+ ♔g8 7 h6 etc.

6 ♖c7+ ♔g8

7 ♔g4

and White wins easily by advancing his king to h6.

In this context it is worth quoting the following study by Kasparian:

188

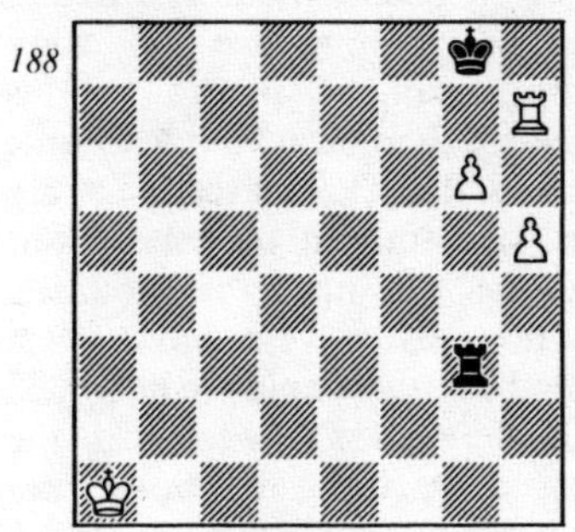

H.Kasparian 1946

White to move has only one way to win, by playing **1 ♔a2!** when Black is in zugzwang. He can only oscillate with his rook between h3 and g3, and after **1 ... ♖h3 2 ♔b2 ♖g3 3 ♔c2 ♖h3 4 ♔d2 ♖g3 5 ♔e2 ♖h3 6 ♔f2!** we arrive at diagram 186, with Black to move, which is of course won for White. It is scarcely credible that the owner of two connected pawns can have such problems!

However, even less credible is the fact that it is sometimes impossible to win even with two pawns standing next to each other and neither of them a rook's pawn. Diagram 189 show us that such positions are possible.

189

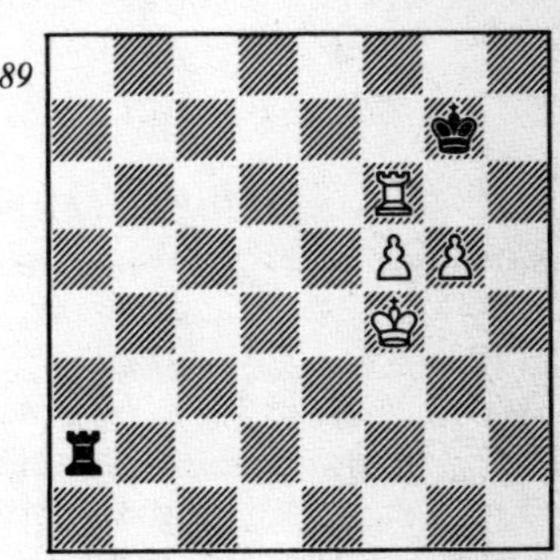

H.Kasparian 1946

White appears to have all elements in his favour and Black seems on the verge of resignation. However, Black can skilfully exploit the fact that the white rook is momentarily placed in an awkward position.

1 ... ♖f2+

Of course, White to move would win comfortably by 1 ♖d6. Horizontal checks are pointless here, as the white king can shelter on h5.

2 ♔e3

White would shorten the solution by playing 2 ♔e5, but we wish to show that other attempts lead nowhere. If 2 ♔g3 ♖f1 3 ♔g2 ♖f4

4 ♔h3 ♖f1 draws.

2 ... ♖g2

Whereas now it is the g-pawn which is attacked.

3 ♖g6+ ♔f7
4 ♔f3 ♖g1
5 ♔f2 ♖g4

The black rook cannot be driven away, so White's king must now head for d7.

6 ♔f3 ♖g1
7 ♔e4 ♖e1+
8 ♔d5 ♖g1
9 ♖f6+

Or 9 ♔d6 ♖g2 10 ♔d7 ♖g2 transposing.

9 ... ♔g7
10 ♔e6 ♖e1+!

After 10 ... ♖xg5 11 ♖f7+ wins, e.g. 11 ... ♔h6 (or 11 ... ♔g8 12 ♖a7 ♖g1 13 ♖a8+ ♔h7 14 f6 etc) 12 ♖f8 ♖g1 13 f6 ♖a1 (or 13 ... ♖e1+ 14 ♔f7 ♔h7 15 ♖e8 wins) 14 ♖h8+ ♔g6 15 ♖g8+ and 16 f7 wins.

11 ♔d6

Black draws at once after 11 ♔d7 ♖e5 12 ♔d6 ♖a5 etc.

11 ... ♖g1
12 ♖g6+

Or 12 ♔e7 ♖xg5 13 ♖f8 ♔h7! 14 f6 ♖e5+ 15 ♔f7 ♖a5 drawing.

12 ... ♔f7
13 ♔d7 ♖g2
14 ♖f6+ ♔g7

White makes his final attempt by sacrificing his g-pawn in order to advance the f-pawn.

15 ♖d6 ♖xg5
16 ♔e6 ♖g1
17 ♔e7

Or 17 f6+ ♔g6 18 ♔e7 ♖f1 19 ♖e6 ♖f2 20 ♖e1 ♖a2! 21 ♖g1+ ♔h7 drawing.

17 ... ♖f1
18 ♖g6+ ♔h7

and the game is clearly drawn.

There are many other interesting positions in which Black manages to draw with two pawns down. However, as these are usually distinguished by a badly placed white piece, they can be classed as exceptional. As such they are of little practical value and beyond the scope of this book.

Rook and Pawn(s) on both sides

Let us now consider positions in which both sides have one or more pawns. This type of ending naturally occurs the most often in practice and almost all rook endings can be placed in this category. It is clear that a volume such as this can scarcely classify this vast amount of material or evaluate the many possibilities. For this reason, we intend to select only basic examples which will show the reader how to tackle the most important situations that can arise.

A: ROOK AND PAWN AGAINST ROOK AND PAWN

Equally balanced material usually means a drawn result, so we are here mainly interested in special cases where one side has sufficient positional advantage to win. The most well-known example of such ending is the following study composed by a former World

Champion, Lasker:

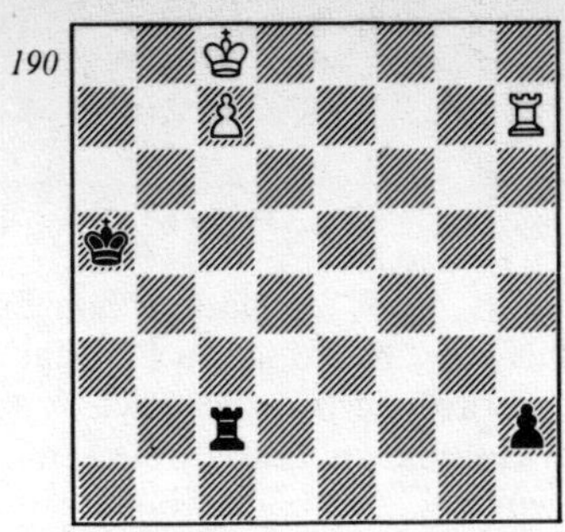

190

Dr Em. Lasker 1890

If White's king steps out into the open, he is checked away from the pawn which is then attacked again by ... ♖c2, forcing the king back to its defence. However, White can still win by an instructive manoeuvre which occurs with surprising frequency in practical play.

1	**♔b7**	**♖b2+**
2	**♔a7**	**♖c2**

All forced, as is clear.

3	**♖h5+**	**♔a4**

After 3 ... ♔b4 4 ♔b7 wins at once. White now repeats his previous manoeuvre.

4	**♔b7**	**♖b2+**
5	**♔a6**	**♖c2**
6	**♖h4+**	**♔a3**
7	**♔b6**	**♖b2+**

White was threatening 8 ♖xh2.

8	**♔a5!**	**♖c2**
9	**♖h3+**	**♔a2**
10	**♖xh2** wins.	

This is the point, as Black's rook is now pinned and cannot take the pawn.

191

P.Keres 1944

Lasker's idea has since been repeated in various forms by tournament players who have introduced further subtleties. Consider diagram 191 in which the winning idea is used with a central pawn, although admittedly the black rook is passively placed in front of his own pawn.

White first uses the black king's position in order to advance his pawn to the 7th rank.

1	**♔e8+**	**♔g6**

As we shall see later, White wins fairly easily if his rook can reach the second rank without Black's king being too near the a-pawn. For this reason 1 ... ♔g8 would lose more quickly.

2	**e7**	**♔h5**

In order to answer 3 ♖a3 with 3 ... ♔h4 preventing 4 ♖h3+ and 5 ♖h2. If Black plays passsively here is what happens:

1) **2 ... ♔g7 3 ♖a3 ♖b1** or variation 2 **4 ♖xa2 ♖b8+ 5 ♔d7 ♖b7+ 6 ♔d8 ♖b8+ 7 ♔c7** wins.

2) **2 ... ♔h6 3 ♖a3 ♔g5** or 3 ... ♔h5

4 ♖h3+ ♔g4 5 ♖h2 ♔g3 6 ♖d2 ♔f3 7 ♔d7 ♔e3 8 ♖xa2 wins **4 ♖g3+ ♔f4 5 ♖g2 ♔f3** or 5 ... ♔e3 6 ♖b2 wins, as the black king cannot go to the d- or f-files, and 6 ... ♔e4 7 ♔d7 transposes **6 ♖b2** but not 6 ♖d2 ♔e3 7 ♔d7 ♔xd2 8 e8♕ ♖d1! etc **6 ... ♔e3 7 ♔d7 ♖d1+ 8 ♔c7 ♖c1+ 9 ♔b7** winning, for the pawn queens with check.

In other words, Black dare not allow White's rook to reach the 2nd rank. The question now is whether White can make any progress. He succeeds in an interesting way by bringing about a zugzwang position.

3 ♖a3 ♔h4!

The best defence. After 3 ... ♔g4 4 ♔f7 gains a tempo on the main line, whereas now 4 ♔f7 ♖f1+ 5 ♔g6 ♖g1+ 6 ♔h6 ♖e1 7 ♖a4+ ♔g3 draws. Because the black king has an extra file at his disposal, Lasker's manoeuvre does not appear to work. However, White wins by a cunning move.

4 ♖a5!

Placing Black in zugzwang, as his king cannot retreat, nor can it go to the 6th rank when White can employ the Lasker stratagem. It is incredible what subtleties can be hidden in the simplest looking positions!

4 ... ♔g4

5 ♔f7!

The point is that Black no longer has a check on the g-file, so Lasker's idea is now successful!

5 ... ♖f1+

6 ♔g6 ♖e1

7 ♖a4+ ♔h3!

Again the best. White wins easily after 7 ... ♔g3 8 ♔f6 etc.

8 ♔f6 ♖f1+

9 ♔g5 ♖g1+

10 ♔h5 ♖e1

Unfortunately for Black, although he has driven the white king far enough away from the pawn, his own king has advanced one rank too much.

11 ♖a3+ ♔g2

12 ♖xa2+

In Lasker's study, the capture of this pawn finished the game immediately, whereas here it is only the end of the beginning. By using the fact that White's king is two files away from the pawn, Black can set up a stubborn defence.

12 ... ♔f3

13 ♖a7 ♖e6

An important move, cutting off the white king from the sixth rank and threatening to play his own king over to d6. To win this position, White has to create another endgame study.

14 ♔g5 ♔e4

15 ♖b7!

But not the obvious 15 ♖d7? ♔e5! when it is White who is in zugzwang and the position is drawn. However, 15 ♖c7 is also possible.

Black is now in zugzwang, as he cannot allow White's king to reach f5 and 15 ... ♖e5+ fails to 16 ♔f6 with an easy win.

15 ... ♔e5

16 ♖d7

Only now is this move played, leading to a forced win.

16 ... ♔e4
17 ♖d1! ♔f3
18 ♖f1+ ♔e2
19 ♖f7 and
20 ♔f5 winning easily.

Who would have thought that the solution would be so long?

Here is another example in which the Lasker idea only occurs after some complex preliminary manoeuvres.

192

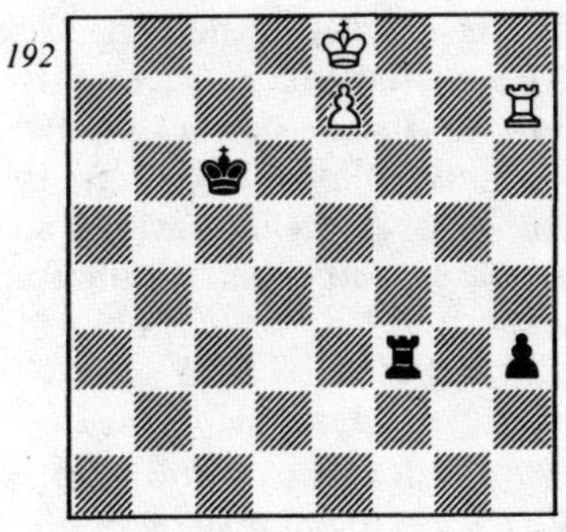

The black pawn is still on the 6th rank, which gives White various advantages. Firstly, to carry out the Lasker plan, he needs to drive the black king back one rank. Secondly, he can now in certain circumstances use his rook to protect his king from checks, as his pawn queens one move earlier. These factors lead to an instructive win.

1 ♔d8 ♖d3+
2 ♔c8 ♖e3
3 ♖h6+

Beginning our well-known manoeuvre, but surely Black's king has too many files at his disposal on the queenside? As will be seen, White must utilize some hidden resources to back up the main plan.

3 ... ♔c5!

The best square for the king. 3 ... ♔d5 allows 4 ♔d7, and 3 ... ♔b5 fails to 4 ♔d7 ♖d3+ 5 ♖d6! and White's pawn queens with check! However, this means that Black's king can now be driven further back.

4 ♔d7 ♖d3+
5 ♔c7

White achieves nothing with 5 ♔e8 when Black plays 5 ... ♖e3 or 5 ... ♖a3.

5 ... ♖e3
6 ♖h5+ ♔b4!

The king must now leave the c-file, as 6 ... ♔c4 loses at once to 7 ♔d7 ♖e3 8 ♖h4+, 9 ♖h4+ and 10 ♖xh3.

7 ♔d7 ♖d3+
8 ♔c6 ♖e3

Once again 8 ... ♖c3+ allows 9 ♔b6 ♖e3 10 ♖h4+ and 11 ♖xh3 winning. It now seems that White can make no progress, but there is one final resource in the position.

9 ♖h4+! ♔a5

Forced, as other moves lose to 10 ♖xh3.

10 ♔d6!

If 10 ♔d7 ♖d3+ 11 ♔e8 threatening 12 ♖h8 Black saves himself by 11 ... ♖b3! etc, when White must come back with his king.

10 ... ♖d3+

Black can set a trap with 10 ...

♔b6 11 ♖xh3? ♖xh3 12 e8♕ ♖d3+ followed by 13 ... ♖e3+ drawing, but 11 ♖h8! wins easily.

11 ♔c5! ♖e3

Or 11 ... ♖c3+ 12 ♔d4 ♖c8 13 ♖xh3 and 14 ♖e3.

12 ♖xh3! wins.

After 12 ... ♖xe7 13 ♖a3 is mate! A surprising twist.

There are other interesting and instructive positions on the same theme, but these would take us too far afield. The keen reader can find many examples of such endings both in games and in studies. Here is one final illustration of rook and pawn against rook and pawn, underlines once again the need to understand elementary endings. This example shows us that even in World Championship matches errors can occur in endgame play.

193
B

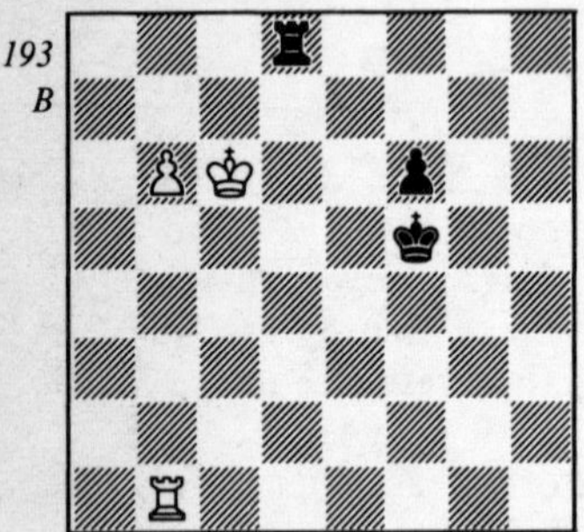

Alekhine-Bogoljubow 1929

This is taken from the 19th game of the Alekhine-Bogoljubow match, 1929. White clearly stands better, for his passed pawn, supported by king and rook, cannot be stopped and is only two squares away from queening. Black must soon give up his rook, so the only chance lies in his own pawn. The game continued:

1 ... ♔g4

Forgetting the important rule which we gave earlier. When time is of the essence, both kings must position themselves so as to restrict as far as possible the approach of the enemy king. In our example it is clear that Black must soon give up his rook on the b8 square, when the white king will have to cross over the d-file as quickly as he can, if he wishes to stop Black's pawn. This points to Black's correct defence. He should play his king to the e-file by **1 ... ♔e4!** blocking the white king's approach, when he draws after **2 b7** or 2 ♖e1+ ♔f4 3 ♖f1+ ♔e5 4 b7 f5 5 ♔c7 ♖f8 6 b8♕ ♖xb8 7 ♔xb8 f4 8 ♔c7 ♔e4 9 ♔d6 f3 draws **2 ... f5 3 b8♕** or 3 ♖a1 ♖b8 etc **3 ... ♖xb8 4 ♖xb8 f4 5 ♖b4+** or 5 ♖e8+ ♔d4 6 ♖f8 ♔e3 and 7 ... f3 draws **5 ... ♔e3 6 ♔d5 f3 7 ♖b3+ ♔e2** but not 7 ... ♔f4? 8 ♔d4 f2 9 ♖b1 ♔f3 10 ♔d3 winning **8 ♔e4 f2 9 ♖b2+ ♔e1 10 ♔e3 f1♘+!** with a book draw.

2 b7 f5

Or 2 ... ♖b8 3 ♔c7 ♖xb7+ 4 ♔xb7 f5 5 ♔c6 wins.

3 b8♕ ♖xb8
4 ♖xb8 f4
5 ♔d5 f3
6 ♔e4 f2
7 ♖f8 ♔g3
8 ♔e3

1-0

Even the simplest endings must be played with precision!

B: ROOK AND TWO PAWNS AGAINST ROOK AND PAWN

This is another type of situation in which it is difficult to state general rules, as so much depends upon the placing of the pieces. Once again we shall therefore restrict ourselves to examples of most practical value to the average chessplayer.

Let us begin with White having two connected pawns, as against Black's single pawn.

194
W

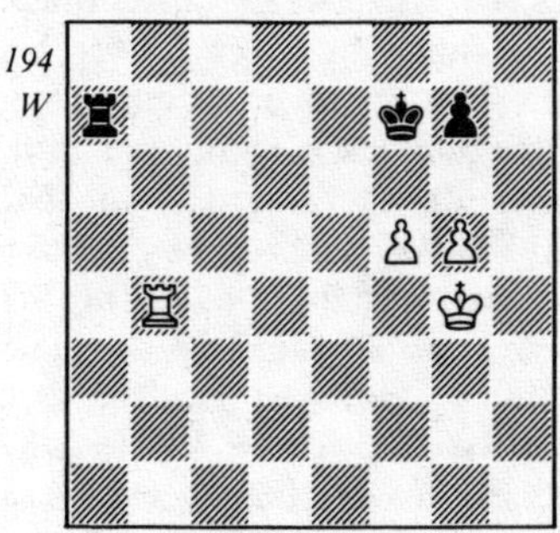

Chekhover-Kasakevich 1949

Usually when none of the pawns is passed, the defender has good drawing prospects. White has chances only if his pawns are reasonably far advanced or if his king can occupy vital squares in front of the pawns. The play from the diagram shows us an interesting win based on the favourable position of White's pieces:

1 ♔h5

A strong square for the king, limiting Black's choice of moves.

1 ... ♖c7

Tempting is 1 ... g6+ in order to obtain a drawn position after 2 fg+ ♔g7. However, this is refuted by 2 ♔h6! gf 3 g6+ ♔f6 4 ♖b6+ (if 4 g7 ♖a1! draws) 4 ... ♔e5 5 g7 ♖a8 6 ♖g6 ♖g8 7 ♔h7 ♖a8 8 g8♕ ♖xg8 9 ♖xg8 f4 10 ♔g6 f3 11 ♔g5 winning.

Equally hopeless is 1 ... ♖a1 2 ♖b7+ ♔f8 3 ♔g6 ♖a6+ 4 f6 gf 5 gf ♖a8 6 ♖h7 with an easy win. If Black plays 1 ... ♖a6 2 ♖b7+ we are back in the main line.

2 ♖b8 ♖c6

Giving White the most difficulties. The actual game continued 2 ... ♖a7 3 g6+ ♔f6 4 ♖f8+ ♔e5 5 f6! (if 5 ♖f7 ♖a1 White dare not play 6 ♖xg7 when 6 ... ♔f4! even wins for Black!) 5 ... gf 6 ♔h6 ♖a1 7 g7 ♖h1+ 8 ♔g6 ♖g1+ 9 ♔f7 1-0. The finish might have been 9 ... f5 10 g8♕ ♖xg8 11 ♖xg8 f4 12 ♔g6 f3 13 ♔g5 ♔e4 14 ♔g4 with an easy win.

3 g6+

If Black had played 1 ... ♖a6 2 ♖b7+ ♔f8 3 ♖b8+, he would now have 3 ... ♔e7 at his disposal. White would then win by 4 f6+! gf 5 g6 ♖a1 6 g7 ♖h1+ 7 ♔g6 ♖g1+ 8 ♔h7 ♖h1+ 9 ♔g8 f5 10 ♖b7+ ♔e6 (or 10 ... ♔f6 11 ♔f8 ♖g1 12 ♖f7+! ♔e5 13 g8♕ ♖xg8+ 14 ♔xg8 f4 15 ♔g7) 11 ♔f8 ♖g1 12 g8♕+ ♖xg8+ 13 ♔xg8 f4 14 ♖f7 and the black pawn is again stopped.

3 ... ♔e7
4 ♖g8 ♔f6
5 ♖f8+ ♔e5

6 f6!

Given by Chekhover and surprisingly strong. White makes no progress with 6 ♖f7 ♖c1 (7 ♖xg7? ♔f4!) or with 6 ♔g5 ♖c1 7 ♖e8+ ♔d6 etc.

6 ... ♖xf6
7 ♖f7 ♔e6

Or 7 ... ♖f5+ 8 ♔g4 ♖c6 9 ♔g5 ♖a6 10 ♖xg7 wins.

8 ♖xg7 ♖f1
9 ♖a7 and wins easily.

As can be seen from this example, Black has great difficulties if White has managed to advance his pawns far enough. Of course, White has even better chances if the pawns are on the central files, as his king then has more room to manoeuvre. Diagram 195 gives us some idea of the dangers facing Black in such a situation.

195
W

From a game played in 1956

This position arose in a game played in Moscow, 1956. It had to be adjudicated and was given a win for White. However, Levenfish later pointed out the following draw:

1 ♔g5 ♖c5!

The only defence to prevent White setting up a winning position similar to diagram 194 by playing 2 f5. This means that Black loses after **1 ... ♖c1 2 ♖b7+ ♔f8** or 2 ... ♔e6 3 f5+ ♔xe5 4 ♖e7+ ♔d6 5 ♖xf7 winning **3 f5 ♖h1** or 3 ... ♖c6 4 ♖b8+ wins easily, e.g. 4 ... ♔e7 5 f6+ ♔e6 6 ♖e8+ ♔d5 7 ♔h6 winning. Or 4 ... ♔g7 5 f6+ ♔h7 6 ♖e8 when both 6 ... ♖c1 7 e6 and 6 ... ♖c5 7 ♖e7 ♔g8 8 ♔h6 ♖c8 9 e6! fe 10 ♔g6 win for White **4 ♖a7!** but not at once 4 ♖b8+ ♔e7 5 f6+ ♔d7 6 ♖f8 ♖g1+ and Black checks until he frees f5 for his king. The text move uses zugzwang to drive Black's rook one rank further up the board **4 ... ♖h2 5 ♖a8+ ♔e7** or 5 ... ♔g7 6 f6+ ♔h7 7 e6! etc **6 f6+ ♔d7 7 ♖f8 ♖h7** now 7 ... ♖g2+ fails to 8 ♔f4 ♔e6 9 ♖e8+ ♔d5 10 ♖d8+ ♔c6 11 ♖f8 **8 ♔f5 ♖h5+ 9 ♔f4 ♖h7 10 ♔g5 ♔e6** or 10 ... ♔c6 11 ♖e8 wins **11 ♖e8+ ♔d5 12 e6 fe 13 ♔g6** and **14 f7** winning.

2 ♔h6

If 2 ♖b7+ then Black does not play 2 ... ♔e6? 3 f5+ ♔xe5 4 ♖e7+ and 5 ♖xf7 winning, but 2 ... ♔f8! 3 f5 ♖xe5 4 ♔f6 ♖e1 5 ♖xf7+ ♔g8 6 ♖g7+ ♔h8 7 ♖a7 ♖f1! with a book draw. The text move threatens 2 ♔g7, so Black's reply is forced.

2 ... ♖c1
3 ♖b7+ ♔f8
4 f5

White has now apparently reached his goal and is threatening to win by 5 ♖b8+ and 6 f6+. However, in order to obtain this position, White's king has to leave the pawns. Black can use this circumstance to set up a successful defence.

4 ... ♖g1!

Again the only defence, cutting off White's king.

5 ♖b8+ ♔e7
6 f6+

There is no other way to make progress.

6 ... ♔e6
7 ♖e8+ ♔f5
8 ♔h7

If 8 e6 ♔xf6 draws. Or 8 ♖e7 ♖g2 9 ♖xf7 ♔xe5 10 ♖g7 ♖f2 11 f7 ♔e6 12 ♔g6 ♖f6+ draws.

8 ... ♖g2
9 ♖e7 ♖g5!

Black must be careful, as after 9 ... ♖g1 10 ♖xf7 ♔xe5 11 ♖g7! ♖h1+ 12 ♔g6 ♖g1+ 13 ♔f7 wins. The text move zugzwangs White, for if now 10 ♔h8 ♖g1! 11 ♖xf7 ♔xe5 12 ♖g7 ♖h1+ draws.

10 ♖xf7 ♔xe5
11 ♖g7 ♔xf6

½-½

We shall now consider a position in which one of White's connected pawns is also passed. In this case his winning chances are far better and only rarely can Black draw. Diagram 196 shows us a frequently occurring situation.

This position (with colours reversed) arose in the game Keres-Smyslov, 1949, and cannot be won, mainly because White's king is short of an extra file to penetrate down the right. The game continued:

196
W

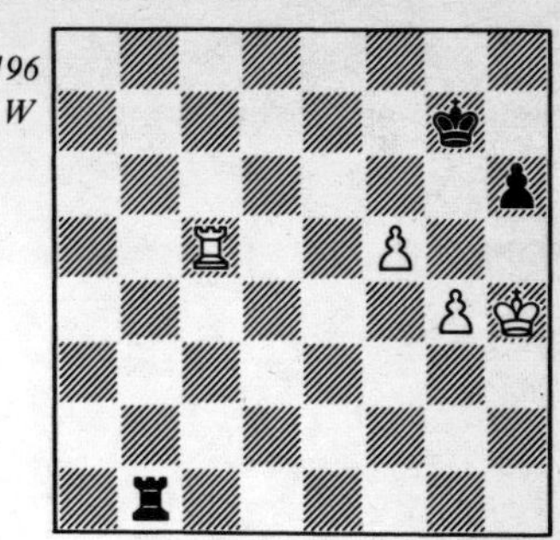

(Keres-Smyslov 1949)

1 ♖c7+ ♔f6

Black's king must not go to the back rank, as 1 ... ♔g8 loses to 2 ♔h5 ♖b6 3 ♖e7 and ♖e6.

2 ♖c6+

Or 2 ♖h7 ♖h1+ 3 ♔g3 ♖g1+ 4 ♔f3 ♖h1 draws.

2 ... ♔g7
3 ♖g6+ ♔h7
4 ♖e6 ♔g7
5 ♔g3 ♖f1

The simplest, giving White's king no chance of reaching the centre.

6 ♖e7+ ♔f6
7 ♖h7 ♖h1
8 ♔g2 ♖h4
9 ♔f3 ♖h1

White has made no progress. After the further moves 10 ♖h8 ♔g7 11 ♖d8 ♖f1+ 12 ♔g2 ♖f4 13 ♖d7+ ♔f6 14 ♖d6+ ♔g7 15 ♔g3 a draw was agreed.

It is worth noting that White could not have won even if his king had managed to advance down the centre.

197

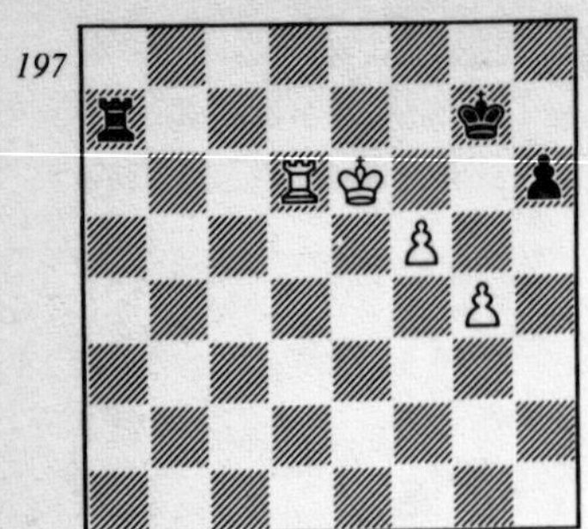

White can do little. The pawn ending after **1 ♖d7+ ♖xd7 2 ♔xd7 ♔f6**, followed by **3 ... h5**, is drawn, and 1 f6+ ♔g6 does not improve matters, whereas **1 ♖b6** fails to **1 ... ♖c7 2 ♖b8 ♖c6+ 3 ♔e7 ♖c7+** 4 **♔e8 ♖f7** threatening 5 ... h5 etc.

As already mentioned, White can do little in such positions because his king has insufficient manoeuvring room to the right of the pawns. This means that if we move diagram 196 one file to the left (diagram 198), White has good winning chances assuming he can advance his king in time.

198

Play might go **1 ♖b7+ ♔e6** or 1 ... ♔f8 2 ♔g5 ♖a6 3 ♖d7 and 4 ♖d6 wins **2 ♔g5 ♖g1+ 3 ♔h6** the vital square! **3 ... ♖g4 4 ♖b6+ ♔e7 5 ♖f6 ♔d7 6 ♔h7!** White must gain the opposition, as we shall see **6 ... ♔e8 7 ♔g8! ♔e7** or 7 ... ♖g1 8 ♔g7 ♖g4 9 ♖f7 wins **8 ♔g7 ♔e8 9 ♖f7 ♔d8** or 9 ... ♖g1 10 ♔f6 ♖g4 11 f5! gf 12 ♖a7 wins **10 ♔f8 ♖h4** the threat was 11 e6 **11 e6 ♖h8+ 12 ♔g7 ♖h4 13 ♔xg6** wins. Black to move can of course stop White's king advancing and draw by 1 ... ♖g1+ 2 ♔f3 ♔e7 etc.

Next we shall examine positions in which both of White's connected pawns are passed. White usually wins here, but there are a number of exceptions, especially if one of the pawns is a rook's pawn. Let us begin our discussion with an interesting example, shown in diagram 199.

199

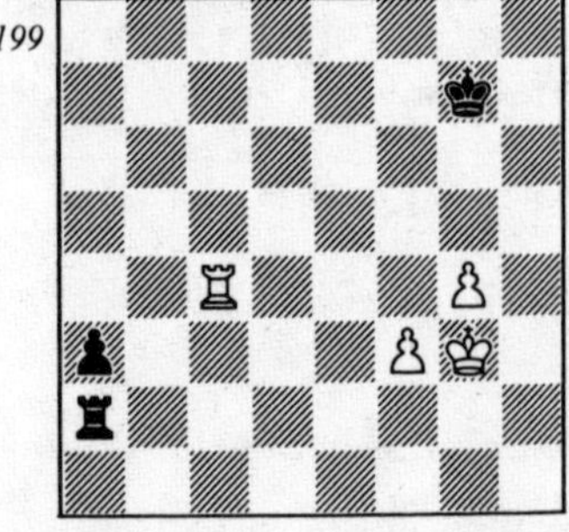

White has no rook's pawn, so should win, as we have stated. However, what is instructive here is that Black has the choice of keeping his rook in front of his pawn or guarding it from the side. Neither method can save the game, as the following analysis shows:

1 ... ♖a1

White has even further problems if Black guards the pawn from the side, e.g. 1 ... ♖b2 2 ♖a4 a2 3 ♖a6 (but not 3 ♔f4? ♖b4+!) 3 ... ♔f7 4 g5 ♔g7 5 ♔g4 ♔f7 (Black can only wait) 6 f4 ♔g7 7 f5 ♖g2+ 8 ♔f4 ♖f2+ 9 ♔e4 ♖e2+ 10 ♔f3 ♖b2 11 ♖a7+ ♔f8 12 g6 ♔g8 13 f6 wins, for to begin with Black's pawn is lost.

2 ♖a4 a2
3 ♔g2!

The only way to win! The plausible 3 ♔f4 only leads to a draw after 3 ... ♔f6 4 ♖a6+ ♔g7 5 g5 (or 5 ♔g5 ♖f1 6 ♖a7+ ♔g8 7 ♖xa2 ♖xf3 draws) 5 ... ♔f7 when White cannot play 6 ♔f5 because of 6 ... ♖f1 etc. However, if White's f-pawn were on f2, 3 ♔f4 would be the simplest way to win. White would advance his king and g-pawn, until Black would be forced to give up his pawn to avoid mate. On f2 White's pawn would be ideally placed, as the white rook guards it when the black pawn is captured.

3 ... ♔f6
4 f4 ♔e6
5 ♖a5

White must be careful in advancing his pawns, for if 5 ♖a6+ ♔d5 6 g5 ♔e4 7 g6 ♖b1! draws.

5 ... ♔f6
6 ♖a6+ ♔g7
7 f5 ♔f7

Or 7 ... ♖b1 8 ♖xa2 ♔f6 9 ♖a6+ wins.

8 g5 ♔g8

Or 8 ... ♖b1 9 ♖xa2 ♖b5 10 ♖f2 wins.

9 ♖a7 ♔f8
10 g6 wins.

White threatens 11 f6 followed by mate, and 10 ... ♖b1 loses to 11 ♖xa2 ♖b5 12 ♖f2 etc.

This example teaches us that Black can cause most problems with his rook in front of his pawn rather that at its side. White on the other hand should try to keep one of his pawns on its original square, when the win is easy.

Now let us turn to the more difficult situation when one of White's pawns is a rook's pawn. In this case, Black's defensive chances are far greater, as White's king has insufficient shelter against horizontal checks. A classic example of this is seen in diagram 200.

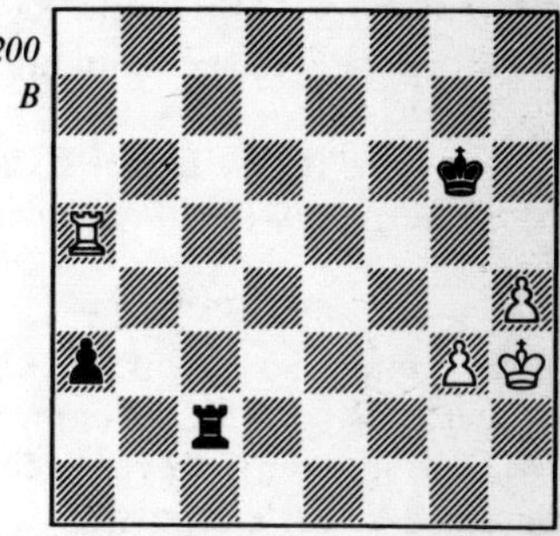

Tarrasch-Chigorin 1893

This position occurred in the Tarrasch-Chigorin match, 1893. Here also Black had the choice of placing his rook in front of or alongside his pawn. In contrast with diagram 199, however, the rook is best placed guarding the pawn on the rank, so as to be ready to check White's king from the side. He can then draw, whereas he would lose with his rook in front of the pawn.

In the game Chigorin selected the wrong plan and lost after 1 ... ♖a2? 2 ♔g4 ♖a1 3 ♖a6+ ♔f7 4 ♔g5 a2 5 g4 (White's pawns are now too far advanced) 5 ... ♔e7 6 ♖a7+ ♔e8 7 h5 ♔f8 8 h6 ♖b1 (or 8 ... ♔g8 9 ♔g6 etc) 9 ♖xa2 with an easy win. The loser pointed out later the correct defence in an instructive piece of analysis:

1 ... a2!

This ties White's rook to the a-file, which would not be the case after 1 ... ♖c3.

2 h5+ ♔f6

An alternative is 2 ... ♔h6 3 ♔h4 ♖h2+ 4 ♔g4 ♖b2 5 ♖a6+ ♔g7 6 ♔g5 ♖b5+ 7 ♔h4 ♖b2 8 g4 ♔f7! transposing to the main line.

3 ♔h4

The only try. If 3 g4 ♖c5! 4 ♖xa2 ♔g5! Black has a theoretical draw.

3 ... ♖h2+

Black could also play a waiting move with his rook, as he cannot in the long run prevent the advance of White's g-pawn.

4 ♔g4 ♖b2
5 ♖a6+ ♔f7

Or 5 ... ♔g7 6 ♔g5 ♖b5+ 7 ♔h4 ♖b2 8 g4 ♔f7! draws.

6 ♔g5 ♖b5+

An important move, as Black dare not allow his king to be driven to the back rank, e.g. 6 ... ♖c2? 7 ♖a7+ ♔g8 8 g4 followed by h6 and 10 ♔h5 wins. White's king must now retreat as 7 ♔h6? allows 7 ... ♖b6+!

7 ♔h4 ♖b2
8 g4 ♖c2

And not 8 ... ♔g7? 9 h6+ and 10 ♔h5 winning. In this defence, it is vital for Black to have his king on f7, with White's rook on a6, in order to prevent 9 ♔g5 ♖c5+ 10 ♔h6? because of 10 ... ♖c6+! White can now make no progress.

9 h6

Or 9 ♖a7+ ♔f6 10 g5+ ♔f5 11 h6 (11 ♖a5+ ♔f4 etc) 11 ... ♖h2+ 12 ♔g3 ♖h1 13 ♖xa2 ♔xg5 draws. Or 9 g5 ♖c4+ 10 ♔g3 ♖c3+ 11 ♔f4 ♖c4+ 12 ♔e3 ♖h4 13 h6 (13 g6+ ♔g7 14 ♖a7+ ♔g8 etc) 13 ... ♖g4 draws.

9 ... ♖c6!

and draws.

As Black's main defence here consisted of checks along the rank, it is worthwhile asking ourselves if White can do better by advancing his g-pawn first. This would then serve as a protection for his king while he advances both pawns. In most cases, this is indeed the correct winning procedure, failing only when the pawns are too far back. Diagram 201 is an excellent example of this type of position.

One can scarcely credit that the result of this position depends upon who has the move! Apparently Black can do little against White's plan of g4, ♔g3, h3, ♔h4, ♖a6+, g5, ♔g4 etc. This is indeed the case with White to move, when he wins as follows:

201

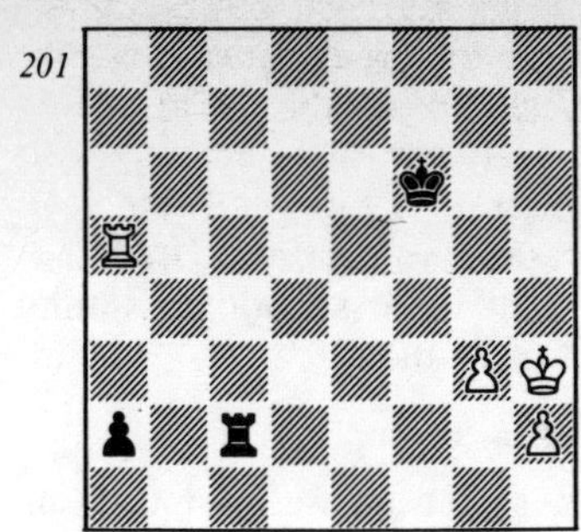

1 g4 ♔e6

Black's only chance is to play his king over to the queenside. If 1 ... ♖b2 2 ♔g3 ♖c2 3 h3 ♖b2 4 ♔h4 ♖h2 (White threatened 5 ♖a6+ and 6 ♔h5) 5 ♖a6+ ♔e5 (or 5 ... ♔f7 6 g5, and 7 ♔g4 wins) 6 ♔g5 ♖xh3 (or 6 ... ♔d4 7 h4 ♔c3 8 h5 ♔b2 9 ♔h6 followed by the advance of the g-pawn winning) 7 ♖xa2 ♖h1 8 ♖e2+ and 9 ♔f6 wins.

2 ♔g3 ♔d6

3 h3

Surprisingly enough, White cannot play 3 h4, when Black checks from the side until White's king leaves his pawns, then plays ... ♖c4! drawing. Or 3 g5 ♖c5 etc draws.

3 ... ♔c6

4 ♔h4

Again White must not bare his king, as after 4 g5 ♔b6 5 ♖a8 ♔b5, Black threatens horizontal checks and the white king dare not play to the 4th rank because of ... ♖c4+ and ... ♖a4. The g-pawn cannot be advanced until White's king is in safety.

4 ... ♔b6

5 ♖a8 ♔b5

The threat was 6 g5 followed by 7 ♔h5.

6 ♔h5 ♔b4

7 g5

Again White must be careful, for Black threatened to play 7 ... ♖c5+ and 8 ... ♖a5.

7 ... ♔b3

8 h4!

Exact to the end! 8 g6? would only draw after 8 ... ♖c8! 9 ♖a7 ♖h8+ 10 ♔g4 ♖h6! etc.

8 ... ♖c1

Or 8 ... ♖c8 9 ♖xa2 ♔xa2 10 g6 ♔b3 11 g7 ♔c4 12 ♔g6 ♔d5 13 h5 ♔e6 14 h6 wins. The black king is too far away.

9 g6 a1♕

10 ♖xa1 ♖xa1

11 g7 ♖g1

12 ♔h6 ♔c3

13 h5

Avoiding the last trap 13 ♔h7? ♖h1! drawing.

13 ... ♔d4

14 ♔h7 ♔e5

15 g8♕ wins.

The black king is just one tempo too late.

The reader will now realize that if Black has the move in diagram 201, he can begin his queenside counterplay at once. Note that Black would draw easily if White's rook were placed less favourably, for instance on a4 instead of a5. He would play 1 ... ♔f5 2 ♖a5+ ♔e4 3 g4 ♔f4 4 ♖a4+ (or g5 a1♕) 4 ... ♔g5 drawing. Let us return to diagram 201, with Black to move:

1 ... ♔e6!
2 g4 ♔d6
3 ♔g3

Premature is 3 g5 ♔e6! threatening 4 ... ♖c5 etc.

3 ... ♔c6
4 h3

As we saw before, White cannot advance his pawns more quickly, because after 4 g5 ♔b6 5 ♖a8 ♔b5 gives White no defence against horizontal checks.

4 ... ♔b6
5 ♖a8 ♔b5
6 ♔h4

The same plan as before, using the g-pawn as a shield in order to advance his king.

6 ... ♔b4
7 g5 ♔b3
8 g6

Or 8 ♔h5 ♖c1 transposing.

8 ... ♖c1

Simpler than 8 ... ♖c4+ 9 ♔h5 ♖a4 10 ♖xa4 ♔xa4 11 g7 a1♕ 12 g8♕ which is also drawn.

9 ♔h5

But not 9 g7 ♖g1 etc.

9 ... a1♕
10 ♖xa1 ♖xa1
11 g7

It is clear that 11 h4 ♔c4 makes no appreciable difference.

11 ... ♖g1
12 ♔h6 ♔c4
13 ♔h7 ♔d5
14 g8♕ ♖xg8
15 ♔xg8 ♔e5

and the draw is clear with the inevitable capture of the last pawn.

Although there are many more interesting rook and pawn endings, we feel that the reader now has sufficient basic theory to enable him to tackle these endings with confidence. Let us finally look at a few examples from practice to see how our basic knowledge can be applied to them.

Practical examples

We shall begin with an interesting position taken from a game Alatortsev-Chekhover, 1937.

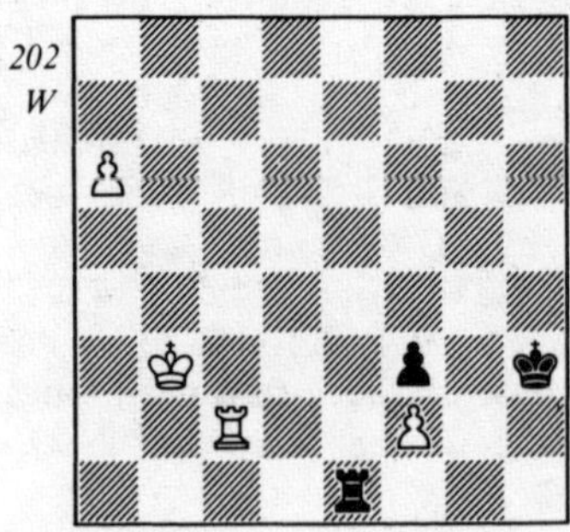

Alatortsev-Chekhover 1937

At first sight, Black's position seems hopeless. White's a-pawn is very strong and will sooner or later cost Black his rook, whereas an attack on White's f-pawn appears to have little chance of success, with the white rook guarding it. What can Black do?

However, rook endings are notoriously tricky and contain unexpected resources which a superficial analysis seldom reveals. Upon closer examination, we find tht Black has a chance of winning the f-pawn once he has been forced to sacrifice his rook for the a-pawn. Secondly, Black can effectively use his rook for checking along the ranks if the white king tries to win without using his rook. Thirdly, if White attempts to defend against checks by playing his rook to c2, Black in some cases can play ... ♖e2.

When we proceed to a more detailed analysis, we shall discover that Black's counterchances are very nearly sufficient to save the game for him. It is only by extremely precise play that White succeeds in winning, as follows:

1	**a7**	**♖e8**
2	**♖a2**	**♖a8**

These and the next few moves require little in the way of explanation.

3	**♔c4**	**♔g2**
4	**♔c5!**	

It is now time to work out how far away from the f-pawn White's king dare go without having to fear ... ♖xa7. The text move just works after 4 ... ♖xa7 5 ♖xa7 ♔xf2 6 ♔d4 etc, but 4 ♔b5 allows Black to draw by 4 ... ♖xa7! 5 ♖xa7 ♔xf2 6 ♔c4 ♔e2!etc. In other words, White's king cannot go beyond the c-file or the 5th rank, whenever Black can play ... ♖xa7.

4	**...**	**♖c8+**

Or 4 ... ♔f1 5 ♔b6 ♖e8 transposing. As White threatens ♔b6-b7, Black must play his rook away.

5	**♔b6**	**♖e8** *(203)*

203
W

Alatortsev-Chekhover 1937

Again confronting White with problems, as 6 a8♕ ♖xa8 7 ♖xa8 ♔xf2 is drawn, as we know, and 6 ♔b7 allows 6 ... ♖e7+ 7 ♔b6 ♖e8 etc. However, White has a subtle plan at his disposal. If his rook is on c2, he can play ♔b7-b8 to escape the checks, when ... ♖xa7 is no good, as White's rook guards his f-pawn, and ... ♖e8+ fails to ♖c8. Still, if White now plays 6 ♖c2 Black can defend by 6 ... ♖e6+ 7 ♔b7 (or 7 ♔c7 ♖e8!) 7 ... ♖e2! the point being that after 8 ♖xe2 fe 9 a8♕ is no longer check and 8 a8♕ ♖xc2 followed by 9 ... ♖xf2 is clear draw.

A further idea is needed before White can win ...

6	**♔c6!**

This beautiful move places Black in zugzwang! If now 6 ... ♖c8+ 7 ♔b7 or 6 ... ♖e6+ 7 ♔d7 both win. Nor can Black's king move away from White's f-pawn because of 7 a8♕. Finally, if the rook leaves the e-file (say, 6 ... ♖h8), White plays 7 ♔b7 ♖h7+ 8

♔b6 ♖h8 (or 8 ... ♖h6+ 9 ♔c5! ♖h8 10 a8♕ wins) 9 ♖c2 ♖e8 10 ♔c7! transposing to the main line.

6 ... ♔f1 (g1)
7 ♔b7 ♖e7+
8 ♔b6 ♖e8

Again 8 ... ♖e6+ fails to 9 ♔c5! ♖e8 10 a8♕, when White's king is near enough to stop the pawn.

9 ♖c2!

Exploiting the position of Black's king with the threat of 10 ♔b7 ♖e2 11 ♖c1+ (the point!), or here 10 ... ♖e7+ 11 ♔b8 ♖e8+ 12 ♖c8 wins. So Black's king must go back to g2.

9 ... ♔g2
10 ♔c7!

Again placing Black in zugzwang. Against king moves by Black, or if the rook leaves the e-file, White wins by 11 ♔b7, e.g. 10 ... ♔h2 11 ♔b7 ♖e2 12 ♖c6 winning easily, as the black king will not be in a position to capture the f-pawn after 12 ... ♖e8 13 a8♕ ♖xa8 14 ♔xa8.

10 ... ♖e7+
11 ♔b8 ♖e8+

White now queens with check after 11 ... ♖e2 12 ♖xe2 fe 13 a8♕+ ♔xf2 and 14 ♕a2+ gives him a win, as we have already demonstrated (diagram 57).

12 ♖c8 ♖xc8+
13 ♔xc8 ♔xf2
14 a8♕

and Black resigned a few moves later. A most instructive and well-played ending.

Our next example has the same balance of material. Notice that without Black's g-pawn and White's h-pawn, we would have the well-known Philidor position (diagram 130) which is drawn.

204
W

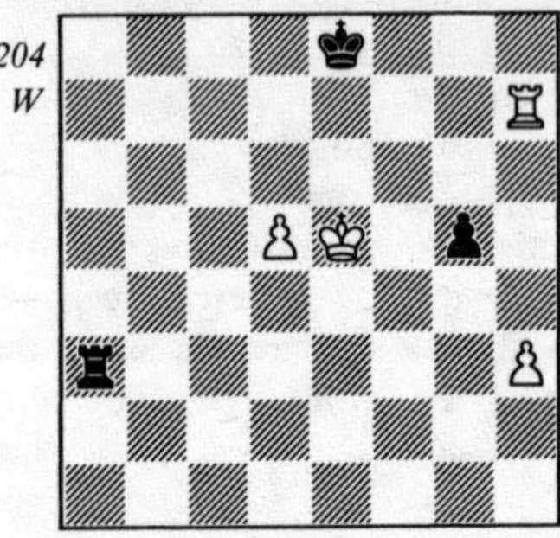

Keres-Mikenas 1937

As it is, White has various important advantages. Firstly, he is a healthy passed pawn up. Secondly, his pieces are actively posted. Thirdly, Black's king is cut off on the back rank. His only weakness is the h-pawn and strangely enough this gives Black excellent counterchances.

What can White do? We already know from the Philidor position that he must not advance his d-pawn which only helps the defender. Nor can he exchange the kingside pawns, when the position is clearly drawn. So he must try to strengthen his position by means of threats.

1 ♔e6 ♖e3+
2 ♔f6

Before playing his king to d6, White sets a little trap, for if now 2 ... ♖f3+ 3 ♔xg5 ♖d3, then

4 ♔f6! ♖xd5 5 ♔e6 wins. But Black is not falling for this.

2 ... ♖d3!
3 ♔e6 ♖e3+
4 ♔d6 ♖a3!

The most active place for the rook. It would be a mistake to play, for example, 4 ... ♖f3 5 h4! gh (or 5 ... g4 6 ♖g7 g3 7 h5! winning, e.g. if 7 ... ♖f6+ 8 ♔c5 ♖h6 9 d6 ♖xh5+ 10 ♔c6 wins, or 7 ... ♔f8 8 ♖g4 ♖f6+ 9 ♔c5 ♖h6 10 ♖xg3 ♖xh5 11 ♖e3 wins) 6 ♖h8+ ♔f7 (or 6 ... ♖f8 7 ♖xh4 ♔d8 8 ♔c6 winning) 7 ♖xh4 ♖a3 8 ♖e4! with a book win.

An alternative defence is 4 ... ♖d3, albeit demanding extreme precision on Black's part. We shall be coming back later to this interesting position, when we analyse diagram 207.

5 ♖h5

After 5 ♖h8+ ♔f7 6 h4 gh 7 ♖xh4 White obtains a won position, but Black does not need to exchange pawns. By 6 ... ♖h3 7 h5 ♔g7 8 ♖c8 ♖xh5 9 ♔c6 ♖h1! his g-pawn guarantees him sufficient counterplay. Or he can even try 6 ... g4 7 ♖h5 ♖a6+ 8 ♔c7 g3 9 d6 (or 9 ♖g5 ♖g6!) 9 ... ♖a7+ 10 ♔b6 ♖a1 etc.

5 ... ♖a6+

Also possible is 5 ... ♖d3 when 6 ♖xg5 ♖xh3 7 ♖g8+ ♔f7 8 ♖d8 ♖a3! 9 ♖b8 ♖d3! gives us the well-known Kling and Horwitz draw (diagram 162), or 6 ♔e6 ♖e3+ 7 ♔f6 ♖d3 8 ♖h7 ♖g3 and White can make no progress.

6 ♔e5 ♖g6

Making his task more difficult. He could tranpose to the variation in the previous note by playing 6 ... ♖a3 7 ♔e6 ♖e3+ 8 ♔d6 ♖d3.

7 ♔f5

After 7 d6 g4 8 ♖h8+ ♔d7 9 ♖h7+ ♔e8 (not 9 ... ♔d8? 10 ♔d5 and 11 ♔c6 winning) 10 d7+ ♔d8 11 ♔f5 Black saves himself by the neat 11 ... g3! etc. The alternative 7 ♖h8+ ♔d7 8 ♖h7+ ♔e8! 9 ♔f5 ♖d6 etc transposes to the main line.

7 ... ♖d6
8 ♖h7 ♔d8!

The only defence. 8 ... ♖xd5+ fails to 9 ♔e6, and if 8 ... ♔f8 9 ♔e5 followed by 10 d6 wins. We have already met the variation 8 ... ♖a6 9 ♔xg5 ♖d6 10 ♔f5 ♖xd5+ 11 ♔e6 winning.

9 ♔e5 ♖a6!

Again the only move. After 9 ... ♖g6 10 d6 g4 11 ♔d5! wins.

10 ♖h5 ♖a3
11 ♔e6 ♖e3+

Forced, as White threatened 12 ♖h8+ and 13 d6+, and if 11 ... ♖d3 12 ♖xg5 can be played.

12 ♔d6 ♔e8 *(205)*

And not 12 ... ♔c8 13 ♖h8+ ♔b7 14 ♔d7 followed by the advance of the pawn. Because of his inexact 6th move, Black has reached a position similar to the one after White's 5th move, with the difference that his rook on e3 is not well placed. Nevertheless, even here Black has sufficient defensive possibilities.

13 ♖h8+

White could probably give

205
W

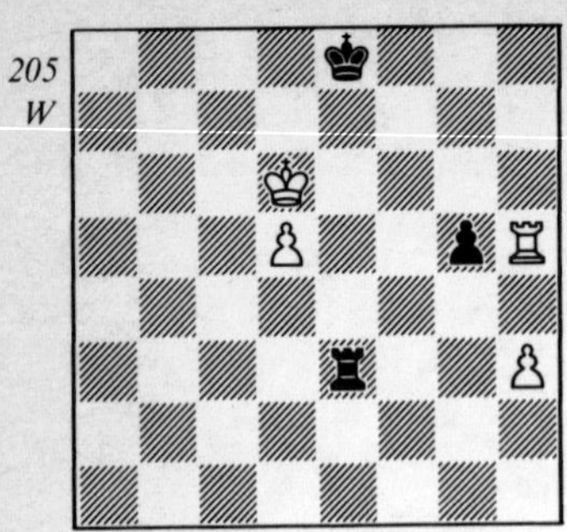

Keres-Mikenas 1937

Black more trouble with 13 h4 when both 13 ... gh 14 ♖h8+ ♔f7 15 ♖xh4, and 13 ... g4 14 ♖g5 g3 15 h5 win for White. However, Black can play 13 ... ♖h3! 14 ♖xg5 ♖xh4 15 ♖g8+ ♔f7 16 ♖b8 ♖d4! drawing, or here 14 ♖h8+ ♔f7 15 h5 ♔g7 16 ♖e8 ♖xh5 17 ♔c7 ♖h1! and Black should be able to hold the position, e.g. 18 d6 ♖c1+ 19 ♔d8 ♖d1 20 d7 ♔f6 21 ♔c7 g4 etc.

13 ... ♔f7
14 ♔d7 ♔g7

Winning the h-pawn and thus giving himself enough counterplay with his g-pawn.

15 ♖c8 ♖xh3
16 d6 ♔g6!

The most exact, although 16 ... ♖d3 17 ♔c7 ♔f6 18 d7 g4 is also possible. Not, however, 16 ... g4? 17 ♖c4 g3 18 ♔c7 winning.

17 ♖c5 ♖h8
18 ♔e7 ♔h5!

In endings with rook against pawn, we know that the rook always wins, if the enemy king can be cut off along the 5th rank. This would apply if Black now played 18 ... g4? as after 19 d7 White would capture the rook for the pawn, then calmly bring his king back whilst Black can do nothing.

19 d7 *(206)*

206
B

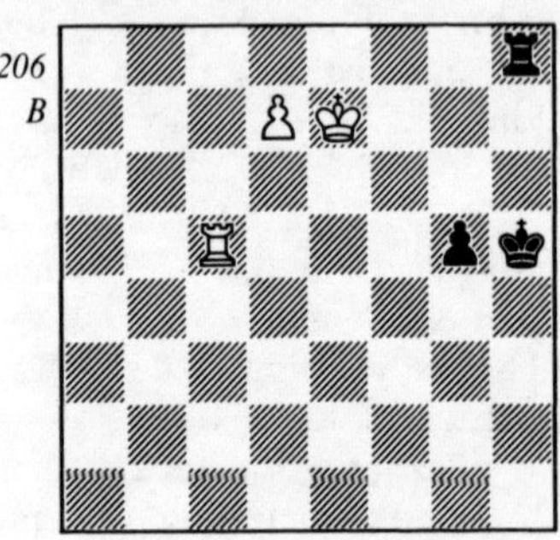

Keres-Mikenas 1937

19 ... ♔g4!

The natural 19 ... ♔h4? loses to 20 ♖c8 ♖h7+ 21 ♔e6 ♖xd7 22 ♔xd7 g4 23 ♔e6 g3 24 ♔f5 g2 25 ♔f4. Black's king must be used to block the approach of White's king.

20 ♔f6

Or 20 ♖c8 ♖h7+ 21 ♔e6 ♖xd7 22 ♔xd7 ♔f4! and now Black draws, e.g. 23 ♔e6 g4 24 ♖c4+ ♔f3 25 ♔f5 g3 26 ♖c3+ ♔f2 27 ♔f4 g2 28 ♖c2+ ♔f1 29 ♔f3 g1♘+! with a book draw.

20 ... ♖f8+

Even now Black could spoil everything with 20 ... ♖h6+? 21 ♔e5 ♖h8 22 ♖c8! winning.

21 ♔e6 ♖d8

White was still threatening to win by 22 ♖c8.

22 ♖d5 ♔f4
23 ♖f5+ ♔g4
24 ♖f7 ♔h3
25 ♔f5

White has no more winning chances and after the further moves 25 ... g4 26 ♔f4 g3 27 ♔f3 ♔h4! a draw was agreed.

Let us now return to the position after White's 4th move and consider the alternative black defence by 4 ... ♖d3, giving us diagram 207.

207
W

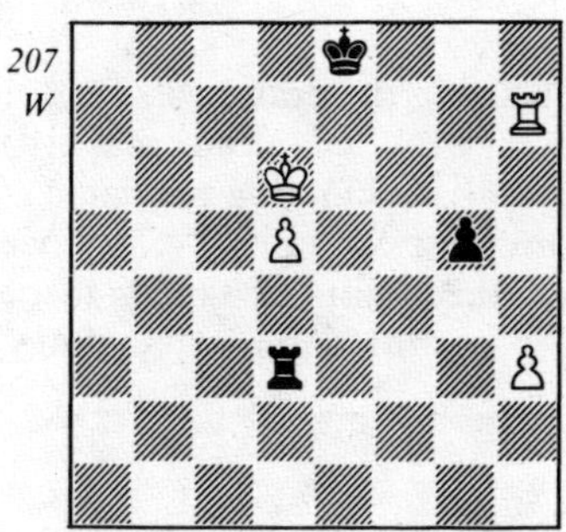

Keres-Mikenas 1937 (variation)

The idea of Black's last move is to bring about the Kling and Horwitz position (diagram 162) after 1 h4 gh 2 ♖h8+ ♔f7 3 ♖xh4 ♔e8! with his rook in the correct place. However, White can try other ideas.

1 ♖e7+ ♔d8

It seems that Black can even try 1 ... ♔f8 2 ♖e5 ♖xh3 3 ♔d7 (3 ♖xg5 ♔e8! draws) when he must play neither 3 ... g4 4 ♖f5+ ♔g7 5 ♖g5+ and 6 ♖xg5, nor 3 ... ♖h7+ 4 ♔d8 g4 5 d6 g3 6 d7 g2 7 ♖g5 ♖g7 8 ♔c8! winning for White in both cases. However, with 3 ... ♖g3! 4 d6 ♔f7 Black can draw, e.g. 5 ♖f5+ ♔g6 6 ♔e6 ♖e3+ 7 ♖e5 ♖xe5+ 8 ♔xe5 ♔f7, or 5 ♖c5 ♔f6 6 ♔c7 ♖d3 7 d7 ♔e7 8 ♖e5+ ♔f6 9 ♖e3 ♖d1 10 d8♕ ♖xd8 11 ♔xd8 g4 etc.

2 ♖g7 ♔c8!

Forced, as 2 ... ♔e8 3 ♖g8+ ♔f7 4 ♖xg5 ♖xh3 5 ♖e5 or 5 ♔d7 wins easily. White has now at least driven Black's king away from the kingside.

3 ♖g8+

White could also try to place Black in zugzwang with 3 ♖h7, when both 3 ... ♖d1 4 ♖c7+ ♔b8 (or 4 ... ♔d8 5 ♖g7) 5 ♖c3, and 3 ... ♖g3 4 ♖h8+ ♔b7 5 ♔d7 g4 6 hg ♖xg4 7 d6 win for White. However, Black has 3 ... ♔b8!, e.g. 4 ♔c6 ♖c3+ 5 ♔d7? ♖c7+ or 4 ♔e6 ♔c8 5 d6 ♖e3+ 6 ♔f5 ♖d3 7 d7+ ♖xd7 etc. If White exchanges pawns on the kingside, then Black's king is correctly placed, on the shorter side of the pawn.

3 ... ♔b7
4 ♖h8 ♔b6

Black is again in zugzwang. If 4 ... ♖d1 (or 4 ... ♖g3 5 ♔d7 etc) 5 ♖h7+! ♔b6 (or 5 ... ♔c8 6 ♖c7+ ♔b8 7 ♖c3 etc. Or 5 ... ♔b8 6 ♖h5 ♖d3 7 ♔c6 and White advances his d-pawn) 6 ♔e6 ♖d3 7 d6 ♔c6 8 ♖c7+ ♔b6 9 ♖c8 ♖e3+ 10 ♔f6 ♖d3 11 ♔e7 ♖e3+ 12 ♔d8 ♖xh3 13 d7 wins.

5 ♖b8+

Black is continuously on the brink of defeat, but always

appears to be able to hold the draw. An alternative winning attempt is 5 ♖h7, placing Black in zugzwang, but 5 ... ♔b5! (after 5 ... ♖d1 6 ♔e6 we have the variation from the previous note, and 5 ... ♖g3 6 ♔d7 equally wins for White) 6 ♔e6 ♔c5 7 ♖c7+ ♔b6 8 d6 ♖xh3 gives Black the draw. The text move gives Black even greater difficulties.

5 ... ♔a6

Weaker is 5 ... ♔a7 (or 5 ... ♔a5 6 ♔c5 ♖c3+ 7 ♔d4 ♖xh3 8 d6 ♖h1 9 d7! ♖d1+ 10 ♔c5 wins) 6 ♖b4 ♖xh3 7 ♔c7 ♖c3+ 8 ♔d7 ♖g3 9 d6 g4 10 ♖e4! ♔b7 11 ♔e7 winning.

6 ♔c6

Or 6 ♖b4 ♔a5 7 ♖g4 ♖xh3 8 ♔c6 (8 ♖xg5 ♔b6 etc) 8 ... ♖c3+ 9 ♔d7 ♔b6 10 ♖xg5 (or 10 d6) 10 ... ♖h3! draws.

6 ... ♖c3+
7 ♔d7 ♖xh3
8 d6 g4
9 ♖b4

Or 9 ♖b1 ♖d3! (but not 9 ... g3? 10 ♔c6 and 11 d7 winning) 10 ♖e1 ♔b6! (again 10 ... g3? loses after 11 ♔e7 g2 12 d7 ♖e3+ 13 ♖xe3 g1♕ 14 ♖e6+ and 15 d8♕) 11 ♔e7 ♔c6 12 ♖c1+ ♔b7 13 d7 ♖e3+ 14 ♔d8 g3 15 ♖b1+ ♔a7 and White can make no progress.

9 ... ♔a5!

At first sight pointless, but in reality the only sure way to draw. 9 ... g3? loses to 10 ♔c6 ♔a5 11 ♖g4, and after 9 ... ♖g3 10 ♖e4! ♔b7 11 ♔e7 wins. However, Black can also draw with 9 ... ♖h1! in order to answer 10 ♖xg4 with 10 ... ♔b6.

10 ♖xg4

An interesting try is 10 ♖b2 g3? 11 ♔c6 ♖h2 12 d7! winning, but 10 ... ♔a6! 11 ♔d8 ♖e3! 12 d7 g3 draws.

10 ... ♔b6
11 ♖b4+

The thematic winning attempt. We have already seen that White can achieve nothing with 11 ♖e4 ♖h7+ 12 ♖e7 ♖h8.

11 ... ♔c5
12 ♖e4 ♔d5!

Ensuring the draw after 13 ♖e1 ♖h7+ 14 ♖e7 ♖h6 etc. An unusually fascinating endgame.

Our next example reveals once again the fighting chances to be found in rook and pawn endings.

208
B

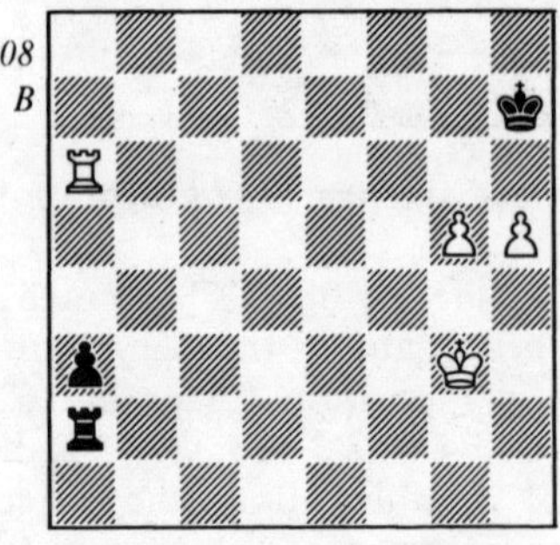

Bernstein-Cukiermann 1929

Black's position seems hopeless, as White's pawns are far advanced and Black's king is in danger of being mated once he is driven to the back rank. Black's only counterchance lies in forcing White's king to retreat, which explains his first few moves:

1 ... ♖a1
2 ♖a7+ ♔g8
3 g6?

A casual move. White wrongly asssumes that the win is easy, a common error in such situations. Kopayev has pointed out the following instructive way to win: **3 h6! a2** White threatened 4 ♔g2 ♖a2+ 5 ♔f3 and 6 g6 **4 ♔h2** if 4 ♔g2 ♖b1! 5 ♖xa2 ♖b5 draws! **4 ... ♖b1 5 ♖xa2 ♖b5 6 ♖g2** but not 6 ♖a8+ ♔h7 7 ♖a7+ ♔h8 8 ♖g7 with perpetual check, because the black king is in a stalemate position **6 ... ♔h7** threatening 7 ... ♔g6 and 8 ... ♖b6 drawing **7 g6+ ♔g8 8 ♖g3 ♖h5+ 9 ♖h3 ♖g5 10 h7+ ♔h8 11 ♖g3 ♖h5+ 12 ♔g2 ♔g7 13 ♖h3 ♖g5+ 14 ♔f3 ♖f5+** or 14 ... ♔h8 15 ♖g3 ♖f5+ 16 ♔e4 and 17 g7+ **15 ♔g4 ♖f8 16 ♔g5** winning.

3 ... a2
4 ♔g2 ♖b1

White was threatening 5 h6.

5 ♖xa2 ♖b5
6 ♖a8+

The only way to guard the h-pawn, as 6 h6 fails to 6 ... ♖g5+.

6 ... ♔g7
7 ♖a7+ ♔g8
8 ♖h7 ♖g5+?

And now it is Black's turn to go wrong. He could draw by 8 ... ♖b3! and if 9 ♔f2 ♖h3! obtaining diagram 186 which we have already analysed as drawn.

9 ♔h3 wins.

Let us turn to a position containing many more pawns, which arose in the famous game Capablanca-Tartakower, 1924.

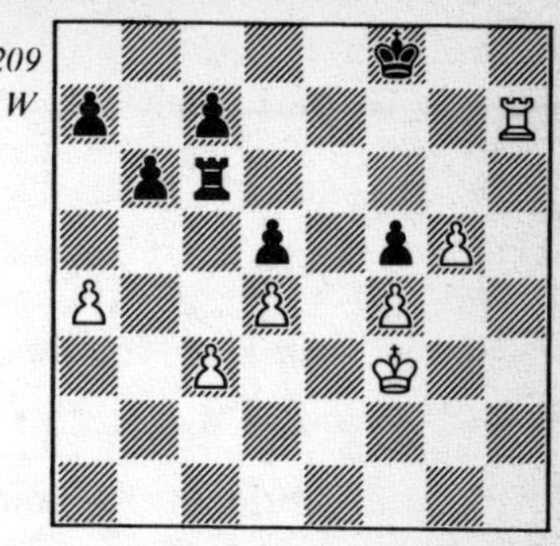

Capablanca-Tartakower 1924

A very interesting situation, difficult to assess at first sight. White has two main advantages: Black's king is cut off on the back rank and the g-pawn is a strong protected passed pawn. Black on the other hand is about to pick up some of White's weak queenside pawns. It is a question of whose advantages are the most important.

A basic rule in rook endings, although to a slightly lesser extent than in queen endings, is to create a passed pawn as soon as possible. There are hundreds of examples of endings in which one side sacrifices a great deal of material in order to create a strong passed pawn and saves or even wins the game with it. Diagram 209 is an excellent example of such an ending.

However, whereas in queen endings a passed pawn can be pushed through with the help of the queen alone, in rook endings the king is usually required to give additional help. In fact, a passed pawn supported by the king and by a rook on the seventh rank restricting the enemy king to the back rank, is an extremely powerful weapon, often enough to win the game in itself.

In our example White's rook is already on the seventh rank, but the support of the king is required. Only by following the above logic will the reader understand Capablanca's brilliant winning plan:

1 ♔g3!

The only way to win, combining attack and defence. On no account must he allow his king to be cut off by Black' rook. For example the plausible continuation 1 ♔e2 ♖xc3 2 ♖h6, winning Black's f-pawn, fails to 2 ... ♖c4 3 ♖f6+ ♔g7 4 ♖xf5 (or 4 ♔e3 c5) 4 ... ♖xd4 which gives Black excellent counterchances.

1 ... ♖xc3+
2 ♔h4 ♖f3

White's main threat was 3 g6 and 4 ♔g5, which he still plays despite the loss of another pawn.

If 2 ... c5 3 g6 cd 3 ♔g5 d3 5 ♖d7 ♖c5 6 ♔h6 wins.

Or 2 ... ♖c1 3 ♔h5 and Black cannot exchange rooks, so must play 3 ... ♖f1 4 ♔g6 ♖xf4 5 ♔f6 which is no improvement on the game continuation.

Even a mixture of the two plans by 2 ... ♖c1 3 ♔h5 c5, relying on the fact that White cannot play 4 g6 at once, does not help Black much after 4 ♖d7.

3 g6!

Note how White heads straight for his goal, without wasting unnecessary time by playing 3 ♖xc7.

3 ... ♖xf4+
4 ♔g5 ♖e4

Another important idea in such endings would be seen if Black played here 4 ... ♖g4+. White would not capture the pawn (5 ♔xf5? ♖xd4) but would use it to protect his own king from the rear, winning at once by 5 ♔f6! The alternative 4 ... ♖xd4 loses to 5 ♔f6 ♔e8 6 ♖xc7 when White picks up more pawns before winning Black's rook for the g-pawn.

5 ♔f6

White has now reached the ideal position he originally envisaged. Black's king is in a mating net, and to avoid the worst he must eventually hand back more material than he has gained. A classic piece of endgame strategy!

5 ... ♔g8
6 ♖g7+ ♔h8
7 ♖xc7 ♖e8
8 ♔xf5

Only now is this pawn captured; Black is positionally lost, the remainder being purely a matter of technique.

8 ... ♖e4

Or 8 ... a6 9 ♖b7 b5 10 ab ab 11 ♖xb5 ♖d8 12 ♔e6 wins. Or White can play here 9 ♖a7 b5 10 a5 winning.

9 ♔f6 ♖f4+

10 ♔e5 ♖g4
11 g7+! ♔g8

Black obviously dare not exchange rooks.

12 ♖xa7 ♖g1

The d-pawn cannot be held, as 12 ... ♖g5+ 13 ♔f6, with the threat of 14 ♖a8+ and 15 ♖h8 mate, wins instantly. For the two pawns sacrificed, White now wins back four!

13 ♔xd5 ♖c1
14 ♔d6

The game is of course won, and Tartakower resigned after 14 ... ♖c2 15 d5 ♖c1 16 ♖c7 ♖a1 17 ♔c6 ♖xa4 18 d6.

Finally, we must quote the famous example given in diagram 210, which occurred in the game Taimanov-Larsen, Palma de Mallorca Interzonal, 1970. This underlines the fact that even leading grandmasters are not always acquainted with basic endings.

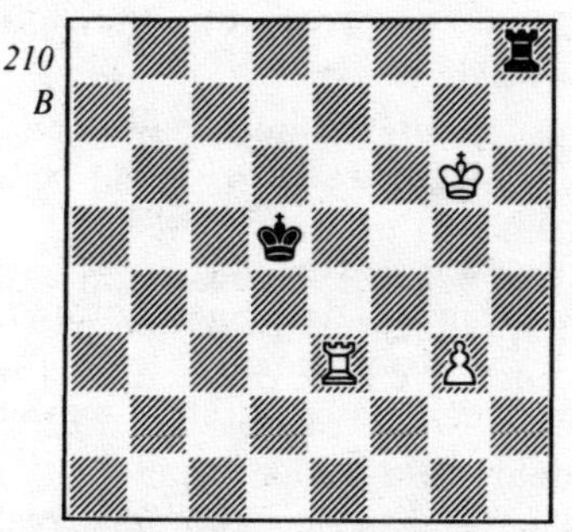

Taimanov-Larsen 1970

If we cast our minds back to diagrams 167 and 170, we know that Black should have no trouble drawing this position. For White to have winning chances, Black's king must be at least three files away from the pawn.

The usual plan for Black in such positions is to drive White's king back by checking with the rook. If the king advances, then the rook stays in front of the pawn to prevent its advance. As the pawn is only on the third rank, the draw is always clear after **1 ... ♖g8+ 2 ♔f5 ♖f8+ 3 ♔g6 ♖g8+ 4 ♔f7 ♖g4** or here **2 ♔f6 ♔d4! 3 ♖a3 ♔e4 4 ♖b3 ♖g4!** etc.

This would have been the logical continuation but Black is so well-placed here that he can even allow the pawn to reach the fourth rank, without risking a loss.

However, let us see how play went:

1 ... ♔d4

Not a mistake, but the most exact move was 1 ... ♖g8+, as we have already seen. The text move allows White to advance his pawns one square.

2 ♖a3 ♔e4

Now 2 ... ♖g8+ would be pointless because after 3 ♔f7 ♖g5 4 ♔f6 ♖g8 White can play 5 g4! (5 ... ♖xg4? 6 ♖a4+). Or 2 ... ♔e5 3 ♖a5+ ♔e6 (e4) 4 ♔g7 wins, as White's pawn reaches g5.

3 g4

The alternative 3 ♔g7 would only waste time after 3 ... ♖h3 4 ♔f6 ♖h6+ 5 ♔f5 ♖h8 because 6 ♖a5 is effectively answered by

6 ... ♔f3.

3 ... ♖g8+

Forced, because Black is lost if the pawn reaches the fifth rank.

4 ♔h5 ♖h8+

5 ♔g5 ♖g8+

6 ♔h4 *(211)*

211
B

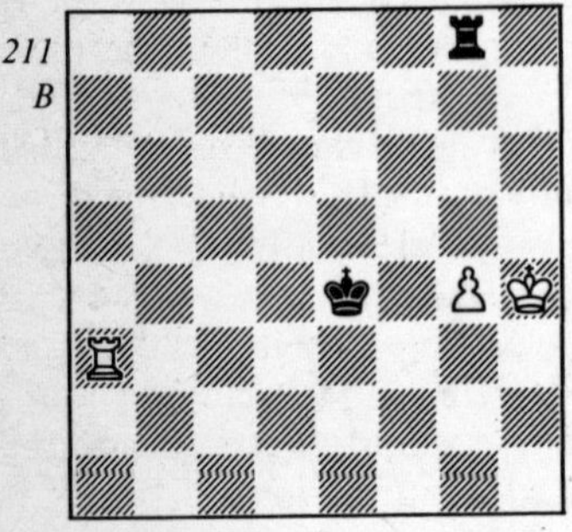

Taimanov-Larsen 1970

6 ... ♔e5??

It is clear that White had to retreat his king in order to avoid the checks and Black's logical continuation is to drive the king back as far as possible before using the rook to prevent the advance of the pawn. After **6 ... ♖h8+ 7 ♔g3** ♖g8, however, 8 ♖a5! wins, so Black would draw by **7 ... ♔e5!** threatening 8 ... ♔f6. Continuing our analysis, play might go **8 ♖a6** (8 g5 ♔f5!) cutting off Black's king, but White can make no progress because his own king cannot advance. Black simply waits by **8 ... ♖h1** (not 8 ... ♖g8? 9 ♔h4 winning) with an easy draw.

The other possibility is **8 ♖f3** when Black's simplest is **8 ... ♖g8** also possible is 8 ... ♔e6 9 g5 ♔e7 10 ♔g4 ♖f8! **9 ♖f4 ♔e6 10 ♔h4 ♔e5! 11 ♖f5+ ♔e6 12 ♔h5 ♖h8+**, or here 9 ♖f5+ ♔e6, with well-known drawing positions.

Apart from this thematic defence, Black could also play **6 ... ♔f4! 7 ♖a4+ ♔f3!** which would have at least justified Larsen's original plan. White can make no progress as 8 g5?? allows mate in one, whereas after **8 ♔h5 ♖h8+ 9 ♔g6 ♖g8+ 10 ♔f5 ♖f8+ 11 ♔e6 ♖g8!** the draw is clear.

7 ♖a6!

Perhaps Larsen failed to appreciate the strength of this move which cuts off his king and allows the white king to advance. The game is now lost.

7 ... ♔f4

Or 7 ... ♖h8+ 8 ♔g5 ♖g8+ 9 ♔h5 ♖h8+ 10 ♖h6 and 11 g5 winning.

8 ♖f6+ ♔e5

9 g5

1-0

After 9 ... ♖h8+ 10 ♔g4 followed by 11 ♖f2 and the advance of White's pawn and king. A defeat which should be a warning to us all.

This example brings to an end our treatment of rook and pawn endings. We have devoted a great deal of space to this part of the endgame but have still had to omit much useful and interesting material. We make no apologies for stressing the importance of such endings which occur most frequently in practice. The keen reader would do well to spend even more time on them, by consulting more specialized endgame volumes.

Rook against minor pieces

The ending of rook against bishop or knight is usually drawn, but there are some positions in which the unfavourable placing of the pieces allows the holder of the major piece to win. This is mainly when the defending king is on the edge of the board.

ROOK AGAINST BISHOP

As we have said, the rook can only hope for success if the enemy king has been driven to the edge of the board. Diagram 212 offers us two basic examples:

212

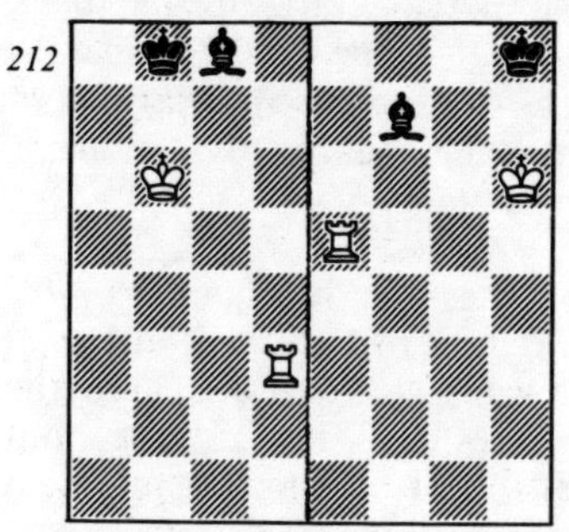

White cannot win from the right-hand position, even though his pieces have reached maximum efficiency. The point is that 1 ... ♝g8 2 ♖e8 gives stalemate, and if instead 2 ♖b5 ♝e6 3 ♖b8+ ♝g8, White can similarly make no progress.

However, in the left-hand position White wins quickly. After 1 ... ♝f5 2 ♖d8+ ♝c8 3 ♖e8 it is mate next move. The moral is clear: the possessor of the bishop should aim to place his king in the corner not controlled by the bishop, assuming, of course, that he is compelled to go to the edge of the board.

It is not always easy to bring about positions such as diagram 212 if the bishop has freedom. Diagram 213 is a typical set-up which White must try to obtain.

213

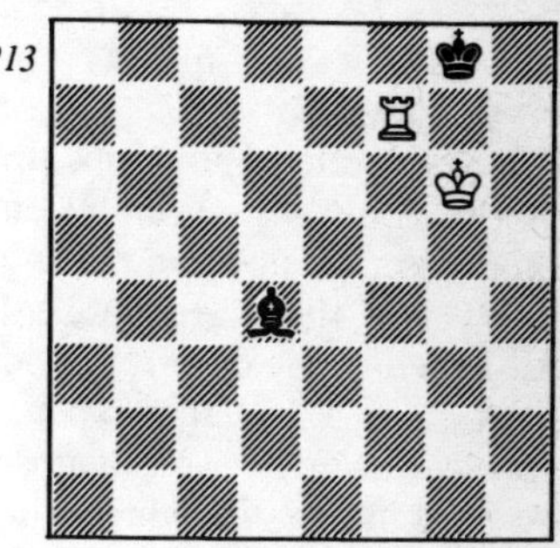

Kling and Horwitz 1851

White wins this type of position, wherever the bishop may be, but he must not allow Black's king to cross the f-file and head towards the 'safe' corner.

1 ... ♝g1

The only move to prevent a double attack by White's rook, threatening mate and the bishop, e.g. 1 ... ♝b2 2 ♖b7 ♝e5 3 ♖e7 wins.

2 ♖f1

Driving the bishop out into the open. But not 2 ♖d7 or 2 ♖c7 when the black king escapes by

2 ... ♔f8!

2 ... ♗h2

3 ♖f2 ♗g3

Or 3 ... ♗g1 4 ♖g2 etc with similar play.

4 ♖g2!

This wins the bishop. If now 4 ... ♗f4 (or 4 ... ♗h4) then 5 ♔f5+ (5 ♔h5+) wins. Or 4 ... ♗c7 (or 4 ... ♗b8) 5 ♖c2 wins, or 4 ... ♗e5 5 ♖e2 wins.

4 ... ♗d6

5 ♖d2 ♗e7

Or 5 ... ♗c7 6 ♖d7 ♗b6 (or 6 ... ♗a5) 7 ♖b7 (♖a7) wins.

6 ♖a2 wins.

There are other positions in which the rook wins even when the enemy king is not in a mating net. However, these are unusual situations which we do not intend to discuss here. Nor shall we spend time on positions of rook against bishop and pawn, in which the rook manages to do more than draw.

However, it is worth paying some attention to positions in which rook and pawn face a single bishop. Of course, these positions are usually won for White, but there are a number of exceptions when the bishop manages to draw. Let us first consider a general case.

The correct normal winning method for White is to advance his king as far as possible before moving the pawn, but here White has pushed his pawn on too early. This means that he has great technical difficulties to overcome before he can force the win.

214

A.Philidor 1777

1 ♖a1

It is not so much individual moves which matter, but the general winning plan. White can win only if his king succeeds in occupying c5 or e5, so that he can drive Black's king to the back rank. To achieve this, he has to chase the bishop away from important squares, by no means an easy task.

1 ... ♗g3

He has not much choice. 1... ♗h2? loses to 2 ♖a7+ ♔d6 3 ♖g7, and 1 ... ♗d6? to 2 ♖a7+ ♗c7 3 ♔f5 followed by 4 ♖xc7+ and 5 ♔e6. If 1 ... ♗b6 2 ♖f1 ♗c7 3 ♖f7+ ♔d6 4 ♖f6+ ♔d7 5 ♔d4 ♗h2! 6 ♖g6 ♗f4 7 ♖g4, or here 2 ... ♗a5 3 ♖f7+ ♔d6 4 ♖f6+ ♔d7 5 ♔d4 ♗d2 6 ♖f2, both giving the same positions which later occur in the main variation. Similarly, 1 ... ♗b8 2 ♖g1 gives Black nothing better than to transpose to our main line by 2 ... ♗c7.

2 ♖g1

This position has an interesting

history. Philidor originally considered it drawn, then Guretzky-Cornitz demonstrated a win by 2 ♖a7+. Finally, Berger pointed out the text move which is the quickest method.

2 ... ♗c7

The only move. If 2 ... ♗h4 3 ♔e5 wins. Or 2 ... ♗f2 3 ♖g7+ ♔d6 4 ♖g6+ ♔d7 5 ♔e5 wins. Or 2 ... ♗h2 3 ♖g7+ ♔d6 4 ♖g2 etc. And of course 2 ... ♗d6 fails to 3 ♖g7+. There is an interesting way to win after 2 ... ♗b8 White plays 3 ♖g7+ ♔d6 4 ♖g6+ (but not 4 ♔d4 ♗a7+! when 5 ♖xa7 is stalemate) 4 ... ♔d7 5 ♔f5! placing Black in zugzwang. The threat is 6 ♖g7+ ♔d6 7 ♖b7 ♗c7 8 ♖xc7, and after 5 ... ♗h2 6 ♖g7+ ♔d6 7 ♔e4! produces another zugzwang.

3 ♖g7+ ♔d6
4 ♖g6+ ♔d7
5 ♔d4

The best square for the king from where he is eyeing both c5 and e5. If instead 5 ♔f5 then 5 ... ♗a5 etc.

5 ... ♗f4

Again the only move. The threat was 6 ♔c5 which would be the reply to 5 ... ♗a5, 5 ... ♗h2 or 5 ... ♗d8. If 5 ... ♗b8 6 ♖g7+ ♔d6 7 ♔c4 ♗c7 8 ♖g6+ ♔d7 9 ♔c5 wins.

6 ♖g4! *(215)*

Driving the bishop from the b8-h2 diagonal, as 6 ... ♗h2 (or 6 ... ♗c7) allows 7 ♔c5, and if 6 ... ♗b8 7 ♖g7+ etc.

6 ... ♗d2

Or 6 ... ♗c1 (6 ... ♗h6 7 ♔e5)

215
B

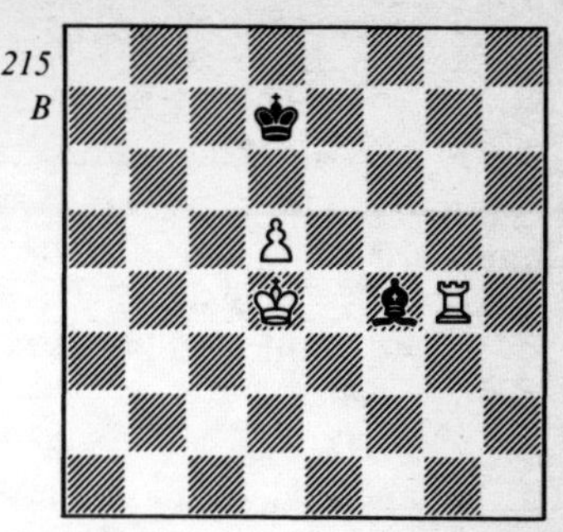

7 ♖g7+ ♔d6 8 ♖g2! zugzwangs Black, as the following lines show:
a) 8 ... ♗f4 (or 8 ... ♔d7 9 ♔e5) 9 ♔e4 ♗c1 10 ♖a2! ♗g5 (or 10 ... ♔d7 11 ♔e5) 11 ♖a6+ ♔d7 12 ♔e5 wins.
b) 8 ... ♗a3 9 ♖g6+ ♔d7 10 ♖b6 ♗f8 (the threat is 11 ♔e5, and if 10 ... ♔c7 11 ♖a6 wins) 11 ♖b7+ ♔d6 12 ♔e4 (again not 12 ♖a7 because of 12 ... ♗g7+!) 12 ... ♗e7 13 ♖b6+ ♔c7 (or 13 ... ♔d7 14 ♔e5 wins) 14 ♖a6 wins.

7 ♖g2

On the surface White appears to win by 7 ♖g7+ ♔d6 8 ♖g6+ ♔d7 9 d6 threatening 10 ♔d5. In reality, however, this throws away the win after 9 ... ♔c6! 10 ♔e5 ♗b4! when White's rook cannot leave the sixth rank nor can his king cross it. An instructive drawing position!

7 ... ♗f4

The only alternative is 7 ... ♗b4, as 7 ... ♗a5 (e1) 8 ♔c5, or 7 ... ♗h6 (c1) 8 ♔e5 both lose. After 7 ... ♗b4 8 ♖b2! we have a position symmetrical to the main variation, e.g. 8 ... ♗a3 (or 8 ... ♗a5 or 8 ... ♗e1 9 ♔c5, or 8 ...

♗e7 9 ♔e5. We have already examined 8 ... ♗f8 9 ♖b7+ in our variation to Black sixth move) 9 ♖b7+ ♔d6 10 ♖b6+ ♔c7 (or 10 ... ♔d7 11 ♔e5) 11 ♖a6 winning after both 11 ... ♗b2+ 12 ♔c5, and 11 ... ♗d6 12 ♖a7+ ♔b6 13 ♖d7 followed by ♔e4-f5-e6 etc.

8 ♖f2

The symmetrical variation. Black is now just as short of bishop moves as in the line 7 ... ♗b4 8 ♖b2.

8 ... ♗b8

Or 8 ... ♗c1 9 ♔e5. Or 8 ... ♗h6 9 ♖f7+. Or 8 ... ♗c7 9 ♖f7+ ♔d6 10 ♖f6+ ♔e7 (if 10 ... ♔d7 11 ♔c5 wins) 11 ♖g6 ♗d6 12 ♖g7+ etc. Or 8 ... ♗g3 9 ♖f7+ ♔d6 10 ♖f6+ ♔e7 (10 ... ♔d7 11 ♔c5) 11 ♖g6 ♗d6 12 ♖g7+ ♔f6 13 ♖d7 wins.

9 ♖f7+ ♔d6
10 ♔c4

Not the recurring possibility 10 ♖h7 ♗a7+!

10 ... ♗c7
11 ♖f6+ ♔d7
12 ♔c5 ♗e5
13 ♖h6 with an easy win.

As can be seen, the whole winning method is necessarily long-winded and demands careful planning.

Before dealing with exceptional positions, let us consider one more interesting example of a winning position.

Surprisingly, despite his advanced pawn, White has great technical difficulties to overcome before he can win. Although there are

216

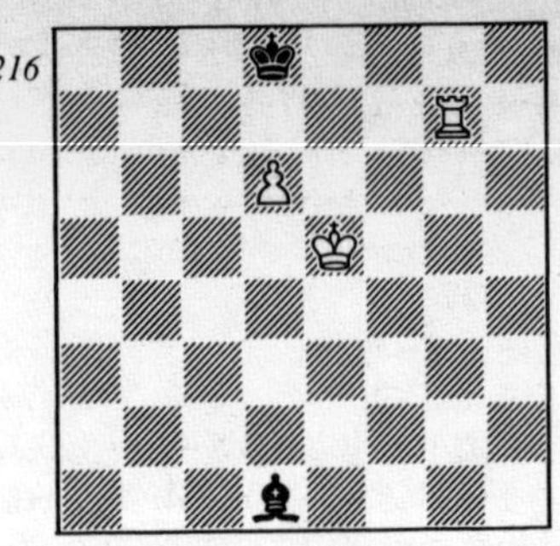

Guretzky-Cornitz 1860

various ways of winning, none of them is simple. We shall select the line which gives Black the least amount of choice:

1 ♖g1

The most interesting of all the winning methods is undoubtedly 1 ♖a7 ♗h5 2 ♖b7! ♗f3 3 ♖h7! placing Black in zugzwang. The keen reader can analyse the further play for himself.

1 ... ♗a4!

To understand the following analysis, it is important to see why the bishop can never go to e2. After 1 ... ♗e2 2 ♖g8+ ♔d7 3 ♖g7+ ♔d8 4 d7 ♔c7 5 d8♕+! ♔xd8 6 ♔d6 ♔c8 (if 6 ... ♔e8 7 ♖e7+) 7 ♖c7+ ♔d8 (or 7 ... ♔b8 8 ♔c6 and 9 ♔b6 with the diagram 213 winning position) 8 ♖c2 ♗d1 (or 8 ... ♗d3) 9 ♖d2 Black loses his bishop in a few moves.

If 1 ... ♗c2 (1 ... ♗f3 or 1 ... ♗h5 lose to 2 ♔e6) 2 ♖g8+ ♔d7 3 ♖g7+ ♔d8 4 ♖b7! wins. The threat is 5 ♔e6 and after 4 ... ♗d3 (d1) 5 d7! ♔e7 6 ♖b4! and

7 ♖d4 wins. Black would also lose after 1 ... ♗b3 2 ♖b1 ♗c4 (if 2 ... ♗c2 or 2 ... ♗a4, then 3 ♖b8+ ♔d7 4 ♖b7+ ♔d8 5 ♔e6 wins) 3 ♖b8+ ♔d7 4 ♖b7+ ♔d8 5 d7 ♔e7 6 ♖b4 and 7 ♖d4 wins (or here 6 ... ♗e6 7 d8♕+).

2 ♖g4! ♗b5

Again forced. If 2 ... ♗d1 3 ♖d4 and 4 d7 wins. If 2 ... ♗c6 3 ♖g8+ ♔d7 4 ♖g7+ ♔d8 5 ♔e6 wins. If 2 ... ♗e8 3 ♖g8 ♔d7 4 ♖xe8 ♔xe8 5 ♔e6 wins. If 2 ... ♗b3 3 ♖b4 ♗a2 (or 3 ... ♗d1 4 d7) 4 ♖b8+ ♔d7 5 ♖b7+ ♔d8 6 d7 ♔e7 7 ♖b2 and 8 ♖d2 wins.

3 ♔d5

The bishop must be driven from the e8-a4 diagonal so that White can set up mating threats with ♔c6. Black cannot prevent this, as all the important squares are guarded by the rook.

3 ... ♔d7

After 3 ... ♗a6 or 3 ... ♗d3 or 3 ... ♗f1 White plays 4 ♔c6, and we know that Black's bishop cannot go to e2 because of the variation we gave in our note to Black's first move. If 3 ... ♔c8 White can play as in the main line or win by 4 ♔c5 ♗d7 5 ♖g8+ ♔b7 6 ♖d8 ♗e6 7 ♔d4 and 8 ♔e5.

4 ♖g7+

Simpler than the line given by Guretzky-Cornitz, 4 ♔c5 ♗d3 5 ♖g7+ ♔d8 6 d7 ♔c7 7 ♖e7! ♗f5 8 d8♕+ ♔xd8 9 ♔d6 ♔c8 10 ♖c7+ winning. There is no need to allow the bishop to d3.

4 ... ♔d8

5 ♖g3! ♗a4

The bishop has no other moves, and after 5 ... ♔d7 6 ♔c5 ♗a4 (if 6 ... ♗f1 or 6 ... ♗a6 7 ♖g7+ and 8 ♔c6 wins) 7 ♖g7+ ♔d8 8 ♖g4! ♗d1 9 ♖d4 and 10 d7 wins.

6 ♖a3

Also possible is 6 ♖g4 (if 6 ♔c5 ♗c2) 6 ... ♗d1 7 ♖d4, or here 6 ... ♗b5 7 ♔c5 etc.

6 ... ♗b5

Or 6 ... ♗d1 7 ♔c6. Or 6 ... ♗c2 7 ♔e6.

7 ♔c5 ♗f1

8 ♖g3! wins.

Black has no defence to the threat of 9 ♔c6, and after 8 ... ♔d7 9 ♖g7+ ♔d8 10 ♔c6 wins for White. A complex winning method.

Our last two examples have shown that the win is made much more difficult if White advances his pawn too far without bringing his king up first. If the pawn is not so advanced, it is easier for White, for the rook can check vertically as well as horizontally.

We shall now leave this type of position and turn to the exceptions.

217

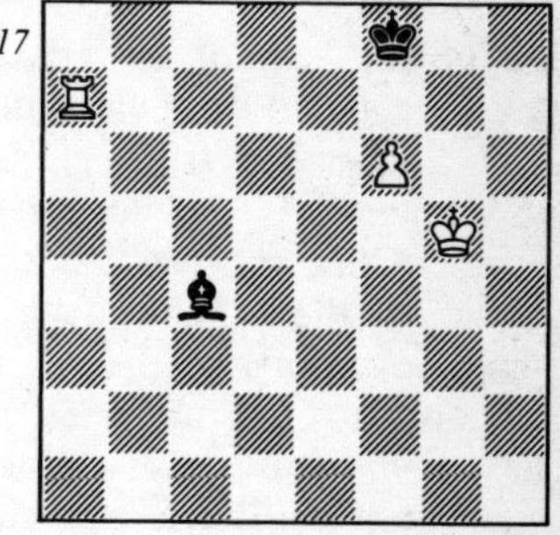

del Rio 1831

Against correct defence, White

can make no progress, as Black's bishop has plenty of manoeuvring room on the g8-a2 diagonal and can always check White's king away from g6. The pawn sacrifice offers no chances either, because Black's king is in the 'safe' corner (see diagram 212, right). Play might go:

1 ♖c7

Or 1 f7 ♔g7! Or 1 ♖h7 ♗b3 2 f7 ♔e7! 3 ♔g6 ♗c4. In both lines White can make no progress.

1 ... ♗a2

Or 1 ... ♗d5. But not 1 ... ♗b3 or 1 ... ♗e6 when 2 ♔g6 wins. Black also loses if he moves his bishop away from the g8-a2 diagonal, e.g 1 ... ♗b5? 2 f7! ♔g7 3 ♔f5 ♗a4 (or 3 ... ♗d3+ 4 ♔e6 ♗g6 5 f8♕+ ♔xf8 6 ♔f6 wins) 4 ♖b7 ♗d1 (or 4 ... ♗c6 5 ♔e6! ♗xb7 6 ♔e7 wins) 5 ♔e6 ♗h5 6 ♖a7 ♗g6 7 f8♕+ ♔xf8 8 ♔f6 wins.

2 ♖c2 ♗d5
3 ♖c8+ ♔f7
4 ♖c7+ ♔f8
5 ♔f5 ♗a2

The bishop cannot be driven away or prevented from checking White's king away from g6. A draw is unavoidable. Of course, if the f-pawn has not reached the sixth rank, then White wins, although not always easily. Let us turn to our next exception.

The left-hand position cannot be won because Black has the 'correct' bishop and White's pawn, although on the fifth rank, is too far advanced.

218

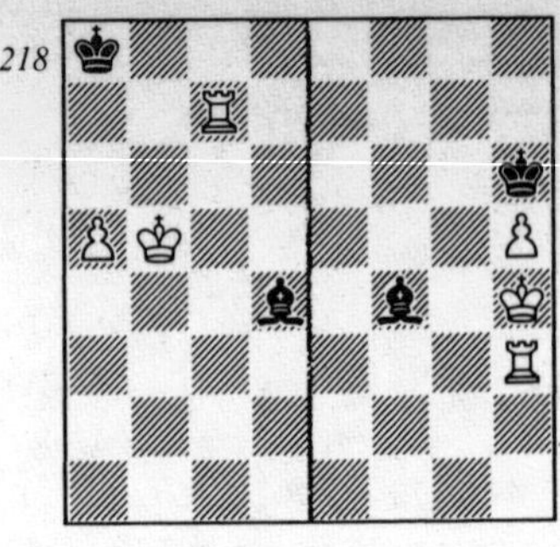

1 ♔a6

If the pawn were on the sixth rank, even this move would not be possible, whereas there are now some chances of the defence going wrong.

1 ... ♔b8
2 ♖b7+ ♔c8!

Black must avoid 2 ... ♔a8? which loses: 3 ♖d7! ♗e5 (or 3 ... ♗f6 4 ♖f7 etc) 4 ♖d8+ ♗b8 5 ♔b5 ♔b7 6 ♖d7+ ♔a8 7 ♔b6! ♗g3 (7 ... ♗f4 or 7 ... ♗h2 8 ♖a7+ ♔b8 9 ♖e7 or 9 ♖g7 winning) 8 ♖a7+ ♔b8 9 ♖f7! (stopping any checks on the bishop's a7-g1 diagonal!) 9 ... ♔a8 (or 9 ... ♔c8 10 a6 etc) 10 a6 ♗e5 11 a7 ♗d4+ 12 ♔a6 wins.

3 ♖b4 ♗e3

The bishop now remains on the diagonal whilst the black king sticks to the c8, c7 and b8 squares.

4 ♖b6 ♗f2

Not of course 4 ... ♗xb6 5 ab winning.

5 ♔a7 ♔c7! draws.

White was threatening to win by 6 ♔a8, whereas now after 6 ♔a6 ♔c8 we are back where we started and White can make no progress.

However, if Black has the 'wrong' bishop (i.e. controlling the pawn's queening square) White wins without any trouble, as we see in the play from the right-hand position of diagram 218:

1	**♔g4**	**♗c1**
2	**♔f5**	

Or first 2 ♖c3 and 3 ♖c6 followed by 4 ♔f5.

2	**...**	**♗d2**
3	**♖b3**	**♗c1**
4	**♖b6+**	**♔h7**

Or 4 ... ♔xh5 5 ♖b1 winning the bishop.

5	**h6!**	**♗d2**

If 5 ... ♗xh6 6 ♖b7+ ♗g7 7 ♔g5 wins.

6	**♖g6!**	

This is simpler than 6 ♖f6 ♗c1 7 ♔g4 ♗xh6 8 ♔h5 to be followed by 9 ♖f7+ and 10 ♔g6 winning.

6	**...**	**♗c1**

If 6 ... ♗xh6 7 ♔f6 and 8 ♔f7 wins. Or 6 ... ♗c3 7 ♔g5 and 8 ♔h5 wins. So Black plays a waiting move.

7	**♖g7+**	**♔xh6**

Or 7 ... ♔h8 8 ♔g6 ♗xh6 9 ♖h7+.

8	**♖g6+**	**♔h7**

After 8 ... ♔h5 9 ♖g1 the bishop is lost.

9 **♔f6** and
10 **♔f7** wins.

Once again we have a variation of the winning set-up in diagram 213.

White also wins, even against the 'correct' bishop, if his rook's pawn is on the fourth rank or lower, as in our next example:

219

Guretzky-Cornitz 1863

First of all White plays a few preliminary moves before beginning his main plan.

1	**♔h6**	**♔g8**

We have already seen that Black loses after 1 ... ♗d5 2 ♖d7 ♗e6 3 ♖d8+ ♗g8 4 ♔g5 ♔g7 5 ♖d7+, as given in our analysis of diagram 218, left, note to Black 2nd move.

2	**♖g7+**	**♔f8**

Or 2 ... ♔h8 3 ♖e7 ♗d5 4 ♖e8+ etc, as in the previous note.

3	**♖g5!**	

Beginning the main plan. To win, White's king must reach f6, but the bishop stops him going via g6, and ♖g1 followed by ♔g5 would allow ... ♔g7. So White must play with more subtlety. The text move already threatens 4 ♔h5 5 ♔g4 (now we see why White's pawn must not be on the fifth rank!) If Black then plays 4 ...

♗f3+ then 5 ♔g6 wins, for if 5 ... ♔g8 6 ♔h6+ Black's king must go into the corner, as 6 ... ♔f8 7 ♖f5+ wins the bishop.

3 ... ♔f7

If 3 ... ♗d3 (c2) 4 ♔h5 ♗e2 (d1)+ 5 ♔g6 ♔g8 6 ♖d5 (c5) wins, for his king reaches g7. Now 4 ♔h5 fails to 4 ... ♗f3+.

4 ♖g3!

Threatening 5 ♔g5 ♔g7 6 ♔f4+.

4 ... ♗c2 *(220)*

Or 4 ... ♗b1 5 ♖g7+ ♔f8 (if 5 ... ♔f6 6 ♖g1 ♗d3 7 ♖d1 followed by 8 ♖f1+ or 8 ♔h7 wins) 6 ♖g5! and Black cannot prevent 7 ♔h5.

220

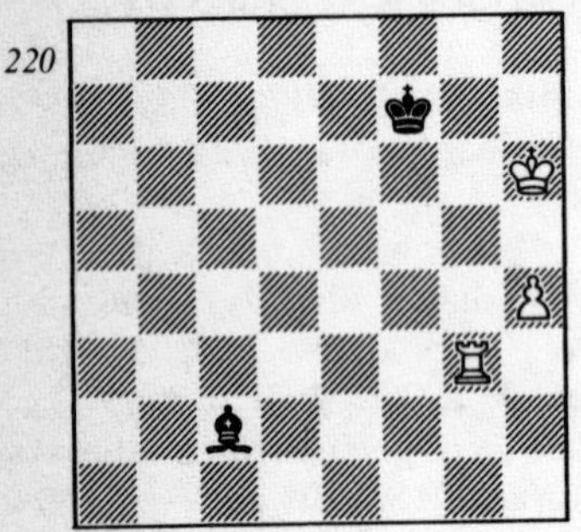

5 ♔h5

The line suggested by Guretzky-Cornitz. Simpler is the method given by Kling: **5 ♖f3+ ♔g8 6 ♖c3!** when 6 ... ♗e4 7 ♖g3+ ♔f7 8 ♔g5! wins. Or 6 ... ♗b1 7 ♖g3+ ♔f7 8 ♖g7+ ♔f8 9 ♖g5! and 10 ♔h5 wins. Or finally 6 ... ♗a4 7 ♖c8+ ♔f7 8 ♔h7 ♗b5 (if 8 ... ♗b3 9 ♖c1, or 8 ... ♗d1 9 ♖c4 etc) 9 ♖d8! ♗c6 (a4) 10 ♖d4 (d2) wins.

5 ... ♔f6

The point of this variation lies in the fact that after 5 ... ♗d1+ 6 ♔g5 ♔g7 7 ♖c3! the bishop cannot return in time to the g8-b1 diagonal, e.g. 7 ... ♗e2 8 h5 ♗b5 (f1) 9 h6+ ♔h7 10 ♖c7+ ♔h8 11 h7 and 12 ♔h6 wins.

If 5 ... ♗b1 (h7) 6 ♖g5. Or 5 ... ♗e4 6 ♔g5. Or 5 ... ♗a4 6 ♔g5 ♔g7 7 ♖c3! when there is no defence to the advance of the pawn.

6 ♖g5 ♗d1+

Or 6 ... ♗f5 7 ♔h6 ♗d3 8 ♖g3 ♗e4 9 ♖g4 and 10 ♖f4+ wins.

7 ♔h6 ♔f7

White was threatening to bring his rook to the f-file with gain of time, e.g. 7 ... ♗f3 8 ♖g1 ♗e2 9 ♖g2, or 7 ... ♗b3 8 ♖b5 etc.

8 ♖g7+ ♔f6

Or 8 ... ♔f8 9 ♔g6 and 10 ♔f6 wins.

9 ♖g1 ♗e2
10 ♖g2 ♗d3
11 ♖f2+ wins.

This example ends our discussion of rook and pawn v bishop. Apart from the few exceptions given, this type of ending is won for White, but can sometimes require extremely precise handling. Endings with rook against bishop and pawn or bishop and two pawn are usually drawn, although in certain positions either side can win, depending on the piece configuration. From among the many possibilities, we select a position in which both sides have two pawns and which has great practical value.

All the pawns are on the same wing, with none being passed, and

221

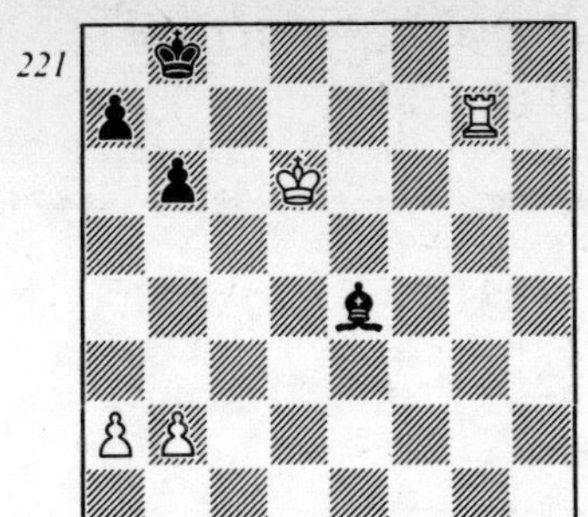

Black has the 'correct' bishop. He has set up the correct defensive formation of pawns on the black squares combining with his bishop to prevent the entry of White's king. The question is whether White can achieve anything by advancing his pawns or whether Black can defend his hedgehog position.

1 b4!

Only by immediately preventing 1 ... a5! can White win the game, as it is difficult to see how he could proceed after this, if Black had the move. The bishop would remain on the long diagonal; it could not be driven away, and if White's king tried to penetrate via b5 Black would place his bishop on c6 and move his king between the first and second ranks.

White's only try would be 2 a4 ♗f3 3 ♖f7 in order to answer 3 ... ♗e4 with 4 b4 ab 5 ♖f4. The situation would then be critical for Black, although 5 ... ♗d3! 6 ♖xb4 ♔a7 7 ♔c6 ♔a6 8 ♖xb6+ ♔a5 9 ♖b3 ♗g6! would draw. However, Black need not even allow this, and can play 3 ... ♗g2 4 ♖f2 ♗h1 in order to answer 5 b4 with 5 ... ab 6 ♖b2 ♔b7 7 ♖xb4 ♔a6 8 ♖b5 ♗f3 9 ♔c7 ♗d1 10 ♖xb6+ ♔a5 etc. White would have no real winning chances.

1 ... ♗f3

If 1 ... a5 2 ba ba 3 ♔c5 a4 4 ♔b6 ♔c8 5 ♖c7+ and 6 ♖c4 wins Black's pawn.

2 a4 ♗e4
3 a5!

An interesting position arises after 3 b5 ♗f3. If White then makes a non-committal move such as 4 ♖g1, Black can cleverly reply with 4 ... a5! If then 5 ba Black plays 5 ... ♔a7 and 6 ... ♔xa6, and if White does not capture the pawn, Black maintains his bishop on the long diagonal and White's king can never attack the b-pawn. This idea was seen in a game Stein-R.Byrne, Moscow 1971 (with colours reversed). However, even without this possibility, Black can probably hold the position after 3 b5. To make any progress, White would have to play a5 and after ... ba recapture with his king. Black must then place his bishop on the c8-h3 diagonal in order to play ... ♗c8+ as soon as White's king goes to a6. On the other hand, if the king returns to c5, Black's bishop goes back to the long diagonal. It is difficult to see how White can make any progress.

3 ... ba
4 ba a6

Black must play this move

sooner or later. If 4 ... ♗d3 5 ♖g3 followed by either 6 a6 or 6 ♔c6. After the text move, a fresh situation has arisen, posing tricky problems for White. He must drive Black's king far enough away from the pawn for the sacrifice ♖xa6 to win. The following analysis by Enevoldsen shows that this is in fact possible:

5 ♔c5 ♗d3
6 ♔b6 ♔c8
7 ♖c7+ ♔d8

White has made the first step, as 7 ... ♔b8? loses to 8 ♖d7, but Black's king must be driven even further away.

8 ♖c5 ♗e2

Not of course 8 ... ♗b5 9 ♖xb5 etc. If 8 ... ♔e7 9 ♖d5 and 10 ♔c7 gains time on the main line.

9 ♔b7 ♔d7
10 ♖d5+ ♔e6
11 ♖d2 ♗c4

It makes no appreciable difference which square the bishop chooses, as White pursues his strategic plan unhindered.

12 ♔c7 ♗b5
13 ♖d4!

Placing Black in zugzwang, so driving hs king further afield. If now 13 ... ♔e5 14 ♖d6 transposes to our main line.

13 ... ♗f1
14 ♖d6+ ♔e5

Or 14 ... ♔e7 15 ♖d1 and 16 ♖e1+ wins.

15 ♔c6 ♗e2
16 ♔c5 ♗b5
17 ♖b6 ♗e2

If 17 ... ♗d3 18 ♖b3 or 17 ... ♗f1 18 ♖b1, the rook equally reaches the d-file.

18 ♖b8

Quicker than 18 ♖b2 ♗d3 19 ♖b3 etc, as 18 ... ♗b5 now fails to 19 ♖xb5.

18 ... ♗d3
19 ♖e8+ ♔f6

Or 19 ... ♔f5 20 ♔d4 winning more quickly.

20 ♔d6

Translator's note: 20 ♔b6 followed by 21 ♖a8 and 22 ♖xa6 would shorten the solution by 8 moves.

20 ... ♔f5

Or 20 ... ♔f7 21 ♖e7+ ♔f8 (if 21 ... ♔f6 22 ♖e3) 22 ♔e6 and 23 ♔f6 wins.

21 ♖e5+ ♔f4
22 ♔d5 ♗b5
23 ♔d4 ♗a4

Or 23 ... ♗f1 24 ♖e8 etc.

24 ♖e6 ♗b5
25 ♖f6+ ♔g5
26 ♖f8

Black's king is now far enough away, otherwise White could have continued the process with 26 ♔e5 etc.

26 ... ♔g6
27 ♔c5 ♔g7
28 ♖a8 ♔f7
29 ♔b6 ♔e7
30 ♖xa6 wins.

A lengthy solution but easy to follow once we have seen the basic idea of driving away Black's king.

ROOK AGAINST KNIGHT

This ending also is usually drawn. A win is only possible in exceptional circumstances. Let us examine a few possibilities from diagram 222.

Here are two examples in which White has driven the enemy king to the edge of the board. Nevertheless, there is no win to be had. In the bottom position, play might go:

1 ♖b2+ ♚a1
2 ♖b8

Or 2 ♖h2 ♚b1 3 ♖d2 ♚a1 4 ♔b4 ♚b1 5 ♔c3 ♞a2+ etc.

2 ... ♞e2!

The only move. Black loses after both 2 ... ♞d3 3 ♔b3 ♞c1+ 4 ♔c2 ♞a2 5 ♖b1 mate, and 2 ... ♞a2 3 ♔b3 ♚b1 4 ♖b7 ♞c1+ 5 ♔c3+ and 6 ♔c2.

3 ♔b3 ♚b1!

Threatening to escape via c1.

4 ♖e8 ♞c1+
5 ♔c3 ♞a2+

White must now allow perpetual check or else let the black king out. The position is drawn.

The top position in diagram 222 is also a typical drawing position.

1 ♖b7 ♞h6
2 ♖h7 ♞g8!

The black knight must stay close to the king. In a game Steinitz-Neumann, 1870 (with colours reversed), Black wrongly continued 2 ... ♘g4 and lost after 3 ♖h4 ♘e3 4 ♖e4! ♘d1 (or 4 ... ♘g2 5 ♔f5, or 4 ... ♘c2 5 ♔d5) 5 ♖f4+ ♔g7 6 ♖f3 ♔g6 (or 6 ... ♘b2 7 ♔d5 ♔g6 8 ♔d4 ♔g5 9 ♖f1 ♘a4 10 ♖b1 etc) 7 ♔e5 ♔g5 8 ♔d4 ♔g4 9 ♖f1 ♘b2 10 ♖b1 ♘a4 11 ♖b4 winning the knight.

3 ♖f7+ ♚e8
4 ♖g7 ♚f8!

Again this is the only move, as 4 ... ♞h6 5 ♖g6 wins the knight.

5 ♖h7 ♚e8
6 ♖f7 ♞h6
7 ♖f1

Or 7 ♖g7 ♚f8 8 ♔f6 ♞g8+ 9 ♔g6 ♞e7+ etc.

7 ... ♞g8

and White can do nothing further.

It is clear that if this last position were moved one square to the right, with Black's knight on h8, Black would be completely lost. White also has winning chances if the knight is separated from the king, or is placed unfavourably near the corner on the second rank. However, the reader can look up this material in more specialized endgame books.

When we have rook and pawn against knight, it is only rarely that Black can save himself. This can only occur when the pawn is blockaded and separated from its own king, as the couple of positions given in diagram 223.

223

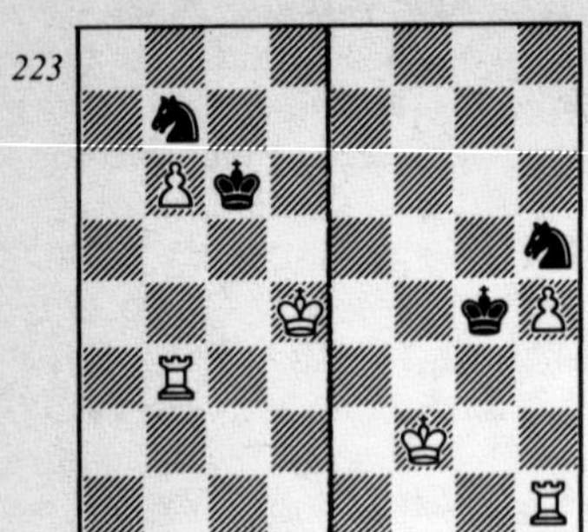

In the left-hand position, Black is blockading the pawn, and it is difficult to see how White can proceed. His only chance lies in approaching with his king along the top of the board, and Black must defend very carefully to hold the position. (Note that if the pieces are moved one rank further up, even this white plan would be impossible).

1 ♖b4 ♘a5!

Berger suggested the following drawing line: 1 ... ♘d6 2 ♔e5 ♘b7 3 ♔e6 ♘c5+ 4 ♔e7 ♘b7 (if 4 ... ♔b7 5 ♔d6 ♘a6 6 ♖b1 ♘b8 7 ♔c5 ♘d7+ 8 ♔b5 wins) 5 ♖b1 ♘a5 6 ♔d8 ♔b7 7 ♔d7 ♘c4 winning the pawn.

224

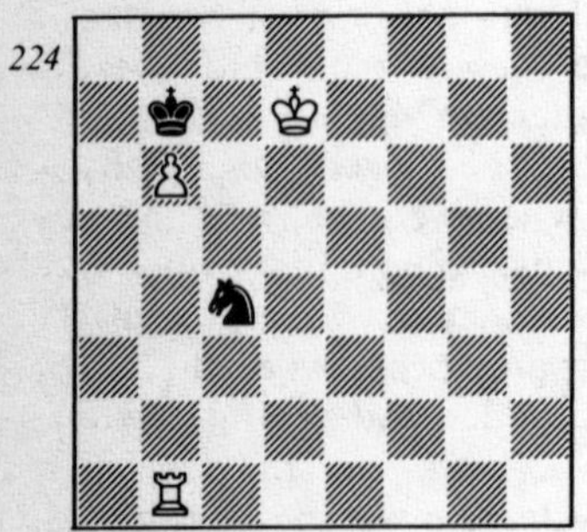

However, as Chéron pointed out, White wins here by 8 ♖b4! ♘xb6+ (or else White's reaches c5) 9 ♔d6 ♔a7 10 ♔c6 etc. The text move was analysed by Frink.

2 ♔e4

If 2 ♔e5 then 2 ... ♔c5! 3 b7 ♘c6+ and 4 ... ♔xb4 draws at once.

2 ... ♘b7
3 ♔e5 ♘c5

So that if 4 ♔f6 ♘d7+ follows.

4 ♔f5 ♘d7!

After 4 ... ♔b7 5 ♔f6 ♘d7+ 6 ♔e7 ♘xb6 7 ♔d6 we have Chéron's winning position.

5 b7 ♔c7

and Black has reached the position we mentioned earlier, in which White's king has no manoeuvring space, e.g. 6 ♖b5 ♘b8 7 ♔e4 ♔c6 8 ♖b1 ♔c7 9 ♔d5 ♘d7 10 ♔c4 ♘b8 11 ♖b5 ♘d7 12 ♔b4 ♔b8 13 ♔a5 ♔a7 drawing.

If this position is moved towards the centre, it is still drawn. Black defends, as we have shown, by placing his king on whichever side the white king threatens to penetrate. He does not even have to fear Chéron's winning line which of course does not work with bishop's pawn, king's pawn or queen's pawn.

When we come to the rook's pawn, Black's chances are far worse for the simple reason that White can sometimes even advantageously give up the pawn. The right-hand position in diagram 223 is an interesting case in point. Black will lose if he allows White's king to reach g6. His only chance lies in the fact that White's rook has little space to manoeuvre behind the pawn, which makes the pawn hard to defend. White wins in the following instructive way:

1 ♖h2

Not of course 1 ♔e3 ♘g3 drawing at once.

1 ... ♘f4

After 1 ... ♘f6 Berger gives a win as follows: 2 ♔e3 ♔g3 3 ♖h1 ♔g2 (or 3 ... ♘g4+ 4 ♔e4 ♘f2+ 5 ♔f5 ♘xh1 6 h5 and the pawn cannot be stopped, or 3 ... ♘h5 4 ♔e4 gives a line we shall see later) 4 ♖d1 ♔g3 5 ♖d4 wins, as 5 ... ♘g4+ is answered by ♔e4.

2 ♔e3 ♘h5

But not 2 ... ♔g3 3 h5! ♘d5+ 4 ♔e4 ♘c3+ 5 ♔e5 and the pawn runs through.

3 ♔e4 ♘g3+

Weaker is 3 ... ♔g3 4 ♖h1 ♔g2 5 ♖d1 ♔g3 (h3) 6 ♔f5! and the pawn cannot be captured.

4 ♔e5 ♘h5

Or 4 ... ♘f1 5 ♖f2 ♘e3 6 ♔e4 etc.

5 ♔e6 ♔g3

Black cannot stop White's king reaching g6. For example, if 5 ... ♘f4+ 6 ♔f6 ♔h5 7 ♔f5 ♘g6 8 ♖h1 and again the pawn cannot be taken.

6 ♖h1 ♔g4

Or 6 ... ♔g2 7 ♖d1 ♔g3 8 ♔f5! etc.

7 ♔f7 ♘g3

Black seems to have defended successfully, as 8 ♖h2 ♘f1 9 ♖f2 ♘g3, or here 9 h5 ♘xh2 10 h6 (10 ♔g6 ♘f3) 10 ... ♘f3! draw for him. However, there is a surprise in store.

8 ♔g6!

This decides matters, as the rook sacrifice must be accepted.

8 ... ♘xh1
9 h5 ♘g3
10 h6 wins.

The pawn cannot be stopped.

225

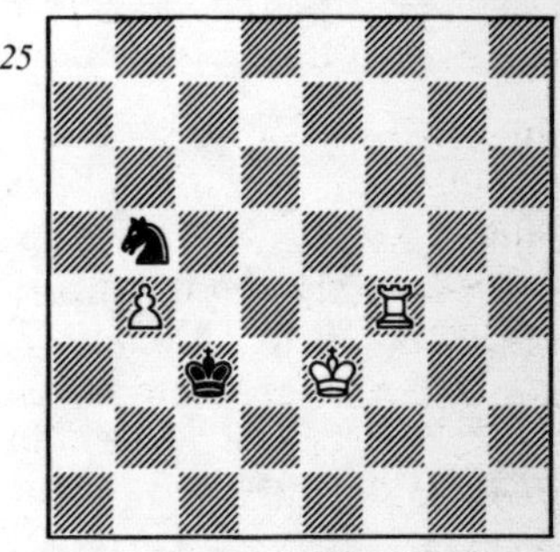

There is another type of drawing position, when the pawn is guarded from the side by the rook. For example, in diagram 225, White cannot win against correct defence. Black must play his king to b3 if the white king stays behind the pawn, but must transfer to b5 if White takes his king up the board. Play might go: **1 ♔f3 ♔b3 2 ♔g4 ♔a4 3 ♔f5 ♘a3 5 ♔e5 ♔b5** and Black is threatening to win the pawn after 5 ... ♘c2.

Common sense tells us that White would win with a rook's pawn in the same situation, for Black has two disadvantages: he now has no file to the left (a4!) to manoeuvre round the pawn, nor can his king attack the rook which is no longer behind the pawn. The reader can try out this position for himself to see how White wins.

Rook against knight and pawn or knight and two pawns is usually drawn, but of course there are exceptions which we shall not discuss here. With equal material, the rook usually wins, unless Black can set up a hedgehog position. Consider the following example:

226

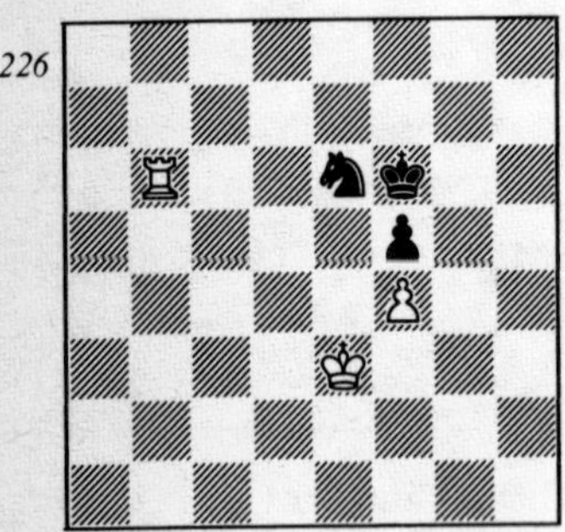

White can make no progress, as one of his pieces is always tied to the defence of the pawn. The most White can do is win the pawn after **1 ♔d3 ♚f7 2 ♖xe6 ♚xe6 3 ♔c4,** but the pawn ending is a book draw. However, the same position one rank further up would result in a winning pawn ending!

Rook and Minor Piece against Rook

The ending of rook and bishop or rook and knight against rook is usually a draw, the rook and knight combination winning only rarely. White's prospects are somewhat better with rook and bishop, although even here there are not many positions from which a win can be forced. However, as we shall soon see, the defence is not always easy to conduct.

ROOK AND BISHOP AGAINST ROOK

Surprisingly enough, this ending occurs relatively often in tournament practice, and is just as often needlessly lost by the defence. It will therefore be worthwhile if we explain here some of the basic principles of defence.

First of all, let us consider a famous position from which Philidor demonstrated a win more than two centuries ago.

227

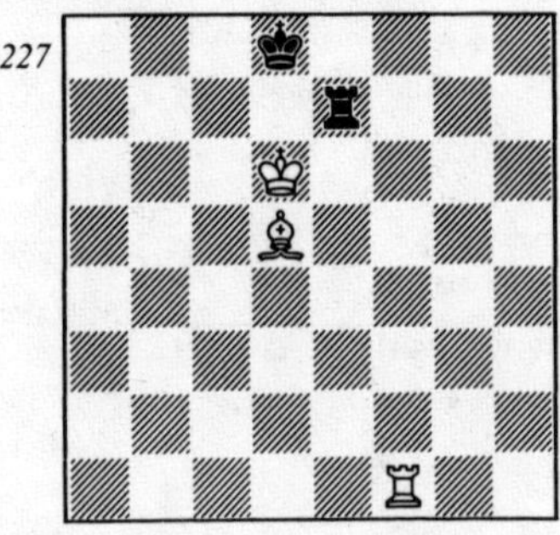

A.Philidor 1749

White wins as follows:

1 ♖f8+

In order to prevent the defensive move ... ♜d7+ which is possible even after 1 ♗c6.

1 ... ♜e8

2 ♖f7 ♜e2!

White was threatening 3 ♖a7. If 2 ... ♚c8 3 ♖a7 ♜d8+ 4 ♔c6 ♚b8 5 ♖a1 and Black is in zugzwang.

2 ... ♖e1 or 2 ... ♖e3 slightly shorten the main variation.

3 ♖h7

A tempo move to force Black's rook to a less favourable square on the e-file.

3 ... ♖e1

A more stubborn defence than 3 ... ♖e3 after which 4 ♖d7+ ♔e8 (or 4 ... ♔c8 5 ♖a7 when Black cannot play 5 ... ♖b3) 5 ♖a7 ♔f8 6 ♖f7+ ♔e8 7 ♖f4! ♔d8 (White threatened 8 ♗c6+ and 7 ... ♖d3 allows 8 ♖g4 when 8 ... ♖f3 cannot be played) 8 ♗e4! wins (8 ... ♔e8 9 ♗c6+).

4 ♖b7 ♖c1

Or 4 ... ♔c8 5 ♖a7 ♖b1 6 ♖g7 ♔b8 7 ♖g8+ ♔a7 8 ♖a8+ and 9 ♖b8+ winning the rook.

5 ♗b3

We now see why the black rook was driven to bottom rank (no check on d1!). Grigoriev gives the alternatives 5 ♖f7 ♖e1 (or 5 ... ♔e8 6 ♖f6 ♖d1 7 ♖f2! ♖d4 8 ♖e2+ and 9 ♖g2 etc) 6 ♗f3 as winning, e.g. 6 ... ♖e3 (or 6 ... ♔e8 7 ♖f4 ♔d8 8 ♗h5 ♔c8 9 ♖b4!) 7 ♗c6 continuing as in the main variation.

5 ... ♖c3

Or 5 ... ♔c8 6 ♖b4 ♔d8 7 ♖f4 ♖e1 (if 7 ... ♔c8 8 ♗d5 ♔b8 9 ♖a4 etc) 8 ♗a4 ♔c8 9 ♗c6 ♖d1+ 10 ♗d5 ♔b8 11 ♖a4 wins. The black rook has now been driven to the unfavourable sixth rank and White can carry out his winning plan.

6 ♗e6 ♖d3+

7 ♗d5 ♖c3

Or 7 ... ♔c8 8 ♖a7 winning.

8 ♖d7+! ♔c8

White mates after 8 ... ♔e8 9 ♖g7 (Black's rook cannot go to f3!).

9 ♖f7 ♔b8

10 ♖b7+ ♔c8

11 ♖b4! ♔d8

Or 11 ... ♖d3 12 ♖a4 etc.

12 ♗c4! wins.

Black can no longer prevent mate.

As can be seen, this winning method is complex and needs to be well planned. There are many similar positions, some of which are won for White, some drawn. We cannot deal with these fully but will just point out that positions similar to diagram 227 are won if the kings are on the rook's or bishop's files, but only drawn with the kings on the knight's file. The reader can find more extensive analysis in specialized endgame books. What interests us here is the practical problem of how to defend such positions.

228

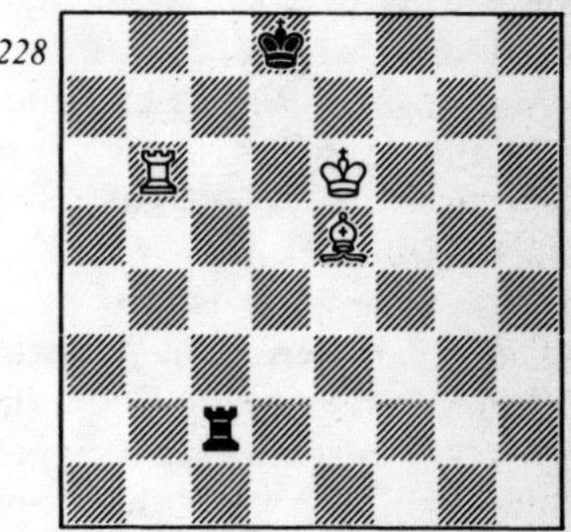

J.Szen

Let us assume that Black's king has been driven to the edge of the board and has reached a position similar to diagram 228.

This is a drawing position given by Szen. It has the following characteristics: the black king is a knight's move away from White's king and on a square of the same colour as the bishop controls, and Black's rook is preventing the threatened mate. White is unable to strengthen his position any further, as the following analysis shows:

1	**Rb8+**	**Rc8**
2	**Bf6+**	**Kc7**
3	**Be5+**	**Kd8**
4	**Rb1**	**Rc2**
5	**Rg1**	**Kc8**
6	**Rb1**	

Otherwise the king escapes. Here is another characteristic of Szen's position; on the side defended by the rook Black's king has sufficient room in which to manoeuvre. If the whole position were moved one file to the left (White's rook on f1). White would now win by 6 Rf8+, when Black would lose his rook in two moves. In other words, Black's king must be on the 'longer' side.

6	...	**Kd8**

and we are back in our original position. The game is drawn.

There is an even simpler drawing position, first given by Cochrane, with the black rook pinning White's bishop to the king. Consider the position in diagram 229.

229

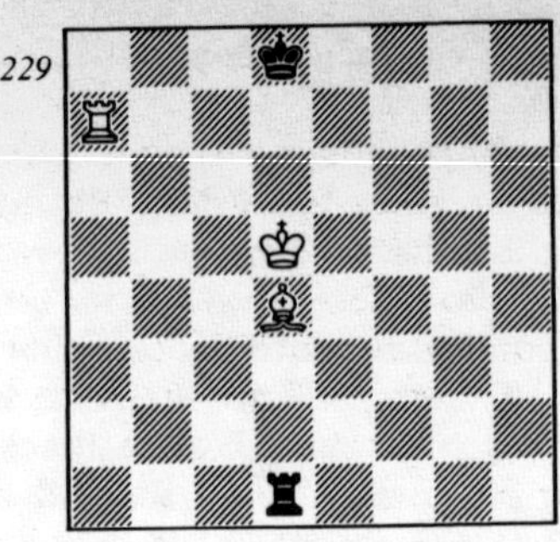

White finds it difficult to set up threats if Black keeps his rook on the d-file. As an example, we quote the continuation of a game Flohr-Reshevsky, 1937, which arose after **1 Rh7**. Black played **1 ... Rd2 2 Ke5 Kc8 3 Bc5 Rd7 4 Be7 Kb7 5 Ke6 Kc6 6 Rh1 Rd2 7 Rc1+ Kb5 8 Bd6 Re2+** and so on.

If both these drawing positions are known, we have little to fear in this type of ending. To learn the whole story, one would have to wade through reams of analysis in bulky endgame tomes, but this knowledge would prove of little practical value.

If in such positions the defending side also has a pawn, this factor can often work against him by cutting out stalemate chances and sometimes interfering with the action of his rook. Rarely can one or two pawns provide effective counterplay.

ROOK AND KNIGHT AGAINST ROOK

The defence here is far easier,

because Black's king cannot be driven to edge of the board. If, however, he is already there, several winning positions are possible, especially if Black's king near a corner. However, as these are exceptional positions, we do not intend to spend much time on them. Here is one interesting example of how White can win such positions:

230

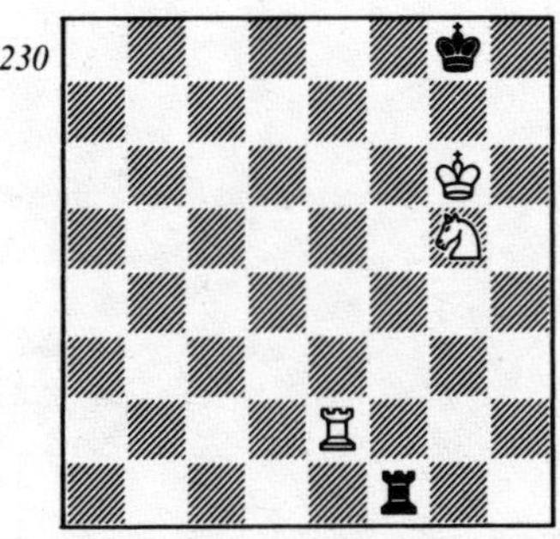

L.Centurini 1888

White achieves nothing with the immediate 1 ♖e8+ ♖f8 2 ♖e7 ♖c1 and yet dare not leave the e-file, allowing ... ♔f8. Once again, the zugzwang weapon is the answer, forcing Black's rook to an unfavourable square on the file.

1 ♖e3 ♖f2

Not of course 1 ... ♔f8 2 ♘h7+ winning. If 1 ... ♖f4 2 ♖a3 ♖f1 3 ♖a8+ ♖f8 4 ♖a1! transposes to our main variation. The disadvantage of Black's rook on f4 is that after 2 ♖a3 the move 2 ... ♔f8 fails to 3 ♘e6+. Finally, if 1 ... ♖f8 2 ♘h7 ♖a8 3 ♖e7 and 4 ♘f6 wins easily.

2 ♖e1 ♖f4

This is the position White was aiming for.

3 ♖a1! ♖f2

There is nothing else.

4 ♘e4 ♖g2+
5 ♔f6 ♔h8

Forced, as White was threatening 6 ♖a8+ and 7 ♘g5+. In order to make progress, White must now drive Black's rook once again to the fifth rank.

6 ♖b1 ♖g4

Not 6 ... ♖g7 because of 7 ♘g5 winning.

7 ♘g5 ♖f4+
8 ♔g6 ♔g8

We now have the same position as after White's 3rd move, but with White to move.

9 ♘e6! ♖g4!
10 ♔f6 ♔h8
11 ♖b8+

Quicker than the composer's 11 ♔f7 ♖h4 12 ♔g6 ♖g4+ 13 ♘g5 which equally wins.

11 ... ♖g8
12 ♘f8

and mates quickly.

White was able to win here only because Black's pieces were most unfavourably placed. Taking diagram 230, we only have to place Black's rook on g1 and Black to move draws by 1 ... ♔f8. The pinned knight cannot join in the action, so White can make no progress.

Even if Black's king can be kept on g8 (diagram 231), the pin of the knight still saves him, e.g. **1 ♔f6 ♖g2** not 1 ... ♔f8? 2 ♘e6+ and

231

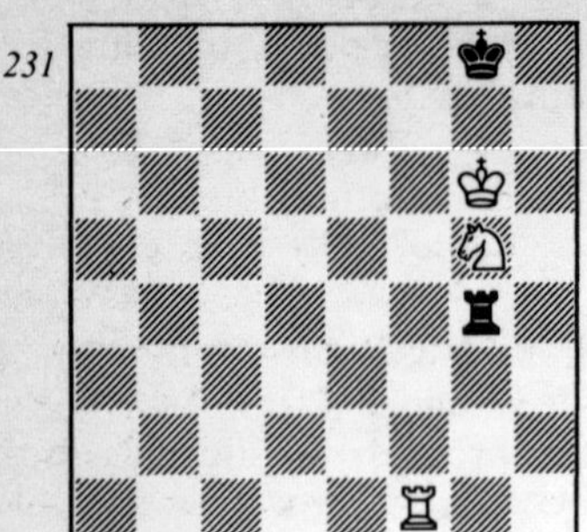

3 ♖d1 winning **2 ♘e6 ♖g3 3 ♖f2 ♖g1** the rook must not go to g4 because 4 ♖a2 threatening 5 ♖a8+ and 6 ♘g5+ **4 ♘f4 ♖a1 5 ♖b2 ♖a6+ 6 ♘e6 ♔h7** and the knight is again pinned, restricting White's possibilities. In other words, Black's best defence in positions of this kind is to pin the knight.

5 Bishop Endings

Along with rook endings, endgames with a bishop on each side constitiute the most difficult part of endgame theory. However, in both types of ending certain general principles have been elaborated which help the player to find his way amid the complexities. Rook endings are much more difficult to analyse, the main difficulty residing in the formulation of a general strategic plan which must then be pursued to its logical conclusion. The following examples will convince the reader of the truth of this statement.

Bishop endings can be divided into two main sections, depending on whether the bishops control squares of the same or opposite colour. Both types of position require drastically different treatment, as we shall see. However, before proceeding with bishop endings proper, let us first see how the bishop fares against pawns alone.

Bishop against Pawns

Because of its long-ranging movement, the bishop is usually successful in its fight against pawns. It is clear that a bishop draws against a single pawn, and this is normally the case also against two pawns. However, against three pawns the bishop can only defend successfully if they are not too far advanced. These are, of course general rules to which there are many exceptions. Let us examine a few positions to see how these points apply.

232

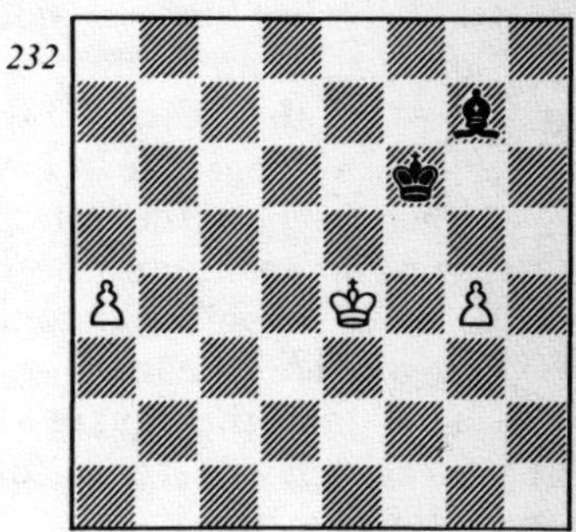

H.Otten 1892

The material immediately leads us to think of a draw, but Black's pieces are so badly placed here that White can in fact queen his a-pawn as follows:

1 a5 ♝f8

Aiming for c5, the only square from which the bishop can stop the pawn. White now prevents this defence.

2 ♔d5 ♝h6

3 g5+!

This surprising sacrifice is the key move. 3 ♔d4 only draws 3 ... ♗f4 4 a6 ♗b8. Note that it is Black's king position which is his undoing. For example, with his king on g8 he would draw.

3 ... ♗xg5

Or 3 ... ♔xg5 4 a6 wins at once.

4 ♔e4 ♗h4

5 ♔f3! wins.

The pawn cannot be stopped. An attractive exception to the rule.

Normally against two isolated pawns, the bishop and king each hold one of the pawns. If, however, both kings are away from the main action, the bishop has the task of holding up both pawns. This can only be done along a diagonal or by controlling at the same time the square in front of each pawn. Take, for example, this position:

233

Neither pawn can advance and the game is drawn. Now move the pawns and bishop one square up the board, and a sacrifice is in the air. White wins easily by **1 e7 ♗xe7 2 a7**, or by **1 a7 ♗xa7 2 e7**. The pawns are too far advanced.

Even against two connected pawns, the bishop can put up a successful defence if they are not too far advanced. As a general rule, the pawns should be no further that the fifth rank, if both kings are not involved. Diagram 234 illustrates this point.

234

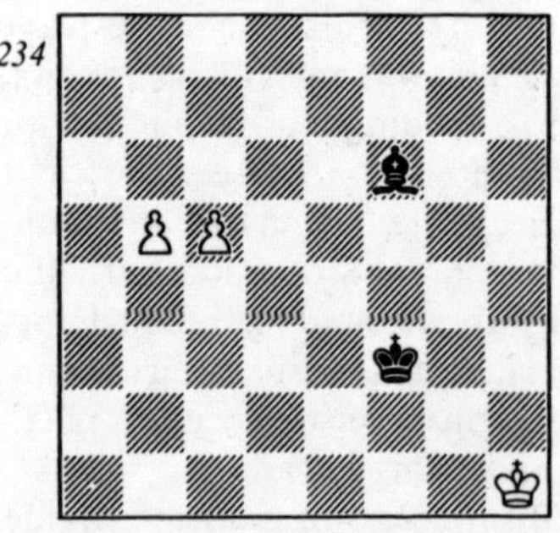

The relatively favourable position of Black's bishop allows him to draw with ease after:

1 b6 ♗d4

White must advance his pawns on squares of the same colour as the bishop controls, or else they can easily be blockaded, e.g. 1 c6 ♗d8 etc.

2 b7 ♗e5

The pawns are held, ensuring the draw.

Now let us examine a few other situations when the bishop is not so well placed. If Black's bishop were on g7, White would win by 1 c6 ♗e5 2 b6, as the bishop cannot reach d8 in time. Or against the bishop on a7, White plays 1 b6 ♗b8 2 c6 winning.

However, if the bishop is on a5, after 1 b6 Black leaves his bishop where it is and draws by coming back with his king 1 ... ♔e4.

If Black has a white-squared bishop in diagram 234, he draws if his bishop can reach the long white diagonal in time. For example, with the bishop on b7 Black draws after **1 c6 ♗a8!** (not 1 ... ♗c8? 2 b6 wins). With his bishop on e2, Black would lose after **1 b6 ♗a6? 2 c6**, but he can utilize the unfavourable position of White's king and draw by **1 ... ♔e3** and **2 ... ♗f3+**.

The whole picture can change if one of the kings is near the pawns. With White's king near the pawns, the win is usually guaranteed, assuming the black king is further away. If Black's king is near the pawns, he usually draws, wherever White's king may be. Of course, there is always the exception.

When Black has a bishop against three pawns, his drawing prospects are good, provided that the pawns are not too far advanced. As a rule, the black king will normally have to join in the fight against the pawns, as our next example shows.

In such positions, Black can draw if the pawns have not reached the fifth rank. However, the defence requires the utmost precision, as the following shows:

235

Y.Averbakh 1954

1 ... ♗e8

For instructional purposes, we give as or main line the faulty passive defence by Black. In the course of our analysis we shall of course indicate the correct defensive measures. For instance, the most exact plan here is to place the bishop on the h5-d1 diagonal by playing 1 ... ♗b3 and 2 ... ♗d1 at once. However, the delay is not yet fatal.

2 f5 ♗f7

3 h5

White would get nowhere by placing his pawns on the black squares h4, g5 and f6, as after 3 ♔f4 ♔f6 4 g5+ ♔g7 5 ♔e5 ♗h5 6 ♔e6 ♗f7+ 7 ♔e7 ♗h5 8 f6+ ♔g8 he has allowed them to be blockaded.

3 ... ♗e8?

An instructive mistake, after which the game is lost for Black. This was the last chance to play the bishop to the more active diagonal h5-d1. After 3 ... ♗b3! Black can still draw, e.g. 4 ♔f4 ♗d1! or 4 f6+ ♔f7 5 ♔h6 ♔xf6 6 g5+ ♔f7 7 ♔h7 ♗c2+ 8 g6+ ♔f6, in both cases drawing comfortably.

4 ♔f4!

The only way to win, pointed out by Karstedt in 1906. Horwitz, who had analysed the position in 1880, gave **4 f6+** as winning, when play might go:

1) **4 ... ♔f7?** 5 h6 ♔g8 6 ♔f5! ♗d7+ 7 ♔f4 ♗e8 (or 7 ... ♗a4 8 ♔e5 wins; Black cannot play both his king to f7 and his bishop to the h7-b1 diagonal in time) 8 ♔e5 ♗g6 9 ♔e6 ♔f8 10 g5 ♗c2 11 f7 ♗b3+ 12 ♔f6 ♗xf7 13 h7 wins.

2) **4 ... ♔g8! 5 ♔f4** if 5 ♔h6 ♔f7 6 g5 ♗b5 White gets nowhere, e.g. 7 g6+ ♔xf6 8 g7 ♗c4 9 ♔h7 ♔g5, or 7 ♔h7 ♗d3+ 8 ♔h8 ♗e4 etc. **5 ... ♗a4 6 g5** 6 ♔e5 ♗d1! **6 ... ♗d1 7 h6** or 7 g6 ♗xh5 8 ♔g5 ♗d1, or here 8 ♔f5 ♔f8! **7 ... ♗c2 8 ♔e5 ♔f7** and Black has reached a drawing position.

4	**...**	**♗f7**

It is now too late for 4 ... ♗a4 5 g5 ♗d1 as after 6 h6+ Black must transpose to the main line by 6 ... ♔h7, or lose at once by 6 ... ♔f7 7 g6+ ♔f6 8 h7. If 4 ... ♔h6 White wins after 5 f6 ♔h7 6 ♔e5 ♔g8 7 h6 etc, or after 5 ♔e5 ♔g5 6 ♔e6 ♗a4 7 f6 etc.

5	**♔e5**	**♗c4**

Or 5 ... ♗e8 6 ♔e6 ♗f7+ 7 ♔e7 ♗c4 8 f6+ ♔g8 9 h6 winning.

6	**g5**	**♗e2**
7	**h6+**	**♔h7**
8	**♔d6!**	

The simplest. White's king reaches e7 without being troubled by the bishop (8 ♔e6 ♗g4 9 ♔f6!).

8	**...**	**♗d3**

Or 8 ... ♗g4 9 f6 ♗h5 10 ♔e7 ♔g8 11 f7+ etc.

9	**f6**	**♔g6**
10	**♔e7**	**♗c4**
11	**f7**	**♗xf7**
12	**h7**	**♔xh7**
13	**♔xf7**	**♔h8**
14	**♔g6!** wins.	

In his fight against the three connected pawns, Black must try to force them to the same diagonal so that he can blockade them with his bishop. Or if they form a triangle, he can use his bishop to blockade two pawns and his king to stop the other. Consider this position:

236

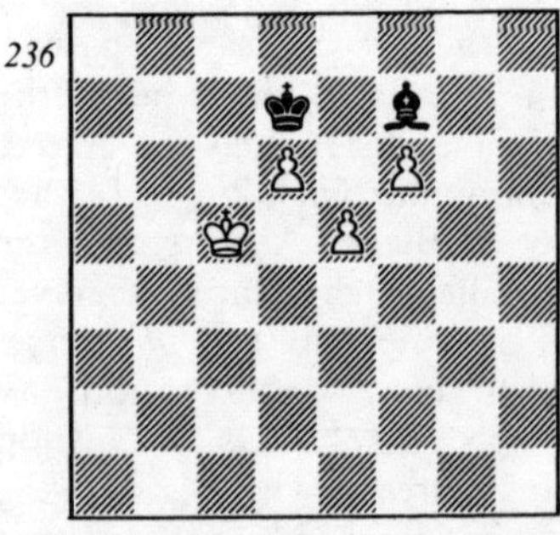

Black can draw if he continues to prevent the approach of White's king. Play might go: **1 ♔d4 ♔e6 2 ♔e4 ♗e8 3 ♔f4 ♗d7 4 ♔g5 ♗e8 5 ♔h6 ♔f7!** (not 5 ... ♗d7? 6 ♔g7 ♗e8 7 f7 ♗xf7 8 d7 winning) and White can make no progress.

If White's three pawns are isolated, it is difficult to give general rules. Black's defence will be trickier, because the bishop has problems stopping the pawns at some distance from each other.

We shall restrict ourselves to one example.

237
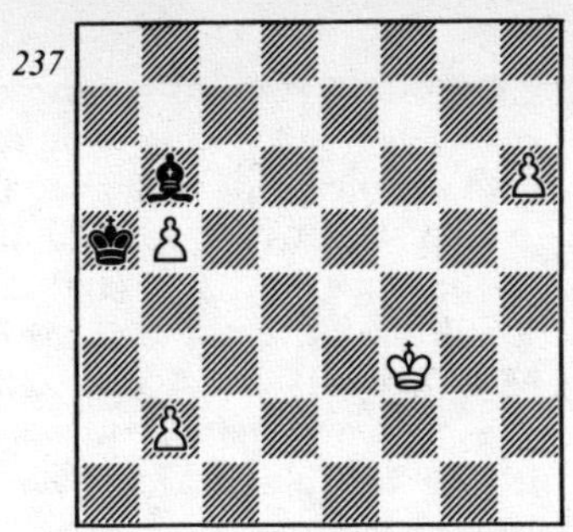

M.Lewitt 1933

As two of White's pawns are doubled, Black has an apparently easy task, for the bishop will only have one pawn to deal with. However, as we saw also in diagram 232, the bishop just cannot do this, and White wins as follows:

1 ♔e4 ♗d8
2 b6!

Again the pawn sacrifice is the answer, creating a self-block after 2 ... ♔xb6 3 ♔f5 when the pawn cannot be stopped. Or if 2 ... ♗xb6 3 h7 wins. However, Black has a cunning defensive idea.

2 ... ♔a6!

Intending to answer 3 h7 with 3 ... ♗f6, and 3 ♔f5 with 3 ... ♗xb6. In a surprising way, however, White's b-pawn now becomes an important factor which White uses cleverly as follows:

3 ♔e5! ♗g5

Black cannot play 3 ... ♗c7+ which would otherwise force White to give up control of d4 or f6. The text move is Black's only chance.

4 h7 ♗c1
5 ♔d6 ♗xb2
6 ♔c7!

Another finesse. After 6 ♔c6? ♗e5! White would be in zugzwang, and Black would draw. Now 7 b7 is the threat.

6 ... ♗e5+
7 ♔c6 ♗d4

Whereas now Black is in zugzwang and 7 ... ♔a5 fails to 8 b7.

8 b7 ♔a7
9 ♔c7 ♗e5+
10 ♔c8 wins.

One of the pawns must queen. A fine study, showing the problems that the bishop has to face against distant passed pawns.

There are many positions in which the side with the bishop also has pawns, but most of them are examples from practical play and difficult to classify. Let us just examine a few exceptional positions which every player must know, beginning with diagram 238.

238
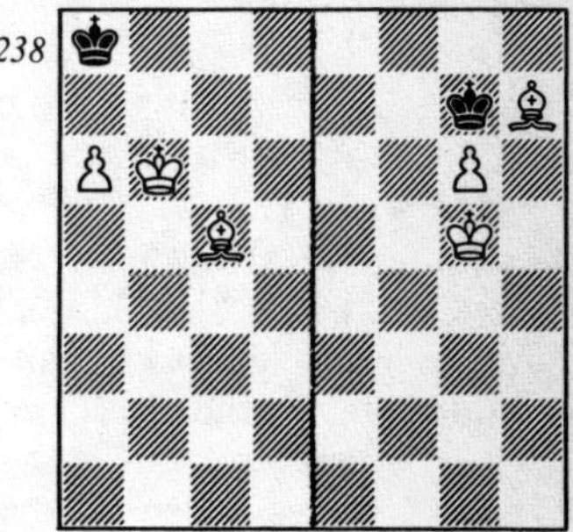

White's material advantage would normally win, but both these positions are drawn. On the left, Black's king cannot be driven out of the corner and is usually stalemated. To win, White's bishop must be able to control the queening square of the pawn. On the right we have an exception known for almost two centuries, in which the bishop cannot win, even with a knight's pawn. As can easily be seen, Black's king cannot be driven from the g7, h8 squares without being stalemated, and sacrificing the bishop on g8 only gives White a drawn pawn ending.

We see similar examples in diagram 239.

239

Black saves himself on the left by the fact that his a-pawn cannot be captured, nor can his king be driven from the corner. White can try **1 ♔c6** when 1 ... ♚a8? allows 2 ♔c7 mate, but after the correct **1 ... ♚c8! 2 ♗e6+ ♚b8 3 ♗f5 ♚a8** White has nothing better than **4 ♔c7 stalemate**, as the reader can verify for himself.

White's bishop also proves useless in the right-hand position. Black's pawn again cannot be captured, and if **1 ♗e4 ♚g8 2 ♔e7 ♚h8 3 ♗d5** or 3 ♔f7 gives stalemate. The position is even drawn when Black's king cannot reach the corner. For instance, if we switch the white king and bishop in diagram 239 (right), Black still draws, e.g. **1 ♔e5 ♚e7 2 ♗d5 ♚f8 3 ♔d6 ♚e8 4 ♗e6 ♚f8 5 ♔d7** stalemate. There is no way of driving the black king away from the pawn.

Surprisingly enough, this pawn setting ensures Black a draw, even if White has a black-squared bishop and can attack the g-pawn. For example, changing White's bishop from f5 to e5, we have **1 ♔d7 ♚g8 2 ♔e7 ♚h8** when **3 ♔f7** again gives stalemate. Nor is **3 ♗f6** any good, as Black does not play 3 ... gf? 4 ♔f7 winning, but **3 ... ♚g8! 4 ♔e6 gf 5 ♔xf6 ♚f8** drawing.

As we have already said, we cannot devote much space to endings of bishop and pawn versus pawn, but here is one final example of great practical value, which has been thoroughly analysed during the last century.

This interesting position was originally analysed by Kling and Horwitz (1851) and poses fascinating problems. We know that Black draws if his king reaches a8, even if he loses his pawn. Can White capture the pawn without allowing Black's king to reach a8? The answer to this question decides

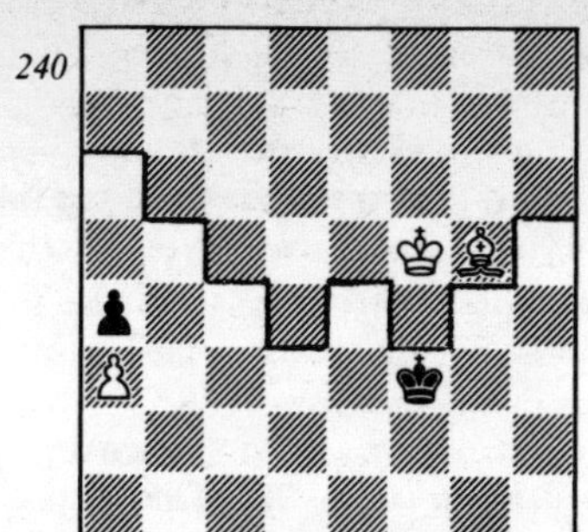

240

Kling and Horwitz 1851

whether White wins or not.

The composers thought that White could win only if he had the move, an opinion also held by other experts, until Rauser proved in 1928 that White wins, whoever has the move. Let us follow the play, first with White to move:

1 ♗f4!

As already mentioned, White aims to capture the pawn without allowing Black's king to reach a8. From Black's point of view, this means that, if White's bishop is, for example, on h2 guarding the long diagonal, Black's king must be in a position to answer a subsequent ♔xa4 by ... ♔c6. So as soon as White threatens to take the pawn, Black must be able to play ... ♔d7. If his king can only reach e6, he loses after 1 ♔xa4 ♔d7 2 ♔b5 ♔c8 3 ♔c6 etc.

All this means that White must manoeuvre his king and bishop so as to drive Black's king as far down the board as possible. White can then capture the pawn before Black's king can occupy d7.

1 ... ♔g2!

Black must keep his options open. Other moves lose quickly, e.g. 1 ... ♔f2 2 ♔e4 ♔g2 3 ♔d4 ♔f3 4 ♗h2 and Black is a move too late.

2 ♔g4!

If White heads straight for the pawn, Black draws after 2 ♔e4 ♔h3 3 ♔d4 ♔g4 4 ♗h2? ♔f5 5 ♔c4 ♔e6 6 ♔b5 ♔d7 obtaining the correct defensive position. White first drives the king further away.

2 ... ♔f2

3 ♗c1 ♔e2

As subsequent play reveals, White has nothing to fear when Black's king moves over to the queenside. However, 3 ... ♔g2 also loses to 4 ♗e3, driving the king to the edge of the board. We shall be coming back to this position.

4 ♔f4 ♔f2

The black king tries to return to his c8-h3 diagonal, in order to reach d7. White's task is easier if the king continues towards the queenside, e.g.:

1) **4 ... ♔d3 5 ♗e3 ♔c4 6 ♔e5! ♔b3** if 6 ... ♔b5 7 ♔d5 **7 ♗c5 ♔c4 8 ♔d6 ♔b5** or 8 ... ♔d3 9 ♔d5 ♔c3 10 ♗d6 ♔d3 11 ♔c5 ♔e4 12 ♔b5 ♔d5 13 ♗h2 wins **9 ♔d5 ♔a5 10 ♔c6 ♔a6 11 ♗e3 ♔a5 12 ♔b7 ♔b5 13 ♗b6!** Black's king has to go back! **13 ... ♔c4 14 ♔c6 ♔b3** or 14 ... ♔d3 15 ♔b5 and 16 ♔xa4 **15 ♗c5 ♔c4 16 ♗d6 ♔d4 17 ♔b5**

♔d5 18 ♗h2 ♔e6 19 ♔xa4 ♔d7 20 ♔b5 ♔c8 21 ♔c6 wins.

2) **4 ... ♔d1 5 ♗e3 ♔c2** if 5 ... ♔e2 6 ♔e4 wins **6 ♔e5!** but not 6 ♔e4? ♔b3 7 ♗c5 ♔c4 drawing **6 ... ♔b3** or 6 ... ♔d3 7 ♗c5 **7 ♗c5 ♔c4 8 ♔d6** as in the previous variation.

5 ♗e3+ ♔g2

After 5 ... ♔e2 6 ♔e4 the black king is driven back to the back rank. With the text move, Black's king still hopes to reach d7.

6 ♔g4! ♔h2

If 6 ... ♔h1 7 ♗f4 transposes. If 6 ... ♔f1 7 ♔f3 ♔e1 8 ♗f4 wins easily.

7 ♗f4+ ♔g2

8 ♗g3!

This recurrent move drives Black's king to the bottom rank.

8 ... ♔g1

9 ♔f3 ♔h1

10 ♗b8

Other moves on the long diagonal also win. As can be seen, Black's king cannot reach d7 in time.

10 ... ♔g1

11 ♔e4 ♔g2

12 ♔d5 ♔f3

13 ♔c4 ♔e4

14 ♔b5 ♔d5

15 ♗h2 wins.

Now let us give Black the move in diagram 240, when it is not so easy to drive his king down the board. This is why it was thought for a long time that White could not win.

1 ... ♔g3!

2 ♗f6 ♔f3

Or 2 ... ♔h3 3 ♔f4 ♔h2 4 ♔g4 ♔g2 5 ♗d4 winning, as we have already seen.

3 ♗e5

Black's king must not be allowed to retreat via the d4 or h4 squares. This move cuts off the latter possibility.

3 ... ♔e3

4 ♗b2!

The only way to win, discovered by Rauser in 1928. The bishop now covers the vital d4 square whilst preparing to occupy the important c1-h6 diagonal to prevent penetration on the kingside. Earlier analysts only considered 4 ♗b8? ♔d4 5 ♔e6 ♔c5 6 ♔d7 ♔b6 7 ♔c8 ♔c5 drawing.

4 ... ♔d3

Or 4 ... ♔f3 5 ♗c1 ♔g3 6 ♗g5 ♔f2 (if 6 ... ♔f3 7 ♗f4 etc, as given above) 7 ♔f4 ♔e2 8 ♔e4 ♔f2 9 ♗f4 wins, as in our analysis to diagram 240 with White to move.

5 ♔e5 ♔e3

We have alread examined 5 ... ♔c2 6 ♗d4 ♔b3 7 ♗c5 ♔c4 8 ♔d6 etc (variation 1 in our note to Black's 4th move of the analysis to diagram 240 with White to move), and after 5 ... ♔c4 6 ♔d6 ♔b3 the simplest is 7 ♔c5! ♔xb2 8 ♔b4 winning.

6 ♗c1+ ♔f3

7 ♔f5! ♔g3

8 ♗g5 ♔f3

If 8 ... ♔h3 9 ♔f4 and 10 ♗h4 drives the king back. We have now reached diagram 240 with White to move!

9 ♗f4! wins.

As we have seen, the black king

must not be allowed into the top half of the board, if White wishes to win. Once there, he cannot be forced back again. In diagram 240 we have indicated the critical zone. If Black's king is above the line, White cannot win. We shall not dwell any longer on this, but instead turn at once to the struggle of bishop against bishop.

Bishop and Pawn against Bishop

A general rule in endings is that a pawn gains in strength as the material on the board is reduced. In other words an extra pawn is worth more if there are weaker pieces on the board; in queen endings it can have relatively little importance, whereas in pawn endings it is usually enough to win the game.

Following this argument, in bishop endings an extra pawn is of great value, especially when the bishops control squares of the same colour, and gives good winning chances. We shall first consider cases in which a single pawn is left on the board. Naturally, Black has fairly good drawing chances and our task is to find out under which conditions the pawn leads to a win.

Let us begin with diagram 241, where White's pawn is already on the sixth rank. To win, White must of course queen his pawn, and this is only possible if Black's king is not immediately in front of the pawn and if his bishop can be prevented from sacrificing itself for the pawn. With bishops of opposite colour there would clearly be no way of stopping this.

241

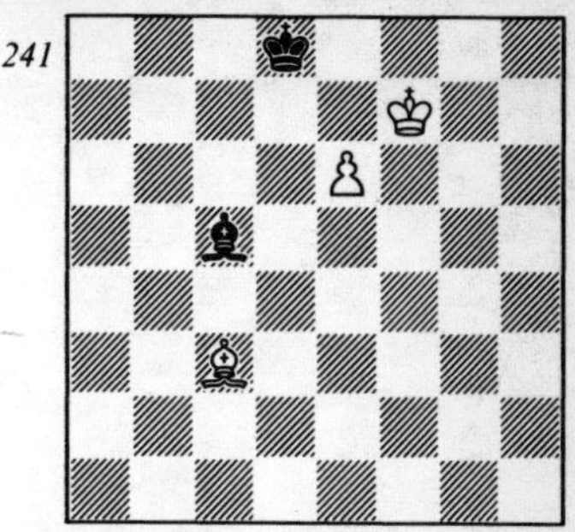

White can always succeed in playing his pawn to e7. The following manoeuvre is typical of such positions:

1 ♗f6+ ♔c8

Or 1 ... ♔c7 2 ♗e7 ♗f2 3 ♗d6+! etc.

2 ♗e7 ♗f2
3 ♗d6 ♗h4

Having been driven from the f8-a3 diagonal, the bishop tries the d8-h4 diagonal, but to no avail.

4 ♗e5 wins.

Black has no defence to threat of 5 ♗f6 and 6 e5.

As we have seen, White can make progress if Black's bishop is driven away from control of e7. However, White also needs to challenge the bishop by playing a later ♗f6. Is this always possible? To find out, let us place Black's king on f5, giving us diagram 242.

The black king is now ideally posted, not only attacking the pawn but preventing a subsequent ♗f6. White cannot win, as the following shows:

242

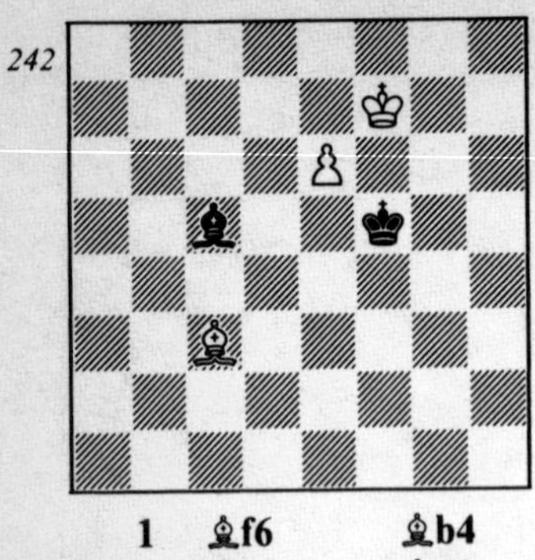

1 ♗f6 ♗b4
2 ♗e7 ♗e1
3 ♗c5 ♗h4

The bishop cannot be driven from the new diagonal.

4 ♗d4 ♗g5

As 5 ♗f6 is now impossible, White can make no progress. Black plays his bishop up and down the d8-h4 diagonal until White plays ♗e7, when he switches back to his original diagonal. The game is drawn.

This means that in positions similar to diagram 242 the result depends on whether Black's king can reach in time the critical square. Consider diagram 243:

243

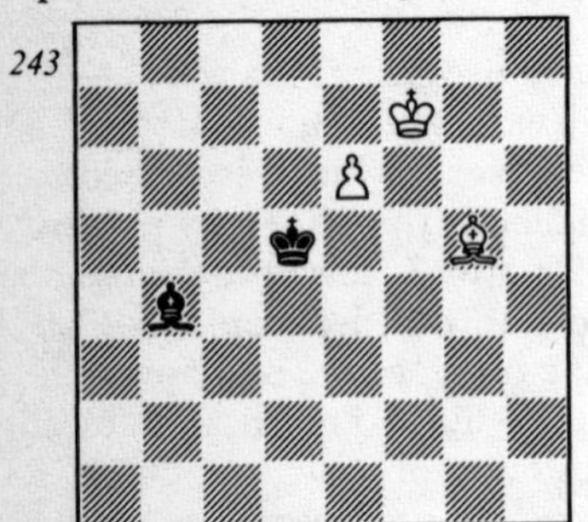

The result depends on who has the move. White to move wins easily, as we have seen, after **1 ♗e7 ♗d2 2 ♗a3 ♗g5 3 ♗b2!** when 4 ♗f6 cannot be prevented. However, Black to move can hold the position, albeit with precise defence, as follows:

1 ... ♔e4!

The only move. Black's king must be ready to go to f5 as soon as White threatens ♗f6. Only knowledge of diagram 242 could help Black to find this move. Note that 1 ... ♔e5? loses to 2 ♗e7 ♗e1 3 ♗f6+ etc.

2 ♗e7 ♗e1
3 ♗a3 ♗h4
4 ♗b2 ♔f5!

The draw is now ensured, as we already know.

These examples have shown us that Black must be in a position to combat on two diagonals the advance of the pawn (f8-a3 and d8-h4 in the ones we have quoted). If the pawn is near the edge of the board, one of these diagonals will obviously prove too short, and this gives White a win when a central pawn would only draw. Consider our next example:

244

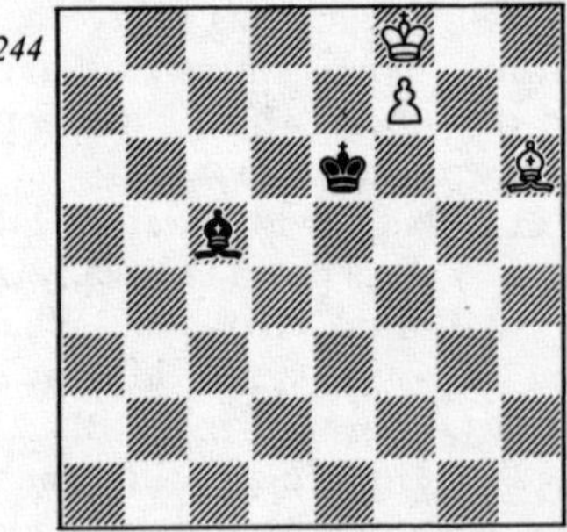

The critical diagonals for Black's

bishop are here f8-a3 and f8-h6, but the latter is only three squares long, which is insufficient for a successful defence, as our following analysis shows:

1 ♔g8!

White's king has a choice of sides, and the result depends upon this decision. 1 ♔e8? only draws after 1 ... ♗d6 2 ♗f8 ♗f4 3 ♗b4 ♗h6 4 ♗c3 ♔d6! etc. Black cannot be manoeuvred into a zugzwang position, as White's bishop cannot prevent at one and the same time the moves ... ♔d6, ... ♔f6 and ... ♗g7. The finish might be: 5 ♗d2 ♗g7 6 ♗e3 ♔e6 7 ♗f4 ♔f6 drawing. As a general rule, we can state that in such positions White's king should always aim for the side where Black's bishop has the shortest defensive diagonal. He can then control squares on it and make it even shorter.

1 ... ♔f5

The threat was 2 ♗f8 ♗e3 3 ♗a3 ♗h6 4 ♗b2 and 5 ♗g7 winning at once.

2 ♗f8 ♗e3
3 ♗b4 ♗h6
4 ♗d2! wins.

White's king controls g7 and Black's bishop is short of squares on the diagonal. Even if Black's king were now on ... g6, he would still lose. For instance, White could play 4 ♗c3 ♔g6 5 ♗d2 ♗g7 6 ♗e3 and Black is in zugzwang (6 ... ♔f6 7 ♗d4+).

So, in order to defend successfully, Black must have at least four squares on the bishop's shortest diagonal. For example, consider the position in diagram 245.

245

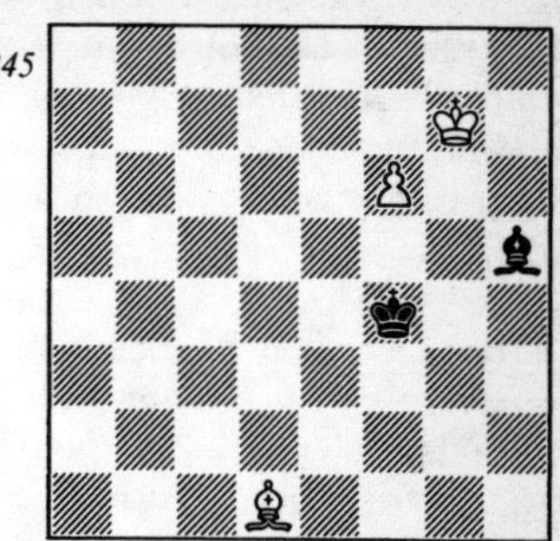

Black can draw, as the bishop's e8-h5 diagonal is long enough. After **1 ... ♗e8 2 ♗c2 ♔g5!** Black prevents ♗g6 and draws easily.

Grandmaster Averbakh has systematized the above points in the form of the zone in diagram 246.

246

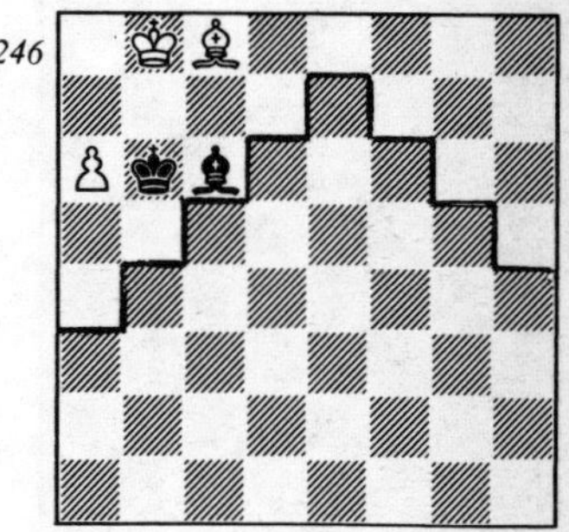

For White to be able to win, the pawn must be above the indicated line. With black-squared bishops, the zone is symmetrically opposite, being drawn above all the white squares in the diagonals a4-d7-h3.

According to Averbakh, this

rule has two exceptions, the first being seen in diagram 244 after White has wrongly played 1 ♔e8?, and the second shown in diagram 246. White cannot win here, despite the fact that his pawn is in the winning zone, because his bishop can never occupy a8. Play might go:

1 ♗b7

After 1 a7 ♗d5 Black's bishop can never be driven from the long diagonal, as there is no b9 available for White's bishop!

1 ... ♗e4!

This is the point. As White cannot capture the bishop, it remains on the long diagonal, and White can do no more than draw.

We can see the logic of all this, if we move the position one rank down the board, giving us diagram 247.

247

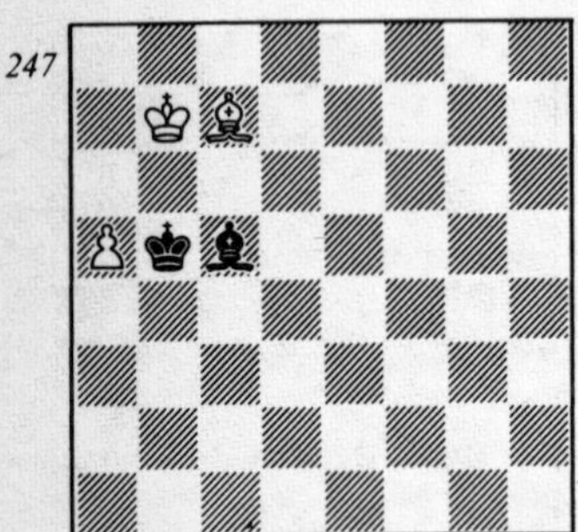

As White's bishop now has b8 at its disposal, White wins, whoever has the move, as follows:

1	**...**	**♗b4**
2	**a6**	**♗c5**
3	**♗b8!**	

The bishop reaches the critical square a7, which was impossible in the previous diagram.

3	**...**	**♗d4**
4	**♗a7**	**♗e5**
5	**♗b6**	**♗b8**
6	**♗d8** wins.	

Black is in zugzwang.

If we again move the position one rank lower, White still wins, as the 'short' diagonal of Black's bishop, c8- a6, is only three squares long. After **1 ... ♗b3 2 a5 ♗c4 3 ♗b7 ♗d3** other bishop moves lead to the same finish **4 ♗a6 ♗f5** or 4 ... ♗e4 5 ♗b5 ♗b7 6 ♗d7 wins **5 ♗b5 ♗c8 6 ♗c6!** and again Black is in zugzwang, e.g. **6 ... ♔c4 7 ♗b7** and **8 a6** wins.

One peculiarity of the rook's pawn can be seen, however, if we hare place the black king on d6 instead of b4:

248

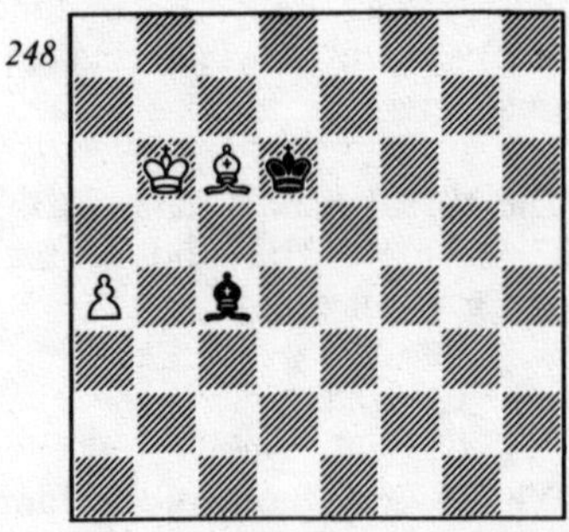

Black draws by **1 ... ♗b3! 2 a5 ♗c4**, as White cannot advance the pawn or play his bishop to b5 or a6, when bishops are exchanged with a drawn pawn ending.

Finally, in diagram 249 we have another interesting position in which White's b-pawn has reached the seventh rank. According to Averbakh's zone, the position is won for White, but the winning method is particularly instructive and by no means easy.

249

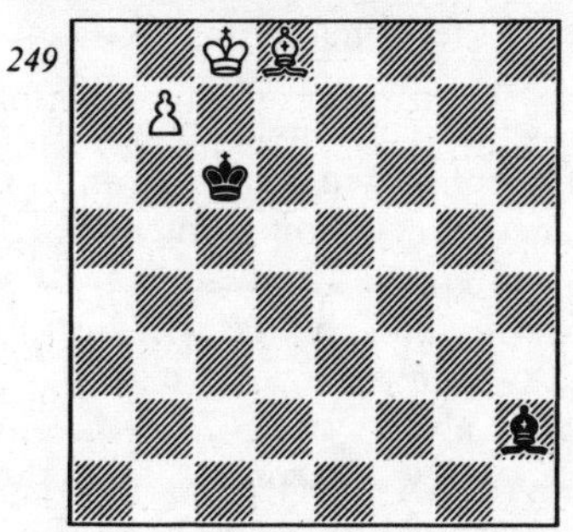

L.Centurini 1847

As Black controls the c7 square, White's bishop must play to b8 to drive the bishop off the long diagonal. After **1 ♗b8 ♗g1 2 ♗g3 ♗a7 3 ♗f2** Black is lost, but how can White's bishop reach b8? If **1 ♗h4** intending 2 ♗f2 and 3 ♗a7 Black plays **1 ... ♔b6! 2 ♗f2+ ♔a6** preventing this plan, and if now **3 ♗h4 ♔b6! 4 ♗d8+ ♔c6**, Black's king is again preventing ♗c7. More subtlety is required.

A moment's thought will convince us that the zugzwang weapon is required. Black to move cannot play **1 ... ♗e5** (f4, g3) because of **2 ♗f6!** (g5, h4), gaining a vital tempo which allows the bishop to reach a7 before Black's king can stop it. However, **1 ... ♗d6! 2 ♗e7 ♗h2** is possible, as White cannot play 3 ♗c5. So in the original position there is no zugzwang, as Black's bishop can oscillate between d6 and h2, and after 1 ♗e7 ♔b5 is good enough.

Well then, how about first playing the bishop to the g1-a7 diagonal, forcing Black's king to a6, so that an eventual ♗c5 is playable? Let us try it: **1 ♗h4 ♔b5 2 ♗f2 ♔a6** and now a waiting move **3 ♗e3**. After, for example, 3 ... ♗g3 4 ♗g5 ♔b5 (White threatened 5 ♗d8 and 6 ♗c7) 5 ♗d8 ♔c6 6 ♗h4! and 7 ♗f2, White wins. However, Black can improve with **3 ... ♗d6! 4 ♗g5 ♔b5 5 ♗d8 ♔c6 6 ♗e7 ♗h2!** when we are back where we started.

From the above analysis, we see that Black's bishop has two critical squares d6 and h2, and so long as it occupies one of these, White can achieve nothing. One of these squares must therefore be taken from the bishop, after which zugzwang will force Black to give way. As ♗g1 fails, because Black can play his bishop anywhere (from g1 White's bishop cannot play to the h4-d8 diagonal), d6 is the all-important one. Now to the winning method:

1	**♗h4**	

Also possible are 1 ♗g5 and 1 ♗f6, but not 1 ♗e7 ♔b5 etc.

1	...	**♔b5**
2	**♗f2**	**♔a6**
3	**♗c5!**	

The key move! Black's bishop is forced out of the corner to a square which will later allow the above-mentioned gain of a tempo. If now 3 ... ♔b5 4 ♗a7 wins.

3 ... ♗g3

The same win follows after 3 ... ♗e5 or 3 ... ♗f4.

4 ♗e7 ♔b5
5 ♗d8 ♔c6

Reaching the original position but with one vital difference: Black's bishop is on longer on h2.

6 ♗h4!

The decisive gain of a tempo. If Black's bishop had gone to e5 or f4 then 6 ♗f6! or 6 ♗g5! would have won.

6 ... ♗h2
7 ♗f2 ♗f4
8 ♗a7 ♗h2
9 ♗b8 ♗g1
10 ♗g3 ♗a7
11 ♗f2! wins.

This beautiful example concludes our treatment of bishop and pawn against bishop. There are other interesting positions in which the pawn is further back, but we must unfortunately close the subject here.

Let us now turn our attention to positions in which White has at least two pawns. Up till now we have assumed that both sides have bishops of the same colour, for the simple reason that there was no point in discussing positions containing bishops of opposite colour, with only one pawn on the board. However, in positions with several pawns, it becomes very important to know whether the bishops are of the same or opposite colour. This is why our next two sections are separated into the two types of ending.

Bishops of the same colour

It is a well-known and easily understood fact that a small material advantage offers more chances of a win when the bishops are of the same colour. We have already seen a number of examples in which a single pawn was sufficient to win. White's winning chances are, of course, increased if his material advantage is greater than this, and endings with bishop and two pawns against bishop are almost always won. There are in fact so few exceptions, and the winning method is so clear, that we do not intend to dwell on this type of ending.

Even endings with pawns on both sides, along with material or positional advantage, offer good prospects. As these are difficult to classify, we intend to restrict ourselves to a few examples which will give the reader some idea of how to handle such endings.

If there is a pawn on either side, a draw is the usual result. White can hope for a win only if he has a positional advantage such as a far advanced pawn, badly posted enemy pieces etc. Diagram 250 is an interesting case in point.

In this study by Troitsky, White's advantage lies in a powerful a-pawn which cannot be stopped. Black must seek chances by advancing his own pawn, whereupon the following exciting solution unfolds:

A.Troitsky 1925

1 a6 c4
2 a7 c3
3 ♗h1!

We can understand the reason for this move by following the variation: 3 ... ♗g6+ 4 ♔e7 c2 5 a8♕ c1♕ 6 ♕g2 mate. However, Black has a more cunning defence.

3 ... ♗a4+
4 ♔f7!

We shall see the reason for this later.

4 ... ♗c6!

It would only help White if the bishop checked again by 4 ... ♗b3+ 5 ♔f6.

5 ♗xc6 c2
6 a8♕ c1♕

Under normal circumstances, this ending would be drawn, but the placing of Black's pieces allows a decisive finish.

7 ♕a2+ ♔g3
8 ♕g2+ ♔f4

If 8 ... ♔h4 9 ♕f2+ ♔g4 10 ♗d7+ ♔h5 11 ♕f3+ ♔h6 12 ♕h3+ ♔g5 13 ♕g4+ mates, or here 9 ... ♔h5 (9 ... ♔g5 10 ♕g3+ and 11 ♕g6+ etc) 10 ♗f3+ ♔g5 11 ♕g3+ ♔f5 12 ♕g6+ winning the queen or mating.

9 ♕f3+ ♔g5

Or 9 ... ♔e5 10 ♕f6 mate.

10 ♕g3+ ♔f5
11 ♕g6+ ♔f4
12 ♕h6+ wins the queen.

In the ending of two pawns agaisnt one, the stronger side has good winning prospects, although much depends on the piece configuration. Here are two instructive examples:

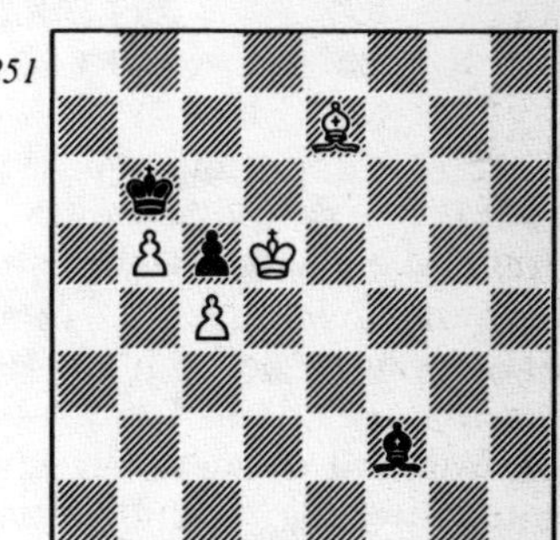

Y.Averbakh 1954

White's extra pawn is protected and passed, whilst the black pawn is an object of attack. These advantages lead to a win as follows:

1 ♗g5

White cannot win the pawn at once, as Black's bishop has enough waiting moves along the a7-g1 diagonal. First of all, White drives this bishop away.

1 ... ♗d4
2 ♔e4 ♗c3

Or 2 ... ♗f2 3 ♗e3 ♗h4 4 ♔d5

♗e7 5 ♗f2! ♗f8 6 ♗h4! and Black is in zugzwang, e.g 6 ... ♔b7 (6 ... ♗h6 7 ♗d8+) 7 ♗g3 ♔b6 8 ♗d6 winning the pawn.

3	**♗e3**	**♗b4**
4	**♔d5**	**♗a3**
5	**♗g5**	**♗b4**

To guard the pawn, Black's bishop has had to occupy a very short diagonal, which is why he will soon be zugzwanged. If 5 ... ♔b7 6 ♗e7 ♔b6 7 ♗d8+ ♔b7 8 ♗a5 we are back in the main line.

6	**♗e7**	**♗a3**
7	**♗d8+**	**♔b7**
8	**♗a5!** wins.	

Black is in zugzwang and loses after both 8 ... ♔a7 9 ♔c6 and 8 ... ♗b4 9 ♗xb4 cb 10 ♔d4 etc.

It is obvious that the same position moved one file to the left would also be a win for White. Black would be zugzwanged as in the note to Black's 2nd move. However, the position is drawn if moved one file to the right. The reason for this is clear, if we follow the above solution, as Black's bishop will now have a longer diagonal to work on, e.g. **1 ♗h5 ♗e4 2 ♔f4 ♗d3 3 ♗f3 ♗c4 4 ♔e5 ♗b3 5 ♗h5 ♗c4 6 ♗f7 ♗b3 7 ♗e8+ ♔c7 8 ♗b5 ♗a2!** etc.

One might be forgiven for thinking that moving diagram 251 two files to the right would also lead to a draw. However, this is not so. Although White cannot win by the method we have shown, he has **1 ♗f8+ ♔d7 2 ♗c5 ♗g3 3 ♗a7!** making use of the fact that b8 is now available for the bishop. There is in fact no defence to 4 ♗b8 winning the pawn.

These examples show us that it is not so easy to utilize the advantage of an extra pawn when both white pawns are near each other. The further these pawns are from each other, the more difficult is the defence. Diagram 252 gives us some idea of the problems involved.

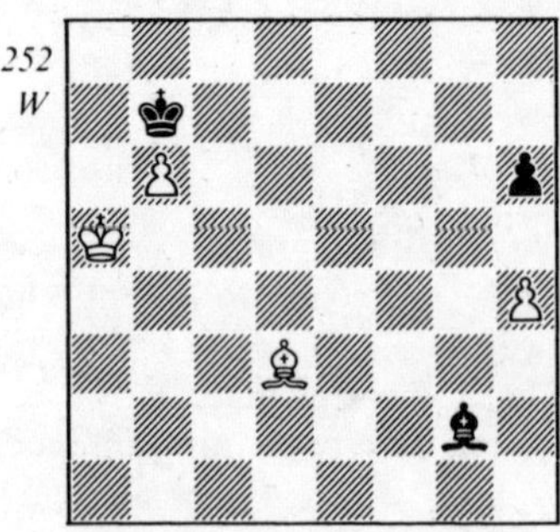

Eliskases-Capablanca 1937

This position arose in the game Eliskases-Capablanca, Semmering 1937. White has an extra pawn which is passed and which should normally win for him. However, there is one factor in Black's favour: White cannot win if he is left with a rook's pawn and the 'wrong' bishop, that is if Black's king reaches h8 in time. In other words, Black draws if he can sacrifice his bishop for White's b-pawn, then play his king to h8.

So White has tricky problems to solve before he can hope for a win. The following analysis will show us whether indeed a win is possible:

1 ♗a6+ ♔c6?

It is usually best to play actively, but here 1 ... ♔b8! would have saved the game because of the tactical point 2 ♔b4 ♗b7! 3 ♗xb7 ♔xb7 4 ♔c5 h5! giving a drawn pawn ending. If instead White plays 3 ♗e2 ♗g2 4 ♔c5, then Black answers 4 ... ♔b7! and his king cannot be driven from this strong square. Admittedly, it is not easy to see at first sight why the text move loses, which makes the following play all the more instructive.

2 ♗c8 ♗f1

White's king must not be allowed to reach a7, when Black is lost at once.

3 ♗g4 ♗d3

The bishop must stay on the diagonal, and if 3 ... ♔b7 4 ♗f3+ ♔b8 5 ♔b4, it is too late for 5 ... ♗a6 6 ♔c5 ♗b7 7 ♗xb7 ♔xb7 8 h5! when the pawn ending is won. White now achieves his first success by driving Black's king away from the pawn.

4 ♗f3+ ♔d6

5 ♗b7

The next stage is to drive Black's bishop from an active to a passive diagonal.

5 ... ♗e2

6 ♗a6 ♗f3

7 ♗f1 ♗b7

8 ♗h3!

Depriving Black's bishop of c8, which means that Black now has nothing but king moves and zugzwang is in the air.

8 ... ♔e7

8 ... ♔c5 seems attractive, but 9 ♗g4 forces Black to give way. After 9 ... ♔d6 10 ♔b5 we transpose to the game, and if 9 ... ♔c4 10 ♗e2+ ♔c5 11 ♗a6 ♗f3 (we now know that the pawn ending is lost after 11 ... ♔c6 12 ♗xb7+ ♔xb7 13 h5!) 12 ♗c8 followed by 13 ♔a6 because 12 ... ♗e2 fails to 13 b7.

9 ♔b5 ♔d6

10 ♗g4 ♔e7

Again Black is in zugzwang and must allow White's king to reach c5. Admittedly his bishop then regains some freedom of movement because ♔a6 will no longer be a threat.

11 ♔c5 ♗g2

He loses quickly after 11 ... ♗a6 12 ♔c6 ♔d8 13 ♗e6, or after 11 ... ♔d8 12 ♔d6 etc.

12 ♗c8 ♔d8

More exact was 12 ... ♗f3, although the game is still lost. Play might continue: 13 ♗a6 ♔d7 14 ♗c4 (but not 14 ♗b5+ ♔c8 15 ♗c6? ♗xc6 16 ♗xc6 h5! drawing) 14 ... ♔c8 (or 14 ... ♗g2 15 ♗d5 ♗f1 16 ♗c6+ and 17 ♔d6 winning) 15 ♗d5 transposing to the game line.

13 ♗a6

Slightly quicker is 13 ♗e6! ♔e7 14 ♗d5! etc.

13 ... ♗f3

For 13 ... ♔d7 14 ♗c4 see the note to Black's 12th move. No matter what Black now does, he cannot stop White taking over the long diagonal with his bishop, then marching his king over to the kingside.

14 ♔d6 ♗g2
15 ♗c4

If 15 ♔e6 at once, Black can later put up some resistance by ... h5 and ♗f3.

15 ... ♔c8
16 ♗d5 ♗f1

After 16 ... ♗xd5 17 ♔xd5 ♔b7 18 ♔e5 Black's king is one move too late.

17 ♔e6

There is now no defence to this move.

17 ... ♗e2
18 ♔f6 ♔d7
19 ♔g6 h5
20 ♔g5 ♔d6
21 ♗f7

It is time to give up the b-pawn.

21 ... ♔c6
22 ♗xh5 ♗c4

Capablanca sealed this move but later resigned, as White wins easily after 23 ♗e8+ ♔xc6 24 h5 ♔c7 25 h6 ♗g8 26 ♔g6 etc.

This ends our discussion of bishops of the same colour. In most cases, as we have seen, the extra pawn gives good winning chances, especially if there are other pawns on the board. There are of course many other points which arise in such endings, and we shall later be examining some of these in our practical examples.

Bishops of opposite colour

As we have already mentioned, with bishops of opposite colour the importance of material advantage is greatly reduced. Sometimes an advantage of several pawns is not enough to win. One reason for this is that the bishops cannot attack each other and thus support the action of the pawns and king. If a breakthrough occurs, this is usually the result of the strength of the pawn alone or through the support of the king. It is not without reason that endings with bishops of opposite colour are noted for their drawing tendencies.

Our task, then, is to ascertain when such endings can be won. Bishop and pawn versus bishop is clearly drawn, but two pawns offer winning chances in certain circumstances.

A: BISHOP AND TWO PAWNS AGAINST BISHOP

It is difficult to give general rules here. Usually connected pawns win if they are far advanced, or if Black's bishop cannot be correctly positioned in time. Let us see how this works in practice:

253

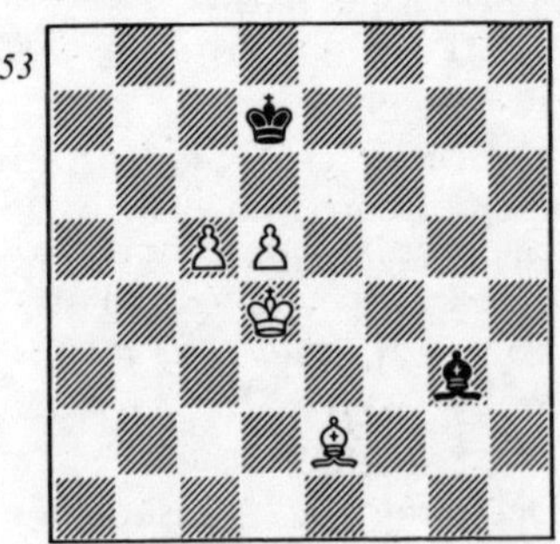

M.Henneberger 1916

We take this as our basic position, with White's pawns already on the fifth rank. It is clear that White must advance his pawns if he is to win and that 1 c6+? ♔c7 would give an immediate draw, as the blockade cannot be broken. The d-pawn is the one we must move, but an immediate 1 d6? fails to 1 ... ♗xd6. So White must prepare this advance which requires the support of his king on e6 or c6. This means that Black's king must first be checked away, so that the white king can penetrate via b5 or f5. Play might go:

1 ♗b5+!

A good rule is to place the bishop to control as many squares as possible in front of the pawns. If White selects the other checking square, he can make no progress after 1 ♗g4+ ♔c7, as 2 ♔e4? ♗f2 3 d6+ ♔c6 draws at once. From b5 the bishop controls c6, thus cutting out this defensive possibility.

1 ... ♔e7

Better than 1 ... ♔c7 when 2 ♔e4 ♗h2 (or 2 ... ♗f2 3 d6+ and 4 c6) 3 ♔f5 ♗g3 4 ♔e6 followed by 5 d6+ wins.

2 ♗a4 ♗f4
3 ♔c4 ♗g3

Black's bishop dare not leave this diagonal, when d6+ follows, and if 3 ... ♗c7 4 ♔b5 ♔d7 5 ♔a6+ ♔e7 6 ♔b7 wins.

4 ♔b5 ♔d7
5 ♔b6+ ♔e7
6 ♔c6 ♗f4
7 ♗b3

Or 7 d6+ ♔e6 8 ♗b3+ ♔e5 9 ♔d7 etc wins.

7 ... ♗g3
8 d6+ ♔d8
9 ♔d5 and
10 c6 wins.

Is, therefore, diagram 253 always lost for Black? No, this is only because his bishop is wrongly placed in the b8-h2 diagonal. Black must post his bishop, with his king on c7, so that it not only prevents d6+ but at the same time attacks the c-pawn. In other words, the bishop must be on e7 or f8, when White cannot win. After **1 ♗b5+ ♔c7!** White's king cannot leave the bishop's pawn, and Black just plays his bishop from f8 to e7 and back.

This gives us an important defensive idea in the fight against two connected pawns. It is easy to see that if the pawns are on the sixth rank, they must always win, because Black's bishop will have only one square available. Consider diagram 254.

254

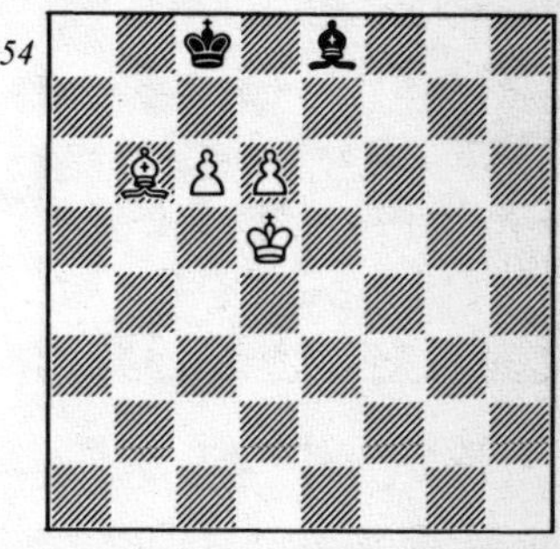

The bishop has reached the correct square, but after **1 ♔c5**

Black is in zugzwang and must allow the d-pawn to advance. The only exception to this rule is found in diagram 255.

After **1 ... ♗xh6 2 ♔xh6** gives **stalemate**.

255

In our analysis of diagram 253, we saw that, to win, White's king had to be in a position to penetrate on both sides of the pawns. Let us see how this fact gives Black a defence, if we move diagram 253 one file to the left.

256

M.Henneberger 1916

There seems to be no difference, but in reality White's king has insufficient room to manoeuvre on the queenside in his efforts to reach b6. Black draws as follows:

1 ♗a5+ ♔d7

But not 1 ... ♔b7? 2 ♔d4 followed by ♔e5-d6 winning easily.

2 ♗b6 ♗g2
3 ♔b4 ♗f3
4 ♔a5 ♗b7!

White's king cannot advance any further and after 5 ♗a7 ♔c7! draws.

White has another winning try which demands precise defence from Black:

1 ♔b4 ♗g2
2 ♔a5

Threatening 3 ♔a6. If now 2 ... ♗b7 then 3 ♗f4+ and 4 ♔b6 wins. Black has only one move.

2 ... ♔b7!
3 ♗g5 ♗f3
4 ♗d8 ♗g2
5 ♗b6 ♗f3

White has now succeeded in driving Black's king to the unfavourable square b7, but he cannot profit from this, as his own king is too far away from the kingside to penetrate via e5 and d6. If he had tried 5 ♔b4 then 5 ... ♔c8! 6 ♗a5 ♔d7! would have followed.

6 ♔b4

If White's bishop were now on a5, he would win as from diagram 233, but ...

6 ... ♗h5!

Black makes clever use of the fact that White cannot play 7 c6+, because the bishop is loose, in order to bring his bishop to the correct defensive square e8.

7 ♗a5 ♗e8!

The draw is now clear, as we have already shown.

We have now seen enough of this type of ending. Diagrams 253 and 256 have illustrated the proper defensive procedure. If the pawns are not so far advanced, Black's task is easier, for he has more time to set up the correct defence.

Let us next turn to positions in which White has isolated pawns. A good rule to remember here is that White usually wins if the pawns are at least two files away from each other, as our next example shows:

257

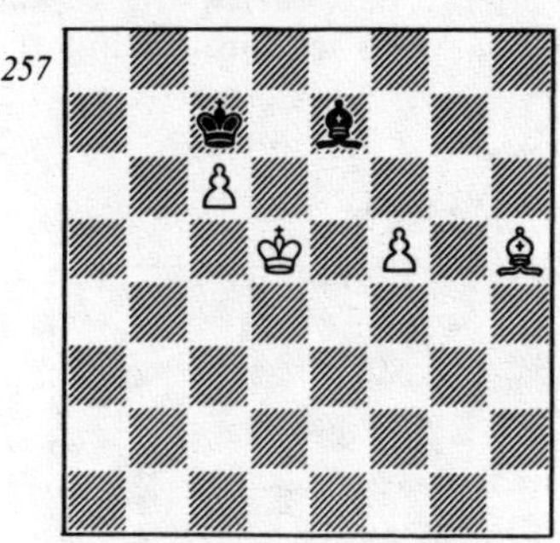

C.Salvioli 1889

White wins because his king can support one of the pawns and win the bishop for it. Each of Black's pieces can blockade a pawn, but this blockade cannot be maintained.

1 ♗f3

To allow 2 ♔e6, when the bishop guards the c-pawn. Black cannot prevent the advance of White's f-pawn.

1	...	♗h4
2	♔e6	♔d8
3	f6	♗g5
4	f7	♗h6

White's pawns are only temporarily held up.

5	♔f6	♗f8
6	♔g6	♔e7
7	♔h7	♔d8
8	♔g8 wins.	

The bishop is lost.

We can see from this example why it is advantageous for White to have his pawns as far apart as possible. If the pawns are nearer, Black can draw.

258

After **1 ♗e4 ♗h4 2 ♔e6 ♗g5 3 ♔f7 ♔d8! 4 e6 ♗h4**, the most White can do is win the bishop for both pawns, giving a draw.

Black can also set up a successful defence if he manages to hold up the pawns on a single diagonal, stopping them both advancing (Diagram 259).

White can make no progress, as Black will not relinquish control of the b4 and e7 squares. He defends passively by **1 ♗e2 ♗f8**

259

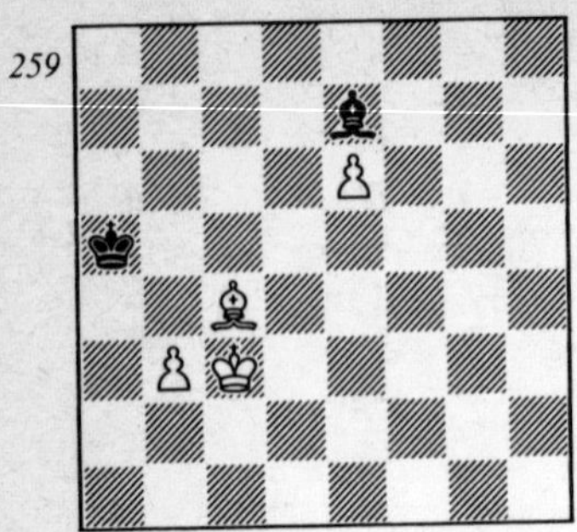

2 ♔c4 ♗e7 3 ♔d5 ♔b6! and if the white king goes to f7, Black plays ... ♔d8, holding everything.

When the pawns are blockaded, it is sometimes impossible to win even with three pawns. Consider this example:

260

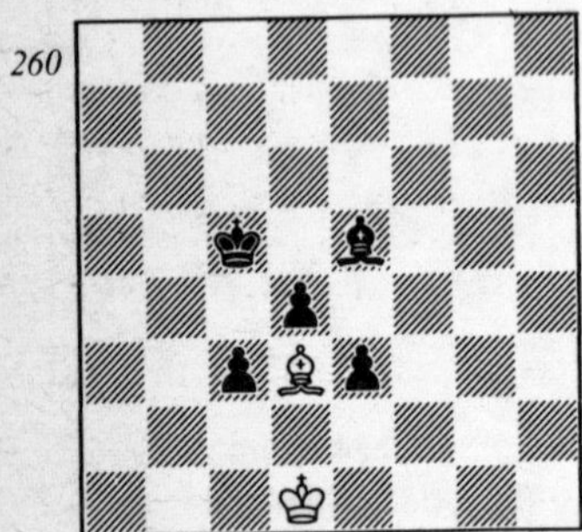

Black cannot lift the blockade. After **1 ... ♔b4 2 ♔c2!** White maintains his bishop on the f1-a6 diagonal, and if Black's king goes to the other wing, the reverse process applies after ♔e2! etc. Such endings are exceptions but point to the importance of not allowing our pawns to be blockaded.

B: BISHOP AND PAWN(S) ON BOTH SIDES

When both sides have pawns, subtle lines are often possible, some of which seem incredible at first sight. Such endings belong more to the practical side, however, so we shall here discuss a few easier examples illustrating the basic principles which govern this type of ending.

We must again stress the fact that bishops of opposite colour are not much good at supporting the advance of their own pawns, as they cannot challenge the opponent's bishop. For this reason, the bishop usually holds up enemy pawns, leaving to the king the task of supporting the advnce of his own pawns. Consider diagram 261 which resembles a game position:

261

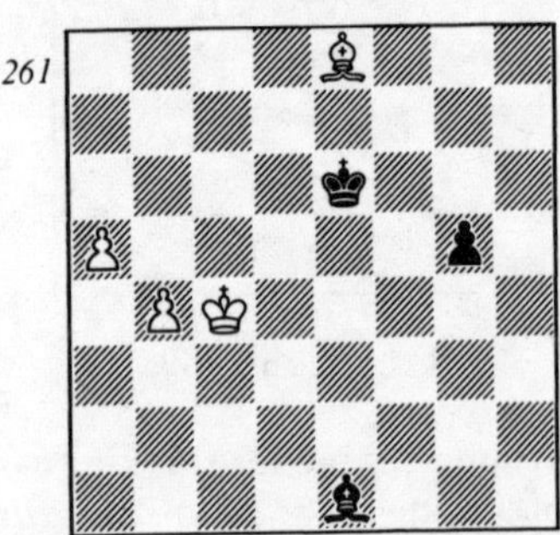

J.Berger 1895

White's winning chances appear slight, as Black's king is near the pawns and his own pawn is threatening to advance.

Nevertheless, by precise play White can achieve a win as follows:

1 ♔c5

He must first prevent Black's king from reaching the queenside. After 1 a6? ♗f2 and 2 ... ♔d6 the draw is clear.

1 ... ♔e7
2 ♔c6!

The point. Black cannot play 2 ... ♗xb4 3 a6 followed by 4 a7, so is practically forced to take the bishop. It is also possible to play these moves in reverse order, 2 a6 and 3 ♔c6, but 2 ♗h5? only draws after 2 ... ♔d7 3 a6 ♔c7 etc.

2 ... ♔xe8
3 a6 ♗f2
4 b5 g4

Black's only counterchance.

5 b6 g3
6 a7 g2
7 a8♕+ wins

The finish might be **7 ... ♔e7 8 ♕a3+** or 8 ♕a7+ ♔f6 9 ♕a1+ and 10 b7, or here 8 ... ♔f8 9 ♕b8+ ♔g7 10 ♕e5+ etc. **8 ... ♔e8 9 b7** etc.

Even in endings with several pawns, it is important to have isolated passed pawns as far apart as possible, so that they cannot be stopped by the enemy bishop. Diagram 262 gives us an interesting example of this.

Black's pawns are very powerful and cannot be stopped by the bishop alone, e.g. 1 ♗d1 c3 2 ♗c2 f4 3 ♗d1 f3! etc. So White must use his king, but after **1 ♔c6 ♔c8!** the threat was 2 b7 ♗f4 3 ♗c2 etc

262

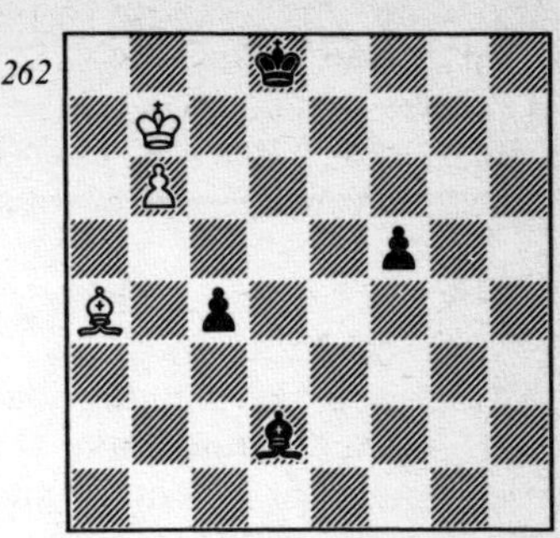

J.Behting 1895

2 ♔d5 c3 3 ♗c2 f4 4 ♔e4 he has paid too high a price. Black merely captures the b-pawn after **4 ... ♔b7** and wins as from diagram 257.

This means that White can stop Black's pawns only by giving up his own, when he loses! Is there another solution? In apparently simple endings there are hidden possibilities often revealed by study composers. This example is a case in point, as the following play shows:

1 ♔a6!

As already mentioned, the plausible 1 ♔c6 does not work, and 1 ♔a7 ♗e3 would lose a vital tempo. White now threatens 2 b7 ♗f4 3 ♗c2.

1 ... ♔c8

Black has no choice, as 1 ... ♗b4 or 1 ... ♗c3 loses the c-pawn after 2 ♔b5, whereas the f-pawn falls after 1 ... ♗e1 2 b7 ♗g3 3 ♗c2 etc. Black now threatens 2 ... ♔b8.

2 ♔a7! ♗e3
3 ♔a8!

Apparently madness, for White not only gives up his pawn, but also plays his king as far as possible from Black's pawns. White's plan will soon become clear.

3 ... ♗xb6

4 ♗b3!!

Only now is the cunning idea revealed. Black cannot take the bishop because of stalemate, and if 4 ... c3 5 ♗e6+ and 6 ♗xf5 draws.

Such ideas occur far more than is generally thought, because of the unusual nature of endings with bishops of opposite colour. However, for our final example we choose an instructive endgame which shows in methodical fashion how an advantage can be converted into a win.

263

B

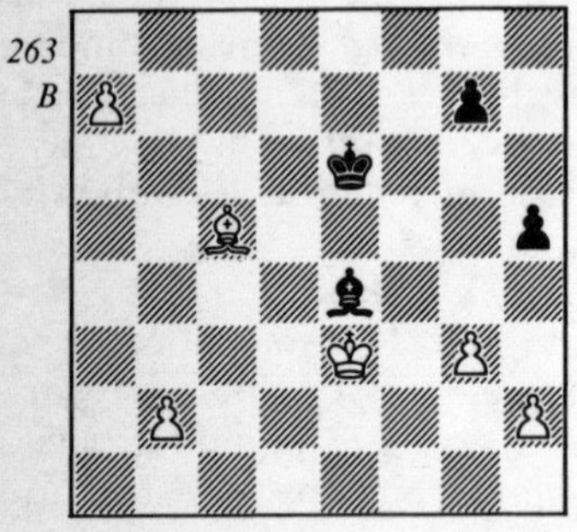

Euwe-Yanofsky 1946

This position arose in the game Euwe-Yanofsky, Groningen 1946. White has two extra connected passed pawns, but these are effectively blockaded at the moment by Black's bishop. Nor does the kingside seem to offer any chances. This example is one of many with bishops of opposite colour in which a clear material advantage proves insufficient against the best defence. However, Black must not assume that it is too easy, as the following play shows:

1 ... ♗g2?

Surprisingly enough, this natural move turns out to be the decisive mistake. Black must have thought that it was immaterial which move he selected, as he can prevent White's queenside play after 2 ♗f8 g6 3 ♔d4 ♔d7 etc, with excellent defensive possibilities.

However, as the game continuation reveals, there is also danger for Black on the kingside. Not that he loses material here, but his king will be forced to f2 from where he will be forced to return to the queenside in time. The whole play is like an endgame study, as the reader will see.

Black could have drawn by **1 ... ♔f5!** blocking the white king's path to the kingside. After **2 ♗f8 g6 3 ♔d4 ♗a8 4 ♔c5 ♔e6 5 ♔b6 ♔d7**, White can make no progress and the game is drawn. Even in this position, however, Black must still be careful. If we continue **6 b4 ♔c8 7 b5 ♔d7 8 ♗b4**, Black should play **8 ... ♔c8!** guaranteeing the draw. A casual move by the bishop instead would lose, e.g. 8 ... ♗f3? 9 a8♕ ♗xa8 10 ♔a7 ♗f3 11 ♔b8! ♗e4 12 b6 ♔c6 13 ♔a7 etc winning.

Accuracy in endgames is even

more important than in the middlegame, for there is rarely a second chance given.

2 ♔f4! g6

3 g4!

The h-pawn is part of the plan and must not be exchanged.

3 ... hg

Or 3 ... ♗a8 4 gh gh 5 ♔g5 ♗f3 6 h4 ♔d7 7 b4 ♔c7 8 a8♕ ♗xa8 9 ♔xh5 wins.

4 ♔xg4 ♗h1

Black cannot prevent ♔g5, for if 4 ... ♔f6 5 ♗d4+. Or 4 ... ♔d7 5 ♔g5 ♗e4 6 h4 ♔c7 7 a8♕ etc gives us a win similar to the previous note.

5 ♔g5 ♔f7 *(264)*

264
W

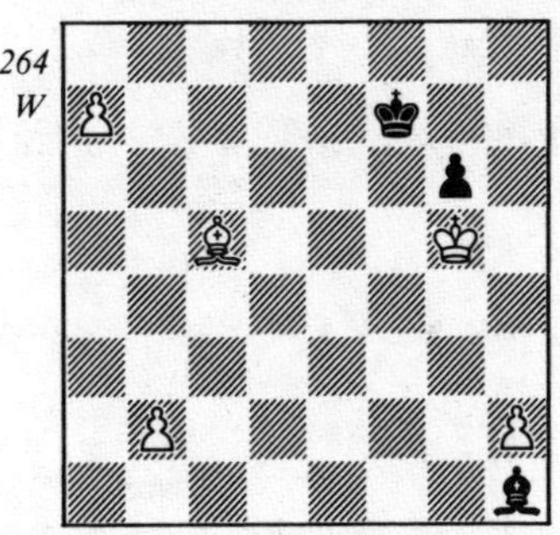

Euwe-Yanofsky 1946

This is the position White was aiming for. He now prepares his final plan.

6 ♗d4 ♗g2
7 h4 ♗h1
8 b4 ♗g2
9 b5 ♗h1
10 ♗f6!

The most important of his preparatory moves, preventing Black's king going to e7, whilst at the same time holding up Black's eventual passed pawn on the kingside.

10 ... ♗g2

Or 10 ... ♗e4 11 h5! gh 12 ♔f4 and 13 ♔e5 wins.

11 h5 gh
12 ♔f5!

1-0

Black's king cannot reach the queenside (12 ... ♔e8 13 ♔e6), his h-pawn is stopped and there is no defence to the advance of White's pawns.

This concludes our discussion of endings with bishop against bishop. There are, of course, many more interesting positions which we have no time to consider, but we shall later give a few examples in our section on practical endings.

Bishop and Pawn(s) against Knight

For a long time theoreticians argued as to the respective merits of bishop and knight in the endgame. We know, for example, that Chigorin preferred the knight, whereas Steinitz and later Tarrasch preferred the bishop. There is probably no absolute truth in the matter, as everything depends on the position. Generally, the bishop is stronger in open positions with play on both wings. The knight's advantages come to the fore in closed positions, especially if the bishop is restricted by the pawns. Finally, we must mention that the bishop can trap a knight on the edge of the board (white bishop on d5, black knight on a5), but the knight cannot imitate this.

Of course, with no pawns on the board, the game is drawn, but even one pawn is usually not enough to win, whichever side has it. However, if one side has two pawns more, or one pawn more with game is normally won. In such cases, the possessor of the bishop can usually defend the most effectively.

In endings with bishop and pawn against knight, there are no general rules about when a position is won or drawn. We will therefore give individual examples which illustrate the way to play such endings, beginning with diagram 265.

265

Chess Player's Chronicle 1856

In positions like this, White can hope for a win only in two situations. Either the pawn cannot be stopped by Black's king and knight, or else the knight can be tied down so that a zugzwang position is reached. In our example, White wins by the second method. It is clear that the knight has no moves, so White must try to drive Black's king away from the pawn, when ♔xe8 would be a threat. Zugzwang can be used, because if Black now had the move, both 1 ... ♔b5 and 1 ... ♔d5 fail to 2 ♗d4! etc.

1 ♗c3

White is himself zugzwanged after 1 ♗d4+ ♔d5 or 1 ♗e5 ♔b6 2 ♗d4 ♔b5, so he has to drive the black king from c5 and b6.

If Black had the move, the solution would be a little longer: after 1 ... ♔b6 White waits by 2 ♗e5 ♔c5 3 ♗c3! transposing to our main variation.

1 ... ♔b6

Forced, as we have shown.

2 ♗a5+

Taking control of one of the vital squares, as 2 ... ♔xa5 fails to 3 ♔xe8.

2 ... ♔b5

After 2 ... ♔c5 3 ♗d8 White wins a little more quickly.

3 ♗d8 ♔c5
4 ♗h4 ♔b5

If 4 ... ♔d5 5 ♗e7 wins. If 4 ... ♔b6 5 ♗f2+ ♔b5 6 ♗d4 zugzwangs Black.

5 ♗g5! ♔c5
6 ♗e3+ ♔d5

The same happens after 6 ... ♔b5.

7 ♗d4! ♘d6
8 c7 wins.

The nearer the pawn is to the edge of the board, the more difficult it is for the knight to defend. Diagram 266 is a good example of this. Although White's pawn is only on the fifth rank, it is a win, because Black's knight has insufficient space to the left of the pawn.

266
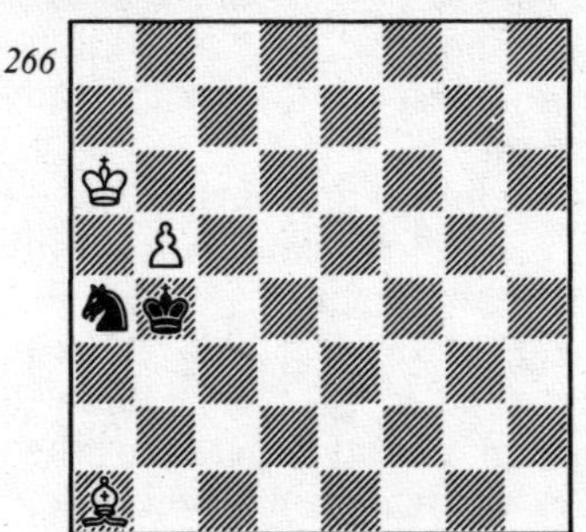

White begins by tying down the knight.

1 ♗d4 ♔c4

After 1 ... ♔b3 (a3) 2 ♔a5 we transpose into the main line.

2 ♔a5 ♔b3
3 ♗f6 ♔a3

Or 3 ... ♘c5 4 b6 ♔c4 5 ♗e7, again transposing.

4 ♗g5 ♔b3
5 ♗c1!

Forcing the knight to move, after which White can advance the pawn. 5 ♗e7 would not do because of 5 ... ♘b2! followed by 6 ... ♘c4 with a clear draw.

5 ... ♘c5
6 b6 ♔c4

The best move, denying White's king the use of b5. If, for example, 6 ... ♘b7+ then 7 ♔b5 wins quickly.

7 ♗a3 ♘d7

Or 7 ... ♘b7+ 8 ♔a6 ♘d8 9 ♗e7 wins.

8 b7 ♔d4

Or 8 ... ♔d5 9 ♔b5 etc.

9 ♔b5 ♔d5
10 ♗c1

White must now play his bishop back to the help h2-b8 diagonal, after which Black will soon be zugzwanged. If now 10 ... ♘b8 11 ♗f4 ♘c6 12 ♔b6 wins at once.

10 ... ♔d6
11 ♗f4+ ♔d5
12 ♗g3

This allows the king to occupy c6.

12 ... ♔e6
13 ♔c6 ♔e7
14 ♔c7 ♔e6
15 ♗d6! wins.

Black has no more moves left.

The rook's pawn gives White the greatest winning chances, for the knight finds it extremely difficult to defend in such circumstances.

267

P.Bilguer 1843

Diagram 267 shows us a position form which White can win, even with the pawn on its original square.

1 ♔g5 ♘f2

Black must rely on his knight for defence, for his king cannot retreat in time, e.g. 1 ... ♔e4 2 h4 ♔d5 3 h5! ♔e6 (or 3 ... ♔xd6 4 h6 etc) 4 h6 ♔f7 5 ♗e5 ♔g8 6 ♔g6 and the pawn queens. 1 ... ♘c3 would amount to the same thing after 2 h4! etc.

2 h4! ♘e4+

If 2 ... ♘g4 3 h5 Black is in zugzwang.

3 ♔g6 ♘xd6

Or 3 ... ♘f2 4 h5 ♘g4 5 ♔g5 wins.

4 h5 ♘c4

Here we see clearly how helpless a knight is against a rook's pawn. Although the pawn takes three moves to queen, Black cannot prevent this.

5 h6 ♘e5+

6 ♔g7 wins.

There is, however, an exceptional case in which White is in great danger of losing. In diagram 268 it is the materially stronger side which has to defend very carefully to avoid mate!

268

K.Richter 1910

Black's knight only has to reach b6 and it is mate, so White's bishop must somehow prevent this. Black's knight has five squares from which he can reach b6. These are a4, c4, d5, d7 and c8. The bishop has to play so as to control these white squares at any moment.

If we look a little further, we see that the knight can threaten only two of these squares at any one time. For example, from b2 he can play to a4 or c4, from c3 he will threaten a4 and d5, etc. So when Black's knight is on b2, the bishop must be in a position to go to b3 or b5; with the knight on c3, the bishop's critical squares are b3 or c6, etc. In other words we have a set of related squares, as in pawn endings. (To complete the picture: knight on e5, bishop on e6 or b5; knight on d6, bishop on e6 or a6; knight on f6, bishop on e6 or c6; knight on e7, bishop on e6 or b7; knight on c5, bishop on the a4-e8 diagonal).

As can be seen, the majority of these related squares lie on the a2-g8 diagonal, so this is clearly the best diagonal for the bishop. We can now look at the solution:

1 ♗a2 ♘f2

2 ♗g8 ♘d3

3 ♗c4

White must already be careful not to be zugzwanged. If he carelessly plays to one of the critical related squares b3 or e6, he is lost! e.g. 3 ♗b3? ♘b2 or 3 ♗e6? ♘e5! In both cases the knight mates in two moves Black is also threatening 3 ... ♘c5 for which the bishop is required on the a4-e8 diagonal. So 3 ♗a2? would lose to 3 ... ♘c5! White has alternatives in 3 ♗f7 or 3 ♗d5.

3	**...**	**♘c5**
4	**♗b5**	**♘e4**
5	**♗c4**	

The bishop returns to the important a2-g8 diagonal.

5	**...**	**♘d6**
6	**♗e6**	**♘b5**
7	**♗g8**	**♘c3**

If 7 ... ♔c8 White has 8 ♗e6+!

8 ♗b3! draws.

If White has bishop and two pawns against knight, the win is usually assured. The defence can draw only if one of the pawns is the 'wrong' rook's pawn (with a queening square not controlled by the bishop) and the knight can sacrifice itself for the knight's pawn. Or, of course, if the pawns have been advanced in the wrong way and are blockaded by Black's pieces.

Let us consider a straightforward example of a White win which offers no technical difficulties:

269

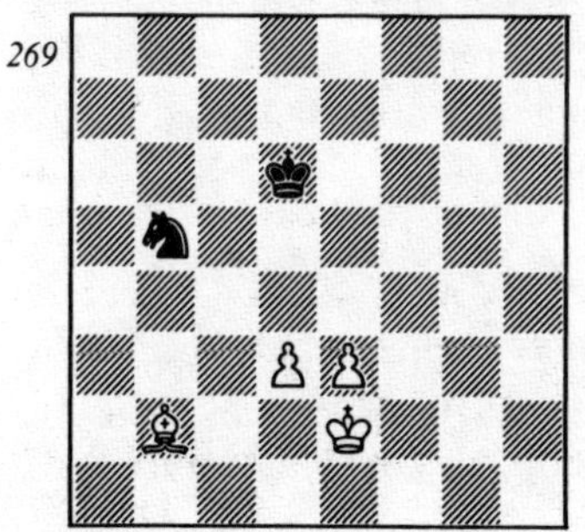

A useful rule here is to advance the pawns on squares of opposite colour to the bishop, or else there is a great danger of their being blockaded. If, for instance, 1 d4? ♔d5 2 ♔d3 ♘d6 followed by 3 ... ♘e4, White cannot lift the blockade, for it is impossible for the bishop to control all the knight's retreat squares.

1	**e4!**	**♔c5**
2	**♔e3**	**♔d6**

2 ... ♔b4 would be pointless, as White would first play 3 ♗g7 before advancing his d-pawn.

3	**d4**	**♘c7**
4	**♔d3**	

Not of course 4 d5? ♘xd5+, but 4 ♗c3 and 5 ♗a5 could also be played.

4	**...**	**♔c6**
5	**♔c4**	**♔d6**
6	**d5**	

Black can do nothing to stop the pawns.

6	**...**	**♘e8**
7	**e5+**	**♔e7**
8	**♗a3+**	**♔f7**
9	**♔c5** wins.	

It is important to follow the rule of not playing both pawns on to squares controlled by the bishop, and with the 'wrong' rook's pawn, the knight must not be allowed to sacrifice itself for the knight's pawn. Here is a position given by Fine.

According to our rule, White should begin by 1 h4, but in this case it makes his task extremely difficult. After 1 ... ♔h6 White cannot advance his g-pawn until

270

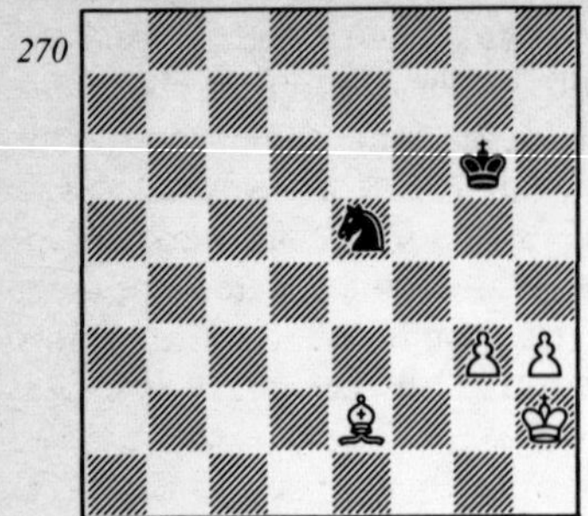

he has driven the knight away from its dominating position.

Best is therefore **1 g4!** so that this pawn is defended by the h-pawn, cutting out the knight sacrifice. There is no danger in the blockade by 1 ... ♔g5 2 ♔g3 ♘g6, for after 3 ♗d3 ♘h4 4 ♗e4 Black is in zugzwang and loses at once. So after 1 g4! White can gradually advance his pawns, e.g. **1 ... ♘c6 2 ♔g3 ♘d4 3 ♗d3+ ♔f6 4 h4 ♘e6 5 ♗c4 ♘c5 6 ♔f4 ♘d7 7 ♗d3 ♔g7 8 g5 ♘f6 9 ♗e4 ♘h5+ 10 ♔g4 ♘f6+ 11 ♔f5 ♘h5 12 ♗f3 ♘g3+ 13 ♔f4** etc, winning easily.

If White's pawns are isolated, the win is easier, unless they are very close together and one of them is the 'wrong' rook's pawn, or unless the pawns can be effectively blockaded. There is little point in examining these exceptions.

It is also clear that bishop and pawn versus knight and pawn must end in a draw, unless one pawn is running through fast or the enemy pieces are badly posted. Again, the exceptions do not concern us here. Let us turn immediately to diagram 271, a more normal position with bishop and two pawns agaist knight and pawn.

271
W

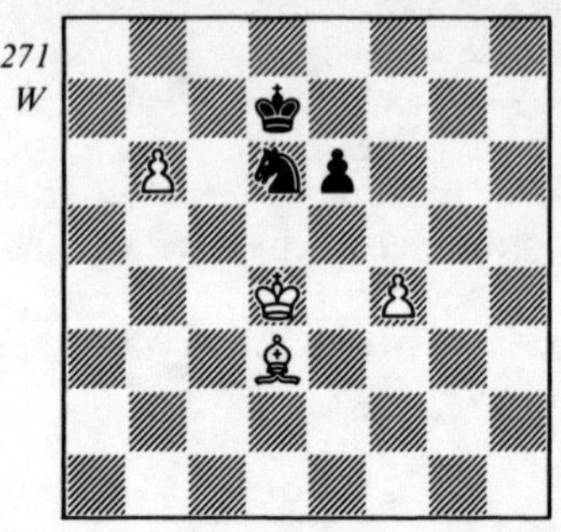

Eliskases-Euwe 1947

White is a healthy pawn to the good and should win, but how can he best proceed? There are only two plans worth consideration: either support the b-pawn with the king, or else try to attack Black's pawn. Let us analyse:

1 ♔c5!

Surely the simplest way, as the b-pawn is a decisive weapon. White would obtain nothing tangible after 1 ♔e5 ♔e7 followed by 2 ... ♘f7+.

1 ... ♘b7+

Black is already forced to give ground, so he drives the king to the edge of the board rather than allow 2 ♗b5+ and 3 ♔c6.

2 ♔b5 ♘d8

If 2 ... ♘d6+ 3 ♔a6 ♔c6 4 ♗c4! and as Black cannot take the bishop, his king must return to d7. Or 2 ... ♔d6 3 ♗e4 ♘c5 4 b7 ♘d7

5 ♔a6 ♔c7 6 ♔a7 wins easily.

3 ♔a6

Even simpler is to cut out Black's counterattack by 3 ♗e4! ♔d6 4 ♗g2, e.g. 4 ... ♘f7 (or 4 ... ♔d7 5 ♔a6 ♔d6 6 b7 transposes) 5 ♔a6 ♘d8 6 b7 ♘xb7 7 ♔xb7 ♔c5 8 ♔c7 ♔d4 9 ♔d6 ♔e3 10 ♔e5 winning.

3 ... ♔c6

Passive play loses more quickly, e.g. 3 ... ♔c8 4 ♔a7 ♘c6+ 5 ♔a8 ♘a5 6 ♗b5 etc. Black now hopes to give up his knight for the b-pawn, then capture the f-pawn.

4 ♗e4+

Tempting is 4 ♗c4 to answer 4 ... ♔c5 with 5 ♗xe6! but after 4 ... ♔d6 the bishop would be misplaced. It is more effective on the long diagonal.

4 ... ♔c5

5 ♗h1

Not of course 5 b7 ♘xb7 6 ♔xb7 ♔d4 and 7 ... ♔e3 drawing, but also possible is 5 ♔a7 ♔d4 6 ♗h1, or even here 6 ♔b8 ♔xe4 7 ♔c7 and the b-pawn queens.

5 ... ♔d4

6 ♔a7 e5

The last attempt. If 6 ... ♔e3 7 ♔b8 ♔xf4 8 ♔c7 wins.

7 f5

The two passed pawns win easily, as Black's e-pawn will be stopped by the bishop.

7 ... e4

8 ♔b8

Or 8 f6 e3 9 ♗f3 threatening 10 b7 and 11 f7 winning.

8 ... e3

9 ♗f3 ♘c6+

White threatened 10 ♔c7.

10 ♔c7 ♘b4

11 ♔d6 wins.

Bishop and two connected pawns usually win against knight and pawn. If White's pawns are both passed, the bishop can effectively support them, whilst stopping the enemy pawn. Only when White has no passed pawn and Black's king is in front of the pawns, are the winning chances minimal. It is even easier for the defence if one of White's pawns is a 'wrong' rook's pawn, or the pawns can be blockaded. Let us consider just one example in which Black has the bishop and must play very carefully to win the game.

272
W

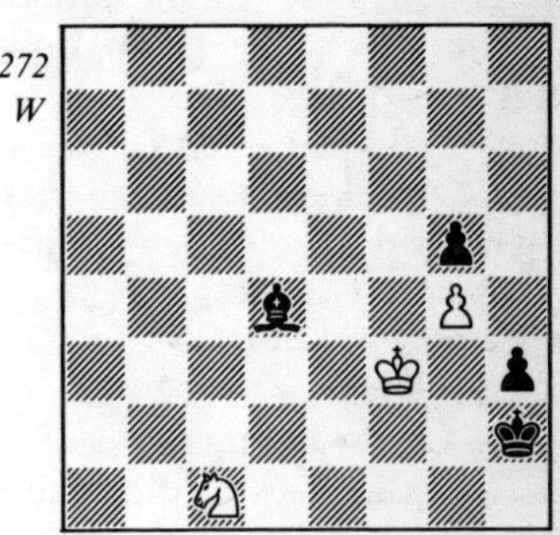

Mohnke-Heinrichs 1926

Black's h-pawn is very strong, supported as it is by the king. The only problem is that his own king is in the way and has difficulty in moving away. To win, Black must carry out a subtle bishop manoeuvre.

1 ♘e2 ♗e3!

Beautifully played. White of course cannot take the bishop, for after 2 ♔xe3 ♔g2 the h-pawn queens. Also possible was the less effective 1 ... ♗c5.

2 ♘g3 ♗d2

This bishop heads for the strong square e1. If here 2 ... ♗f4 3 ♘e2 ♔h1? 4 ♘xf4 gf 5 ♔f2! it is Black who is fighting for the draw. However, if the bishop remains on the b8-h2 diagonal, White has tempo moves with his king to f2 and f3.

3 ♘e2

Not of course 3 ♔f2 ♗e1+. Or 3 ♘f1 ♔g1 4 ♘xd2 h2 and the pawn queens.

3 ... ♗e1

This square is good because it takes g3 from the knight and f2 from the king. The pawn now cannot be stopped.

4 ♘d4 ♔h1

Not 4 ... ♔g1 5 ♘e2+ ♔f1 6 ♘g3+ and Black's king must go back, as 6 ... ♗xg3 7 ♔xg3 draws.

5 ♘e2 h2

White is now in zugzwang and must allow Black's king out of the corner.

6 ♘d4 ♔g1
7 ♘e2+ ♔f1
8 ♘g3+

The last joke!

8 ... ♗xg3
9 ♔xg3 h1♖!

Of course, 9 ... h1♕ would give stalemate, but promotion to a minor piece, or 9 ... ♔g1 would also win.

Bishop against Knight and Pawn(s)

In fighting against pawns the bishop is usually much more effective than the knight, which means that bishop versus knight and pawn normally draws. The side with the knight has chances only if the pawn is well advanced and the enemy king is far enough away. Even in this case the bishop can defend against a centre pawn, because he then has two good diagonals at his disposal. Consider our next example:

273

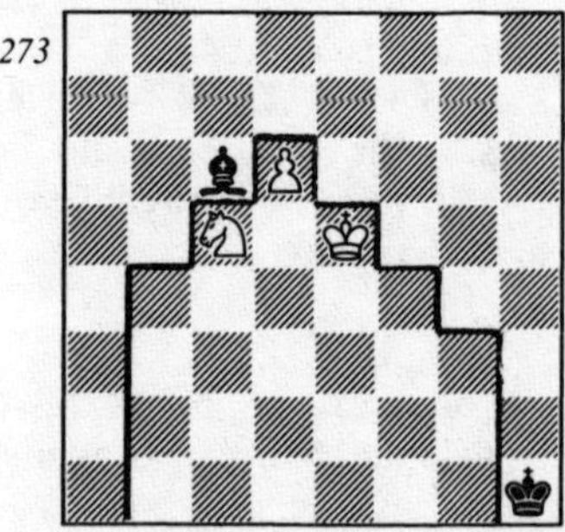

White cannot win, even though Black's king takes no part in the play. The bishop can control the vital d7 by using both the e8-a4 and c8-h3 diagonals. Play might go:

1 ♔e6 ♗b5
2 ♔e7 ♗c6
3 ♔d8

The only chance, as the knight alone cannot guard the a4-e8 diagonal.

3 ... ♗b5
4 ♔c7 ♔g1
5 ♘d3 ♔h1

6 ♘e5 ♗e8!

Forced, as White was threatening 7 ♘c6 winning.

7 ♘d7 ♔g1

8 ♔d8 ♗g6

The bishop must momentarily leave both critical diagonals but heads straight for f5.

9 ♔e7 ♗f5

The threat was 10 ♘f8 ♗f5 11 ♘e6 winning.

10 ♘c5 ♗c8!

Using the same defensive method on a different diagonal. White can make no progress, e.g. 11 ♔d8 ♗f5, or 11 ♘d7 ♔h1 12 ♔d8 ♗a6 13 ♔c7 ♗b5 14 ♘e5 ♗e8! etc.

Grandmaster Averbakh has indicated the zone that the pawn must be in, if it is to be stopped by the bishop without the help of the king (see diagram 273). This is valid for a white-squared bishop controlling the square in front of the pawn. In the case of a black-squared bishop, as symmetrical zone applies bounded by the squares b3, c4, d5, e6, f5 and g4. The bishop cannot stop a rook's pawn without the help of the king.

However, if the white pawn is over the critical line, the win depends upon how far away Black's is. Analysts have even indicated a zone for Black's king, within which he must be in order to draw against various positions of the pawn. We have no space here to analyse such possibilities but advise any interested reader to refer to more specialized works on the endgame. Meanwhile here is one example of this type of ending.

274

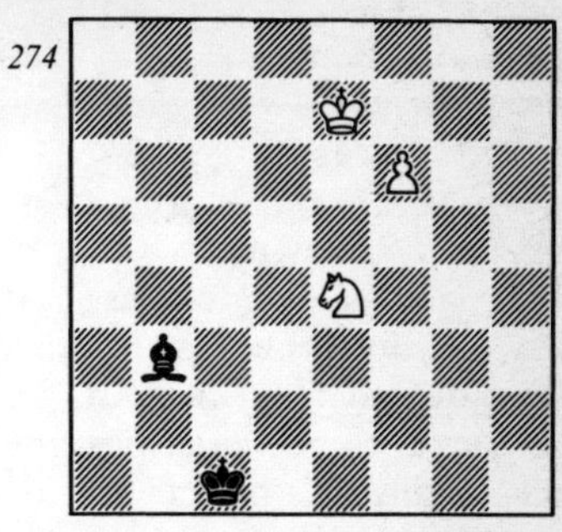

V.Košek 1921

White's pawn has crossed the critical f5 square, which means that the result depends upon the position of Black's king. We shall see that Black's king is too far away to control f4 in time, as the following analysis shows:

1 ♘g5 ♗g8

Forced, as White was of course threatening 2 ♘e6.

2 ♘f7 ♔d2

Heading for f4, but he is too late. After 2 ... ♗h7 3 ♘h6 ♗g6 4 ♘f5 ♔d2 5 ♘h4 ♗h5 6 ♘g2! wins for White, as Black's king cannot prevent the decisive threat of 7 ♘f4. We can now see why this square is so important; White's knight controls g6 and h5, and as White's king guards f7 and e8, the black bishop is driven from the diagonal.

3 ♔f8 ♗h7

4 ♘g5 ♗d3

If 4 ... ♗g6 5 ♔g7 ♗h5 6 ♔h6 ♗e8 7 ♘e4+ and 8 ♘d6 wins, or

here 5 ... ♗e8 6 ♘e4+ ♔e3 7 ♘d6 ♗h5 8 ♔h6 wins.

5 ♘e6 ♗g6

Or 5 ... ♗f5 6 ♔e7 ♗g6 7 ♘f4 wins.

6 ♘f4 ♗c2

7 ♔e7 ♗b3

8 ♘e6 wins.

This analysis shows us that Black only loses because his king cannot defend f4 in time. If, for example, in the original position Black's king is placed on d1 instead of c1, White cannot win, e.g. **1 ♘g5 ♗g8 2 ♘f7 ♗h7! 3 ♘h6 ♗g6 4 ♘f5 ♔e2 5 ♘h4 ♗h5 6 ♘g2 ♔f3!** draws.

The nearer the pawn is to the side of the board, the more difficult is the defence. The reason for this is clear: the bishop has virtually only one diagonal for defence, so the knight can easily cut it off. A successful defence is possible only if Black's king can support his bishop.

The rook's pawn allows the defence new possibilities. Firstly, it means that the bishop can sometimes be exchanged for the knight, because of drawing chances in the pawn ending. Secondly, there is sometimes the opportunity for a bishop sacrifice in order to force White's king to block the pawn. Our next example illustrates these points.

It is clear that White's only plan is to play his king to b8 and knight to b7, to cut off the bishop from the long diagonal. This plan fails, however, if Black's king reaches b6 or a6, preventing ♘b7. White's aim, therefore, is to keep Black's king away, whilst improving the position of his knight.

275

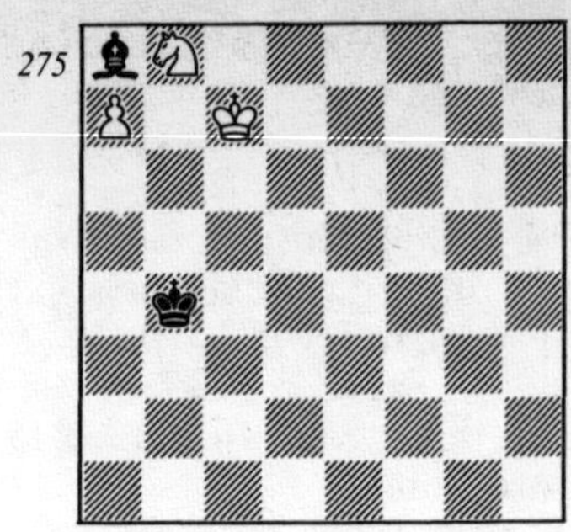

B.Horwitz 1885

1 ♔b6!

White gets nowhere with the immediate 1 ♘a6+ ♔b5 2 ♔b8 ♗g2 3 ♘c7+ ♔b6 etc drawing as White's knight can never play to b7.

1 ... ♔c4

Passive defence would be hopeless, as White would play his knight to d6, force Black's bishop to a8 because of the threat of ♘b7, then win by ♘b7 followed by ♔c7-b8. Black intends to defend against this manoeuvre, which is why his king needs to reach the d8-d6 squares.

2 ♘a6 ♔d4

3 ♘c7 ♗f3

4 ♘e6+ ♔e5

5 ♘d8 ♗a8

The threat was 6 ♘b7. It now seems that White still wins with this move, followed by ♔c7-b8, but matters are not so simple.

6 ♔c7 ♚d5

Any bishop move would allow 7 ♘b7. *(276)*

276 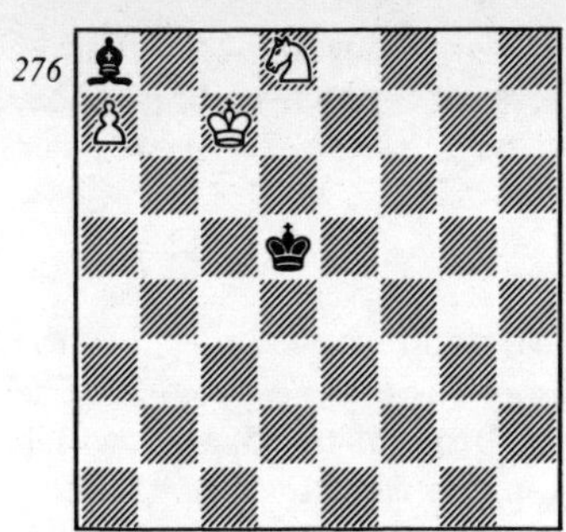

7 ♘b7!

Apparently, White can also win by 7 ♔b8 when the bishop cannot move, but Black's defensive plan 7 ... ♚d6! 8 ♔xa8 ♚c7! forcing a draw. This drawing position is characterized by the stalemate situation of White's king in front of the pawn, and by Black's king being placed on the same coloured square as the knight, with White to move. It is a well-known fact that the knight can never lose a tempo (i.e. hand the move over to Black), so Black's king can never be driven away from the c8 or c7 squares. A most surprising draw!

Now that we know the position, the following play is easier to understand. White intends to capture the bishop only when Black cannot bring about the above drawing position.

7 ... ♚e6

The only move, as Black must be prepared to answer 8 ♔b8 with 8 ... ♚d7.

8 ♘a5!

As already seen, White only draws after 8 ♔b8 ♚d7 9 ♔xa8 ♚c8! etc, so he plans a subtle knight manoeuvre.

8 ... ♚e7

9 ♔c8!

After 9 ♔b8 Black cannot play 9 ... ♚d7? 10 ♘b7! ♚c6 11 ♔xa8 ♚c7 12 ♘d6! winning, but he draws by 9 ... ♚d8! 10 ♘b7+ ♚d7, or here 10 ♔xa8 ♚c7! etc.

9 ... ♚e8

The bishop cannot move because of ♘b7, and if 9 ... ♚d6 10 ♔b8 ♚d7 11 ♘b7! again zugzwangs Black.

10 ♘c4! ♚e7

Again forced, as bishop moves allow 11 ♘d6+ and 12 ♘b7.

11 ♔b8 ♚d8

The king has to go to the 'wrong' square, as 11 ... ♚d7 fails to 12 ♘b6+ winning the bishop, and 11 ... ♝f3 allows 12 ♘a5 etc.

12 ♘d6 ♚d7

13 ♘b7!

and wins after 13 ... ♚c6 14 ♔xa8 ♚c7 (the correct square is c8!) 15 ♘d6! etc. A neat ending.

There are many more interesting endings of knight and pawn against bishop which will not concern us here. Instead, we turn at once to positions in which the bishop is fighting against a knight and two pawns. Whereas a bishop and two pawns almost always win against a knight, the weaker side has greater drawing chances with a bishop against knight and two pawns. If the pawns are connected, the stronger side usually wins, but even here there are exceptions, especially when one of the pawns is a rook's pawn and the bishop and king have managed to set up a successful blockade. Let us first turn to diagram 277 to see how the win is normally brought about.

277

White must clearly advance a pawn sooner or later if he is to win, but must be careful to avoid certain drawing positions. First of all, he must not allow Black to give up his bishop for both pawns, and secondly he must not allow them to be blockaded after, for example, 1 b4+ ♔c4. With methodical preparation, however, the win is not difficult:

1 ♔b2

In order to advance the pawns, the king is best placed on a3, with the knight guarding c4.

1 ... ♗g8
2 ♘c2 ♗f7

Or 2... ♔d5 3 c4+ and 4 ♔c3 winning.

3 ♘e3 ♗g8
4 ♔a3 ♗f7

Black can only remain passive whilst White completes his preparations for advancing the pawns.

5 b4+ ♔b5
6 c4+!

Driving Black's pieces further back, as the pawn ending is lost after 6 ... ♗xc4 7 ♘xc4 ♔xc4 8 ♔a4.

6 ... ♔b6
7 ♔b3

Also good was 7 ♘d5+, but the text move is the most logical. The king is brought to d5, after which the c-pawn can advance.

7 ... ♗e6
8 ♔c3 ♗f7
9 ♔d4 ♗e8

Black can do nothing but wait.

10 ♘d5+ ♔c6
11 b5+

The most methodical plan is 11 ♘c3 followed by 12 c5 and 13 b5+, but the text move leads to a slightly quicker finish.

11 ... ♔b7
12 ♔c5 ♗f7
13 ♔b4 ♗e6
14 ♘e7 ♗g4
15 c5 ♗f3
16 ♔a5 wins.

Black has no defence against the threat of 17 b6 followed by 18 c6+ winning easily.

Matters are far more complex, however, if the pawns are advanced prematurely and have become partially blockaded. Diagram 278 offers us an interesting and instructive example of this.

This position has been known for almost a century as an unusual draw. Its composer made a few

278

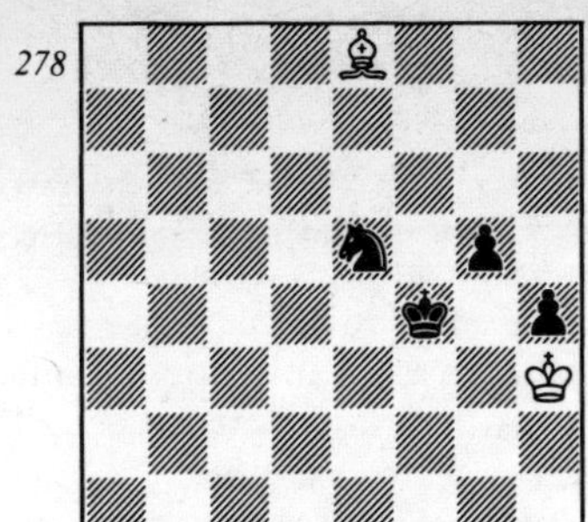

B.Horwitz 1880

mistakes in his original analysis, but later analysts have nevertheless demonstrated that White can draw with the best defence. The following variations are very instructive, and illustrate the defensive possibilities in such positions:

1 ♗b5!

The only move. King moves would clearly allow the g-pawn to advance, as would 1 ♗h5 ♘f3!, bringing about a zugzwang position, whereas 1 ♗a4 fails to 1 ... g4+ 2 ♔xh4 ♘f3+ 3 ♔h5 g3 and 4 ... g2 winning.

1 ... ♘g4

The best chance. If 1 ... g4+ 2 ♔xh4 ♘f3+ 3 ♔h5 g3 White plays 4 ♗f1 ♔e3 5 ♔g4 ♔f2 6 ♗h3! (not 6 ♔h3? ♘e1! 7 ♔g4 ♘g2 8 ♔h3 ♘e3 winning) 6 ... ♘g1 7 ♗f1! and Black can make no progress.

If Black tries the alternative **1 ... ♘g6**, threatening 2 ... g4+ in order to answer 2 ♗d7? with 2 ... ♔f3! 3 ♗c6+ ♔f2 4 ♔g4 ♘e5+ etc, reaching a winning position from the main line, White replies **2 ♗e2! ♔e3 3 ♗a6!** e.g. **3 ... ♔f2** or 3 ... ♔f3 4 ♗b7+ ♔f2 5 ♔g4 etc **4 ♔g4 ♘e5+ 5 ♔xg5!** but not 5 ♔h3 g4+! 6 ♔xh4 g3 7 ♗f1 ♘f3+ 8 ♔h3 ♘e1! winning as shown above **5 ... ♔g3** or 5 ... h3 6 ♔f4 h2 7 ♗b7 ♘d3+ 8 ♔g4 ♘e1 9 ♔h3 draws **6 ♗c8** and White draws comfortably.

Finally, we must mention that after 1 ... ♘f3 2 ♗d7 ♘d4 (threatening 3 ... ♘f5) 3 ♗g4 ♘f5 4 ♗e2 Black has obtained nothing, and after 1 ... ♔f3 2 ♗a6 White's bishop can again reach the correct squares.

2 ♗a6!

Again the only move to draw. The bishop must be ready to prevent the advance of the pawns by playing to c8 and b7, and must keep as far away as possible from the kingside to avoid forks by the knight.

Horwitz thought that **2 ♗d7** was the correct move here, but Karstedt later pointed out that Black then wins as follows: **2 ... ♘f2+ 3 ♔g2 ♘d3! 4 ♔h3** or 4 ♗b5 ♔e3 5 ♔h3 ♘f2+ and 6 ... g4 wins **4 ... ♔f3! 5 ♗c6+** or 5 ♗g4+ ♔f2 6 ♗c8 ♘f4+ when both 7 ♔g4 h3 8 ♔xg5 h2 9 ♗b7 ♘g2 and 7 ♔h2 ♔f3 8 ♗b7+ ♔g4 win for Black **5 ... ♔f2 6 ♔g4 ♘e5+ 7 ♔xg5 ♔g3!** not 7 ... h3? 8 ♔h4 h2 9 ♔h3 drawing **8 ♗g2! ♘g4 9 ♔h5 ♘e3 10 ♗h1 h3 11 ♔g5 h2** wins. An interesting piece of analysis which can occur later also.

2 ... ♘f2+
3 ♔g2 ♔e3

4 ♗c8!

Preventing 4 ... g4 because of 5 ♗xg4! ♘xg4 6 ♔h3 drawing.

4 ... ♘d3

5 ♔h3 ♘f4+

Or 5 ... ♔f3 6 ♗b7+ ♔f2 7 ♔g4, and after 7 ... ♘e5+ 8 ♔xg5 ♔g3 the bishop is not attacked, so that 9 ♗c8 draws easily.

6 ♔g4 h3

7 ♔g3

The simplest, although 7 ♔xg5 h2 8 ♗b7! and 9 ♔g4 was also playable. Black can now do nothing to strengthen his position, as White maintains his bishop on thc h3-c8 diagonal and simply captures the h-pawn if Black's king gives up control of f4 or f3. The position is drawn.

With isolated pawns White usually wins, if they cannot be effectively blockaded or one of them captured, but here again there can sometimes be great technical difficulties if one is a rook's pawn. Rather than concern ourselves with such positions, let us conclude with an example of knight and two pawns against bishop and pawn.

279

All the pawns are on one wing, with White having a protected passed pawn. Such an ending could not be won with bishops only, but the knight gives White a definite advantage. This is mainly because the bishop can only control squares of one colour whereas the knight can attack all squares. For example, in the diagram the bishop can do nothing to drive White's king from its dominating position, whereas the knight can switch squares and create problems for the defender.

It is clear why the knight is at its best when all the pawns are on the same wing. For instance, if Black's pawn were on b5 instead of f5, he would draw easily, as this pawn would tie down one of White's pieces while Black's king and bishop hold up the pawns.

The diagrammed position is a variation from the game Romanovsky-Verlinski 1925, and the following instructive analysis is the work of Grandmaster Averbakh:

1 ♘d7+

White must proceed methodically if he is to win. It is clear that his king must advance via e5 or g5, which means that Black's king must be driven away from f6 without it being possible for him to return immediately. To bring this about, White has to play h5, but to do so at once allows 1 ... ♗e6! followed by 2 ... ♗f7, capturing the h-pawn, once the knight has moved. White first improves the position of his knight.

1 ... ♔e6

If 1 ... ♔g6 2 h5+! wins the pawn immediately.

2 ♘c5+ ♔f6

3 h5! ♗h7!

The best defence. Black cannot prevent the knight check on d7, and if 3 ... ♗f7 (a2) 4 ♘d7+ ♔e6 5 h6! wins, or here 4 ... ♔e7 5 h6 ♗g8 6 ♔xf5! ♗h7+ 7 ♔g5 ♔xd7 8 ♔f6 wins.

Note that after the text move, Black would lose if he had the move, e.g. 4 ... ♗g8 5 ♘d7+ ♔e7 (or 5 ... ♔e6 6 h6! ♔xd7 7 ♔xf5 ♔e7 8 ♔g6 etc) 6 ♔xf5 ♗h7+ 7 ♔g5 ♔xd7 8 ♔f6! wins, as the pawns cannot be stopped. However, as we know, the knight cannot lose a tempo, and 4 h6 would give Black's king the use of g6. So further preparation is required.

4 ♘d7+ ♔e7

5 ♘e5 ♔f6

Or 5 ... ♔e6 6 ♘f3 ♔f6 7 ♘d4 wins the pawn.

6 h6!

Now that the knight has a strong central post, this pawn advance is decisive, as Black is in zugzwang. Averbakh points out that 6 ♘f3 ♗g8 7 ♘h4 fails to 7 ... ♗e6! 8 h6 ♗c8! etc, but not here 7 ... ♗f7? 8 h6 ♗e6 9 h7 ♔g7 10 ♘g6! ♔xh7 11 ♘f8+ and 12 ♘xe6 winning.

6 ... ♗g8

Or 6 ... ♔e6 7 ♘f3 ♔f6 8 ♘d4 wins the pawn.

The text move leads to a beautiful finish.

7 ♘d7+ ♔g6 *(280)*

If 7 ... ♔e6 8 h7 wins, or 7 ... ♔e7 8 ♔xf5 wins, as we saw in the note to Black's 3rd move.

280

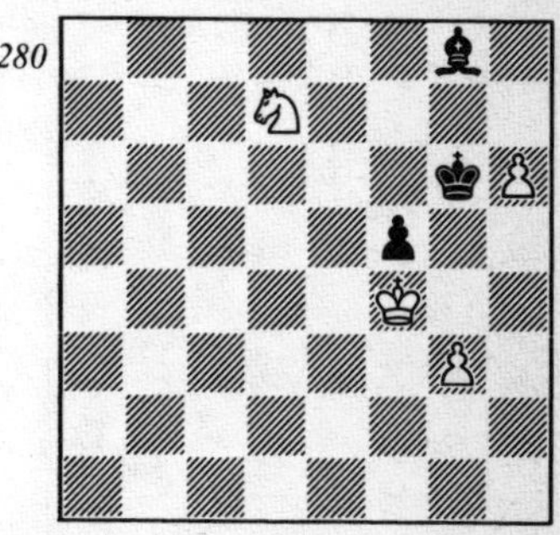

8 h7!

This surprising move wins at once, as capture by either piece allows a knight fork, exchanging pieces and bringing about an easily won pawn ending.

This example concludes our theoretical discussion of bishop endings. We have seen that in many cases it is impossible to lay down general rules. It is best for the reader to recognize certain key positions on which he can base his analysis. We now give a selection of endings from practical play to show how these principles are applied.

Practical examples

The reader may feel that our basic positions are of limited practical value, as they hardly ever occur as such in actual games. This is faulty reasoning; although many endings never reach this stage, these key positions are a vital part in any analysis, and a player must know them thoroughly before he can even begin to understand more complex endgames. Our next example shows us that even leading masters are not above reproach in this respect.

281
W

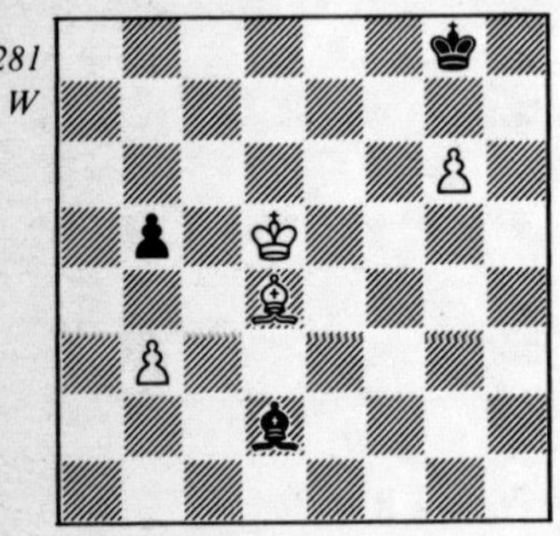

Capablanca-Janowski 1916

This ending occurred in the game Capablanca-Janowski, New York, 1916. White has an extra pawn but has great difficulties in converting this advantage to a win. The g-pawn cannot be queened, so White must devote his attention to the capture of Black's pawn in the best possible circumstances. Black cannot guard this pawn but he can force the white bishop to leave the a1-h8 diagonal, when ... ♔g7 is possible. Clearly a bishop ending will then arise in which White will try to force his b-pawn through.

It is now that our basic positions come in. We must think back to which positions are won and drawn in bishop endings with a knight's pawn! In our notes to diagram 246 we indicated the zone within which the pawn must be if Black is to draw, with black-squared bishops. This means that the pawn must be stopped before it reaches b6. All this will help us to understand the following analysis:

1 ♔e4

A typical waiting manoeuvre, designed with the practical purpose of allowing Black to go wrong. Capablanca was no doubt aware that his only winning chances lay in **1 ♔c5 b4 2 ♔c4 ♗e1 3 ♗c5 ♔g7 4 ♗xb4** (diagram 282) but he does not play this at once. He first waits to see if Black defends correctly; only then will he come back to the main plan.

282
B

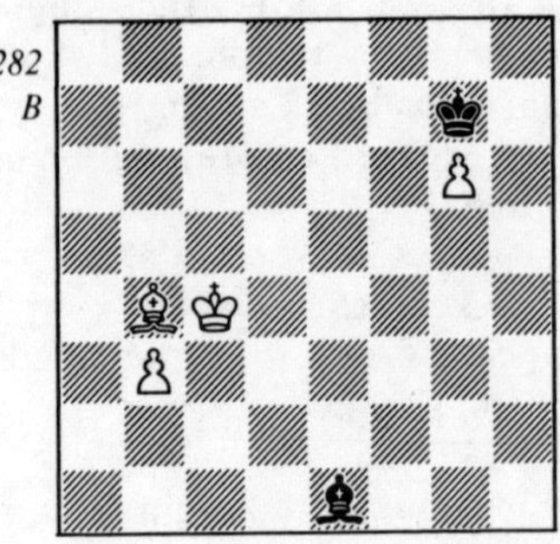

Capablanca-Janowski 1916
(variation)

Let us see how the game would proceed if White goes at once for the win of the pawn. We follow Averbakh's analysis. After 4 ♗xb4 Black has three bishop moves giving three different variations:

1) **4 ... ♗h4?** leads surprisingly to a loss after **5 ♗c3+ ♔xg6 6 b4 ♔f7** Black's king must help, and 6 ... ♔f5 7 ♔d5 ♔f4 8 b5 ♗d8 9 ♗e5+ ♔e3 10 ♔c6 and 11 ♗c7 wins for White **7 b5 ♗d8** the pawn must be stopped before it reaches b6; if 7 ... ♔e6 8 b6 ♔d7 9 ♔b5 ♗g3 10 ♔a6 wins **8 ♔d5 ♔e8 9 ♔c6** and there is no defence to the threat of **10 ♗e5** and **11 ♗c7**.

2) **4 ... ♗g3!** the best defence **5 ♗c3+ ♔xg6 6 b4 ♔f7 7 b5 ♗c7! 8 ♔d5 ♔e7 9 ♔c6 ♔d8** we now see the difference, as in the first variation Black's bishop blocked its own king **10 ♔b7** otherwise 10 ... ♔c8 draws at once **10 ... ♔d7 11 ♗d4 ♗d8 12 ♗b6 ♗g5 13 ♗a5 ♗e3 14 ♔a6 ♔c8 15 ♗b6 ♗g5 16 ♗d4 ♗d8 17 ♗c3 ♗c7** and White can make no progress as **18 ♗a5 ♗xa5** gives a drawn pawn ending.

3) **4 ... ♗f2** weaker than 4 ... ♗g3, but playable **5 ♗c3+ ♔xg6 6 b4 ♔f7 7 ♗d4 ♗g3 8 b5 ♗c7! 9 ♔d5 ♔e7 10 ♔c6 ♔d8!** and after **11 ♗b6 ♔c8!** stalemate saves Black.

1	**...**	**b4**
2	**♗e3**	**♗c3**
3	**♔d3**	**♗e1**
4	**♗d2**	**♗f2**

Clearly the pawn ending would be lost, whereas now 5 ♗xb4 ♔g7 6 ♗c3+ ♔xg6 7 b4 ♔f5 8 ♗d4 ♗g3 etc gives White no winning chances. So Capablanca tries another plan.

5	**♔e4**	**♗c5?**

A success for White's crafty waiting policy! This move gives White a decisive tempo. White threatened 6 ♗xb4, but Black should have interposed 5 ... ♔g7 6 ♔f5 and only then 6 ... ♗c5. Capablanca would have had to revert to the original plan after driving Black's king away from the g-pawn (see note to move 1).

6	**♔d5!**	

Gaining the all-important tempo, as shown in the line 6 ... ♗f2 7 ♗xb4 ♔g7 8 ♗c3+ ♔xg6 9 b4 ♔f7 when Black's king arrives too late, e.g. 10 ♗d4 ♗g3 (or 10 ... ♗e1 11 b5 ♗a5 12 ♔c6 ♔e8 13 ♗f6! ♔f7 14 ♗e5 etc) 11 b5 ♗c7 12 ♔c6 ♗a5 13 ♗e5 and 14 ♗c7 winning easily.

6	**...**	**♗e7**

The only chance, as 6 ... ♗f8 leads to the exchange of bishops after 7 ♔c4 ♔g7 8 ♗xb4.

7	**♔c4**	**♔g7**
8	**♗xb4**	**♗d8** *(283)*

Janowski does his best, but his bishop has been driven to the wrong diagonal. If, for example, 8 ... ♗h4 9 ♗c3+ ♔xg6 10 b4 we have the winning variation 1 given in our note to move 1.

283
W

Capablanca-Janowski 1916

9 ♗c3+?

Averbakh has demonstrated, in the following subtle analysis, that this natural move throws away the win. We can see why this is so if we turn to diagrams 241 and 242. We saw there that the bishop alone cannot defend against the pawn, and that the help of the king is required. We also saw from diagram 242 that Black's king must not support the bishop from the side but from behind. In the present case this means that, with White's king on c6, the black king must reach c4 in time, and with White's king on a6 the black king has to occupy a4. Capablanca's move does nothing to stop Black's king reaching c4. If he had remembered the basic positions, he would have found the correct **9 ♗d2!** giving two variations:

1) **9 ... ♔xg6 10 b4 ♔f5** 10 ... ♔f7 11 ♔d5 ♔e8 12 ♔c6 etc **11 ♔d5 ♔g4** here is the point; Black's king cannot go to f4 in this variation **12 b5 ♔f3 13 ♔c6 ♔e4** or 13 ... ♔e2 14 ♗f4 and 15 ♗c7 wins **14 ♔b7!** or else Black's king would reach c4 in time, whereas now a4 is too far away for him **14 ... ♔d3 15 ♗e1 ♔c4 16 ♔a6** and there is no defence to the threat of **17 ♗a5** and **18 b6**.

2) **9 ... ♗e7** to stop White's pawn **10 ♗e3 ♔xg6 11 ♗c5 ♗d8 12 b4 ♔f5 13 ♔d5 ♔f4 14 b5** and Black's king arrives too late.

9	**...**	**♔xg6**
10	**b4**	**♔f5**
11	**♔d5**	

In this position Janowski resigned, one of the countless such incidents in international chess! As Grandmaster Averbakh has shown, however, Black can draw in the following instructive way.

11	**...**	**♔f4!**

At first sight pointless, but our basic positions tell us that the king must head for c4! Incredible though it may seem, the king arrives there just in time.

12	**♗d4**	

The last try. We already know from diagram 242 that the game is drawn after 12 b5 ♔e3 13 ♗e5 ♔d3 14 ♔c6 ♔c4.

12	**...**	**♔f3**
13	**b5**	

Or 13 ♗c5 ♔e2 14 ♔c6 ♔d3 15 ♔d7 ♗h4 16 b5 ♔c4 17 ♔c6 drawing.

13	**...**	**♔e2!**

The diagonal route is just as short as the horizontal.

14	**♔c6**	**♔d3**
15	**♗b6**	**♗g5**
16	**♔b7**	

Still trying. The king heads for a6 so that he can carry out the manoeuvre ♗f2-e1-a5. If 16 ♗c7 ♗e3 17 ♗d6 ♔c4! the draw is clear.

16	**...**	**♔c4**
17	**♔a6**	**♔b3!**

The king must reach a4! The reader can see for himself that there is no other defence against 18 ♗f2.

18	**♗f2**	**♗d8**
19	**♗e1**	**♔a4!**

and the black king's long journey

is crowned with success. White can make no progress, so the game is drawn. This instructive example is yet a further proof of the need to play endings with the utmost precision.

Now let us consider a position in which White again has an extra pawn, but all the play takes place on the kingside.

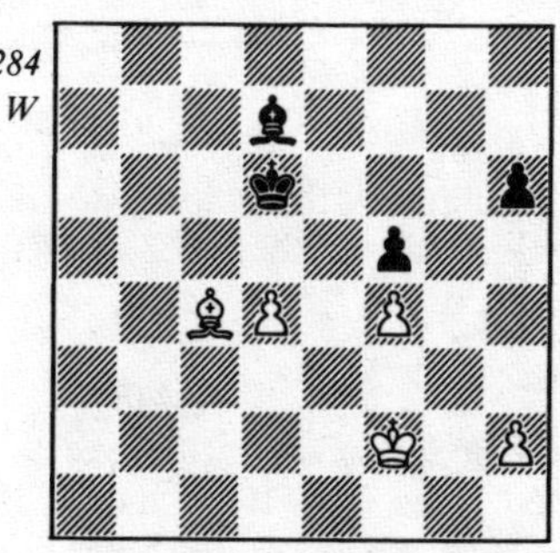

Keres-Lilienthal 1945

This position comes from the game Keres-Lilienthal, Tallinn 1945. We know that bishops lose in strength when the field of action is limited, so White has relatively few winning chances despite his extra pawn. It is clear that his d-pawn s effectively blockaded, so his only chance is to penetrate with his king down the h-file. However, as only a few squares are available for the king, this manoeuvre offers few prospects of success.

1 ♔g3 ♗e8

Black dare not allow White's king to reach h5, as this would tie his own king down to g7 and free White's d-pawn.

2 ♔h4 ♔c6

3 ♗e6!

To make any progress, White's bishop must reach h5, but if immediately 3 ♗e2 ♔d5 4 ♗h5 ♗b5 5 ♗f7+ ♔xd4 6 ♔h5 ♔e4 Black draws. Black's bishop must first be driven to g6.

3 ... ♗g6

At first sight, it appears that 3 ... ♔d6 4 ♗xf5 ♔d5 is the simplest defence, for neither 5 ♗h7 ♔xd4 6 f5 ♔e5 7 ♗g6 ♗d7, nor 5 ♗g4 ♔xd4 6 ♗h5 ♗c6 7 ♗g6 ♗f3 8 ♗f5 ♔e3 gives White anything. However, 5 ♔g4 ♔xd4 6 ♗c2 and 7 ♔f5 would cause Black difficulties.

In such endgames, Black's trouble is that he has a number of continuations, none of which directly loses, but which do not give a clear draw. Practice tells us that in such situations it is easy to make a mistake, and our example is good proof of this.

4 ♗b3 ♔d6

5 ♗d1 ♔e7

Already Black misses a simpler defence by **5 ... ♗e8! 6 ♗h5 ♗b5** with a cunning idea **7 ♗g6** or 7 ♗f7 ♗e2 etc **7 ... ♔d5 8 ♔h5** or 8 ♗xf5 ♔xd4 9 ♔h5 ♔e3 **8 ... ♔e4! 9 ♔xh6 ♔xf4 10 h4 ♗e2!** and it is difficult to see how White can do anything. However, as we stated above, it is by no means easy to select the best of several plausible lines.

6 ♗e2! *(285)*

White's logical move would be 6 ♗h5, transposing into the main variation, but as we saw in the Capablanca-Janowski game, it is sometimes useful to tack about before proceeding with the main plan. Assuming, of course, that there is no danger and that your opponent has chances of going wrong. The waiting move 6 ♗e2! forces Black to defend with great care, and Lilienthal is equal to the situation.

285
B

Keres-Lilienthal 1945

6 ... ♔f8!

The only correct defence. Black's king protects the two critical squares e8 and f7, the importance of which is seen in the following line: 6 ... ♔f6 (d6) 7 ♗h5 ♗h7 8 ♗e8 ♔e7 9 ♔h5! ♔xe8 10 ♔xh6 ♗g8 11 ♔g6 and White wins the other pawn, as 11 ... ♗e6 12 ♔f6 ♗c8 13 h4 is even worse for Black. White should have good chances with three pawns against a bishop.

It is interesting to note that Black also loses if he moves his bishop from the h7-g6 diagonal, e.g. 6 ... ♗f7 7 ♗h5 ♗e6 8 ♗g6 ♔f6 9 ♔h5 ♔g7 10 h3 ♗c8 11 d5 wins.

7 ♗h5 ♗h7
8 ♔h3

It is difficult to make any progress. The bishop has no squares on the h5-e8 diagonal, and if it retreats, Black plays ... ♗g6. The only remaining chance is to play d5 to lure Black's king away from the critical squares on the diagonal. However, an immediate 8 d5 is premature and after 8 ... ♔e7 White is in zugzwang. This is why he first triangulates with his king, so that Black's king will be on e7 when d5 is played.

8 ... ♔e7
9 ♔g3 ♔f8

As we saw on the 5th move, 9 ... ♔d6 loses to 10 ♔h4 ♔d5? 11 ♗f7+ ♔xd4 12 ♔h5 winning the bishop.

10 ♔h4 ♔e7
11 ♗d1

The next few moves were only played to take White past the time control. The situation remains unchanged.

11 ... ♗g6
12 ♗e2 ♔f8
13 ♗f3 ♔e7
14 ♗h5 ♗h7
15 d5! *(286)*

At last White plays his trump card.

15 ... ♗g8?

and Black immediately makes a decisive error, after which the game is lost. He could draw by **15 ... ♔d6!** with the following possibilities:

286
B

Keres-Lilienthal 1945

1) 16 ♗e8 ♔e7! (not 16 ... ♔xd5? 17 ♔h5 ♔e4 18 ♔xh6 ♔xf4 19 h4 and 20 h5 winning) 17 ♔h5 (the only chance) 17 ... ♔xe8 18 ♔xh6 ♗g8 19 d6 ♔d7 20 h4 ♗f7 draws. 2) 16 ♗f7 ♔e7 17 ♔h5 (after 17 ♗e6 ♗g6 18 ♔g3 ♔d6 19 ♔f2 Black can calmly play 19 ... ♗e8 20 ♗xf5 ♔xd5 with a clear draw) 17 ... ♔xf7 18 ♔xh6 ♗g8 19 d6 ♔f6 draws.

16 ♗g6 ♗xd5

Or 16 ... ♔f6 17 ♔h5 ♔g7 18 d6 ♗e6 19 ♗e8 wins.

17 ♔h5! ♔f6
18 ♔xh6 ♗e6

White has made definite progress but still has problems, because his king is in the way of the powerful h-pawn. The whole question is whether the king can escape from the h-file. Apparently he cannot do so because Black's bishop controls the exit square on g8, but a little combination comes to his aid.

19 ♔h7 ♗d5
20 h4 ♗c4
21 h5 ♗d5 *(287)*

Black could try 21 ... ♗b5 to prevent 22 ♗e8, when White would continue 22 h6 (but not 22 ♔g8 ♗c4+ 23 ♔f8? ♗f7! drawing, as 24 ♗xf7 gives stalemate) 22 ... ♗d7 23 ♗h5 ♗e6 24 ♗e8, as in the game.

287
W

Keres-Lilienthal 1945

22 ♗e8!

White must be careful not to throw away the win. After 22 h6? ♗f7! Black clearly draws, but play is much more subtle after the other winning attempt of **22 ♔h8** intending ♗h7-g8 etc.

Black defends by **22 ... ♗c6! 23 ♗h7** we already know the defensive point in 23 ♔g8 ♗d5+ 24 ♔f8? ♗f7!, but White can still revert to the game continuation by playing 23 ♔h7 **23 ... ♗e8! 24 h6 ♗f7!** or 24 ... ♗g6 25 ♗g8 ♗e8 as below, or here 25 ♗xg6 ♔xg6 26 ♔g8 ♔xh6 27 ♔f7 ♔h7! 28 ♔f6 ♔g8 etc **25 ♗g8 ♗e8! 26 ♗c4** if 26 h7 ♗f7, or 26 ♔h7 ♗g6+ **26 ... ♔g6 27 h7 ♗f7 28 ♗d3 ♗e6!** and White's king is permanently shut in. An interesting variation.

22 ... ♗e6

The waiting move 22 ... ♗c4 resists a little longer, but a simple winning plan then is 23 ♗d7 ♗b3 24 h6 ♗f7 (the threat was 25 ♗xf5! ♔xf5 26 ♔g7, and if 24 ... ♗c2 25 ♗e6! wins) 25 ♗c8 ♗g6+ (if 25 ... ♗e8 or 25 ... ♗h5 26 ♔g8 wins) 26 ♔g8 ♗f7+ 27 ♔f8 ♗g6 28 ♗d7 ♗h7 29 ♗e8 ♗g6 and now White wins with either 30 ♗xg6 ♔xg6 31 ♔e7 or 30 ♗f7 ♗h7 31 ♗g8 etc.

23 h6 ♗f7

Or 23 ... ♗d5 24 ♗d7 ♗f7 25 ♗c8 etc wins.

24 ♗d7! ♗c4

25 ♗xf5!

The point! Black cannot play 25 ... ♔xf5 because of 26 ♔g7 followed by 27 h7, but with two pawns down Black is now lost.

25 ... ♔f7

26 ♗d7 ♗d3+

27 f5 ♔f8

Hoping for 28 ♔g6? ♔g8 followed by 29 ... ♗xf5 drawing against the 'wrong' rook's pawn.

28 ♗e6

1-0

Our last two examples have shown us the difficulties that can arise when little material is left on the board or when all material is placed on one side of the board. In general, with bishops of the same colour, the extra pawn guarantees the win.

However, we may have a positional advantage which is often no less important than a material one. Such advantages as the better pawn position, a more effectively placed bishop or king, a strong passed pawn, enemy pawns or squares which are weak, are often sufficient to ensure the win. We have no time here to illustrate all these positional elements, but diagram 288 shows a number of them.

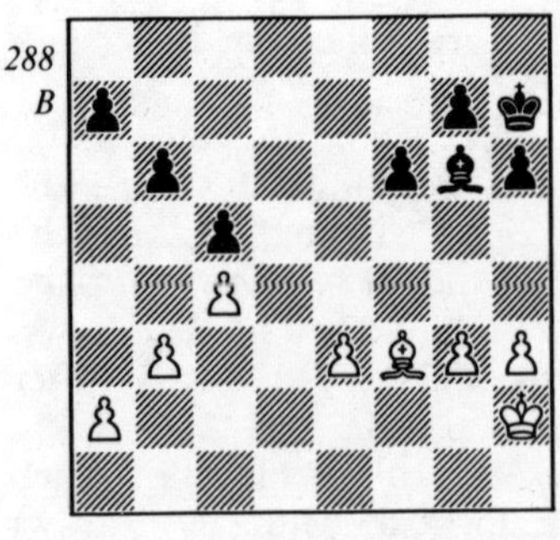

288

B

Smyslov-Keres 1951

This position occurred in the game Smyslov-Keres, 1951. Both sides have equal material, but Black has several important positional advantages. Firstly, White's pawns on the queenside are badly placed on the same colour as his bishop. Let us explain this point further: although such pawns can of course be defended more easily by the bishop, a grave disadvantage is that all the squares of opposite colour are seriously weakened. This allows the penetration of the enemy king who can be stopped only by the opposing king. This is why it is usually advisable to place one's pawns on squares of opposite colour to one's own bishop.

Secondly, Black's king can reach the unassailable post on e5. From here he controls the centre and can penetrate via d4 or f4 after playing ... g5 and ... f5-f4. As White must use his bishop to defend his queenside pawns, he is soon in zugzwang and compelled to give way to the black king.

We can see Black's winning plan already, and can easily understand the game continuation:

1 ... ♗b1

Gaining a tempo by attacking the a-pawn.

2 a3 a5!

A vital move, preventing b4 once and for all and threatening to win the b-pawn after 3 ... ♗c2.

3 ♗d1

Bitter necessity. The white bishop remains here for the rest of the game, tied down to the defence of the b-pawn. The black bishop, on the other hand, is free to move along the h7-b1 diagonal whilst maintaining the threat of ... ♗c2. In other words White is practically playing minus a piece, so can hardly avoid an eventual zugzwang.

3 ... ♔g6
4 ♔g2 ♔f5
5 ♔f3 ♔e5 *(289)*

Making his task more difficult. The immediate 5 ... g5! would have prevented White's counter-chance of 6 h4, when Black would exchange and prepare ... f5-f4 followed by an attack on the h-pawn or on the queenside. It is important that the pawns are left on the h-file, as we shall see.

289
W

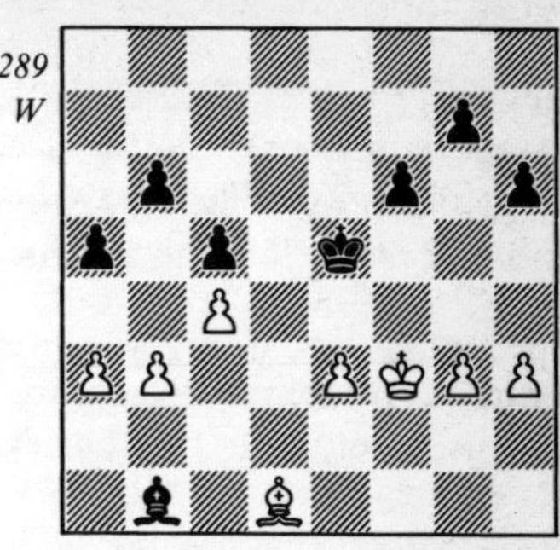

Smyslov-Keres 1951

6 a4

White neglects the opportunity to play 6 h4!, placing this pawn on a black square and making Black's task extremely difficult. The main reason for this is that, if Black then plays 6 ... g5 followed by the advance of his f-pawn to f4, all the kingside pawns are exchanged, giving White good drawing chances. If instead Black plays 6 ... g5 7 hg fg, then 8 g4! blocks the kingside pawns.

Nevertheless, even **6 h4** should not be sufficient to draw the game if Black pursues a logical plan. He plays **6 ... ♗d3** forcing **7 a4** because of the threatened 7 ... a4, then continues **7 ... g6!** The idea is to play ... ♗f5 and h5, taking away the e2 and f3 squares from White's king and allowing Black's king to penetrate via e4. However, with White's king on f2, he can answer ... ♔e4 with ♗c2+, so Black must bring about this position with White to move. It is then zugzwang, as the bishop cannot move and the king must leave the defence of his e-pawn (the pawn ending is lost after ♔e2 and the exchange of bishops). For instance, if White plays ♔e1 Black plays his king to e4 and, if ♔d2, ... ♗g4 winning.

The plan is clear but its execution is fraught with technical problems. The point is that after, for example, 8 ♔f2 h5 9 ♔f3 ♗f5 10 ♔f2! it is Black who is in zugzwang and 10 ... g5 does not lead to a clear win. Black must therefore manoeuvre with more subtlety to bring about the same position with White to move. Play might go: **8 ♔f2** 8 g4 only helps Black after 8 ... g5! 9 hg hg and 10 ... f5, creating an outside passed pawn **8 ... ♔e4! 9 ♗f3+ ♔f5! 10 ♗d1 ♔e5 11 ♔f3** or 11 ♔e1 ♗f5! 12 ♔f2 h5, or here 12 ♔d2 ♔e4 threatening 13 ... h5 and 14 ... ♗g4 **11 ... ♗f5!** if 11 ... h5 12 ♔g2! can be played **12 ♔f2 h5** the required position **13 ♔e1 ♔e4 14 ♔d2 ♗g4!** and Black wins after both 15 ♗c2+ ♔f3 and 15 ♗xg4 hg 16 ♔e2 f5 etc.

After the text move, anticipating the threat of ... ♗d3 and ... a4, Black's task is far easier.

6 ... g5!
7 ♔e2

Now 7 h4 is too late, as 7 ... gh 8 gh f5 9 ♔f2 ♔e4 10 ♔e2 f4 wins easily. If instead 7 ♔f2 Black's simplest plan is to play ... f5-f4.

7 ... ♗f5!

Forcing White to advance the g-pawn, as 8 h4 allows Black to exchange bishops.

8 g4 ♗b1
9 ♔f3 f5
10 gf

Or 10 ♔e2 f4 11 ♔f3 fe 12 ♔xe3 ♗e4 and Black's king reaches d4 or f4.

10 ... ♔xf5

After 10 ... ♗xf5 11 ♔g3 Black cannot play 11 ... ♔e4 because of 12 ♗c2+.

11 ♔f2 ♗e4

11 ... ♔e4 would be pointless after 12 ♗h5. The text move restricts the activity of White's king and prepares the decisive advance of the h-pawn.

12 ♔g3 ♔g6
13 ♔f2

If 13 h4 h5! 14 ♔h3 ♗d3 15 ♔g3 ♗f5! forces the exchange of pawns, when the h-pawn wins quickly.

13 ... h5
14 ♔g3 h4+
15 ♔f2 ♗f5

White's new weakness on h3 ties his king down and gives Black's king a way through the centre.

16 ♔g2 ♔f6
17 ♔h2 ♔e6!

The final point. If at once 17 ... ♔e5 18 ♔g2 Black is in zugzwang (18 ... ♔e4 19 ♗c2+), whereas now the opposite is the case. **0-1**, for after 18 ♔g2 ♔e5 19 ♔h2 ♗b1 20 ♔g2 ♔e4 21 ♔f2 ♔d3 22 ♔f3 ♔d2 23 ♗e2 ♗f5 Black wins easily.

Let us now consider a few examples of endings with bishops of opposite colour. As we have already mentioned there is a strong drawing tendency here, mainly because the bishops can never challenge each other. If the weaker side manages to blockade the enemy pawns, he can draw even with a great material deficit. Take the following position:

290

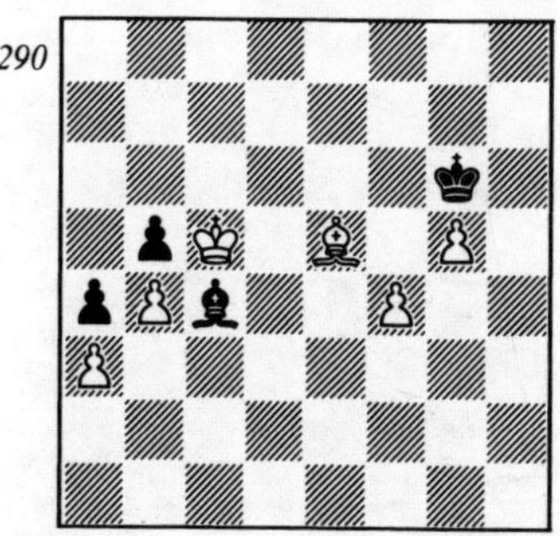

White can do nothing, as Black's bishop guards the queenside pawns, and the kingside pawns are permanently blockaded. The extra material is useless.

However, if we now place the black king on g8, White wins easily after **1 ... ♗d3 2 f5!** etc. Or if Black's a-pawn is on a6 and White's on a5, the black bishop cannot defend his backward pawn.

Our first example comes from the game Nimzowitsch-Tarrasch, Kissingen 1928.

White has an extra pawn but the win is still a long way off. He has no passed pawn yet and the few weaknesses in Black's position seem difficult to exploit because

291
W

Nimzowitsch-Tarrasch 1928

the bishop can guard the kingside pawns. One might imagine that Black has little to fear if he uses his bishop to protect his kingside pawns while his king holds up the eventual passed pawn on the queenside.

However, matters are not so simple, as the instructive game continuation shows us. The reason for this is that Black's bishop finds difficulty in defending without the help of the king, precisely because of the weak pawn position. For instance, if his e-pawn were on g7, he would have no trouble at all. Let us see what dangers are lurking in this position:

1 ♔h2 c4?

It is understandable that Black wishes to place his queenside pawns on the same colour as his bishop, so that his king can cross over to the kingside. (As we shall see later, the bishop cannot guard his weak f- and h-pawns without the help of the king.) However, the disadvantage of marching the king over to the kingside is that White can create a passed pawn on the queenside. There are admittedly some technical problems to overcome, but once White has a passed pawn, Black's defence crumbles.

Apparently Tarrasch did not recognize the danger in time, or else he would have taken specific measures against it. Of course, he could not play 1 ... f4 2 ♗g5 f3 3 g4! and White can eventually create a passed pawn on both wings. Grandmaster Averbakh pointed out the correct defence: 1 ... ♗b5! 2 ♔g3 ♗f1 preventing the advance of White's king. After 3 h4 h5 4 ♔f4 ♗xg2 5 ♔xf5 ♗f3 Black's bishop protects both his kingside pawns. The same happens after 2 g4 fg 3 hg ♗e2 etc. After missing this chance, Black has a lost position.

2 ♔g3 ♔c8
3 ♔f4 ♔d7
4 ♗b4 ♔e6
5 ♗c3 ♗d7

If Black tries 5 ... ♗g6, then the advance of White's h-pawn soon brings him into difficulties. Fine gives the following interesting continuation: 6 ♔g5 ♔d5 7 g3 b5 8 h4 (if 8 ♔h6 Averbakh gives 8 ... f4! 9 gf e3 10 ef ♗xc2 etc) 8 ... ♔c6 9 b3! cb (or 9 ... ♔c5 10 a4 and White still obtains a passed pawn) 10 cb ♔b6 11 a4 ba 12 ba ♔a6 13 a5 ♔b5 14 h5 ♗e8 15 ♔xf5 ♗xh5 16 ♔xe4 and White wins by advancing his f-pawn.

This variation clearly shows us why Black's bishop cannot defend the kingside pawns on its own. Black has decided to switch the roles of his king and bishop, but this plan too proves unavailing.

6 g3 b5
7 ♔g5 ♔f7

Forced, as 8 ♔h6 was threatened.

8 h4 ♗c8
9 ♔h6 ♔g8

Black is now holding everything on the kingside, so White turns his attention to the queenside where he creates a passed pawn.

10 b3! cb

Or 10 ... ♗e6 11 a4! and White still obtains a passed pawn.

11 cb *(292)*

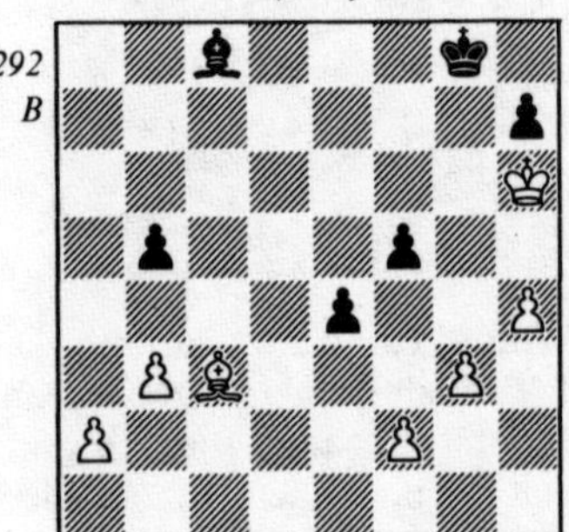

Nimzowitsch-Tarrasch 1928

11 ... f4

Despair, but there was no defence. After 11 ... ♗d7 12 ♗e5 Black is in zugzwang, e.g. 12 ... ♗e6 13 a4! ba 14 ba ♗d7 15 a5 ♗c8 16 ♗d4 ♗a6 17 ♔g5 ♗c8 18 ♔f6 wins. Or 12 ... ♗e8 13 ♔g5 ♗d7 14 ♔f6 ♔f8 15 ♗d6+ ♔g8 16 ♔e7 ♗c6 (or 16 ... ♗c8 17 a4 etc) 17 ♔e6 and Black's f-pawn falls. Tarrasch's move doubles White's pawns but the passed f-pawn is now decisive.

12	**gf**	**♗d7**
13	**♔g5**	**♔f7**
14	**f5**	**♗c6**
15	**♔f4**	**♔e7**
16	**♔e5**	**♗e8**

He cannot hold the e-pawn, e.g. 16 ... ♔f7 17 ♔d6 ♗e8 18 ♔d5 wins, or here 17 ... ♗b7 18 ♔c5 etc.

17 ♔xe4

This virtually ends resistance. The game finished: 17 ... ♗c6+ 18 ♔e5 ♗e8 19 ♔d5 ♗f7+ 20 ♔c5 ♗e8 21 ♗e5 ♗d7 22 ♔b6 ♔f7 23 f6 ♗e8 24 f4 ♔e6 25 ♔a6 ♔f7 26 b4 ♔e6 27 a4 ba 28 b5 1-0. A very interesting and instructive ending.

In such endings, passed pawns play a vital part, and surprising sacrifices of material are often necessary to create these passed pawns, even if it means giving some to the enemy. Connected pawns or pawns standing on the same diagonal can be held by the bishop, so it is much better to have passed pawns which are far apart. Our next beautiful example shows how this works out in practice.

293

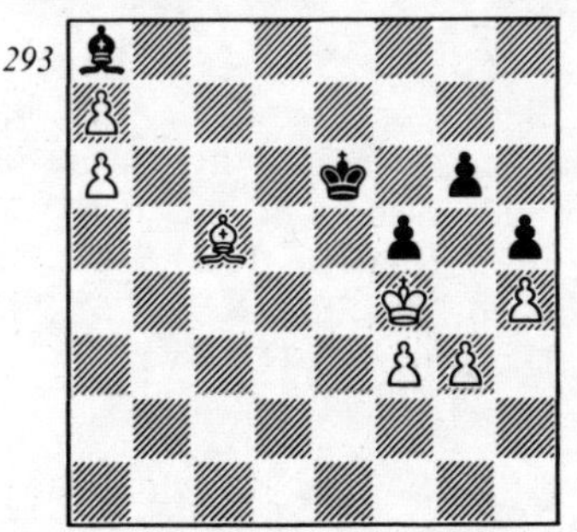

Y.Averbakh 1951

This position occurred in a variation of the game Smyslov-Averbakh, Moscow 1950. In the actual game Smyslov only drew, but Averbakh pointed out afterwards that White could have obtained the diagrammed position which is won for him. White has two extra pawns, but they are doubled. He can undertake nothing on the kingside and Black's king bars the way to the queenside. No wonder that Smyslov felt he could make no progress and gave up the game as drawn, after a few unsuccessful attempts at a win.

Nevertheless, there is a surprising way to win, as we see in the following analysis by Averbakh:

1 ♔g5 ♔f7

If 1 ... ♗xf3 2 ♔xg6 ♔e5 3 ♗e3 ♔e6 4 ♗f4 White wins another pawn. Black now threatens 2 ... ♗xf3.

2 f4!!

A bizarre-looking move, blocking in his own king, but it is the only way to win. After **2 g4** Black draws by **2 ... fg!** if 2 ... ♗xf3 3 gf gf 4 a8♕ ♗xa8 5 ♔xh5 f4 6 ♔g5 f3 7 ♔f5 and 8 ♗f2 followed by the transfer of the king to the queenside, winning **3 fg hg 4 ♔xg4 ♔e6 5 ♔g5 ♗e4!** not 5 ... ♔f7 6 ♗d4 ♗h1 7 ♗f6 threatening 8 h5 and 9 ♔f5 etc **6 a8♕ ♗xa8 7 ♔xg6 ♔d7 8 h5 ♔c7** and Black draws by giving up his bishop for the h-pawn.

The idea of White's move is to break through with g4, creating another passed pawn on the kingside, even though this means giving Black two connected passed pawns. These will be held by the bishop, as the following exciting play shows.

2 ... ♗e4

Guarding the f-pawn, so that after 3 g4 hg 4 h5 gh White would have to give up one of his doubled pawns in order to win the f-pawn. At all events, White must make preparations before he can break through.

3 ♗f2

This is the best square for the bishop in the coming fight against Black's future passed pawns. After, for example, 3 ♗d4 ♗f3 4 g4 hg 5 h5 gh 6 ♔xf5 h4 Black draws.

3 ... ♔g7

Or 3 ... ♗f3 4 g4! hg (4 ... fg 5 ♗g3! ♔g7 6 f5 gf 7 ♔xh5 f4 8 ♗xf4 g3+ 9 ♔g5 g2 10 ♗e3 wins, as the white king heads for the queenside) 5 h5 gh 6 ♔xf5 winning even more easily than in the main line.

4 g4!

The key move of the whole plan. Black cannot prevent the creation of another passed pawn.

4 ... hg

Giving White more problems than 4 ... fg 5 f5 gf 6 ♔xh5, e.g. 6 ... ♔f6 7 ♗g3 ♗f3 8 ♔h6 ♗e4 9 h5 ♗f3 10 ♗h4+ ♔f7 (or 10 ... ♔e5 11 ♔g5 f4 12 h6 etc) 11 ♔g5 ♗e4 12 ♗g3 ♔g7 13 ♗e5+ ♔h7 14 h6 ♗a8 15 ♔xf5 ♔xh6 16 ♔e6 wins easily.

5 h5 gh

6 a8♕!

White has no time for 6 ♔xh5 ♔f6 7 ♗h4+ ♔e6 8 ♔g6 ♗a8 9 ♔g7 ♗c6 10 ♔f8 ♔d5! 11 ♔e7 ♔c5 12 ♗f2+ ♔b5 13 ♔d6 ♗e4 14 ♔c7 ♔xa6 15 ♔b8 ♔b5 drawing, as given by Averbakh.

6 ... ♗xa8

7 ♔xf5 *(294)*

294

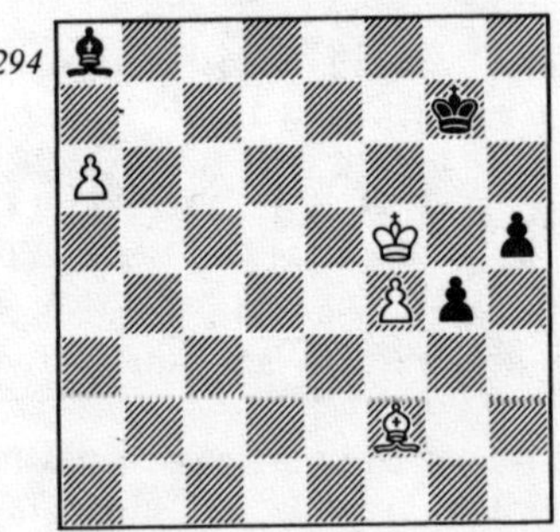

White has now given up his two extra pawns but has reached a very favourable ending with his passed pawns far apart and effective, whilst Black's pawns are easily held by the bishop.

7 ... ♔f7

White was threatening 8 ♔e6 followed by the advance of his f-pawn.

8 ♔g5 ♗f3

Black could draw if only his king could reach the queenside and his bishop be sacrificed for White's f-pawn. But he has no time for this, e.g. 8 ... ♔e7 9 f5 ♔d7 10 f6 ♗d5 11 a7 wins.

9 a7 ♗d5

10 ♗h4

Not 10 ♔xh5 ♔e6! 11 ♔xg4 ♔d7 12 f5 ♔c7 13 f6 ♔b7 and

Black's king arrives time to draw.

10 ... ♗f3

11 f5

If 11 ♔xh5 g3+ 12 ♔g5 g2 13 ♗f2 ♗e4 Black draws, for if White's king heads for the queen-side, his bishop cannot maintain a guard on the f-pawn.

11 ... ♔g7

12 ♗g3 ♔f7

13 ♗e5 ♗e4

Or 13 ... ♔f8 14 ♔f6 h4 15 ♗d6+ ♔e8 (if 15 ... ♔g8 16 ♔e7) 16 ♔g7 wins. Or 13 ... ♔e7 14 ♔g6 wins. Black is in zugzwang.

14 ♔xh5

Apparently allowing Black to win the f-pawn.

14 ... g3

15 ♗xg3 ♔f6

16 ♔g4! ♗xf5+

17 ♔f4 wins.

White's a-pawn queens. An attractive finish, the whole play being typical of the subtleties involved in endings with bishops of opposite colour.

And now, to conclude this section on practical endgames let us analyse a few very useful examples of the struggle between knight and bishop. We have already mentioned that the bishop is superior to the knight when the centre is open and there are pawns on both wings. The advantage of the bishop is also clear when the knight has strayed into the enemy camp and is threatened with capture. Our next example shows us that a win is even possible with limited material on the board and all the pawns on the same wing.

295
B

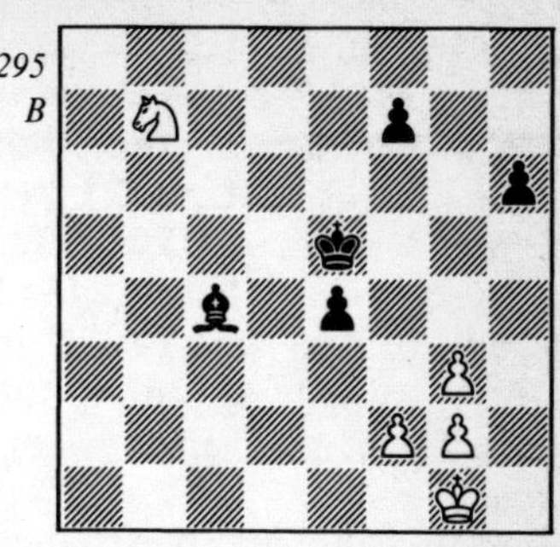

Marshall-Nimzowitsch 1928

This position occurred in the game Marshall-Nimzowitsch, Berlin 1928. Although material is even, and a Black victory would normally be out of the question, the position of White's knight is a serious handicap to him. It has no way of getting back into the game and could even be lost. Nimzowitsch skilfully uses this factor to win as follows:

1 ... ♔d5!

Cutting out the knight's retreat to c5 and threatening to capture it by 2 ... ♗a2 and 3 ... ♔c6.

2 ♔h2

Why does White choose to ignore the threat? The following analysis shows that if White tries to save his knight he still loses the ending: **2 ♘d8 ♔d6 3 ♘b7+ ♔c6! 4 ♘a5+ ♔d5** if 4 ... ♔b5 5 ♘b7 and the threat of 6 ♘d6 forces the king to go back **5 ♘xc4** or 5 ♔h2 ♗a2! and White has insufficient compensation for his piece after both 6 g4 ♔c5 7 ♔g3 ♔b6 8 ♔f4

♔xa5 9 ♔xe4 ♔b4 10 ♔f5 ♔c3, and 6 ♔h3 ♔c5 7 ♔g4 ♔b5 8 ♔h5 ♔xa5 9 ♔xh6 ♔b4 **5 ... ♔xc4 6 ♔f1 or 6 f3 e3 7** ♔f1 ♔d3 8 ♔e1 f5 followed by 9 ... e2 and 10 ... ♔e3 winning easily **6 ... ♔d3 7 ♔e1 h5 8 ♔d1 e3! 9 fe** or 9 f3 f5 wins **9 ... ♔xe3 10 ♔e1 ♔e4 11 ♔e2 ♔f5 12 ♔f3 ♔g5 13 ♔e3 ♔g4 14 ♔f2 f6** and Black wins by capturing the g-pawn then advancing his h-pawn.

Marshall is hoping to exchange all the pawns while Black is using time to capture the knight.

2	**...**	**♗a2**
3	**g4**	**f6**

Winning more easily than after **3 ... ♔c6 4 ♘d8+ ♔c7 5 ♘xf7 ♗xf7**. However, as this position could have arisen if Marshall had played 2 ♘d8 ♔d6 3 ♘b7+ ♔c6 4 ♘a5+ ♔d5 5 ♔h2 ♗a2 6 g4 ♔c5 7 ♘b7+ ♔c6 8 ♘d8+ ♔c7 9 ♘xf7 ♗xf7, let us examine it more closely:

296
W

Marshall-Nimzowitsch 1928 (variation)

White must of course continue with **6 ♔g3 ♔d6 7 ♔f4** attacking the e-pawn. Black guards it by **7 ... ♗g6** and play goes **8 f3** 8 g5 h5 only helps Black **8 ... ef** if 8 ... ♔d5 9 fe+ ♗xe4 10 g5 h5 11 g6! ♗xg6 12 ♔g5 and 13 g4 draws. Or 8 ... ♔e6 9 g5! h5 10 fe ♔d6 11 ♔g3! ♔e5 12 ♔h4 ♔f4 13 g3+ ♔f3 14 e5 ♗e8 15 e6 ♗g6 16 ♔h3! draws **9 gf** when Black still has several technical problems to overcome. The winning method is as follows: **9 ... ♔d5 10 ♔e3** or 10 ♔g3 ♔e5 11 f4+ ♔e4 wins **10 ... ♗c2 11 ♔f4** or 11 f4 ♗d1 12 g5 h5 etc **11 ... ♗b1** waiting **12 ♔e3** or 12 ♔g3 **12 ... ♗g6!** and White is in zugzwang, giving us two variations:

1) **13 ♔f4 ♔d4 14 ♔g3** easier for Black is 14 g5 h5 **14 ... ♔e3 15 f4 ♔e4! 16 f5 ♗e8! 17 g5 h5 18 f6 ♔f5** wins.

2) **13 f4 ♗e8!** so that 14 f5 is not played with gain of time **14 ♔f3** or 14 g5 h5 15 f5 ♔e5 winning the pawns **14 ... ♔d4 15 ♔g3 ♔e4 16 f5 ♔e5** wins, or here 15 g5 h5 16 f5 ♔e5 wins.

Returning to the actual game, Black's last move preserves his f-pawn. His task is thus made a little easier, but the finish is still interesting.

4	**♔g3**	**♔c6**
5	**♘a5+**	

As the knight is lost anyway, it is best to drive Black's king as far away as possible from the kingside.

5	**...**	**♔b6**
6	**♔f4**	**♔xa5**
7	**♔xe4**	

White dare not let Black keep the strong e-pawn. For example, after 7 ♔f5 Black wins by 7 ... ♔b4 8 ♔xf6 ♔c3 9 g5 hg 10 ♔xg5 ♔d2 11 ♔f4 ♗b1! 12 g4 ♔e2 13 ♔g3 ♗a2 14 g5 ♗f7 15 ♔g2 ♗g6 and Black's king comes in decisively at f1 or f3.

7 ... ♗e6
8 ♔f4 ♔b4
9 ♔g3 ♔c5
10 ♔h4 ♗f7

Black must not allow White's king to reach h5. White now manages to exchange one of his pawns.

11 f4 ♔d6
12 g5 hg+

Not of course 12 ... fg+ 13 fg h5 14 g4 etc.

13 fg f5 *(297)*

297

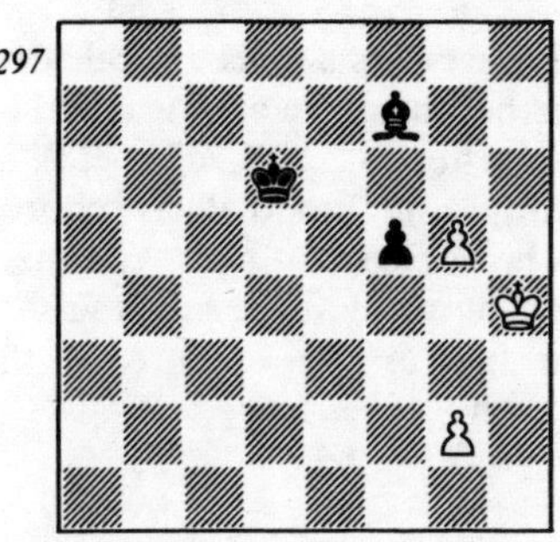

Marshall-Nimzowitsch 1928

14 g6! ♗e6

Again White draws after 14 ... ♗xg6 15 ♔g5 and 16 g4.

15 ♔g5 ♔e5
16 ♔h6 ♔f6

The more active 16 ... ♔f4 only leads to a draw after 17 ♔h5 ♔g3? 18 ♔g5 f4 19 g7 ♗g8 20 ♔f5 ♗h7+ 21 ♔g5 etc.

17 g3

Sooner or later White is compelled to make this disadvantageous move, e.g. after 17 ♔h5 ♗d5 etc White loses at once after 17 ♔h7 ♔g5 18 g7 f4 or 18 ♔g5 ♗e6.

17 ... ♗d7
18 ♔h5

If 18 ♔h7 ♔g5 19 g7 ♗e6, or 18 g7 ♗e6, as given in the last note.

18 ... ♔g7

A little quicker is 18 ... ♗e8 19 ♔h6 ♗xg6 20 g4 f4 21 g5+ ♔f5 etc.

19 ♔g5 ♗e6
20 ♔h5 ♗c8
21 ♔g5 ♗d7!

Black has now lost a tempo and White is forced to give way.

22 ♔h5 ♔f6

Not of course 22 ... ♗e8 23 ♔g5 ♗xg6 24 g4 drawing.

23 ♔h6 ♗e8
24 g7 ♗f7

and White resigned in view of the continuation 25 ♔h7 ♔g5 26 g8♕+ ♗xg8 27 ♔xg8 ♔g4 winning. A remarkable ending whose outcome one could hardly suspect from looking at the original diagram.

Our next example illustrates most clearly the advantage of the bishop in positions with play on both wings.

Again material is even. White has little to fear on the kingside at the moment, but his queenside pawns could easily become weak. Not in the sense that they can be captured, but that they cannot

298
W

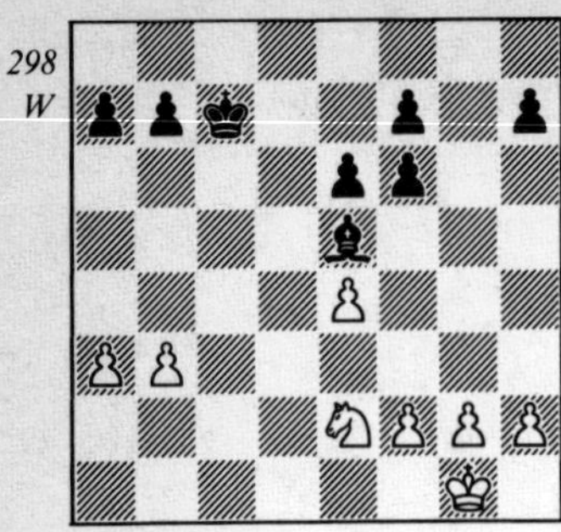

Chekhover-Lasker 1935

prevent the entry of Black's king. So White must try to strengthen his queenside. If his a-pawn were on a4, for example, he could play 1 ♘c1 and 2 ♘d3, covering all points of entry, with a reasonable position. However, he has no time for 1 a4 because of 1 ... ♔c6 2 ♘c1 ♔c5 penetrating via b4 or d4. White's only chance is to bring his king over a quickly as possible to the queenside.

1 ♔f1 b5!

With the idea of creating a weak white pawn on a4. 1 ... ♗b2 loses time, as after 2 a4 ♔c6 3 ♔e1 ♔c5 4 ♔d2 ♔b4 5 ♔c2 White guards his weak b-pawn.

2 ♔e1 ♗b2
3 a4 ba
4 ba ♔c6!

Or, of course, 4 ... ♔b6, but after 5 ♔d2 Black must not play 5 ... ♔a5? 6 ♔c2 ♗e5 7 f4 ♗d6 8 ♔b3 with a perfectly acceptable position for White, instead, 5 ... ♔c5! transposes to our main line. Lasker's deep positional understanding tells him that it is not enough to attack a single weakness, so he plans to centralize his king, aiming also at White's e-pawn.

5 ♔d2 ♔c5!
6 ♘c3

Lasker's idea would be clearly seen in the variation 6 ♔c2 ♗d4 7 f3 ♔c4! when Black's pieces dominate the whole board and White must lose material, e.g. 8 ♘c1 ♗e5 9 h4 ♔b4 winning a pawn. Or 8 ♘xd4 ♔xd4 9 ♔b3 a5 with an easily won pawn ending.

With the text move White seeks counterplay, but in so doing he plays his knight too far away from the queenside and allows Black a powerful passed a-pawn.

6 ... ♔b4

Lasker does not need to calculate whether the pawn ending could be won after 6 ... ♗xc3+ etc. In endings one should always choose the most clear-cut plan, and there is no doubt that the safest way to win lies in the capture of the a-pawn.

7 ♘b5 a5
8 ♘d6 ♔xa4
9 ♔c2

After 9 ♘xf7 ♔b3 the a-pawn costs at least the knight, e.g. 10 ♘d8 a4 11 ♘xe6 a3 12 ♘c5+ ♔c4 etc. The text move on the other hand loses the h-pawn.

9 ... ♗e5
10 ♘xf7 ♗xh2

Black must now win with his extra passed a-pawn, and Lasker faultlessly solves the technical problems.

11	**♘d8**	**e5**
12	**♘c6**	**♗g1**
13	**f3**	**♗c5**

Restricting the activity of White's knight.

14	**♘b8**	**♔b5**
15	**g4**	**♗e7**
16	**g5**	

The knight was already threatened with capture.

16	**...**	**fg**
17	**♘d7**	**♗d6**
18	**♘f6**	**♔c4**

and White resigned, as 19 ♘xh7 fails to 19 ... ♗e7. A beautiful example of the strength of a bishop in an open position with play on both wings.

Let us now examine the other side of the coin. The knight is often superior to the bishop when the position is of a more closed nature or when the bishop is restricted by its own pawns. It is here that the knight can exploit its ability to control squares of either colour, as our next example shows.

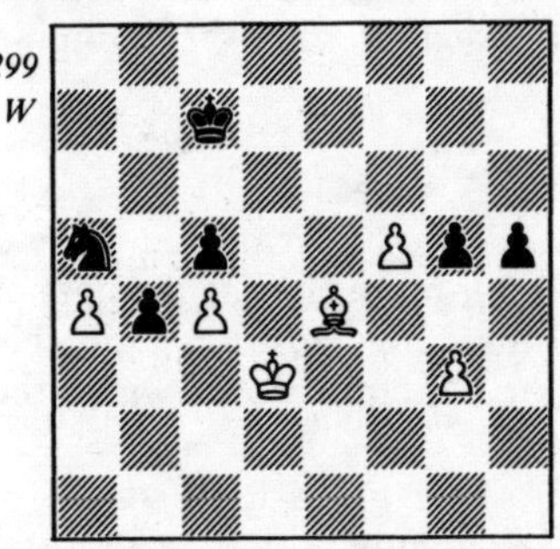

Kan-Keres 1955

This position occurred in the game Kan-Keres, Moscow 1955. At first sight it may seem that White's passed pawns, backed by his centralized bishop, give him a good game. However, on closer examination certain disadvantages appear. Firstly, both passed pawns are effectively blockaded and can be supported only by the bishop, as White's king is tied to the defence of the c-pawn. Secondly, the weakness of the black squares means that Black's king is threatening to occupy e5, when White's f-pawn is lost. If we add to all this the fact that Black also has two possible passed pawns, then the good points of White's position dwindle in importance.

We can conclude that Black's prospects are better, but is White's position lost? Although the situation is difficult, White's long-ranging bishop ensures him good defensive chances, but only if he plays with the utmost precision. The game continued as follows:

1 ♗d5?

This obvious move, protecting the c-pawn and freeing White's king, leads to the loss of the game. It is clear that White use his passed f-pawn as a counter-threat to the advance of Black's h-pawn. Once this pawn reaches h2 it will completely tie the bishop down, so White must play **1 ♗f3! h4 2 gh gh 3 ♗g4!** *(300)* stopping the h-pawn and threatening f6, with the following variations:

1) **3 ... ♔d6** if 3 ... ♘c6 4 f6 ♘e5+ 5 ♔c2, Black's knight dare not

300
B

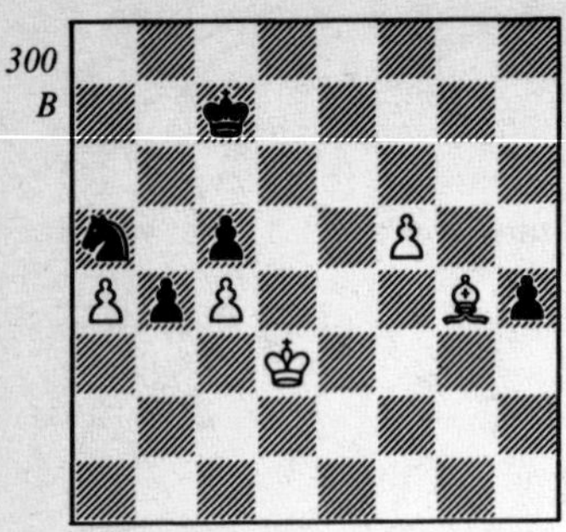

Kan-Keres 1955 (variation)

capture the bishop or the c-pawn **4 f6!** White must not allow this pawn to be blockaded, e.g. 4 ♗h3? ♔e5 5 ♗g4 ♔f6 6 ♗h3 ♔g5 with zugzwang **4 ... ♘c6 5 ♔c2** only this problem move saves White, as 5 ... ♘e5+ was threatened, winning the c-pawn **5 ... ♘e5 6 a5! ♘xc4** not of course 6 ... ♘xg4 7 f7 ♔e7 8 a6 winning, or 6 ... ♔c7 7 ♗e6 ♔b7 8 ♔b3 etc **7 a6 ♘b6 8 ♔b3** and if anyone has the advantage, it is not Black.

2) **3 ... ♔d8** in order to attack the f-pawn via e8 and f7 **4 f6 ♘c6** if 4 ... ♔e8 5 ♗e6 **5 ♗e6!** and it is difficult to see how Black can make any progress. Any attempt to attack the f-pawn or advance the h-pawn would allow White's a-pawn to advance.

This defensive plan may appear simple enough, but in practice it was not so easy to find, when one considers that 1 ♗d5? was the first move played after the time control. Despite long thought during the adjournment, Master Kan failed to grasp all the subtleties of the position. It is interesting and instructive to see how the text move leads to a loss.

1	**...**	**♔d6**
2	**f6**	**h4**
3	**gh**	**gh**

There is not much difference between this position and the one we examined above, except that the bishop is posted less effectively. Unless White wants to lose his f-pawn he has to allow Black's h-pawn to reach h2. The white king is still tied to the queenside because of Black's passed b-pawn.

4 f7

Passive defence is no good either. After 4 ♔d2 h3 5 ♔c2 h2 6 ♔d3 ♔d7! White is in zugzwang, as bishop moves lose the c-pawn. Nor would 4 ♔e4 save White, because Black's b-pawn then becomes too dangerous, e.g. 4 ... h3 5 ♔f3 (or 5 ♔f5 h2 when White loses after both 6 f7 ♔e7 7 ♔g6 ♔f8 and 6 ♔g6 ♘xc4 7 f7 ♘e5+) 5 ... b3 6 ♔g3 b2 7 ♗e4 ♔e6! 8 ♔xh2 ♔xf6 9 ♔g3 ♔e5 winning easily.

4	**...**	**♔e7**
5	**♗e6**	

So White has managed to hold up the h-pawn, but at the cost of an insecure position for his bishop. Black now wins the f-pawn.

5 ... ♘c6!

Threatening both 6 ... ♘e5 and 6 ... ♘d8.

6 ♗d5

Or 6 ♔e4 b3 7 ♔d3 b2 8 ♔c2

♘d4+ winning the bishop.

6 ... ♘e5+
7 ♔c2 ♘xf7

The beginning of the end, for if White exchanges pieces, Black's h-pawn queens first,stopping the a-pawn.

8 a5 ♘d6
9 a6

The attractive idea 9 ♗b7 ♘xb7? 10 a6 fails to 9 ... ♔d7 10 a6 ♔c7 etc.

9 ... ♘c8
10 ♗g2 ♔d6
11 ♔b3 ♔c7

White's a-pawn is now harmless and Black wins easily.

12 ♗b7 h3
13 ♔a4 h2

0-1

However, the knight is really seen at its best in blocked positions, when the bishop can find no scope for its long-ranging movement. This is especially the case when there are no points of attack in the enemy position. Diagram 301 offers us a good example of this.

301
B

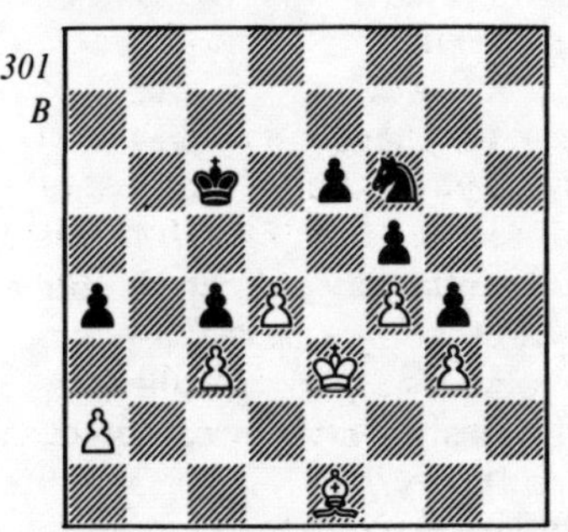

Henneberger-Nimzowitsch 1931

This position comes from the game Henneberger-Nimzowitsch, Winterthur 1931. White has the so called 'bad' bishop, restricted by its own pawns and unable to attack the enemy pawns. It must remain on e1 permanently to guard his c- and g-pawns against the threat of ... ♘e4. Contrast the complete freedom of Black's knight which can attack from various positions.

Nevertheless, despite all this, coupled with a grave weakness on the white squares, it is not easy for Black to exploit his positional advantages. The main reasons for this are that White is for the time being holding all his weak points and can use his king to prevent the entry of Black's king. Black must therefore think of a way of strengthening his position. The usual weapon in such situations is zugzwang. White's bishop can easily be tied down by ... ♘e4 but this knight then blocks the square needed for Black's king.

Careful consideration of the position produces a winning plan: if Black plays his knight to b1 via a3 then places his king on d5, White is in zugzwang, and the pawn ending is lost after ... ♗d2 because of the tempo move ... a3! This is the plan, then, but how can it be executed? The first moves are simple enough to understand:

1 ... ♘e4
2 ♔e2 ♔d5

Apparently Nimzowitsch has not yet seen the winnng idea, or

else he would play 2 ... ♔d6! 3 ♔e3 ♔d5 with a quicker win.

3	**♔e3**	**♔d6!**

He now realizes that there are problems if he immediately plays 3 ... ♘d6. After 4 ♗d2 ♘b5 5 ♗e1 ♘a3 6 ♗d2 ♘b1 (or 6 ... ♘c2+ 7 ♔e2 ♔e4 8 ♗c1 and the knight has no retreat) 7 ♗e1 Black is in zugzwang. If then 7 ... a3 8 ♗d2 ♘xd2 9 ♔xd2 ♔e4 10 ♔e2 draws, as Black no longer has the tempo move ... a3. Black must therefore bring about the same position with White to move. In other words he must lose a move by triangulating with his king (we already know that a knight cannot lose a move).

4	**♔e2**	**♔c6**
5	**♔e3**	**♔d5!**
6	**♔e2**	**♘d6**
7	**♔e3**	**♘b5**
8	**♗d2**	**♘a3**
9	**♗c1**	

If 9 ♗e1 Black has a choice between 9 ... ♘b1 10 ♗d2 ♘xd2 and 11 ... ♔e4, or 9 ... ♘c2+ and 10 ... ♘xe1, winning as we have already seen. So White has no alternative.

9	**...**	**♘b1**
10	**♗b2**	**a3**

Although this completely blocks in his own knight, the fact that White's bishop is immobilized in the corner is more than enough compensation. We now have a curious position which is almost a pawn ending and won by Black without great difficulty.

11	**♗a1** *(302)*	

Or 11 ♗c1 ♘xc3 12 ♗xa3 ♘xa2 winning easily.

302
B

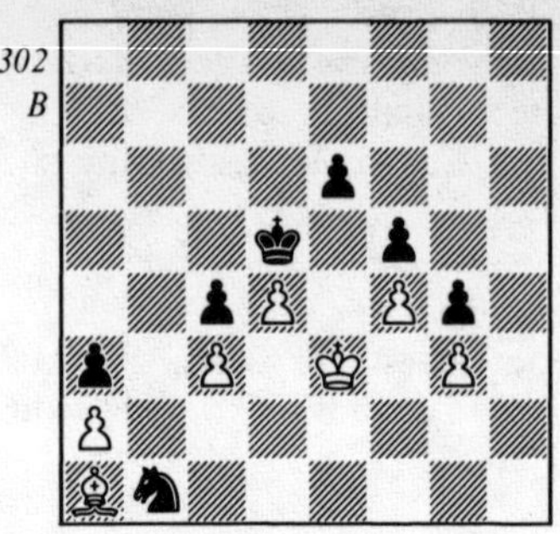

Henneberger-Nimzowitsch 1931

11	**...**	**♔d6!**

Black again manoeuvres to lose a move. White's king cannot do the same without allowing the knight in at d2, e.g. 12 ♔f2 ♘d2 13 ♔g2 ♘b3! etc.

12	**♔e2**	**♔c6**
13	**♔d1**	

The best chance. If 13 ♔e3 ♔d5 White is in zugzwang and loses at once after 14 ♔f2 (14 ♔e2 ♔e4) 14 ... ♘d2 and 15 ... ♘b3 or 15 ... ♘e4. The text move wins the knight, but allows the entry of Black's king.

13	**...**	**♔d5**
14	**♔c2**	**♔e4**
15	**♔xb1**	**♔f3** *(303)*
16	**♗b2!**	

The only way to keep the game alive, creating a passed a-pawn.

16	**...**	**ab!**

The bishop must be captured, as after 16 ... ♔xg3 17 ♗xa3 White could even win.

17	**a4**	**♔xg3**

303
W

Henneberger-Nimzowitsch 1931

18	**a5**	**♔h2!**

Black wants an easily won pawn ending, not the queen ending he would reach after 18 ... ♔xf4 19 a6 etc.

19	**a6**	**g3**
20	**a7**	**g2**
21	**a8♕**	**g1♕+**
22	**♔xb2**	**♕g2+!**

All of which had to be exactly calculated when Black blocked in his knight on b1.

23	**♕xg2+**	**♔xg2**
24	**♔a3**	**♔f3**
25	**♔b4**	**♔xf4**
26	**♔xc4**	**♔e3**
27	**d5**	**ed+**
28	**♔xd5**	**f4**

0-1

White's pawn reaches c7 but his king is wrongly placed for the draw. An excellent example of the strength of a knight in blocked positions.

This concludes our practical examples. We have obviously only shown the reader a small amount of the available material, but hope that he has now acquired the basic knowledge required for handling such endings with some confidence.

6 Knight Endings

In the fight against pawns, the knight usually cuts a poor figure, especially if the pawns are far apart. It takes at least three moves to cross the board and often finds a single pawn more than a match for it. Let us therefore begin with this aspect.

Knight against Pawn(s)

As already mentioned, the knight is not at its best when trying to stop pawns, and is sometimes helpless against a far-advanced pawn. Here are a few examples in which the knight is trying to stop a pawn without the help of the king:

304

It is clear that the knight's task is harder, the nearer the pawn is to the edge of the board, as was also the case with bishop endings. The reason for this is the same: against a rook's pawn the knight's defensive possibilities are halved, as it has only one side of the pawn to work on.

In the left half of diagram 304, we have the classic case of the knight being powerless against the rook's pawn, despite the nearness of its own king. White wins by **1 a6!** when the pawn cannot be stopped; 1 ... ♔c7 2 a7! Contrast this position with the one on the right. Against the knight's pawn Black can draw after **1 ♔e6 ♘g8 2 ♔f7 ♘h6+** 3 **♔g6 ♘g8** etc.

When the rook's pawn has reached the seventh rank, White wins if the black king is not near enough. In the left half of diagram 305, Black cannot prevent the loss of his knight.

305

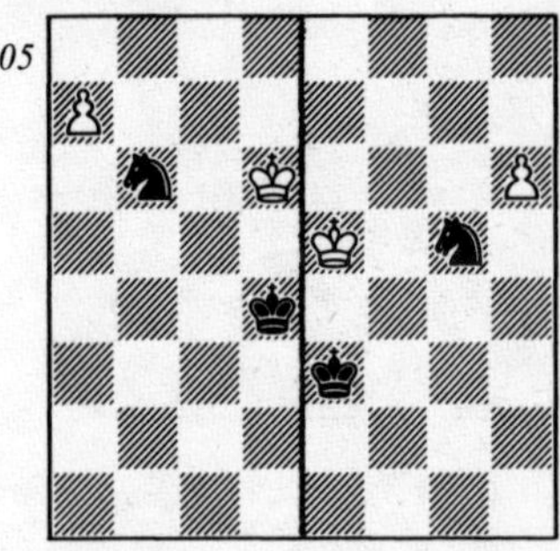

White plays **1 ♔c6 ♘a8 2 ♔b7**

winning. To draw, Black's king must be ready to occupy c8 or c7 as soon as White's king captures the knight.

However, if the pawn is not so far advanced, the knight can draw without the help of the king. For example, in the right half of diagram 305, White cannot win, for after **1 ♔f5 ♘h7 2 ♔g6 ♘f8+ 3 ♔g7 ♘e6+ 4 ♔f7 ♘g5+ 5 ♔g6** Black has the saving resource **5 ... ♘e6! 6 h7 ♘f8+** etc.

In practice, we usually meet positions in which the knight is far away from the pawn. The difficulty then lies in calculating whether the pawn can be stopped. If the pawn is on its own, matters are relatively simple, but if it is supported by the king, extremely complex situations can arise which demand exact calculation. Diagram 306 is a good example of this.

306

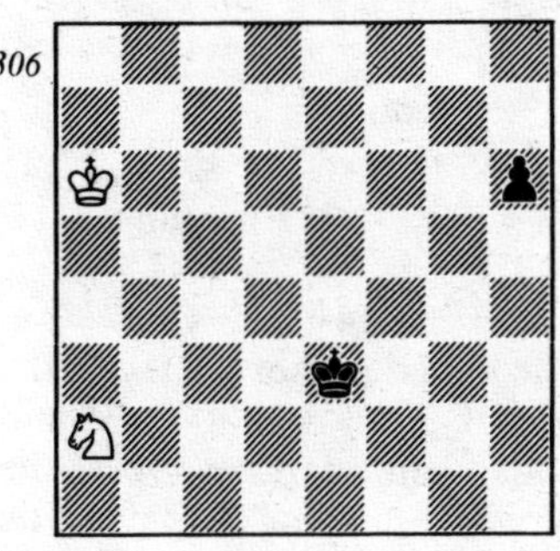

N.Grigoriev 1932

White's task is to stop the pawn. On an empty board, various knight routes are possible, but in the actual position the way is barred by the excellently posted black king. We know from diagram 305 that the knight can hold the game if it reaches f1 or g4 before the pawn reaches the seventh rank. As the presence of Black's king puts f1 out of the question, the white knight must look for ways of reaching g4.

How can this be done? Let us try 1 ♘c3 h5 2 ♘d5+ ♔f3 (it is well known that the king is best placed in diagonal opposition to the knight which then requires 3 moves before it can check him) 3 ♘c7 h4 4 ♘e6 ♔g4! 5 ♘c5 h3 6 ♘e4 h2 7 ♘f2+ ♔f3 8 ♘h1 ♔g2 and Black wins. White's only way to draw is as follows:

1	**♘b4!**	**h5**
2	**♘c6**	

We have already seen that 2 ♘d5+ ♔f3 wins for Black. If instead 2 ♘c2+ ♔e4 3 ♘e1 h4 4 ♘g2 h3 wins.

2	**...**	**♔e4**

Or 2 ... h4 3 ♘e5 and the knight reaches g4 because 3 ... ♔f4 allows 4 ♘g6+.

3	**♘a5!!**	

This bizarre knight move can only be understood in the context of the critical squares f1 and g4. From c4 the knight is excellently placed for reaching either square. The knight cannot reach g4 at once, as after 3 ♘d8 h4 4 ♘e6 ♔f5! 5 ♘d4+ ♔g4 6 ♘c2 ♔f4 Black wins.

3	**...**	**h4**

Black cannot prevent the knight reaching c4. If 3 ... ♔d4 (d3)

4 ♘c6 (+) follows, and if 3 ... ♔d5 4 ♘b3 and the knight reaches f1 via d2.

4 ♘c4

Reaching the ideal square and threatening to draw at once with 5 ♘d2+ and 6 ♘f1. If instead 4 ♘b3 Black wins by 4 ... ♔e3!

4 ... ♔f3!

Giving White the most trouble. If 4 ... h3 5 ♘d2+ and 6 ♘f1 draws, as we have seen.

5 ♘e5+

Precise play is still required. If 5 ♘d2+ ♔e2! 6 ♘e4 h3 7 ♘g3+ ♔f2 Black wins.

5 ... ♔g3

6 ♘c4 h3

If 6 ... ♔f2 then 7 ♘e5 is again played, and 6 ... ♔f4 allows 7 ♘d2 and 8 ♘f1.

7 ♘e3

and we have reached the drawing position seen in our analysis of diagram 305. A beautiful ending.

There is one further point worth mentioning about the struggle of knight versus rook's pawn. We saw from diagram 305 that our knight was powerless against a pawn on the seventh rank, providing that the enemy king was near and our king was too far away. If the enemy king is some distance away, the knight can prevent its approach and create surprising defensive possibilities. Diagram 307 shows us how this is done.

To stop the pawn, White's knight must gain a tempo by checking on e4 or e2. The following solution shows us which square White chooses, and why:

307

N.Grigoriev 1932

1 ♘f7!

It is clear that White cannot stop the pawn reaching the seventh rank, so he must keep open the option of playing to f2 or g3. Only from e4 can the knight do this. For this reason, 1 ♘g6 is wrong. After 1 ... h3 2 ♘f4 h2 3 ♘e2+ ♔d2! 4 ♘g3 ♔e1 and 5 ... ♔f2 Black wins easily.

1 ... h3

2 ♘g5

2 ♘d6 fails to 2 ... ♔d3! 3 ♘f5 ♔e2! 4 ♘g3+ ♔f2 winning.

2 ... h2

3 ♘e4+ ♔c2

The king dare not approach the pawn! If 3 ... ♔d3 4 ♘g3! and Black's king cannot cross the e-file without losing the pawn. His only routes would then be c2-d1-e1 or d4-e5-f4, but this would give White's king time to come nearer. We now see why the black king goes to c2: to gain a tempo in his journey to e1.

Black could also try 3 ... ♔d4 in

order to approach by the other route. White's knight would then go to f2, again preventing the immediate approach of the black king (White's king can stop him taking the d5-e6-f5 route). Equally hopeless would then be 4 ... ♔c3 5 ♔d6 ♔d2 6 ♔e5 ♔e2 7 ♘h1 ♔f3 8 ♔d4 ♔g2 9 ♔e3 ♔xh1 10 ♔f2 stalemate.

The above variations demonstrate that the knight can successfully hold back the enemy king until its own king comes nearer.

4 ♘g3!

It is clear that 4 ♘f2 would allow Black's king to approach by 4 ... ♔d2 5 ♔d6 ♔e2 6 ♘h1 ♔f3 winning.

4 ... ♔d1
5 ♔d6 ♔e1
6 ♔e5 ♔f2
7 ♔f4 draws.

White's king manages to guard the knight. Note that White would have lost if his king had been one square further away in the original position.

Surprisingly enough, the knight is not always on the defending side in such positions. When the enemy king is unfavourably placed in front of his own pawn, there are a few typical positions which are won for the side with the knight. Consider diagram 308.

In both positions White has a mating attack. On the left he wins by **1 ♔c2! ♔a1 2 ♘c1 a2 3 ♘b3** mate. On the right, we have a more complicated form of the same mate: **1 ♔f3!** but not 1 ♔f2

308

♔h1 and White is in zugzwang **1 ... ♔h1 2 ♔f2 ♔h2** or 2 ... h2 3 ♘g3 mate **3 ♘c3 ♔h1 4 ♘e4 ♔h2! 5 ♘d2 ♔h1 6 ♘f1 h2 7 ♘g3** mate. Of course, such positions are rare, but they must be known.

When the knight faces two connected passed pawns, everything depends on the placing of the pieces. When the pawns have reached the sixth rank, the knight can only draw if it is near the pawns and if its own king is in front of them. Our next example illustrates this.

309

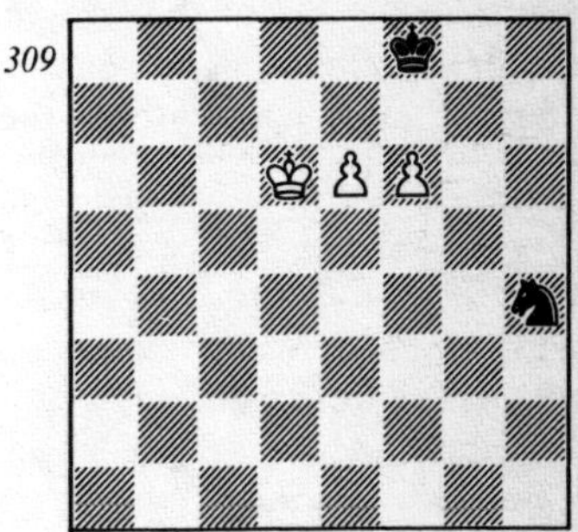

Although the pawns look most dangerous, Black to move can draw by careful defence. White to move would win at once by 1 ♔d7, but even with the move Black's position is difficult. Play goes:

1 ... ♘g6!

The only move. Bad are 1 ... ♘f5+ 2 ♔d7 followed by 3 e7+ and 1 ... ♚e8 2 f7+! ♚f8 3 e7+ ♚xf7 4 ♔d7, both winning. Black also loses after 1 ... ♘f3 2 f7! when he is in zugzwang, e.g. 2 ... ♚g7 3 ♔e7 wins or 2 ... ♘d4 3 e7+ ♚xf7 4 ♔d7 wins.

2 ♔d7

If 2 f7 ♘e7 draws. Or 2 e7+ ♚e8 or 2 ... ♚f7 or 2 ... ♘xe7 all draw.

2 ... ♘e5+

3 ♔d8

Or 3 ♔c7 ♘g4 etc.

3 ... ♘c6+

4 ♔c7 ♘d4

5 ♔d7

Or 5 e7+ ♚e8 6 ♔d6 ♘f5+ and 7 ... ♘xe7 draws.

5 ... ♘xe6

6 ♔xe6 ♚e8 draws.

If the pawns are not so far advanced, the knight's task is easier. For instance, the knight can usually defend against pawns on the fifth rank, even without the help of the king.

310

White plays **1 ♘b3!** stopping the pawns after both **1 ... e3 2 ♘d4** and **1 ... f3 2 ♘d2 f2 3 ♘f1** etc.

A position by Chekhover shows us that the knight can sometimes produce near miracles:

311

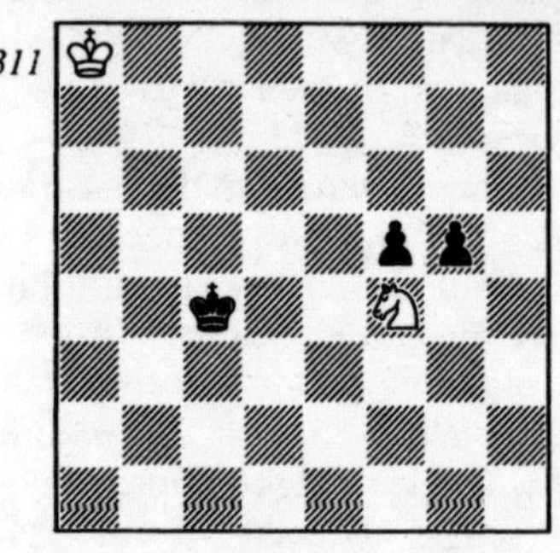

Chekhover

White's position seems hopeless, but he saves himself by the surprising manoeuvre **1 ♘e6! g4 2 ♘g7 f4** if 2 ... g3 3 ♘xf5 g2 4 ♘e3+ **3 ♘h5! f3 4 ♘f6 g3** and now 4 ... f2 fails to 5 ♘xg4 f1♛ 6 ♘e3+ **5 ♘e4 g2 6 ♘d2+** and **7 ♘xf3** draws. A remarkable defence, helped admittedly by the unfavourable position of the black king.

Against isolated pawns the knight usually defends badly and needs the help of the king, especially if the pawns are far apart. There is no space for examples of such positions, but we can consider the case of three connected pawns against knight. The knight draws, provided the pawns have not reached the fifth rank, as we can see in our next example.

312
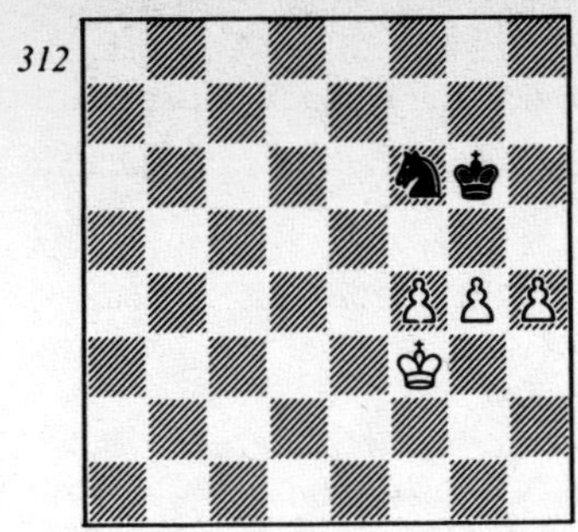

White to move wins because he can play his pawns to the fifth rank. Black to move draws by skilful use of his knight. Let us analyse both these possibilities:

1 f5+

White must not allow Black to blockade the pawns, e.g. 1 g5 ♘d5! 2 ♔e4 ♘e7 3 ♔e5 ♔h5! 4 f5 ♔xh4 5 ♔f6 (or 5 g6 ♔g5 6 g7 ♘g8 etc. Or 5 f6 ♘g6+ 6 ♔f5 ♔h5 etc) 5 ... ♘d5+ 6 ♔g6 ♘e7+ drawing.

1 ... ♔g7
2 g5 ♘d5
3 h5

All pawns are now on the fifth rank and White wins easily.

3 ... ♘c3

If 3 ... ♔f7 4 h6 ♘c3 5 h7 ♔g7 6 g6 wins.

4 ♔f4 ♘e2+
5 ♔e5 ♘g3
6 f6+ ♔g8
7 h6 ♘h5
8 g6

and White wins, e.g. 8 ... ♘g3 9 h7+ ♔h8 10 f7 and one of the pawns queens.

With Black to move, White cannot advance his pawns as he would like:

1 ... ♘d5
2 h5+

Or 2 f5+ ♔f6! 3 ♔e4 ♘c3+ 4 ♔e3 (if 4 ♔d4 or 4 ♔d3, the simplest is 4 ... ♘d1 threatening 5 ... ♘f2) 4 ... ♔e5 5 h5 ♘e4 6 h6 ♘g5 and White can make no progress.

2 ... ♔h6!

The king must blockade the furthest advanced pawn. For instance, 2 ... ♔f6 loses 3 h6 ♔g6 4 g5 ♘e7 5 ♔g4 ♘f5 6 h7! etc.

3 ♔e4

If 3 ♔g3 ♘e3 4 ♔h4 ♘g2+, or here 4 ♔h3 ♘d5, both drawing.

3 ... ♘c3+

This line is given, as it is more intstructive than the simpler 3 ... ♘f6+ 4 ♔f5 ♘d5 when White can do nothing, e.g. 5 ♔e5 ♘e3 etc.

4 ♔e5

There is nothing better. If 4 ♔f5 ♘d5 we have the line given in the last note. If 4 ♔d4 (d3) ♘d1 and the threat is 5 ... ♘f2.

4 ... ♘d1
5 ♔f6

Or 5 g5+ ♔xh5 6 f5 ♔xg5 7 f6 ♔g6 8 ♔e6 ♘e3 9 f7 ♔g7 10 ♔e7 ♘f5+ draws.

5 ... ♘e3
6 g5+ ♔xh5
7 g6

Or 7 f5 ♘g4+ winning the g-pawn.

7 ... ♘g4+

and Black draws, e.g. 8 ♔g7 ♘h6 9 ♔h7 ♘f5 10 g7 ♘xg7 11 ♔xg7 ♔g4. Or 8 ♔f7 ♘h6+ 9 ♔g7 ♘g4

10 f5 ♔g5 etc.

For further examples of knight against pawns, the reader must refer to more specialized volumes. Let us just consider a few exceptional positions in which White cannot force a win with a whole knight up:

313

In the left half of the diagram, White has a knight and a pawn extra, but he cannot win. If the knight moves, the pawn is lost, and if the white king guards the pawn, it is stalemate.

When analysing diagram 275, we met another position in which knight and pawn fail to win against a bare king. Here is the position once again:

314
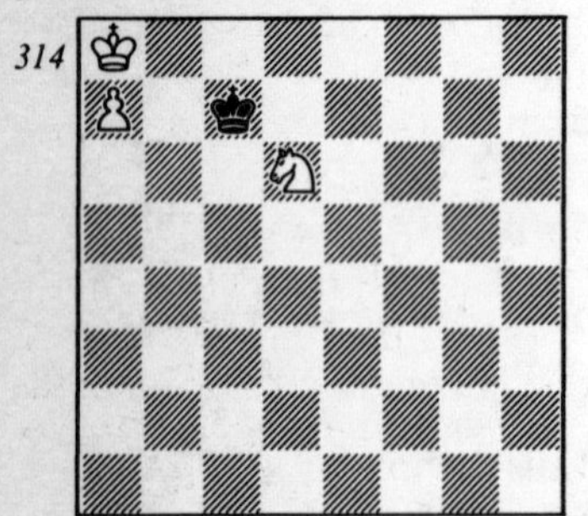

White to move can never force Black's king away from c8 and c7. However, Black to move is in zugzwang and loses. As a rule, in such positions Black must place the king on a square of the same colour as that occupied by the knight, with White to move. As the knight cannot lose a tempo, there is no way of handling the move over to Black.

On the right of diagram 313, we have a most unusual drawing position. Black's king cannot be driven from the corner. After **1 ♘f7 ♔g8** then **2 ♔e7** is stalemate. Of course, if the position is moved from the side of the board, White wins easily. For instance, moving it one square to the left, White wins by **1 ♘c7+ ♔f8 2 ♔d7 ♔g8 3 ♔e7 ♔h8 4 ♘d5 ♔g8 5 ♔e8 ♔h8 6 ♘f6! gf 7 ♔f7** etc.

Finally, it is useful to note that, with knight and pawn against king, when one's own king is far away, the pawn is best guarded by the knight from behind. The enemy king can then never capture the knight without allowing the pawn to queen. Consider, for example, this position:

315

As Black threatens 1 ... ♔b3, the knight must move away. Only **1 ♘b2! ♔b3 2 a4** wins whereas both 1 ♘b6? ♔b3 2 a4 ♔b4 3 ♔d2 ♔a5 and 1 ♘c5? ♔c3 2 ♔e2 ♔c4 3 ♘d3 ♔b3 lead to a draw.

Knight and Pawn against Pawn

Material advantage such as this usually means an easy win for the stronger side. Nevertheless there are a number of positions in which a successful defence is possible. Let us examine a few of the more interesting ones.

316

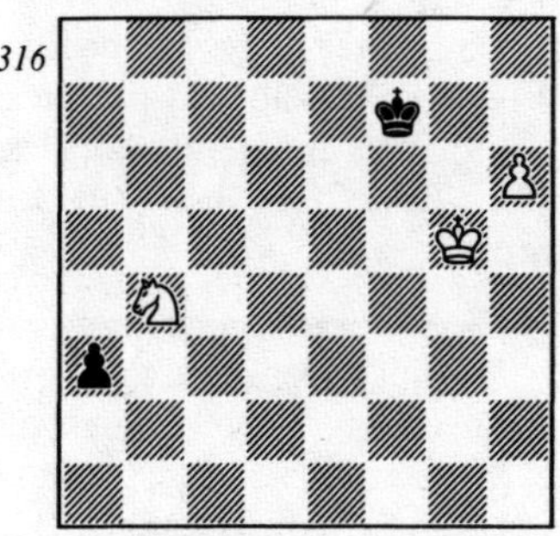

N.Grigoriev 1933

Positions similar to this are quite common in knight endings. Despite his extra knight, White has difficulty in winning, mainly because his rook's pawn cannot be queened without the help of the knight which is apparently tied down on the queenside. White loses his own pawn if his king goes over to the queenside, so the only winning chance lies in stalemating Black's king, then bringing his knight over to mate him. As the following solution shows, the timing is vital:

1 ♘a2!

In order to win, White must reach a position with Black's king on g8, his own king on g6 and knight on b4. He can then play 1 h7+ ♔h8 2 ♘c6 followed by mate in 2. Black on the other hand must bring about the same position with himself to move, when he can play 1 ... ♔h8 stopping White advancing his h-pawn with gain of time. In the diagram position, for instance, Black is threatening to draw by 1 ... ♔g8!, e.g. 2 ♔g6 ♔h8 and White's knight needs to be on a2. Hence the reason for the text move, preparing 3 ♘b4 in the above line, winning as we have seen.

1 ... ♔f8
2 ♔f6!

Not of course 2 ♔g6 ♔g8 and if now 3 ♘b4 ♔h8 4 ♘c6 a2 5 ♘e5 a1♕ 6 ♘f7+ ♔g8 7 h7+ ♔f8 and the black queen controls the queening square of the h-pawn.

2 ... ♔g8
3 ♔g6 ♔h8
4 ♘b4 ♔g8
5 h7+ ♔h8
6 ♘c6

with mate in 2 moves.

Occasionally there are positions in which the enemy king is attacking both the knight and the pawn, and White cannot free his pieces, as in our next example.

This position occurred in a match game between Blackburne

317
B

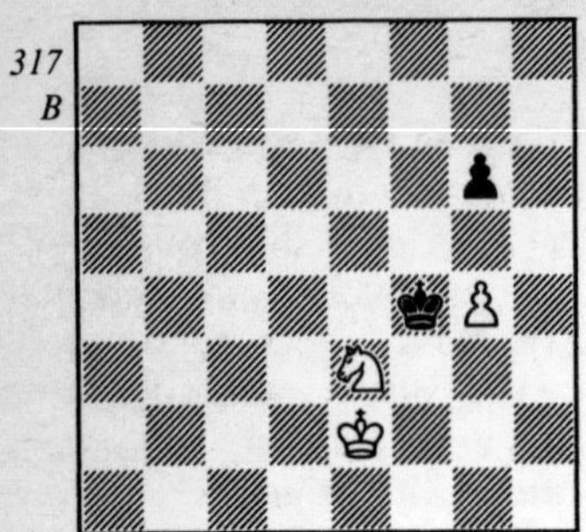

Blackburne-Zukertort 1881

and Zukertort in 1881. The actively placed king can hold the position by maintaining his attack on the pawn. As White can neither advance the pawn nor move the knight, his only chance is to attack Black's pawn with his king. However, this fails against the correct defence, as follows:

1 ... ♔g3!

Black must stop White's king going to f2 and he dare not move his own pawn, e.g. 1 ... g5 2 ♔d3 ♔f3 3 ♔d4 ♔f4 4 ♔d5! ♔xe3 5 ♔e5 wins. Or if 1 ... ♔e4 then 2 ♘g2 and 3 ♔f2 wins easily. In the same position with White to move, he plays 1 ♔f2! practically forcing 1 ... g5 (1 ... ♔e4 2 ♘g2) when 2 ♔e2 ♔g3 3 ♔d3 wins as above.

2 ♔d1 ♔f3!

Black must always take the opposition when his king plays to the f-file. For example, both 2 ... ♔f2 and 2 ... ♔f4 allow White to take the opposition with 3 ♔d2 ♔f3 4 ♔d3 ♔f4 5 ♔d4 ♔f3 6 ♔e5! ♔xe3 7 ♔f6 ♔f4 8 g5 winning.

3 ♔d2 ♔f2

Also sufficient is the diagonal opposition, for after 3 ... ♔f4 4 ♔e2 ♔g3! we are back where started. After the text move, Black has no need to fear 4 ♘f5 ♔f3 5 ♘h6 because of 5 ... ♔f4 and 6 ... ♔g5 etc.

4 ♔d3 ♔f3
5 ♔d4 ♔f4!

and White can make no progress. After 6 ♔d5 ♔xe3 7 ♔e5 ♔f3 White is forced to draw with 8 ♔f6, as 8 g5 even loses to 8 ... ♔g4 9 ♔f6 ♔h5.

This resource is worth noting, as it is often possible in practical play, and saves apparently hopeless games. Take this position for example:

318

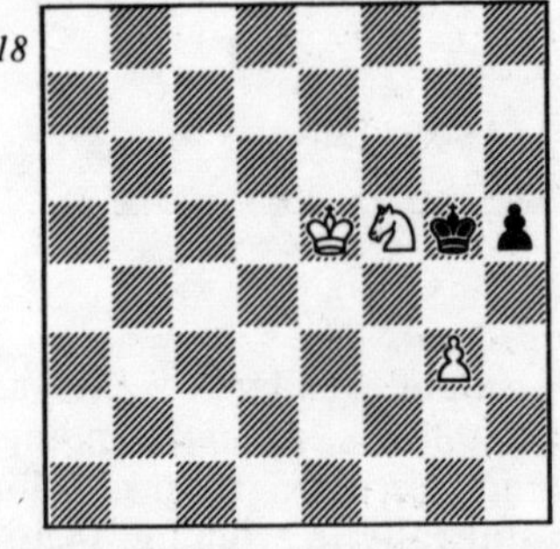

White to move cannot win, e.g. 1 ♔e6 ♔g6! 2 ♔e5 ♔g5 3 ♔e4 ♔g4 draws. Or 1 ♘e3 h4! 2 g4 h3 etc. If Black has the move, White wins easily of course.

Now that we have seen these two positions, we are prepared for our next beautiful study.

White can capture Black's

L.Prokes 1946

remaining pawn, but his own pawn is threatened by 1 ... ♔f2. As White's king cannot guard the pawn in time, the knight must do this job, giving us the following interesting play:

1 e4!

After 1 ♘xe6 ♔f2 2 e4 ♔e3 Black draws, e.g. 3 e5 ♔e4. Or 3 ♘g5 ♔f4. Or 3 ♘c5 ♘d4. The black king must now chase the pawn, as 1 ... e5 fails to 2 ♘d5 ♔f2 3 ♔b2 ♔f3 4 ♘f6 etc.

1 ... ♔f2
2 ♘d5!

The point of this fine move is clear, if we think back to our solution to diagram 317. If 2 ♘b5 ♔e3 3 ♘c3 then Black wins the opposition after 3 ... ♔d3! 4 ♔b2 ♔d2 5 ♔b3 ♔d3 6 ♔b4 ♔d4 with a draw similar to the one already seen. The text move guards the important e3 square, stopping Black's king reaching the queenside so quickly.

2 ... ♔f3

Or 2 ... ♔e2 3 ♘f6 ♔d3 4 e5 ♔d4 5 ♘d7 etc.

3 ♘c3 ♔e3
4 ♔a2!

As we saw in our analysis to diagram 317, White must take the opposition, if he is to win. From a2 White's king eyes the squares b2 and b3, corresponding to Black's d2 (d4) and d3 squares. It is clear that Black draws after both 4 ♔b2 ♔d2! and 4 ♔b1 ♔d3!

4 ... ♔d4
5 ♔b2! ♔d3

If 5 ... ♔e3 6 ♔c2 wins. Or 5 ... ♔c4 6 ♔c2 ♔d4 7 ♔d2 e5 (7 ... ♔c4 8 ♘e2) 8 ♔c2 ♔e3 9 ♔b3 ♔d3 10 ♔b4 ♔d4 11 ♔b5! ♔xc3 12 ♔c5 winning.

6 ♔b3 ♔d4
7 ♔b4 ♔d3
8 ♔c5 ♔xc3
9 e5 and
10 ♔d6 wins.

If the defending side has more than one pawn, very complex situations can arise which are impossible to classify. Usually the extra piece should guarantee the win, but not without difficulty, as the following interesting position shows:

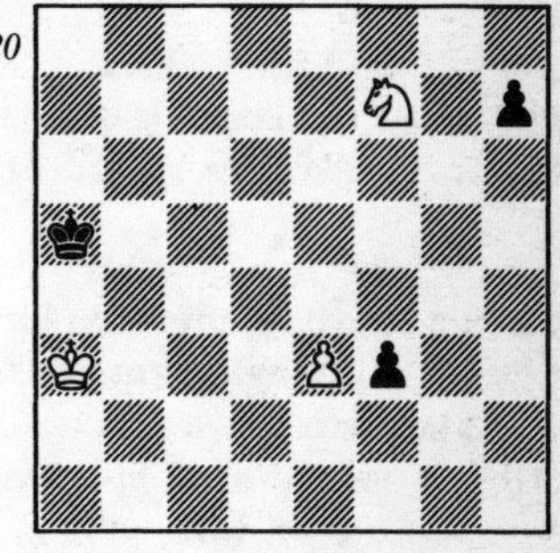

L.Kubbel

It is scarcely credible that White can win, as his knight and king seem badly placed for stopping Black's f-pawn. However, Black's king is badly placed too, and White uses this factor to win in the following instructive fashion:

1 ♘d6!

It is clear that the knight must check on c4 if it is to stop the pawn, but it is important to choose the correct route. For instance, 1 ♘e5 only draws after 1 ... ♔b5! 2 ♘xf3 (or 2 ♘g4 ♔c4 3 ♘f2 ♔c3 4 ♔a4 ♔d2 5 e4 ♔e3 draws) 2 ... ♔c4 3 e4 h5 4 ♔b2 h4 5 ♔c2 (or 5 e5 ♔d5 etc) 5 ... h3 6 ♔d2 h2 7 ♘xh2 ♔d4 and the last pawn falls. The text move stops 1 ... ♔b5 and threatens to win at once by 2 ♘e4 followed by 3 ♔b3.

1 ... f2
2 ♘c4+ ♔b5
3 ♘d2 f1♕!

To create counterplay by making a path for his king. If he tries to cling to his material, both pawns eventually fall, e.g. 3 ... h5 4 ♔b3 h4 5 ♔c3 h3 7 ♘f1 etc.

4 ♘xf1 ♔c4
5 ♔b2 ♔d3
6 ♔c1 ♔e2!

The only chance. If 6 ... h5 7 ♔d1 h4 8 ♔e1 h3 9 ♔f2 wins easily.

7 e4 ♔xf1

Black's play seems to have succeeded, for if White queens his pawn, Black's h-pawn reaches h2 with a book draw. However, White has not yet finished.

8 ♔d2! h5

Or 8 ... ♔f2 9 e5 h5 10 e6 h4 11 e7 h3 12 e8♕ h2 13 ♕e2+ ♔g1 14 ♔e3 h1♕ 15 ♕f2 mate.

9 ♔e3 ♔g2

Black loses his pawn after 9 ... h4 10 ♔f3, and if 9 ... ♔g1 10 ♔f3! (not 10 ♔f4? ♔g2 11 ♔g5 ♔g3! drawing) 10 ... ♔h2 11 e5 wins.

10 e5 h4
11 e6 h3
12 e7 h2
13 e8♕ h1♕

White's subtle play has given him a well known winning queen endgame.

14 ♕g6+ ♔h3

If 14 ... ♔f1 15 ♕f5+ ♔g2 16 ♕g4+ transposes to the main line, and 14 ... ♔h2 15 ♔f2 leads to mate.

15 ♕h5+ ♔g2
16 ♕g4+ ♔h2

Or 16 ... ♔f1 17 ♕e2+ ♔g1 18 ♕f2 mate.

17 ♔f2 wins.

A wonderful ending!

We could quote many similar positions, but feel that the reader now has sufficient ideas of how to handle knight versus pawns endings. Let us turn at once to positions in which both sides possess a knight.

Knight and Pawn(s) against Knight

We shall begin with knight and one pawn against knight. This ending is usually drawn, as the knight can either give itself up for the pawn, or else blockade it. However, if the pawn is far advanced and supported by the king, there are good winning

prospects for the stronger side. Consider our next example.

321

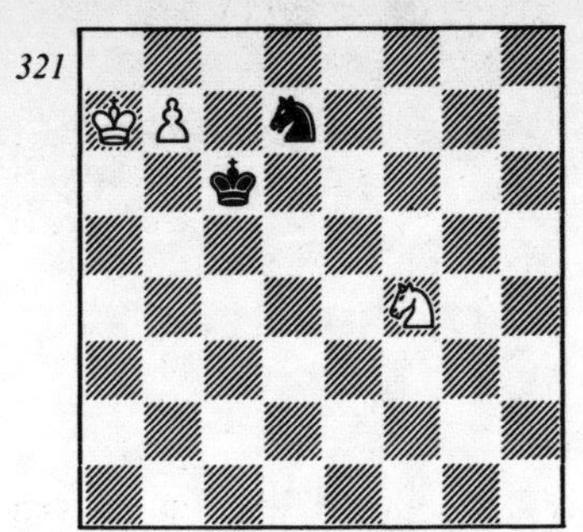

J.Kling 1867

This study is over a hundred years old but has permanent instructional value. White wins as follows:

1 ♘g6

The black knight must be driven away from its control of the pawn's queening square, and White now threatens 2 ♘e5+ or 2 ♘f8 winning immediately. Also possible is 1 ♘e6 ♔d5! 2 ♘f8 etc, transposing.

1 ... ♔d5!

Black prepares to answer 2 ♘f8 with 2 ... ♘e5, so his king must not go to c7 or b5 where will be checked by the new queen.

Also unsatisfactory is 1 ... ♔c5 2 ♘f8 ♘e5 3 ♔a8 ♘c6 4 ♘e6+ and 5 ♘d8.

2 ♘f8 ♘e5

3 ♔b6

Even simpler 3 ♔a8 ♘c6 4 ♘d7 planning ♘b6-c8-a7, 4 ... ♔d6 (4 ... ♔e6 5 ♘b6 ♔d6 6 ♘c8+ ♔c7 7 ♘a7 ♘b8 8 ♘b5+ etc) 5 ♘b6 ♔c7 6 ♘d5+ and 7 ♘b4 wins.

3 ... ♘c6

4 ♔c7

The composer's solution was a little slower, as follows: 4 ♘d7 ♔d6 5 ♘e5! ♘b8 6 ♔a7 ♔c7 7 ♘c4 ♘c6+ (or 7 ... ♘d7 8 ♘b6 ♘b8 9 ♘d5+) 8 ♔a8 ♘b8 9 ♘b6 ♘a6 (or 9 ... ♘c6 10 ♘d5+ and 11 ♘b4 wins) 10 ♘d5+ followed by 11 ♔a7 or 11 ♘b4 winning.

4 ... ♘b4

Or 4 ... ♔c5 5 ♘e6+ ♔d5 (5 ... ♔b5 6 ♘d4+) 6 ♘d8 ♘b4 7 ♔b6 wins.

5 ♘d7 ♘c6

After king moves or 5 ... ♘a6+, then 6 ♔b6 wins.

6 ♘e5! ♘b4

7 ♔b6 wins.

Black's task is far easier if his king is in front of the pawn. In this case he can hope to save the game, even if the remaining pieces are favourably placed for White. Diagram 322 gives us an example of this.

322

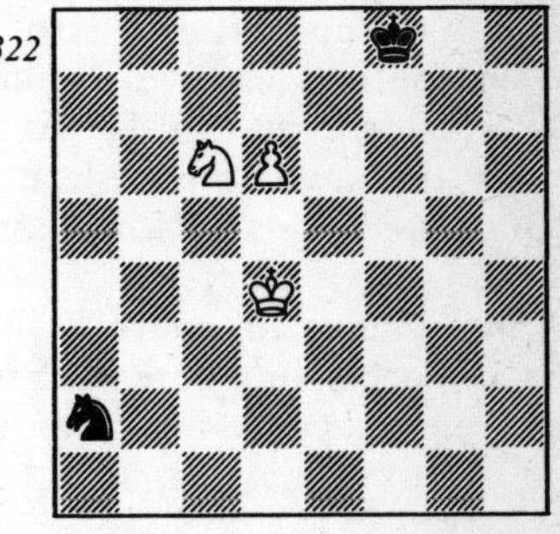

Y.Averbakh 1956

Despite the fact that Black's

knight is badly placed and White's king and knight can support the pawn, it was thought that Black could draw.

1 ... ♔e8
2 ♔d5 ♔d7

Not of course 2 ... ♘c3+ 3 ♔e6 winning at once.

The original solution, now known to be cooked, ran: **3 ♘e5+ ♔c8**. The only defence. Other moves lose to 4 ♔e6, whereas now White cannot play 4 ♔c6 because of 4 ... ♘b4+ **4 ♘d3**. This offers more chances than 4 ♔e6 ♘b4 5 d7+ ♔c7 6 ♔e7 ♘d5+, or here 6 ♘f7 ♘c6, both drawing. **4 ... ♘c3+!** If 4 ... ♔d7? 5 ♘c5+ ♔c8! 6 d7+ ♔c7 7 ♔e6 ♘b4 (or 7 ... ♘c3 8 ♘b7) 8 ♘a6+! ♘xa6 7 ♔e7 wins. **5 ♔c6 ♘e4 6 d7+ ♔d8 7 ♘e5 ♘g5** with a clear draw.

3 ♘b8+!

The point is that 3 ... ♔c8 4 ♔e6 ♘b4 5 d7+ ♔c7 (5 .... ♔d8 6 ♔d6) 6 ♘a6+! ♘xa6 7 ♔e7 and finito!

Like the bishop, the knight has most trouble against the rook's pawn, which can be attacked from one side only. This gives White good winning chances if his king supports the pawn from the front, as illustrated in the following interesting study by Réti.

White would, of course, win easily if Black's king were further away from the pawn, or if it were Black to move, e.g. 1 ... ♔b4 2 ♔b6 ♔c4 3 ♘c3! ♘d6 4 ♔c7 ♔c5 5 a7 winning. The problem, then, is how to hand the move over to

323

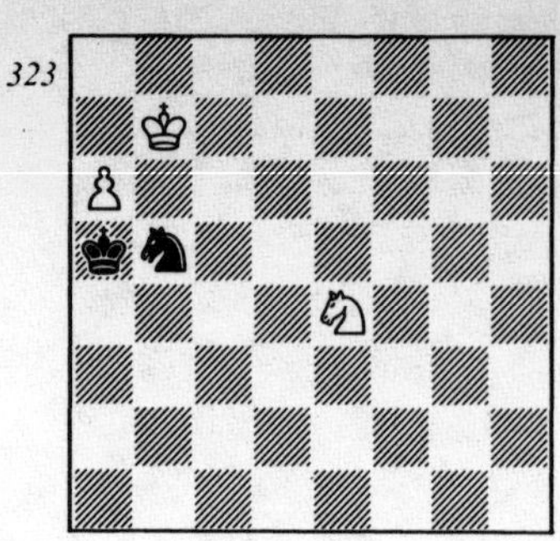

R.Réti 1929

Black. There is clearly no waiting move available, so the following instructive manoeuvre is both forced and forcing:

1 ♘c5!

The only move, as White's pawn must be protected against the threat of 1 ... ♘d6 and 2 ... ♘c8+ drawing.

1 ... ♔b4

After 1 ... ♘d6+ White would triangulate with his king by 2 ♔c7! ♘b5+ 3 ♔c6 ♘a7+ 4 ♔b7 ♘b5 5 ♘e4! reaching the original position with Black to move.

2 ♔b6 ♘d6
3 ♘e4!

Driving the black knight from its key post. If the knight is taken, then 4 a7 wins.

3 ... ♘c8+
4 ♔c7!

Care is still required. If 4 ♔b7 ♔b5! zugzwangs White and draws, e.g. 5 ♘c3+ ♔a5. Or 5 ♘f6 ♘d6+ 6 ♔a7 ♘c8+ etc. After the text move, 4 ... ♘a7 loses to 5 ♔b7 ♘b5 6 ♔b6 ♔c4 7 ♘c3!, so

Black's reply is forced.

4 ... ♔b5

Black loses more quickly after 4 ... ♔a5 5 ♘c5 ♘a7 (or 5 ... ♘b6 6 a7 winning) 6 ♔b7 ♘b5 7 ♘e4! etc.

5 ♔b7 ♔a5
6 ♘c5 ♘d6+
7 ♔c7 ♘b5+
8 ♔c6 ♘a7+

Or 8 ... ♔b4 9 ♘e4 ♘a7+ (if 9 ... ♔a5 10 ♔b7 etc) 10 ♔b7 ♘b5 11 ♔b6 wins.

9 ♔b7! ♘b5
10 ♘e4!

and we have reached the original position with Black to move, which we have already demonstrated as a win. A very fine study.

The ending of knight and pawn against knight and pawn is usually drawn. Wins are possible only if one side a definite advantage such as an unstoppable passed pawn, better piece placing, chances of trapping or stalemating an enemy piece etc. Rather than deal with such unusual situations, let us consider a position in which White has a knight and pawn against knight and two pawns. It is difficult to generalize about such positions, as everything depends upon the placing of the pieces. If the stronger side has a passed pawn supported by the pieces on one wing, whilst the other pawns are on the opposite wing, winning prospects are good, as they are with two connected passed pawns. However, if all the pawns and pieces are on the same wing, the weaker side has drawing chances, despite the fact that knight endings give the stronger side more opportunity of exploiting advantages than is the case with other pieces.

324
B

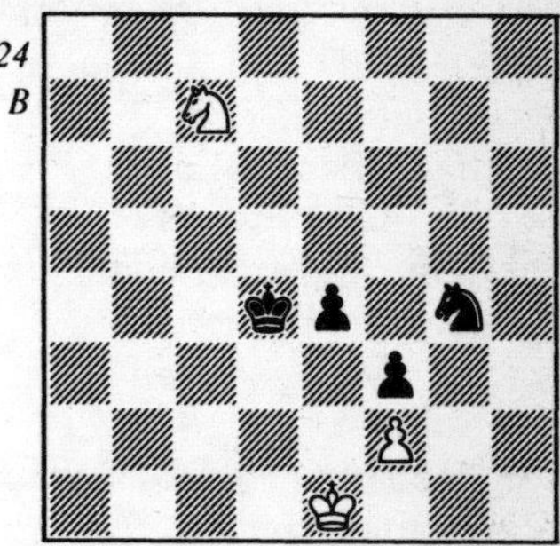

Goldenov-Kan 1946

In this position, all the pawns are together and the white king is favourably placed in front of them. White's only problem is his badly placed knight, but this should not be enough to give Black a win.

1 ... e3

Black makes his last attempt before White's knight returns to the fray, and sets White tricky problems.

2 fe+

Also possible is 2 ♘e6+ ♔e5 (or 2 ... ♔d5 3 ♘f4+ and 4 fe) 3 ♘g5 ef+ 4 ♔f1 ♔f4 5 ♘xf3! ♔g3 6 ♔e2, and it is difficult to see what Black can do.

2 ... ♔e4!

Finely played. 2 ... ♔xe3 allows 3 ♘d5+, whereas now White is in zugzwang.

3 ♔f1! ♘xe3+

4 ♔f2 ♘d1+

Or 4 ... ♘g4+ 5 ♔g3! drawing.

5 ♔e1?

This mistake costs White the game. He could draw by 5 ♔g3! f2 (if 5 ... ♔e3 6 ♘d5+ ♔e2 7 ♘f4+) 6 ♔g2 ♔e3 7 ♘d5+ ♔e2 8 ♘f4+ etc. Even 5 ♔f1 f2 6 ♔g2, or here 5 ... ♔f4 6 ♘d5+ ♔g3 7 ♔e1! would hold the position.

5 ... f2+!

This move was completely overlooked by White.

6 ♔e2 ♔f4

0-1

If 7 ♘d5+ (e6+) Black places White in zugzwang by 7 ... ♔g3, e.g. 7 ♘d5+ ♔g3 8 ♔f1 ♔f3 followed by mate.

Before going over to further practical examples of knight endings, we must mention an endgame which has little practical value but about which the reader should know something: two knights against a pawn. It is well known that two knights alone cannot force mate because of the danger of stalemate. As the pawn removes this danger, in certain positions a win is possible.

A great deal of research has been done on this ending, in particular by the study composer Troitsky, but we do not intend to go into the matter too deeply here. We shall give one diagram to illustrate the main principles to be followed.

It is clear that Black's pawn must be blockaded by a knight until the last possible minute, or

325

else it will simply push forward and sacrifice itself, when the two remaining knights cannot mate. We are left with the important question of on which square the pawn must be stopped. In diagram 325 we have drawn the line which the pawn must not have crossed if White is to win. If the pawn is behind this line White always wins, but if the pawn has advanced further White can only win with his pieces favourably placed. All this assumes, of course, that Black's king cannot lift blockade of the pawn by attacking a knight. Let us now see how play might go from the diagram:

1 ... ♔b5!

We quote Chekhover's analysis. The text move gives White the most problems as the following variations show:

1) 1 ... ♔b7 2 ♘c4 ♔a6 3 ♔c6 ♔a7 4 ♘d6 ♔a6 5 ♘b7 ♔a7 6 ♘bc5 ♔b8 7 ♔d7 ♔a7 8 ♔c7 ♔a8 9 ♘b4 d3 10 ♘c6 d2 11 ♘d7 d1♛ 12 ♘b6 mate.

2) 1 ... ♔a7 2 ♘c4 ♔b7 (or 2 ... ♔a6 3 ♔c6 as above) 3 ♘c5+!

♔a7 (or 3 ... ♔b8 4 ♘e5 etc) 4 ♔c7 d3 5 ♘e5 d2 6 ♘c6+ and mate in 2 moves.

3) 1 ... ♔a6 2 ♔c7! ♔b5 3 ♔b7 ♔a5 4 ♔c6 ♔a6 (or 4 ... ♔a4 5 ♔b6, as in the next variation) 5 ♘c4 transposing into variation 1.

4) 1 ... ♔a5 2 ♔c6 ♔a4 3 ♔b6 ♔a3 4 ♔b5 ♔a2 5 ♔b4 ♔a1 6 ♘c4 ♔a2 7 ♔a4 ♔b1 8 ♔b3 ♔a1 9 ♔c2 ♔a2 10 ♘b4+ ♔a1 11 ♘a3 d3+ 12 ♔b3 d2 13 ♘bc2 mate.

2 ♔c7 ♔a6

3 ♔c6 ♔a5!

It is easier for White after 3 ... ♔a7 4 ♘c4 ♔b8 (or 4 ... ♔a6 5 ♘c5+ and 6 ♔c7) 5 ♘d6 ♔a7! 6 ♘c5! ♔b8 (or 6 ... d3 7 ♔c7) 7 ♔b6 d3 8 ♘d7+ and mate in 2 moves.

4 ♔c5

White would be in zugzwang after 4 ♔b7 ♔b5, so the knight on d2 is needed. However, an immediate 4 ♘c4+ would not be good because of 4 ... ♔a4, threatening to go to b3. As a general rule, the enemy king must be kept away from the blockading knight, whilst the king and the other knight drive him towards the edge of the board.

4 ... ♔a6

If 4 ... ♔a4 5 ♔b6 winning as we saw in variation 4 above.

5 ♘c4 ♔b7

6 ♔d6 ♔c8

7 ♘a5 ♔d8

Black's king cannot be confined to the left corner, so he is driven to the kingside. This move is forced, as 7 ... ♔b8 loses to 8 ♔c6! ♔a7 (or 8 ... ♔c8 9 ♘b7 ♔b8 10 ♘d6 etc) 9 ♘b7 ♔a6 10 ♘b4+ ♔a7 11 ♔c7 d3 12 ♘a5 d2 13 ♘ac6+ and mate in 2 moves.

8 ♘b7+ ♔e8

Or 8 ... ♔c8 9 ♔c6 as in the last note.

9 ♔e6 ♔f8

10 ♘d6 ♔g7

11 ♔f5 *(326)*

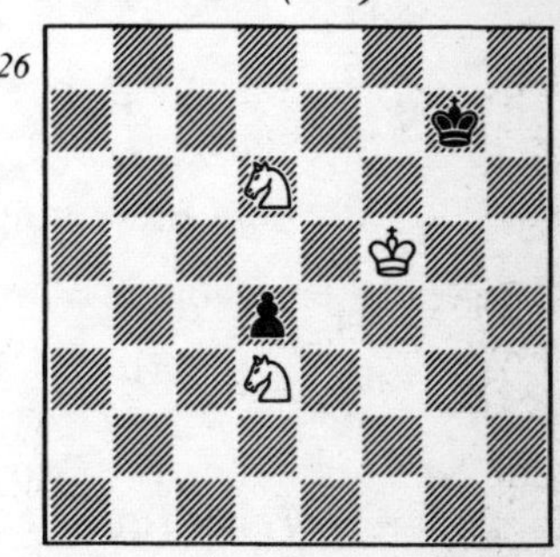

326

11 ... ♔h6

Or 11 ... ♔f8 12 ♔f6 ♔g8 13 ♘f5 ♔f8 14 ♘g7 ♔g8 15 ♘e6 ♔h7 16 ♔g5 ♔g8 17 ♔g6 with a quick mate. Black's king is to be driven to the bottom right corner, whatever he plays, e.g. 11 ... ♔h7 12 ♔f6 ♔h6 13 ♘c4 ♔h7 (or 13 ... ♔h5 14 ♘ce5 ♔h4 15 ♔g6 ♔g3 16 ♔g5 ♔g2 17 ♔g4 ♔f1 18 ♔f3 etc, or here 14 ... ♔h6 15 ♘g4+ ♔h5 16 ♔f5 etc) 14 ♘ce5 ♔g8 15 ♘g6 ♔h7 16 ♘e7 ♔h6 17 ♘g8+ ♔h5 18 ♔f5 ♔h4 19 ♘f6 ♔g3 20 ♔e4 ♔h4 21 ♔f4 and Black's king is restricted to the corner.

12 ♘e8! ♔h5

After 12 ... ♔h7 13 ♔g5 ♔g8 14 ♔f6 ♔h7 (or 14 ... ♔f8 15 ♘g7 ♔g8 16 ♘e6 etc) 15 ♘d6 ♔h6

16 ♘c4! we transpose to the variation given in the previous note.

13 ♘g7+ ♔h4

If 13 ... ♔h6 Black is mated in the top corner after 14 ♔f6 ♔h7 15 ♘f5 ♔g8 16 ♔e7 ♔h7 17 ♔f7 etc. The reader should now be acquainted with the methods used to control the black king's activity.

14 ♔f4 ♔h3
15 ♘f5 ♔g2
16 ♔g4 ♔h2

Or 16 ... ♔f1 17 ♘g3+ ♔g2 18 ♘h5 and 19 ♘hf4 preventing 19 ... ♔e2.

17 ♘h4 ♔g1
18 ♘g6 ♔f1
19 ♘gf4 ♔g1

Both knights stop the king escaping. It is now only a question of preparing the final mate.

20 ♔g3 ♔f1
21 ♔f3 ♔g1
22 ♔e2 ♔h2
23 ♔f2 ♔h1

Finally, the king is trapped in the corner, but White must still be careful, as 24 ♘e5 d3 25 ♘f3 d2 26 ♘h5 fails to 26 ... d1♘+! drawing.

24 ♘e6! ♔h2
25 ♘g5 ♔h1
26 ♘e5! d3
27 ♘ef3 d2
28 ♘e4 d1♘+
29 ♔g3!

and mate next move.

The reader now has sufficient information about this type of ending to be able to handle it, should it arise in practical play.

Practical examples

Let us begin with a classic knight ending from the game Lasker-Nimzowitsch, Zürich 1934.

327
B

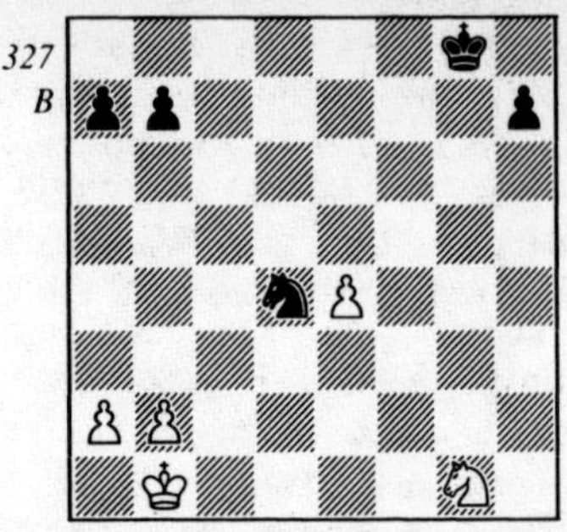

Lasker-Nimzowitsch 1934

Although material is even, Black has several positional advantages. Firstly, his h-pawn is very strong, for as we know it is difficult for a knight to contain a rook's pawn, and if White's king heads for the kingside, the centre and queenside remain unprotected. Secondly, Black's king can quickly reach e5, an excellent central square from which he can eye both sides of the board. Thirdly, Black's knight is posted more actively than White's.

These advantages together are sufficient to give Black a win, as Nimzowitsch convincingly demonstrated:

1 ... ♔f7
2 ♔c1 ♔f6
3 ♔d2 ♔e5

There would be no point in 3 ... ♔g5, as after 4 ♔e3 ♘e6 5 ♔f3 Black can advance neither his king nor his h-pawn. It is also important to blockade White's passed e-pawn.

4 ♔e3 h5

5 a3

As a general rule, one should avoid such weakening pawn moves whenever possible. In this case a hole is created at b3, giving Black's king a further entry point. It seems to me that White should have at least postponed this move, as there is no immediate win against 5 ♘h3. If then 5 ... ♘c2+ White does not have to play 6 ♔f3 ♘b4 7 a3 ♘d3 8 b4 ♘e1+ and 9 ... ♘c2, which is why Lasker played 5 a3. He can instead play 6 ♔d2! (6 ... ♘b4 7 a3). It is difficult to say whether 5 ♘h3 would draw, but it would give Black far more problems than in the game.

5 ... a5

A good move, fixing White's b-pawn and eventually threatening ... a4.

6 ♘h3

White is almost in zugzwang. There is no other knight move, as 6 ♘f3+ ♘xf3 7 ♔xf3 h4 is easily won for Black, and if 6 ♔d3 the e-pawn falls after 6 ... ♘e6 7 ♔e3 ♘g5. Pawn moves would of course only weaken the queenside more.

6 ... ♘c2+

An attempt which succeeds, although in fact it should lead to nothing after 7 ♔d2! If 7 ... ♘xa3 8 ba ♔xe4 9 ♔c3 would clearly be drawn, as the knight can hold the h-pawn without the help of the king (see diagram 305).

Admittedly, the text move was worth trying, as Black can always obtain the same position after **7 ♔d2 ♘d4 8 ♔e3** etc. It is interesting to see how he would then proceed. The key move is **8 ... ♘e6!** limiting the activity of White's knight and threatening to attack the e-pawn. As 9 ♔d3? ♘f4+ wins for Black, and 9 ♘g1 ♘g5 loses the e-pawn, White's only move is **9 ♘f2** (9 ♔f3 ♔d4) when Black plays **9 ... ♘f4!**

328
W

Lasker-Nimzowitsch 1934
(variation)

White would again be in semi-zugzwang. If he plays passively with 10 ♔f3 Black strengthens his position by 10 ... a4 11 ♔e3 b6 12 ♔f3 ♘e6 13 ♔e3 ♘c5 14 ♔f3 ♔d4 etc. White's best move is probably **10 a4** but even then Black has good prospects, e.g. **10 ... b6 11 b3 ♘g2+ 12 ♔f3** or 12 ♔d3 ♔f4 etc **12 ... ♘e1+ 13 ♔e3 ♘c2+ 14 ♔d3 ♘d4 15 ♔c4 h4** and White is in trouble. We are not saying that 8 ... ♘e6 leads to a forced win, but our analysis shows the difficulties with which the defence is faced.

7	**♔f3**	**♘e1+**
8	**♔e2**	**♘g2**
9	**♔f3**	**♘h4+**
10	**♔e3**	**♘g6**

Black has now reached a position similar to the one we gave in the previous note. 11 ♘f2 ♘f4 would now transpose to this line, and 11 ♔d3 ♘f4+ or 11 ♔f3 ♔d4 are not worth serious consideration. Lasker chooses another continuation which does not alter the situation overmuch.

11	**♘g5**	**♔f6**
12	**♘h7+**	

Or 12 ♘h3 ♘e5 13 ♔d4 transposing to the game line.

12	**...**	**♔e7**
13	**♘g5**	**♘e5**
14	**♔d4**	**♔d6**
15	**♘h3**	

White would like to prevent the blockade of his queenside pawns, but 15 a4 ♘c6+ would eventually give Black's king an entry point at b4. Best is probably 15 b3, but Black's outside passed pawn would still guarantee him the win.

15	**...**	**a4!**
16	**♘f4**	**h4**
17	**♘h3**	**b6**

A subtle tempo move. Black later wants to play ... ♘c6+ and ... ♔c5, but only with White's knight on h3, so he takes two moves to play his pawn to b5.

18	**♘f4**	**b5**
19	**♘h3** *(329)*	

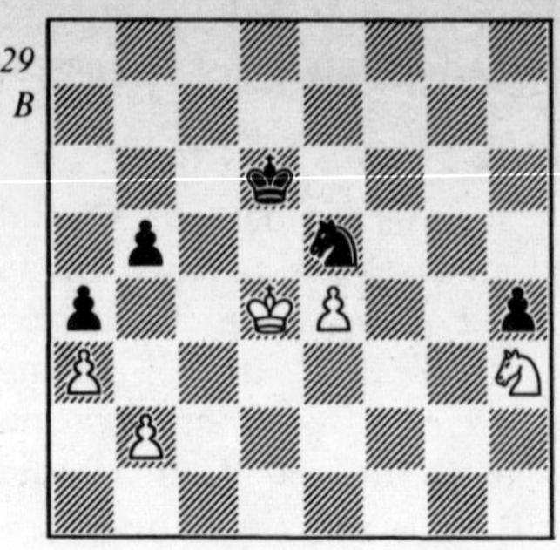

Lasker-Nimzowitsch 1934

19	**...**	**♘c6+**

Pursuing his logical plan of attack on the queenside. An alternative plan is 19 ... ♘c4 20 ♔c3 ♔e5 etc. Black presumably did not want to allow counterplay after 20 ♘f4 ♘xb2 21 e5+, but 21 ... ♔c6! and 22 ... ♘c4 wins for him.

20	**♔e3**	

If 20 ♔d3 ♔e5 21 ♔e3 ♘a5 wins.

20	**...**	**♔c5**
21	**♔d3**	**b4**

With so few pawns on the board, the attacker should usually avoid pawn exchanges, but Nimzowitsch has calculated a forced win. White must now exchange, as 22 ... ♘e5+ is threatened.

22	**ab+**	**♔xb4**
23	**♔c2**	**♘d4+**
24	**♔b1**	

His only chance, intending to attack the a-pawn. If 24 ♔d3 ♘e6, White's king would be forced back by the threat of 25 ... ♔b3, as 25 ♔e3 ♔b3 26 ♘f4 fails to 26 ... ♔xb2! 27 ♘xe6 a3.

24	**...**	**♘e6**

There is no need for 24 ... ♔b3, as the e-pawn is now the target, e.g. 25 ♔c2 ♔c4 26 ♔d2 ♔d4

27 ♘f2 ♘g5 etc. Lasker's last attempt is prettily refuted by Nimzowitsch.

25	**♔a2**	**♔c4**
26	**♔a3**	**♔d4**
27	**♔xa4**	**♔xe4**

Although Black has only one pawn left, White's knight cannot stop it. If now 28 ♘g1 ♔e3 and 29 ... ♔f2 wins. Or 28 ♘f2+ ♔f3 wins.

28	**b4**	**♔f3**
29	**b5**	**♔g2**

0-1

After 30 b6 ♔xh3 31 b7, then 31 ... ♘c5+ wins the pawn, and if here 31 ♔b5 ♘d8 32 ♔c5 ♔g4 33 ♔d6 h3 34 ♔c7 h2 35 ♔xd8 h1♕ wins. A splendidly played ending, well illustrating the strength of a passed rook's pawn against a knight.

This example might lead the reader to think that knight endings are purely a matter of technique, with given advantages being methodically exploited. However, our next position shows us that imagination can also play a part and provide us with interesting tactical possibilities.

330
W

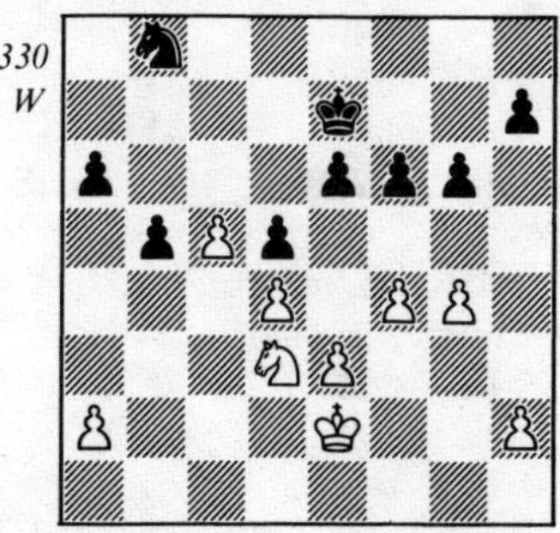

Pillsbury-Gunsberg 1895

This position occurred in the game Pillsbury-Gunsberg, Hastings 1895. White has a strong protected passed pawn on c5, but this in itself is not enough. Much more important is the fact that by energetic play he can successfully attack Black's pawns on e6 and d5. We have here a position in which dynamic elements are more important than static ones. From a static point of view, Black's position seems acceptable. He can create a passed pawn on the queenside and has the blockading move ... ♘c6 available. In fact, if it were Black to move, 1 ... ♘c6 would hold everything. However, in chess we must always examine concrete tactical possibilities along with positional considerations. In this case, White can immediately disorganize Black's position by attacking the pawns on e6 and d5, as follows:

1	**f5!**	

White cannot allow 1 ... ♘c6. His threat is now 2 fe followed by 3 ♘f4+ or immediately 2 ♘f4.

1	**...**	**g5**

Necessary, or else the d-pawn falls, e.g. 1 ... gf 2 gf ef 3 ♘f4 regaining the pawn with a clear positional advantage. Or 1 ... ef 2 gf g5 3 ♘b4 winning the d-pawn.

2	**♘b4!**	**a5**

Selecting the line which leads to beautiful combinational play. There is hardly anything better, for the threat is 3 c6 ♔d6 4 fe, as in the game, and if 2 ... ♔d7 3 fe+ ♔xe6 4 c6! ♔d6 5 c7 ♔xc7 6 ♘xd5+ and

7 ♘xf6 wins easily. With the text move Black hopes to drive the knight away, when 3 ... ♘c6 gives him a good defensive position.

3 c6! ♔d6

Black obviously cannot take the knight because of 4 c7, and 3 ... ♔d8 allows 4 fe! with play similar to the game.

4 fe! ♘xc6

All forced, as 4 ... ab loses to 5 e7 ♔xe7 6 c7, revealing the helplessness of the knight.

5 ♘xc6 ♔xc6 *(331)*

331
W

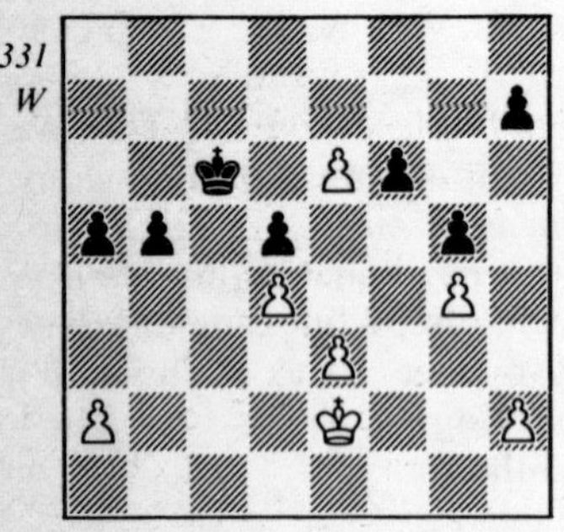

Pillsbury-Gunsberg 1895

We have now reached a pawn ending in which material is even and which superficially still seems all right for Black. He not only threatens to win the e-pawn but has the chance of creating an outside passed pawn. However, White has foreseen that he can guard his advanced passed pawn and set up two powerful passed central pawns before Black has time to use his passed pawns effectively.

6 e4! de

7 d5+ ♔d6

8 ♔e3

It is only now that we realize how far ahead Pillsbury had to calculate. He captures the e-pawn just in time to stop Black's passed queenside pawn.

8 ... b4

9 ♔xe4 a4

10 ♔d4 ♔e7

The best defence. In the actual game Gunsberg continued with 10 ... h5 and had to resign after 11 gh a3 12 ♔c4 f5 13 h6 f4 14 h7. If 10 ... f5 11 gf g4 12 f6 wins easily.

11 ♔c4 b3

Again 11 ... f5 12 gf g4 13 ♔xb4 h5 is too late, as White's pawns are too far advanced, e.g. 14 ♔c5 h4 15 d6+ wins.

12 ab a3

Or 12 ... ab 13 ♔xb3 f5 14 gf g4 15 ♔c3 and White stops the pawn.

13 ♔c3 f5

14 gf g4

Black has at least succeeded in creating a passed pawn on both wings, but has also given White a passed b-pawn which now decides the game.

15 b4! h5

16 b5 h4

17 b6 a2

To force White's king to the back rank where he will be in check from a new queen, but it never comes to that.

18 ♔b2 g3

19 hg hg

20 d6+!

More exact than 20 b7 g2 21 b8♕ a1+ 22 ♔xa1 g1♕+, when

Black could still fight on.

20 ... ♔xd6

Or 20 ... ♔f6 21 d7 ♔e7 22 b7 g2 23 d8♕+ ♔xd8 24 b8♕+ wins, a recurring theme.

21 b7 ♔c7

22 e7 wins.

Again White queens with check. Extremely fine play by White.

Here is another example of how concrete tactical possibilities must be offset against formal advantages:

332

B

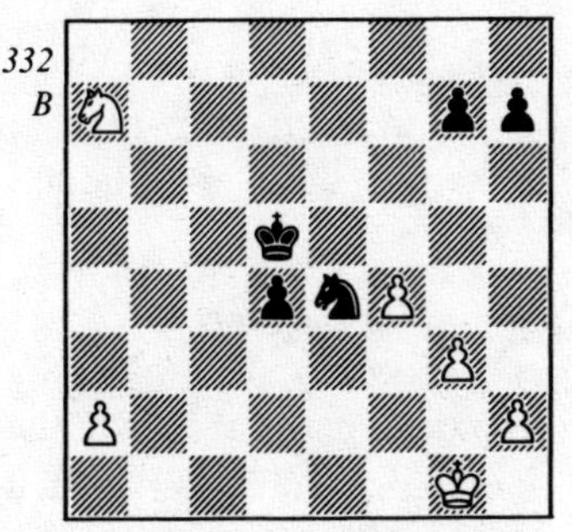

Barcza-Simagin 1949

Not only is White a pawn up, but he has an outside passed a-pawn and can hope to create another on the f-file. Nevertheless, he is lost. Firstly, Black's beautifully centralized pieces lend excellent support to his passed d-pawn. Secondly, White's knight is badly placed for joining in the defence against the d-pawn. These two factors allow Black to win as follows:

1 ... d3

2 ♔f1 ♘c3

3 ♔e1 ♔d4

It is clear that all White's moves are forced, as is his next. 4 ... ♔e3 is now the threat.

4 ♔d2 ♘e4+

5 ♔c1

Other king moves lose at once to 5 ... ♔e3, but what is Black to do now? If 5 ... d2+ 6 ♔c2 follows, and if 5 ... ♔e3 White saves himself by 6 ♘b5 d2+ 7 ♔c2 ♘f2 (or 7 ... ♔e2 8 ♘d4+) 8 ♘c3 etc. Nevertheless, Black can win by the following instructive manoeuvre, reminding us of possibilities arising from diagram 322. How vital it is to be acquainted with basic endings!

5 ... ♘d6!

Heading for c5. We shall soon see the difference this makes.

6 ♔d2

Allowing Black to pursue his winning plan, but other moves also lose, e.g.

1) 6 ♘c6+ ♔c3 7 ♘e7 (the threat was 7 ... ♘e4 and 8 ... d2+) 7 ... d2+ 8 ♔d1 ♘e4 9 ♘d5+ ♔c4 wins, as knight moves allow 10 ... ♔d3.

2) 6 a4 ♔e3 7 ♘c6 ♘c4! 8 ♘b4 (or 8 a5 d2+ and 9 ... ♘b2) 8 ... d2+ 9 ♔c2 ♔e2 wins.

6 ... ♘c4+

7 ♔c1

If 7 ♔d1 (e1) then 7 ... ♔e3 is decisive.

7 ... d2+

8 ♔c2 ♔e3

9 ♘b5

Apparently setting up a successful defence by threatening to go to c3, but we now see the reason why Black played his knight to c4.

9 ... ♘a3+!

The same idea as in diagram 322. White's knight is lured away.

10 ♘xa3 ♔e2

and the pawn queens. It is scarcely credible that Black has a forced win from diagram 332.

We have already mentioned that an extra pawn gains in value when there is less material on the board. In pawn endings an extra pawn is almost always decisive, and in minor piece endings it usually gives good winning prospects. On the other hand, in rook and queen endings the placing of the pieces is usually more important than the extra pawn. Our final example illustrates this basic principle once again. Black has an extra pawn but it seems difficult to exploit this fact, as all the pawns are on the same wing, the passed pawn is effectively blockaded, and at the moment White can defend his weak c-pawn. How is Black to use his material advantage?

333
B

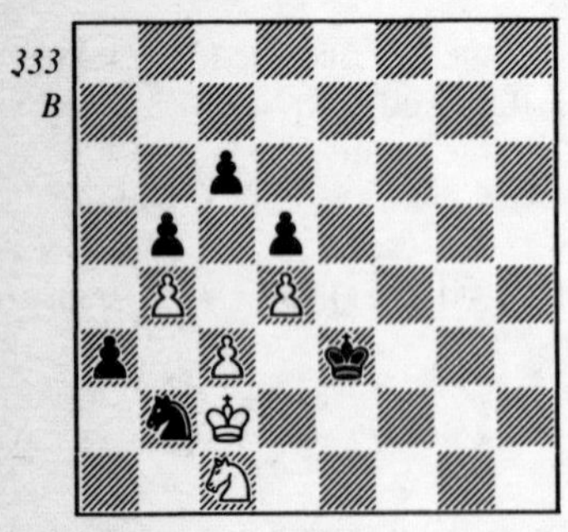

Marco-Maroczy 1899

This position arose in the game Marco-Maroczy, Vienna 1899. Black's passed pawn in itself would not be sufficient without other advantages. Firstly, his king is especially well placed and he could win the pawn ending even if he lost his passed pawn. Secondly, White's knight is badly placed and in some lines blocks his own king. Maroczy exploits these advantages in masterly fashion, as follows:

1 ... ♘d3!

Immediately using the fact that the pawn ending is won after 2 ♘xd3 a2 3 ♔b2 ♔xd3 etc. As White also loses after 2 ♘a2 ♔e2! 3 ♔b3 ♔d2 4 ♔xa3 ♔c2, he has only one move.

2 ♘b3 ♘e1+

It is not so easy after 2 ... a2 3 ♘a1 ♔e2 4 ♘b3, as White's king can stop the a-pawn as soon as the black knight moves, thus freeing his own knight.

3 ♔d1

Or 3 ♔b1 ♔d3 4 ♘a5 ♔xc3 5 ♘xc6 (or 5 ♔a2 ♘c2!) 5 ... ♘c2 winning easily.

3 ... ♔d3!

In endings with pawns on one side only, one must always be on the look-out for such piece sacrifices, to open the way for the king. In this case it is particularly effective, for we know that the knight defends badly against a rook's pawn.

4 ♔xe1 ♔xc3

5 ♘a1!

An imaginative defence. If Black now tries to win the knight, he only draws after 5 ... ♔b2?

6 ♔d2! ♔xa1 7 ♔c1 ♔a2 8 ♔c2 etc.

5 ... ♔xd4

6 ♘c2+

If 6 ♔d2 ♔c4 7 ♘c2 ♔b3 8 ♔c1 a2 etc, we have a situation like the one that occurs later.

6 ... ♔c3!

7 ♔d1

The subtleties of this ending are not yet over. If 7 ♘xa3 ♔b2 and the knight is lost.

7 ... a2

8 ♔c1 d4

9 ♘a1 d3

10 ♘c2

The last trick, as 10 ... dc gives stalemate.

10 ... c5!

0-1

Maroczy was one of the finest endgame artists.

This not only ends our discussion of knight endings but also completes our treatment of the endgame. We hope that by explaining each position in detail, we have succeeded in making endgame theory more palatable. Of necessity, this has meant a rigorous selection of material, making certain omissions inevitable, but we have endeavoured to present all the basic endings of use to the practical player.

We hardly need to stress the importance of this part of the game. One has only to consider the outstanding endgame technique of World Champions and leading Grandmasters to realize the efforts they must have made in this field. If the study of this volume enables the reader to make some progress in his own endgame play, we shall have succeeded in our aim.